CIGARETTE CARD VALUES

1991 Catalogue of Cigarette and other Trade Cards

NANKI-POO.
"THE MIKADO."

"My catalogue is long, through every passion ranging"
W. S. Gilbert (The Mikado)

Compiled and published by

MURRAY CARDS (INTERNATIONAL) LIMITED

51 Watford Way, Hendon Central, London NW4 3JH
Tel: (081) 202-5688
Fax: (081) 203-7878
For International Calls dial (011) 4481 202 5688

Opening hours — 9am-5pm, Monday-Friday

Watford Way is the A41 road into London, and is one mile from the end of the M1 Motorway. It can be reached via Hendon Central Underground Station (Northern Line), which is 100 yards away, and is also served by a number of bus routes and Green Line.

                    ISBN 0 946942 10 2

Introduction

Our 1991 Catalogue has been introduced rather earlier than had been expected. This has been necessitated by a damaging blow to the hobby. Until recently cigarette and trade cards have escaped the V.A.T. (Value Added Tax) net because they were classified as 'leaflets', and therefore zero-rated. The interpretation of a recent V.A.T. Tribunal decision has resulted in a reclassification, and it has been determined that cigarette and other trade cards will bear the standard rate of V.A.T. from September 1st, 1990. This means that all prices would have to increase by the current rate of 15%, without any regard to the normal market trends. Our policy has always been to keep our Catalogue as simple as possible, and show our customers the price that they actually have to pay, without having to add on any of the 'hidden extras' such as postage. We have therefore decided to issue the new Catalogue early, so that the prices, which *come into effect from 1st September 1990,* will include V.A.T.

All cards are now included in the standard rate category, since there is no practical way of treating even the oldest cards as 'antiques' within the strict V.A.T. rules for such items. Therefore the only items which we now offer that do not include V.A.T. are books, which for the time being are still zero rated. Exports by mail (including those to the Channel Islands) are however always zero rated, and a reduction on the prices shown of three twenty-thirds can be allowed, except of course for books. The tax is payable by all dealers who have achieved a fairly modest annual turnover, and will thus separate the 'professionals' from the 'amateurs'; by asking the trader for his V.A.T. Registration Number, or just for a tax invoice, the collector will be able to determine whether there is a reasonable chance of being able to anticipate a quality service backed by adequate stocks.

Our auctions, fortunately, are unaffected by the change. The vast majority of lots that we sell are on behalf of private individuals, who are not registered, and therefore not liable to pay V.A.T. on their cards. Where dealers submit cards to us for auction the bids will be treated as being on a tax-inclusive basis. It may now be deduced in other auctions, where V.A.T. may be charged as an extra on some or all lots, that these are either the property of the auctioneer himself, or else 'dealer lots'. Where a buyers premium is also charged, that has always been subject to V.A.T., but since we have never taken this step we can again offer our auction clients the simple slogan WHAT YOU BID IS WHAT YOU PAY!

Apart from the exceptional price increases, the Catalogue this year has continued with the pattern commenced last year. Part 1 contains a few new series and some corrections and additional information; the demise of the Embassy and Doncella brands will reduce the number of additions in the future. Part 2 has been enlarged, as previously promised, with the addition of many series mainly from the U.S.A. and Commonwealth; where printing varieties occur these have in general been mentioned, but not given separate space in order to keep down costs. Part 3 has of course been increased by a number of new issues, and the 1992 edition of the Catalogue will expand this section further. The fifteen pages of colour illustrations are all of cards not previously shown by us.

The hobby has continued to expand in the last year, with much interest shown in thematic subjects such as boxing and cinema. There has also been considerable interest in cards other than baseball in North America, and our increased business there has resulted in our appointment of a major American Company as our official distributor in North America. An additional facility for our customers is the installation of a Fax machine, which can be used at any time of the day or night to order cards (including-odds lists). We shall of course always try to keep abreast with modern technology in order to improve our service to our clients. 3

HOW TO USE THE CATALOGUE

The Catalogue is in three parts.

Part I contains all known issues by British-based tobacco companies. Thus all cards by the firm W.D. & H. O. Wills, which was located in Bristol, are shown, even though they may have been issued in a Wills brand abroad. Issues from the Channel Islands and the Republic of Ireland are included in this part. Excluded are most post cards and larger non-insert items.

Part II contains tobacco issues by most of the major manufacturers in the English-speaking world, and a selection of other series, including all the sets readily available to collectors.

Part III comprises series issued with commodities other than tobacco (commonly known as ''trade cards''). Although mainly British issues, there are a number of overseas sets included. Each issuer's name is followed by the commodity with which the cards were issued; where the set was not given away free, but produced in order to be sold, the issuer is described as ''commercial''.

Parts I and III commence with an index of brand names, and the issuer's name under which that item appears. Series are listed in alphabetical order of series title under the issuing firm, regardless of country of origin. Where the issuer was not normally located in the United Kingdom the country of origin is given. In the case of certain larger issuers series have been listed in logical groups so that they may be more readily found.

For each set the following information is given: —

(1) **Size information.** Cards are assumed to be standard size unless otherwise stated. Sizes used correspond to the page sizes used for our plastic albums (see separate notice) i.e. when a letter is used it may be assumed that at least one dimension is greater than the size shown by the previous letter. Abbreviations used are: —

K	smaller than standard.	51 x 41 mm.
B	bigger than standard.	80 x 46 mm.
M	medium size.	80 x 52 mm.
L	large size.	80 x 71 mm.
T	Typhoo/Doncella size.	110 x 54 mm.
X	extra large size.	80 x 110mm.
C	book-mark size.	165 x 52 mm.
P	postcard size.	165 x 105 mm.
G	cabinet size.	223 x 165 mm.
E	too large for albums.	
D	dual (more than one) size.	
S	stereoscopic series.	
F	photographic production.	

(2) **Number of cards in set.** When there are several rare numbers in a set the quantity normally available is shown. Thus 35/37 means that the series consists of 37 cards, but that only 35 are usually obtainable.

(3) **Series title.** Where the set has no name then the title accepted by common usage is given. Sect. = sectional series. Silk = silk, satin or canvas. P/C = playing card. When a dimension is shown this may be compared on the ruler printed on page 2.

(4) **Year of issue.** This is approximate only, and should in no way be considered to be binding. Particularly in the case of overseas and pre-1900 issues the date should be treated as merely an indication of the era in which the set was produced.

(5) **Price of odd cards.** Because of high labour costs and overheads it is not an economic proposition to offer odd cards from many post-1945 series. Where shown the price is that of normal cards in the set. End numbers (e.g. numbers 1 and 50 from a set of 50 cards) are DOUBLE the price shown. Known scarce subjects from a

series, and also thematic subjects from general series (e.g. cricketers from general interest series) would be more expensive than the price shown here.

Where no cards from a series were actually in stock at the time of compilation the price is shown in *italics*. It must be borne in mind that many of these prices are only approximate, since the discovery of just a few cards from a scarcer series could greatly affect the price.

(6) **Price of complete sets.** Prices shown are for sets in clean, undamaged condition. Where mint sets are required (and available) there will be a premium of 50% extra for sets 1920-1940, and 100% for pre 1920 sets. Where no set price is quoted we had no complete sets in stock at the time of compilation; however, when available these will be sold at prices based on the odds figure. *With each pre 1940 set the appropriate Nostalgia album pages are presented FREE!*

UNLISTED SERIES

Because our stocks are constantly changing we always have in stock a large number of series which are unlisted. In particular we can presently offer an excellent selection of German sets, loose or in their special albums and also a good choice of Australian trade isues. If you require a specific item please send us a stamped addressed envelope for an immediate quotation.

ALIKE SERIES

There are many instances where affiliated companies, or indeed completely independent groups issued identical series, where the pictures are the same, and only the issuer's name is altered. Examples are Fish & Bait issued by Churchman, I.T.C. (Canada) and Wills; British Cavalry Uniforms of the Nineteenth Century issued by Badshah, Browne, Empson, Rington and Willcocks & Willcocks; or even Interesting Animals by Hignett or Church & Dwight. If wishing to avoid duplication of pictures, please state when ordering which series you already **have**.

SPECIAL OFFERS

10 different Pre 1940 sets, our selection (no pages)	**£35.00**
35 different post 1945 sets, our selection	**£20.00**
100 different post 1945 sets (including the above 35), our selection	**£75.00**
8 different sets of Trucards	**£3.75**
10 different Brooke Bond sets (our selection)	**£12.50**
Liebig starter pack. 1991 Catalogue + 15 different sets	**£15.00**
90 different tobacco playing cards, mainly pre 1940, good selection	**£30.00**
4 different Carreras "Black Cat" sets—value £21.00	**£10.00**
10 different Ice Cream sets—catalogued £30+	**£15.00**

IT'S ON THE CARDS

Our Retail Shop — open to serve you

When in London, why not pay us a visit?

* Fast, courteous service.

* Odds lists filled while you wait.

* Sample albums of cards arranged thematically.

* New Issues and additions to stock.

* Monthly Special Offers.

* Unlisted lines always available.

* Albums without postal charges.

* Second hand books and albums.

* Complete framing service (with glass).

* Packets, playing cards and other ephemera.

* Spot cash for purchases.

Murray Cards (International) Limited

51 Watford Way, Hendon Central, London NW4 3JH

Opening hours 9.00 a.m. to 5.00 p.m., Monday-Friday

Watford Way is the A41 road into London, and is one mile from the end of the M1 Motorway. It is 100 yards from Hendon Central Underground Station (Northern Line), and is also served by a number of bus routes and Green Line. Street parking is largely unrestricted.

6

CENTRAL LONDON BRANCH

For the convenience of our customers we have now opened a branch in Central London. Less than 100 yards from Trafalgar Square, it is in an ideal location for visitors to London. It is three minutes walk from Charing Cross Main Line Station, and just around the corner from Charing Cross and Leicester Square underground (Bakerloo, Jubilee, Northern and Victoria Lines).

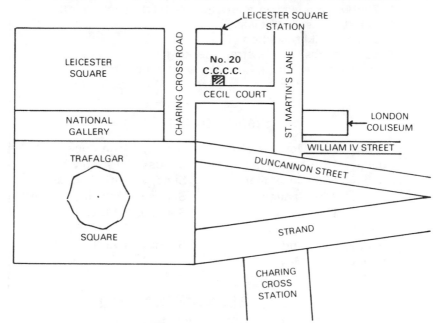

Cecil Court Collectors Centre is open from 10.30 a.m. to 5.30 p.m. Monday to Saturday. As well as cigarette cards you may purchase banknotes, coins, share certificates and stamps all under one roof.

Since we cannot split our stocks of the scarcer and more elusive cards the items available at Cecil Court will be restricted to those shown below. We can however arrange for any specific items not covered by this list to be made available for collection at the new Collectors Centre provided that we have at least 72 hours warning. All correspondence and telephone calls should still be made to our Head Office at 51 Watford Way, Hendon Central (081-202-5688).

Available at Cecil Court Collectors Centre

* A comprehensive selection of cheaper complete sets (up to £60 in price).
* Framed sets and framing kits.
* Nostalgia and Hendon albums.
* Catalogues, books and other accessories.
* Wholesale supplies.

CECIL COURT COLLECTORS CENTRE
20 Cecil Court, Charing Cross Road, London WC2

CIGARETTE CARD AUCTIONS

Our auctions are the largest and most successful in the world!

Every month over 450 interesting lots are sold. These include rare sets and type cards, cheaper sets and mixtures, sets in excellent to mint condition, literature, overseas and trade cards not recorded in our Catalogue and highly specialised collections such as Guinea Golds and silks. Lots are submitted to us from other dealers, collectors disposing of their unwanted cards, estates, overseas sources and antique dealers.

Highlights of recent years have included:—

Sets: Taddy Clowns & Circus Artistes, Actresses with Flowers, V.C. Heroes (125).
Wills Waterloo, The Reign of Edward VIII, Cricketers 1896.
Players Military Series, Old England's Defenders.
Smith Races of Mankind, Boer War Series.
Ogden Guinea Golds 1-1148 complete.
Hudden Soldiers of the Century.
Cope Golfers.

Odds: Player, Wills, Smith Advertisement Cards, Clarke Tobacco Leaf Girls, Kinnear Cricketers, Edwards Ringer & Bigg Eastern Manoeuvres, Taddy Wrestlers etc.

But there is something for everyone each time, from beginner to advanced collector, as the more than 200 participants every month will attest.

You do not have to attend in order to bid. Most of our clients bid by post, knowing that their instructions will be dealt with fairly and in confidence.

How do you bid? Just assess each lot that interests you. Then tell us the maximum amount that you are prepared to pay for it. We will then obtain it (if there are no higher bids) for the cheapest price possible—if for example your bid is £30 and the next highest received is £20 then you will obtain the lot for just £21. If you wish to put a ceiling on your total spending in any auction then we can accommodate this too.

How do you obtain Auction Catalogues? Send £1.00 for a sample, or else £10.00 will cover the cost of all 12 Catalogues for 1991, including Prices Realised Lists. £1.00 is refundable to each successful bidder, each month. Auctions are held on the third Sunday of every month and Catalogues are sent out at least three weeks before sale date.

TERMS OF BUSINESS

All previous lists are cancelled.

Cash with order. Any unsatisfactory items may be returned for credit or refund within seven days of receipt.

Overseas payments can only be accepted by sterling cheque drawn on a British bank, or by Credit Card.

Credit Cards. We can accept payment by Access, Eurocard, Mastercard and Visa. Just quote your card number and expiry date, and we will complete the amount of items actually sent. This is particularly useful for overseas customers, saving bank and currency conversion problems. Minimum credit card order — £5.00

Condition. All prices are based on cards in clean, undamaged condition. Where available mint sets 1920-1940 will be at a premium of 50% above the normal price, and mint sets pre 1920 and all mint odd cards will be an extra 100%.

Minimum Order. We are unable to accept orders totalling less than £2.00.

Postage. Inland second class post is included in all prices quoted. Overseas letter post is sent free by surface mail: overseas parcels and (if requested) air mail are charged at cost.

Value Added Tax at the current rate is included.

When ordering cards please quote the issuer's name, the name of the set, the date of issue, and the price. This will enable us to identify the precise series.

Odd Lists must be submitted on a separate sheet of paper with the name and address clearly shown; this will be returned with the cards for checking. Remember that end cards are double the normal price. Please write all the numbers required, e.g. NOT ''17-20'' but 17, 18, 19, 20. If the cards are required to complete an unnumbered set, and you do not know the missing titles, we can supply them provided that you list all the cards that you HAVE in alphabetical order.

Alternatives. Although this catalogue is based upon current stocks, these are bound to fluctuate. Therefore, whenever possible please give alternatives.

Credit Notes. When items are out of stock a credit note is normally sent. This may be utilised or encashed at any time, but MUST be returned when so doing.

Unlisted series. We are always pleased to quote for series unlisted, or unpriced.

Purchasing. We are always pleased to purchase or exchange collectors' unwanted cards. Please write with full details before sending cards.

Enquiries. We are always pleased to offer our advice on all collectors' queries. Please enclose a stamped addressed envelope with all enquiries.

Callers. Our shop is open from 9.00 a.m. to 5.00 p.m. each Monday to Friday, and collectors are always welcome to select from our complete range of cards and accessories. Watford Way is at Hendon Central (Underground, Northern Line), and is served by a number of buses, including Green Line.

Fax Machine. Our facsimile machine is always on. It can be used to place orders (including odd cards) when a credit card number and expiry date are quoted, and also for auction bids. The number is 081-203-7878 (international 011-4481-203-7878).

Answering machine. For the convenience of customers an answering machine is in operation whenever the shop is closed. Just leave your message, or order with Credit Card number and expiry date, and it will be dealt with as soon as we re-open. Please note we cannot accept telephone orders for odd cards.

No Hidden Extras. Remember that all prices shown include postage, packing, insurance and (where applicable) V.A.T. And that with every pre 1940 set we include Nostalgia pages *absolutely free!*

CARTOPHILIC SOCIETY REFERENCE BOOKS

A number of the earlier Reference Books have been unavailable for some years. However we are now pleased to be able to offer the following paper backed reprints at exceptionally low cost.

No. 1 Faulkner.
No. 2 Hill.
No. 4 Gallaher.
No. 5 Abdulla, Adkin & Anstie.
No. 6 Ardath.
No. 7 Directory of British Cigarette Card Issuers (16 cards illustrated).
No. 8 Glossary of Cartophilic Terms (27 cards illustrated).
No. 9 Lambert & Butler (25 cards illustrated).
No.10 Churchman (29 cards illustrated).
No.12 Taddy (30 cards illustrated).
No.13 Phillips (225 cards illustrated).
No.17 Player (26 cards illustrated).

ONLY £2.50 Per Booklet!

The following reprints have been combined in hard cover. The information contained cannot be found elsewhere, and each book represents excellent value. Each contains lists of unnumbered series, illustrations of untitled cards, and background information to most sets.

The Cigarette Card Issues of Wills. Originally 5 parts, now in one volume. 200 pages, 559 cards illustrated. **PRICE £7.50**

The Ogden Reference Book (including Guinea Golds). 244 pages, 536 cards illustrated. **PRICE £12.50**

The Tobacco War and B.A.T. Book, 336 pages, 2,959 cards illustrated! **PRICE £12.50**

A MUST FOR ALL COLLECTORS
THE WORLD TOBACCO ISSUES INDEX

Published by the Cartophilic Society of G.B. Ltd., this work is now in four volumes, which between them list every card issued by tobacco manufacturers that was known at the end of 1980.

Part I. World Index and Handbook reprinted as one volume. 701 pages, 1,977 cards illustrated. This is the basic reference work for all serious collectors, including details of nearly every British cigarette card. First published in 1956. **PRICE £20.00**

Part II. 452 pages, with 3,600 cards illustrated. This volume covers additions to Part I, which are mainly overseas cards. In particular it includes most of the information from the American Book of Checklists. **PRICE £12.50**

Part III. 504 pages, 666 cards illustrated. Published in 1978, this latest work updates the information in Parts I and II, and also repeats the lists (amended) which were previously in the Churchman, Lambert & Butler, Taddy, Phillips and Australasian Booklets. Also featured are American non-insert cards, blankets and pins. **PRICE £12.50**

Part IV. 688 pages. Lists of U.S. Baseball, photographic, Maltese etc. as well as additions to three previous parts. **PRICE £20.00**

OTHER LITERATURE

GENERAL WORKS

The Story of Cigarette Cards by Martin Murray, Hardback, 128 pages, including 32 in colour. **£7.25**

Collecting Cigarette Cards by Dorothy Bagnall, 112 pages, illustrated. **£4.50**

Cigarette Cards and Novelties by Frank Doggett, 96 pages, 1291 cards illustrated in colour. Paper back reprint. **£5.95**

Burning Bright. The autobiography of E. C. Wharton-Tigar, President of the Cartophilic Society and editor of its reference books. Well written, very cigarette card orientated. 280 pages. **£15.00**

Operation Red Poppy by Jack Nickle Smith. A spy thriller featuring a cartophilist. Hard cover. 158 pages. **£8.50**

Figurine Pubblicita, arte, collezionismo e industria 1867-1985. Italian text. A history of cards 1897-1985. Many pages of colour and black and white illustrations. **£15.00**

REFERENCE BOOKS

Handbook Part I. Published by L.C.C.C. Lists and illustrations of pre-1918 unnumbered and alike series (tobacco only). Essential reference. **£7.50**

Handbook Part II. Published by L.C.C.C. Lists of post-1918 series and all silks, with additions to Part I. **£7.50**

Smith Cigarette Cards. 36 pages with illustrations. Lists all known series, including back varieties. **£2.50**

British Trade Index, Part I. Series up to 1940. 216 pages, many illustrations. **£10.00**

British Trade Index, Part II. 232 pages. Additions to Part I and also issues 1945-1968. **£10.00**

British Trade Index, Part III. 400 pages, many illustrations. Additions to Parts I and II, with new issues to the end of 1985. **£13.50**

Typhoo Tea Cards. 36 pages with illustrations. Lists of back varieties. **£2.50**

A. & B.C. Gum Cards. 40 pages with illustrations. Many lists. **£2.75**

British Silk Issues by Dorothy Sawyer. New Edition, amended, many illustrations, 64 pages with details of all known British Tobacco and Trade silk issues. Essential reading for silk collectors. **£4.50**

Lawn Tennis Cigarette Cards by Derek Hurst. 1986. 37 pages **£3.00**

Lawn Tennis Trade Cards by Derek Hurst. 32 pages **£3.00**

Half Time (Football and the cigarette card 1890-1940) by David Thompson. 104 pages, listing every tobacco issue. **£9.00**

The Illustrated Footballer by Tony Ambrosen, 64 pages. Almost 600 cards illustrated **£7.50**

Errors & Varieties, British Cigarette Cards by W. B. Neilson. Lists all known varieties, corrected or uncorrected. **£7.50**

Errors & Varieties, British Cigarette Cards, Part 2 by W. B. Neilson. 37 pages. Additions to Part 1, plus Guinea Golds, Tabs. **£3.00**

Errors & Varieties, British Trade Cards by W. B. Neilson. 36 Pages, with Illustrations. Include pre & post-1945. **£3.00**

Huntley & Palmers Catalogue of Cards by E. Vansevenant. 63 pages, paper back, many cards illustrated. **£9.00**

Peak Frean Catalogue of Cards available shortly, ask for details.

CRICKET BOOKS

Cricket Cigarette & Trade Cards by Derek Deadman. The definitive work. 254 pages, 16 pages of illustrations. Comprehensive list of all titles known until the end of 1984. 'Monumental'. **£6.75**

Classic Cricket Cards. Reproductions of 154 cards in colour — Wills 1896 onward. Designed to be cut out. **£2.50**

More Classic Cricket Cards. 160 cards, different from above. **£2.50**

Cricket Postcards by Grenville Jennings. 236 Cards illustrated. **£4.50**

FOREIGN CARDS

Australian & New Zealand Index. Published by Cartophilic Society. Over 300 pages—600 cards illustrated. Lists all tobacco and trade cards. Published 1983. **£10.50**
Cigarette Cards Australian Issues & Values by Dion H. Skinner. A truly magnificent work. 245 pages, with coloured illustrations of at least one sample front and back(s) of each series. Lists of every card in each series (or illustrations of untitled sets).
Now only £20.00
Liebig Catalogue in English. 1991 Edition. See page 228 for full details. **£4.00**
Sanguinetti Liebig Catalogue. 1991 Edition. 431 pages, listing all titles from 1,974 sets and menus, Italian text, illustrations of 1,308 series. Indices in various languages.
£20.00
Liebig Menus and Table Cards by L. De Magistris. 118 page listing of all known Table and Menu cards, plus printing varieties. Colour Illustrations of each series. **£20.00**
Baseball Card Price Guide. 1st Edition 1987. Published by Sports Collectors Digest. 65,000 cards listed and individually priced. Many illustrations. **£7.50**
Canadian Trade Card Index by Dale Stratton. 181 pages, soft back, covering 660 sets issued by 142 Companies. **£8.50**

MISCELLANEOUS

Sweet Cigarette Packets by Michael Johnston. 36 pages, 127 packets illustrated. Published 1983. **Now only £1.50**
I.P.M. Postcard Catalogue, 17th Edition (1991). Illustrated, completely revised. The one THEY all use! **£8.00**
Postcard Collecting, a beginner's guide to old and modern picture postcards. **£1.00**
Golf on old Picture Postcards by Tom Serpell. 64 pages heavily illustrated in both black and white and colour. **£5.50**

A MAJOR NEW BOOK
The Story of Cigarette Cards by Martin Murray.

The history and development of cigarette and trade cards from their origins in Europe in the mid-Nineteenth Century to 1987. The story is told in words, and more appropriately in pictures. There are no less than 80 pages of illustrations (32 in full colour), with 48 pages of text by a leading authority on the subject. As befits such an important work, the book is hardbound, with an attractive dust cover.

Price—an astonishingly low £7.25 (post paid).

FRAMING KITS

Best materials — Competitive prices
Easy to do-it-yourself — Cards positioned without damage
— Backs can be read —

MOUNTING BOARDS

(Available in black, brown, green and maroon)

A To hold 25 standard sized cards (horizontal or vertical).
E To hold 25 large cards (horizontal or vertical).
F To hold 50 standard size cards (horizontal or vertical).
K To hold 10 standard size cards (horizontal or vertical).
L To hold 6 Liebig cards (Horizontal or vertical).

PRICES (Rate applied to total quantity ordered).

	1-10	11-50	51 +
Boards E, F	£5.50	£3.70	£3.00
Board A	£3.50	£2.35	£1.90
Boards K. L	£2.00	£1.35	£1.10

COMPLETE KITS — NOW AVAILABLE WITH GLASS

Comprising frame, glass, mounting board, spring clips, rings & screws. We are now able to offer for the first time, a newly designed exclusive frame complete with glass.

Prices — A £23.00 each   E & F £38.50   K & L £16.50

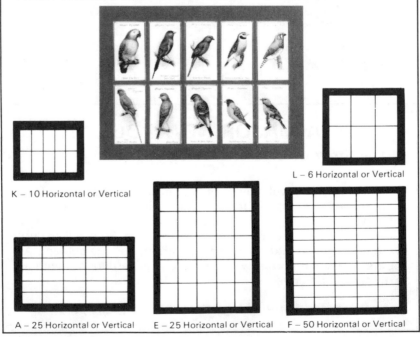

K – 10 Horizontal or Vertical

L – 6 Horizontal or Vertical

A – 25 Horizontal or Vertical   E – 25 Horizontal or Vertical   F – 50 Horizontal or Vertical

14

"NOSTALGIA" REPRINTS

An exciting concept for collectors. Reproductions of Classic cards sets, all of which are almost impossible to obtain, at a price that everyone can afford.

These cards are of the highest quality, and the latest technology has been used to recreate as closely as possible the beauty of the originals. They have received universal acclaim in the cigarette card world, and are indeed becoming collector's items in their own right.

Because of the difficulty of distinguishing our reproductions from the originals each reprint has 'A Nostalgia Reprint' printed on the back of the card.

TITLES CURRENTLY AVAILABLE

Taddy County Cricketers

15 Derbyshire
15 Essex
16 Gloucestershire
15 Hampshire
15 Kent
15 Lancashire
14 Leicestershire
15 Middlesex
15 Northamptonshire
14 Nottinghamshire
15 Somersetshire (sic)
15 Surrey
15 Sussex
15 Warwickshire
14 Worcestershire
15 Yorkshire

ONLY £1.75 per County. Or all 238 cards for £24.00

Allen & Ginter	50	American Indian Chiefs	£7.50
Allen & Ginter	50	Fruits	£7.50
Berlyn	25	Humorous Golfing Series	£6.00
Cope	50	Cope's Golfers	£7.50
Cope	50	Dickens Gallery	£7.50
Cope	50	Shakespeare Gallery	£7.50
Jones Bros.	18	Spurs Footballers	£1.75
Kinney	25	Leaders	£6.00
Player	50	Military Series	£7.50
Wills	50	Cricketers 1896	£7.50
Wills	50	Cricketers Series 1901	£7.50

THE "NOSTALGIA" ALBUM

We believe our album to be the finest on the market — yet now it is even better. Our pages are now being made from a material which contains no potentially harmful plasticiser and has a crystal-clear appearance. Only available from Murray Cards (International) Ltd. and approved stockists. Note also the following features: —

★ ★ Album leaves are made from clear plastic, enabling the entire card to be examined easily without handling!

★ ★ Cards easily removed and inserted!

★ ★ Wide margin enables pages to be turned in album without removing retention clip!

★ ★ A planned range of page formats allows most cards to be housed in one cover. Ten different pages now available!

★ ★ Handsome loose leaf PVC binders for easy removal and insertion of pages. Matching slip cases. Four different colours available.

★ ★ Black or coloured interleaving to enhance the appearance of your cards.

★ ★ Binder with 40 pages only £9.00 ★ ★

Matching slipcase (only supplied with binder) £2.00

Extra pages — 15p each

Pastel interleaving	50p per 8	Black interleaving	£1.20 per 40
Binder	£3.00 each	Tweezers	£1.50 each

Page sizes available: —

K	holds 15 cards smaller than standard. Size up to 51 x 41 mm.
A.	holds 10 standard size cards. Size up to 80 x 41 mm.
B.	holds 8 cards larger than standard. Size up to 80 x 46 mm.
M.	holds 8 medium size cards. Size up to 80 x 52 mm.
L.	holds 6 large size cards. Size up to 80 x 71 mm.
T.	holds 6 Doncella/Typhoo cards. Size up to 110 x 54 mm.
X.	holds 4 extra large size cards. Size up to 80 x 110 mm.
C.	holds 4 long cards. Size up to 165 x 52 mm.
P.	holds 2 post card size cards. Size up to 165 x 105 mm.
G.	holds 1 card cabinet size. Size up to 223 x 165 mm.

Binders, size 303 x 182 x 60 mm., are available in blue, gold, green or red.

Nostalgia — Collect with Confidence!

NOSTALGIA
ALBUMS

Preserve the best of the past in the best of the present. See opposite page for details.

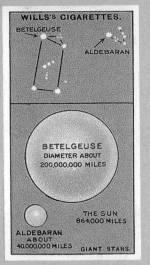

Romance of the Heavens.
Wills. Also B.A.T.

Your Birthday Tells Your Fortune.
Ardath

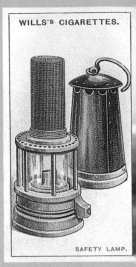

Famous Inventions.
Wills

Polar Exploration.
Player

Strange But True.
Charter Tea, Cooper & Co.

How to do it Series.
Godfrey Phillips

Arms of Companies.
Wills

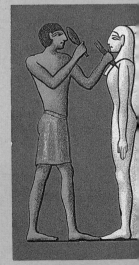

Ancient Egypt.
Cavenders

THE "HENDON" ALBUM

For Postcards, trade cards, and all printed ephemera.
* Page in crystal clear material, free of plasticiser.
* 8 different page formats.
* Handsome loose leaf binders, in choice of blue, brown, green or red.
* Matching slip cases.
* Big enough for BIG cards, small enough for small muscles.

Pages available

1. Pocket.   Cards size 294 x 214mm.
2. Pockets. Cards size 143 x 214mm. Ideal for banknotes.
3. Pockets. Cards size 93 x 214mm. Ideal for banknotes.
4. Pockets. Cards size 143 x 105mm. Especially for postcards.
6. Pockets. Cards size 92 x 105mm.
6. Pockets. Cards size 145 x 70mm. Especially for Medals.
8. Pockets. Cards size 67 x 105mm. Ideal for Gum cards, XL cigarette cards.
9. Pockets. Cards size 94 x 68mm. Suitable for playing cards.

Binder with 25 pages	**£11.50**	(including postage).
Extra pages	**30p**	each.
Matching slip case	**£3.00**	(must be ordered with binder).
Black interleaving, full page size	**£1.25**	per 25.
Black inserts for postcard pages	**£1.25**	per 100.

COLLECTOR'S AIDS

Cleartex strips, for wrapping standard size sets	**200 for £2.60**
large size sets	**200 for £2.80**
extra large sets	**200 for £3.00**
Tweezers, fine quality, with plastic sheath	**£1.50**
Magnifying Glasses, 2¼" diameter	**£3.00**
4" diameter	**£6.00**
Printed wants lists, numbered 1-50 on thin card	**30 for 75p**
Plastic Wallet. Pocket size with 10 postcard size pages. Ideal for carrying odds (and ends)	**£1.60**
Postcard pockets, thin PVC	**100 for £3.00**

INDEX OF BRANDS (Tobacco)

GUARDS CIGARETTES—See Carreras (Part 1)

HAVELOCK CIGARETTES—See Wills (Part 1)
HAWSER Etc.—See Wholesale Tobacco Co. (Part 1)
HEARTS DELIGHT CIGARETTES—See Pritchard & Burton (Part 1)
HERBERT TAREYTON CIGARETTES—See American Tobacco Co. (Part 2)
HOFFMAN HOUSE MAGNUMS—See American Tobacco Co. (Part 2)
HONEST LONG CUT—See Duke or American Tobacco Co. (Part 2)
HUSTLER LITTLE CIGARS—See American Tobacco Co. (Part 2)

ISLANDER, FAGS, SPECIALS, CLUBS—See Bucktrout (Part 1)

JACK ROSE LITTLE CIGARS—See American Tobacco Co. (Part 2)
JERSEY LILY CIGARETTES—See Bradford (Part 1)
JUST MEMBER CIGARETTES—See Pattreiouex (Part 1)

KENSITAS CIGARETTES—See J. Wix (Part 1)

LENOX CIGARETTES—See American Tobacco Co. (Part 2)
LE ROY CIGARS—See Miller (Part 2)
LEVANT FAVOURITES—See B. Morris (Part 1)
LIFEBOAT CIGARETTES—See United Tobacco Co. (Part 2)
LIFE RAY CIGARETTES—See Ray (Part 1)
LITTLE RHODY CUT PLUG—See Geo. F. Young (Part 2)
LOTUS CIGARETTES—See United Tobacco Co. (Part 2)
LUCANA CIGARETTES—See Sandorides (Part 1)
LUCKY STRIKE CIGARETTES—See American Tobacco Co. (Part 2)
LUXURY CIGARETTES—See American Tobacco Co. (Part 2)

MAGPIE CIGARETTES—See Schuh (Part 2)
MANIKIN CIGARS—See Freeman (Part 1)
MATTOSSIANS IMPORTED EGYPTIAN CIGARETTES—See Henly & Watkins (Part 1)
MAX CIGARETTES—See A. & M. Wix (Part 1)
MAYBLOSSOM CIGARETTES—See Lambert & Butler (Part 1)
MECCA CIGARETTES—See American Tobacco Co. (Part 2)
MILLBANK CIGARETTES—See Imperial Tobacco Co. (Canada) (Part 2)
MILLS CIGARETTES—See Amalgamated Tobacco Corporation (Part 1)
MILO CIGARETTES—See Sniders & Abrahams (Part 2)
MINERS EXTRA SMOKING TOBACCO—See American Tobacco Co. (Part 2)
MOGUL CIGARETTES—See American Tobacco Co. (Part 2)
MURAD CIGARETTES—See American Tobacco Co. (Part 2)

NEBO CIGARETTES—See American Tobacco Co. (Part 2)

OK CIGARETTES—See African Tobacco Mfrs. (Part 2)
OBAK CIGARETTES—See American Tobacco Co. (Part 2)
OFFICERS MESS CIGARETTES—See African Tobacco Mfrs. (Part 2)
OLD GOLD CIGARETTES—See American Tobacco Co. (Part 2)
OLD JUDGE CIGARETTES—See B.A.T. or Goodwin (Part 2)
ONE OF THE FINEST—See Buchner (Part 2)
ORACLE CIGARETTES—See Tetley (Part 1)
OUR LITTLE BEAUTIES—See Allen & Ginter (Part 2)
OXFORD CIGARETTES—See American Tobacco Co. (Part 2)

PAN HANDLE SCRAP—See American Tobacco Co. (Part 2)
PETER PAN CIGARETTES—See Sniders & Abrahams (Part 2)
PIBROCH VIRGINIA—See Fryer (Part 1)
PICCADILLY LITTLE CIGARS—See American Tobacco Co. (Part 2)
PICK-ME-UP CIGARETTES—See Drapkin & Millhoff (Part 1)
PIEDMONT CIGARETTES—See American Tobacco Co. (Part 2)
PINHEAD CIGARETTES—See British American Tobacco Co. (Part 2)
PINNACE—See G. Phillips (Part 1)

PIONEER CIGARETTES—See Richmond Cavendish (Part 1)
PIRATE CIGARETTES—See Wills (Part 1)
POLO MILD CIGARETTES—See Murray (Part 1)
PURITAN LITTLE CIGARS—See American Tobacco Co. (Part 2)
PURPLE MOUNTAIN CIGARETTES—See Wills (Part 1)

R. S.—See R. Sinclair (Part 1)
RECRUIT LITTLE CIGARS—See American Tobacco Co. (Part 2)
RED CROSS—See Lorillard or American Tobacco Co. (Part 2)
REINA REGENTA CIGARS—See B. Morris (Part 1)
RICHMOND GEM CIGARETTES—See Allen & Ginter (Part 2)
RICHMOND STRAIGHT CUT CIGARETTES—See American Tobacco Co. (Part 2)
ROSELAND CIGARETTES—See Glass (Part 1)
ROYAL BENGALS LITTLE CIGARS—See American Tobacco Co. (Part 2)
RUGGER CIGARETTES—See United Tobacco Companies (Part 2)

ST DUNSTANS CIGARETTES—See Carreras (Part 1)
ST. LEGER LITTLE CIGARS—See American Tobacco Co. (Part 2)
SCOTS CIGARETTES—See African Tobacco Mfrs. (Part 2)
SCRAP IRON SCRAP—See American Tobacco Co. (Part 2)
SENATOR CIGARETTES—See Scerri (Part 2)
SENIOR SERVICE CIGARETTES—See Pattreiouex (Part 1)
SENSATION CUT PLUG—See Lorillard (Part 2)
SHANTUNG CIGARETTES—See British American Tobacco Co. (Part 2)
SILKO CIGARETTES—See American Tobacco Co. (Part 2)
SMILE AWAY TOBACCO—See Carreras (Part 1)
SOVEREIGN CIGARETTES—See American Tobacco Co. (Part 2)
SPANISH PUFFS—See Mandelbaum (Part 2)
SPINET CIGARETTES—See Hill (Part 1)
SPOTLIGHT TOBACCOS—See Hill (Part 1)
SPRINGBOK CIGARETTES—See United Tobacco Co. (Part 2)
STAG TOBACCO—See American Tobacco Co. (Part 2)
STANDARD CIGARETTES—See Carreras (Part 1) or Sniders & Abrahams (Part 2)
STATE EXPRESS CIGARETTES—See Ardath (Part 1)
SUB ROSA CIGARROS—See American Tobacco Co. (Part 2)
SUMMIT—See International Tobacco Co. (Part 1)
SUNRIPE CIGARETTES—See Hill (Part 1)
SUNSPOT CIGARETTES—See Theman (Part 1)
SWEET CAPORAL—See Kinney or American Tobacco Co. (Part 2)
SWEET LAVENDER—See Kimball (Part 2)

TATLEY CIGARETTES—See Walkers (Part 1)
TEAL CIGARETTES—See British American Tobacco Co. (Part 2)
THREE BELLS CIGARETTES—See Bell (Part 1)
THREE CASTLES CIGARETTES—See Wills (Part 1)
TIGER CIGARETTES—See British American Tobacco Co. (Part 1)
TIPSY LOO CIGARETTES—See H. C. Lloyd (Part 1)
TOKIO CIGARETTES—See American Tobacco Co. (Part 2)
TRAWLER CIGARETTES—See Pattreiouex (Part 1)
TRUMPS LONG CUT—See Moore & Calvi (Part 2)
TURF CIGARETTES—See Carreras (Part 1)
TURKEY RED CIGARETTES—See American Tobacco Co. (Part 2)
TURKISH TROPHY CIGARETTES—See American Tobacco Co. (Part 2)
TWELFTH NIGHT CIGARETTES—See American Tobacco Co. (Part 2)

U.S. MARINE—See American Tobacco Co. (Part 2)
UZIT CIGARETTES—See American Tobacco Co. (Part 2)

VANITY FAIR CIGARETTES—See Kimball (Part 2)
VICE REGAL CIGARETTES—See Wills (Part 1)
VIRGINIA BRIGHTS CIGARETTES—See Allen & Ginter (Part 2)

WINGS CIGARETTES—See Brown & Williamson (Part 2)

YANKEE DOODLE—See British Australasian Tobacco Co. (Part 2)

ZIRA CIGARETTES—See American Tobacco Co. (Part 2)

Part 1

BRITISH TOBACCO MANUFACTURERS

(Including Channel Islands, Eire, and Overseas Issues
by British-based firms)

ABDULLA & CO.
24 Page Reference Book (with Anstie & Adkin)—£2.50

Qty		Date	Odds	Sets
50	Beauties of Today	1938	£3.00	—
L1	Bridge Rule Cards (Several Printings)	1936	—	9.50
25	British Butterflies	1935	50p	£12.50
F52	Cinema Stars, Set 1	1932	£3.00	—
30	Cinema Stars, Set 2	1932	£3.75	—
30	Cinema Stars, Set 3	1933	£3.00	—
32	Cinema Stars, Set 4	1933	£1.60	£50.00
32	Cinema Stars, Set 5	1934	£1.60	£50.00
30	Cinema Stars, Set 6	1934	£2.20	—
P2	Commanders of the Allies	1914	£40.00	—
25	Feathered Friends	1935	50p	£12.50
50	Film Favourites	1934	£3.00	—
50	Film Stars	1934	£5.00	—
P24	Film Stars (Series of Cards)	1934	£6.25	—
P24	Film Stars (Series of 24 Cards)	1934	£6.25	—
P24	Film Stars, 2nd (25-48)	1934	£6.25	—
M3	Great War Gift Packing Cards	1916	£40.00	—
18	Message Cards (Blue Printing)	1936	£6.25	—
18	Message Cards (Green Printing)	1936	£6.25	—
18	Message Cards (Red Printing)	1936	£6.25	—
K18	Message Cards (Two Wordings)	1936	£9.50	—
25	Old Favourites	1936	50p	£12.50
L1	Princess Mary Gift Card	1914	—	£12.50
40	Screen Stars	1939	75p	£30.00
40	Screen Stars (Successors Clause)	1939	£1.50	£60.00
50	Stage and Cinema Beauties	1935	£2.50	—
30	Stars of The Stage & Screen	1934	£3.00	—

GERMAN ISSUES

M150	Autobilder Serie I	1931	75p	—
M150	Autobilder Serie II	1932	75p	—
M160	Im Auto Mit Abdulla Durch Die Welt	1930	50p	£80.00
B110	Landerwappen-Sammlung	1932	50p	£55.00
B110	Landerwappen-Sammlung Serie II	1932	50p	—
B150	Landerwappen-Sammlung Serie III	1932	50p	—
B200	Nationale Und Internationale Sport Rekorde	1931	95p	—
B50	Soldatenbilder Europaischer Armeen	1928	£1.25	—
X80	Wappenkarten	1928	50p	£40.00

ADCOCK & SON

11/12	Ancient Norwich	1928	£2.50	£27.50

ADKIN & SONS
24 Page Reference Book (with Anstie & Abdulla)—£2.50

25	Actresses—French	1898	£125.00	—
12	A Living Picture (Adkin & Sons Back)	1900	£5.00	£60.00
12	A Living Picture (These Cards Back)	1900	£5.00	£60.00
P12	A Living Picture	1900	£75.00	—
12	A Royal Favourite	1900	£10.00	£120.00
15	Beauties "PAC" (7 Brands)	1898	£150.00	—
50	Butterflies & Moths	1924	£1.25	£62.50

ADKIN & SONS — cont.

Qty		Date	Odds	Sets
12	Character Sketches (Black Back)	1901	£5.00	£60.00
12	Character Sketches (Green Back)	1901	£5.00	£60.00
P12	Character Sketches	1901	£75.00	—
P4	Games by Tom Browne	1900	£125.00	—
25	Notabilities	1915	£3.60	£90.00
12	Pretty Girl Series (Actresses)	1897	£37.50	£450.00
12	Pretty Girl Series (12 Calendar Backs)	1900	£37.50	—
12	Pretty Girl Series (6 Verse Backs)	1900	£25.00	—
12	Pretty Girl Series (32 Other Backs)	1900	£21.50	—
25	Soldiers of The Queen (Series of 50, "Issued Exclusively With")	1899	£18.75	—
50	Soldiers of the Queen (Series of 50)	1900	£3.75	—
59	Soldiers of the Queen (Series of 60)	1900	£3.75	£225.00
31	Soldiers of The Queen & Portraits	1901	£4.50	—
30	Sporting Cups & Trophies	1914	£12.50	£375.00
25	War Trophies	1917	£3.60	£90.00
50	Wild Animals of the World	1923	£1.00	£50.00

AIKMAN'S

Qty		Date	Odds	Sets
30	Army Pictures, Cartoons, etc.	1916	£62.50	—

H. J. AINSWORTH

Qty		Date	Odds	Sets
30	Army Pictures, Cartoons, etc.	1916	£62.50	—

ALBERGE & BROMET

Qty		Date	Odds	Sets
25	Boer War & General Interest (Brown Bridal Bouquet)	1900	£75.00	—
	(Green Bridal Bouquet)	1900	£75.00	—
	(Green La Optima)	1900	£75.00	—
40	Naval & Military Phrases (Bridal Bouquet)	1904	£75.00	—
40	Naval & Military Phrases (La Optima)	1904	£75.00	—
30	Proverbs	1903	£75.00	—

PHILLIP ALLMAN & CO. LTD.

Qty		Date	Odds	Sets
50	Coronation Series	1953	40p	£20.00
12	Pin Up Girls, 1st Series (Numbered)	1953	£1.90	£23.00
12	Pin Up Girls, 1st Series (Unnumbered "Ask For Allman—Always")	1953	£1.90	£23.00
12	Pin Up Girls, 1st Series (Unnumbered "For Men Only")	1953	£1.90	£23.00
L12	Pin Up Girls, 1st Series	1953	£2.50	£30.00
12	Pin Up Girls, 2nd Series	1953	£1.90	£23.00
L12	Pin Up Girls, 2nd Series	1953	£2.50	£30.00
24	Pin Up Girls, Combined Series (Numbered "First Series of 24")	1953	£3.75	—

AMALGAMATED TOBACCO CORPORATION LTD. (Mills)

Qty		Date	Odds	Sets
25	Aircraft of the World	1958	—	£6.25
25	A Nature Series	1958	—	£2.00
25	Animals of the Countryside	1958	—	£2.25
25	Aquarium Fish	1961	—	£2.00
25	Army Badges—Past & Present	1961	—	£12.50
25	British Coins and Costumes	1958	—	£5.00
25	British Locomotives	1961	—	£5.00
25	British Uniforms of the 19th Century	1957	—	£12.50
25	Butterflies & Moths	1957	—	£2.00
25	Cacti	1961	—	£7.50
25	Castles of Britain	1961	—	£17.50
25	Coins of the World	1961	—	£2.00
25	Communications	1961	—	£17.50
25	Dogs	1958	—	£9.50
25	Evolution of the Royal Navy	1957	—	£12.50
M25	Famous British Ships, 1st	1952	—	£2.00
M25	Famous British Ships, 2nd	1952	—	£2.00
25	Football Clubs and Badges	1961	—	£17.50
25	Freshwater Fish	1958	—	£3.00
25	Guerriers a Travers Les Ages (French)	1961	—	£12.50
25	Histoire De L'Aviation, Premiere Serie	1961	—	£2.00
25	Histoire De L'Aviation, Seconde Serie	1962	—	£7.50
25	Historical Buildings	1959	—	£12.50
M25/50	History of Aviation	1952	—	£2.00
M50	History of Aviation	1952	—	£37.50
25	Holiday Resorts	1957	—	£2.00
25	Interesting Hobbies	1959	—	£7.50
25	Into Space	1959	—	£3.75
25	Kings of England	1954	£1.00	£25.00
25	Les Autos Modernes (French Text)	1961	—	£7.50
25	Medals of the World	1959	—	£3.75
25	Merchant Ships of the World	1961	—	£7.50
25	Merveilles Modernes (French Text)	1961	—	£7.50
25	Miniature Cars and Scooters	1958	—	£17.50
25	Naval Battles	1959	—	£6.25
25	Ports of the World	1959	—	£2.25
25	Propelled Weapons	1953	—	£2.50
25	Ships of the Royal Navy	1961	—	£6.25
25	Sports and Games	1958	—	£17.50
25	The Wild West	1960	—	£15.00
25	Tropical Birds	1958	—	£20.00
25	Weapons of Defence	1961	—	£12.50
25	Wild Animals	1958	—	£4.50
25	World Locomotives	1959	—	£10.00

THE ANGLO-AMERICAN CIG. MAKING CO. LTD.

20	Russo Japanese War Series	1902	£150.00	—

ANGLO CIGARETTE MFG. CO. LTD.

36	Tariff Reform Series	1909	£20.00	—

ANONYMOUS ISSUES—TOBACCO

Qty		Date	Odds	Sets
PRINTED BACKS				
40	Beauties "KEWA" ('England Expects' Back)	1899	*£85.00*	—
41	V.C. Heroes	1916	£5.00	£200.00
50	War Portraits	1915	£18.50	—
PLAIN BACKS				
25	Actors & Actresses "FROGA"—C	1900	£7.50	—
?25	Actresses "ANGLO"	1896	*£50.00*	—
?20	Actresses "ANGOOD" (Brown Fronts)	1898	£30.00	—
?20	Actresses "ANGOOD" (Grey Fronts)	1898	£17.50	—
20	Actresses "BLARM"	1900	£6.25	£125.00
?50	Actresses "DAVAN"	1902	*£25.00*	—
26	Actresses "FROGA A" (Brown)	1900	£6.25	£165.00
26	Actresses "FROGA A" (Coloured)	1900	£7.50	—
?25	Actresses "HAGG"	1900	£6.25	—
25	Beauties "BOCCA"	1900	£10.50	—
50	Beauties "CHOAB" (Brown)	1902	£7.50	—
50	Beauties "CHOAB" (Coloured)	1902	£7.50	—
50	Beauties "FECKSA"	1903	£6.25	—
20	Beauties "FENA"	1899	£35.00	—
25	Beauties "GRACC"	1898	£10.00	—
26	Beauties "HOL"	1900	£8.00	—
20	Beauties "PLUMS"	1898	£30.00	—
25	Boer War & General Interest	1901	£15.00	—
20	Boer War Cartoons	1900	£10.00	—
20	Boer War Generals "CLAM"	1901	£8.75	—
12	Boer War Generals "FLAC"	1901	£10.00	—
25	Boxer Rebellion—Sketches	1904	£7.50	—
M108	British Naval Crests	1916	£2.50	—
16	British Royal Family	1902	£6.25	—
F?12	Celebrities of the Great War	1915	£12.50	—
50	Colonial Troops	1902	£5.00	—
M108	Crests & Badges of the British Army	1916	£2.00	—
20	Cricketers Series	1902	£150.00	—
50	Dogs (as Taddy)	1900	£18.00	—
30	Flags & Flags with Soldiers (Draped)	1902	£4.40	£132.00
15	Flags & Flags with Soldiers (Undraped)	1902	£5.00	—
24	Flags Arms & Types of Nations	1904	£4.40	—
40	Home & Colonial Regiments	1900	£5.00	—
2	King Edward & Queen Alexandra	1902	£15.00	£30.00
1	Lord Kitchener	1915	—	£12.50
40	Naval & Military Phrases	1904	£5.00	—
F30	Photographs (Animal Studies)	1935	£1.25	—
?50	Pretty Girl Series "BAGG"	1898	£12.50	—
12	Pretty Girl Series "RASH"	1899	£9.50	—
30	Proverbs	1901	£6.25	—
19	Russo Japanese Series	1902	£12.50	—
20	Russo Japanese War Series	1902	£16.00	—
25	Star Girls	1900	£6.25	£160.00
20	The European War Series	1915	£4.40	£88.00
25	Types of British & Colonial Troops	1900	£15.00	—
25	Types of British Soldiers	1914	£5.00	£125.00

E. & W. ANSTIE

24 Page Reference Book (with Abdulla & Adkin) — £2.50

Qty		Date	Odds	Sets
25	Aesop's Fables	1934	£1.50	£37.50
16	British Empire Series	1904	£8.00	£125.00
10	Clifton Suspension Bridge (Sect.)	1938	£1.00	£10.00
B40	Flags (Silk)	1915	£1.00	—
X10	Flags (Silk)	1915	£7.50	—
40	Nature Notes	1939	£5.00	—
50	People of Africa	1926	£2.50	£125.00
50	People of Asia	1926	£2.50	£125.00
50	People of Europe	1925	£2.25	£112.50
40	Places of Interest (Matt Fronts)	1939	50p	£20.00
40	Places of Interest (Varnished Fronts)	1939	95p	—
8	Puzzle Series	1900	£87.50	—
25	Racing Series (1-25)	1922	£2.25	£56.25
25	Racing Series (26-50)	1922	£2.75	£68.75
60/84	Regimental Badges (Silk)	1915	95p	—
M5	Royal Mail Series	1900	£150.00	—
X5	Royal Standard & Portraits (Silk)	1915	£12.50	—
2	Royal Portraits (Silk)	1915	£31.50	—
50	Scout Series	1923	£1.60	£80.00
10	Stonehenge (Sect.)	1936	£1.00	£10.00
10	The Victory (Sect.)	1936	£1.00	£10.00
50	The World's Wonders	1924	£1.25	£62.50
20	Wells Cathedral (Sect.)	1935	£1.00	£20.00
40	Wessex	1938	90p	£36.00
20	Wiltshire Downs (Sect.)	1935	£1.00	£20.00
10	Windsor Castle (Sect.)	1937	£1.00	£10.00

HENRY ARCHER & CO.

Qty		Date	Odds	Sets
51	Actresses "FROGA" (Golden Returns Back)	1900	£45.00	—
51	Actresses "FROGA" (M.F.H. Back)	1900	£45.00	—
50	Beauties "CHOAB" (Brown)	1900	£21.50	—
25	Beauties "CHOAB" (Coloured, Golden Returns)	1900	£55.00	—
25	Beauties "CHOAB" (Coloured, M.F.H.)	1900	£55.00	—
20	Prince of Wales Series	1912	£21.50	—

ARDATH TOBACCO CO. LTD.

28 Page Reference Book — £2.50

Qty		Date	Odds	Sets
50	Animals at The Zoo (Descriptive Backs)	1924	£2.00	—
50	Animals at The Zoo (Double Ace Backs)	1924	£12.50	—
F54	Beautiful English Women	1930	£2.00	£108.00
25	Big Game Hunting (Descriptive Backs)	1930	£2.50	£62.50
25	Big Game Hunting (Double Ace Backs)	1930	£9.00	—
L30	Boucher Series	1915	£2.50	£75.00
50	Britain's Defenders	1936	50p	£25.00
50	British Born Film Stars	1934	£1.00	£50.00
M50	British Born Film Stars	1934	£1.60	
X1	Calendar 1942	1941	—	£1.60
X1	Calendar 1942-3	1942	—	£1.60
X1	Calendar 1943	1942	—	£2.00

ARDATH TOBACCO CO. LTD. — cont.

Qty		Date	Odds	Sets
X1	Calendar 1943-4	1943	—	£1.25
X1	Calendar 1944	1943	—	£1.25
MF36	Camera Studies	1939	90p	£32.00
LF45	Camera Studies	1939	80p	£36.00
L8	Christmas Greeting Cards (Folders)	1943	£1.60	£12.50
X25	Champion Dogs	1934	75p	£18.75
X100	Contract Bridge Contest Hands	1930	*£15.00*	—
50	Cricket, Tennis & Golf Celebrities	1935	£1.00	£50.00
50	Cricket, Tennis & Golf Celebrities (Grey)	1935	65p	£32.50
X25	Dog Studies (State Express etc.)	1938	£2.00	£50.00
X25	Dog Studies (Firm's Name, New Zealand)	1938	*£7.50*	—
25	Eastern Proverbs	1932	£1.00	£25.00
48	Empire Flying Boat (Sect.)	1938	£1.25	£62.50
50	Empire Personalities	1937	50p	£25.00
50	Famous Film Stars	1934	50p	£25.00
50	Famous Footballers	1934	55p	£27.50
25	Famous Scots	1935	65p	£16.25
X25	Fighting & Civil Aircraft	1936	90p	£22.50
50	Figures of Speech	1936	50p	£25.00
50	Film, Stage and Radio Stars	1935	65p	£32.50
X25	Film, Stage & Radio Stars (Different)	1935	75p	£18.75
PF?	Film Stars (State Express)	1938	*£25.00*	—
PF?	Film Stars (Straight Cut)	1938	*£25.00*	—
M50	Flags 4th Series (Silk)	1914	*£37.50*	—
M50	Flags 5th Series (Silk)	1914	*£37.50*	—
M25	Flags 6th Series (Silk)	1914	*£43.75*	—
L40	Franz Hals Series	1916	*£12.50*	—
L40	Franz Hals Series (2.5 Cents Overprint)	1916	*£15.00*	—
X50	From Screen and Stage	1936	50p	£25.00
L30	Gainsborough Series (Multi-Backed)	1915	£2.50	£75.00
L30	Girls of all Nations	1916	£10.00	—
50	Great War Series	1916	£4.40	—
50	Great War Series "B"	1916	£4.40	—
50	Great War Series "C"	1916	£4.40	—
35	Hand Shadows	1930	*£15.00*	—
X25	Historic Grand Slams	1936	*£15.00*	—
L50	Hollandsche Oude Meesters (4 Backs)	1916	£12.50	—
X48	How to Recognise The Service Ranks	1940	£2.50	—
X2	Industrial Propaganda Cards (Black)	1943	£2.50	—
X4	Industrial Propaganda Cards (Coloured)	1943	£2.50	—
X11	Industrial Propaganda Cards (White)	1943	£2.50	—
X150	Information Slips	1940	£2.00	—
L24	It All Depends On Me	1940	95p	£22.50
50	Life in The Services (adhesive)	1938	50p	£25.00
50	Life in The Services (non-adhesive NZ)	1938	90p	£45.00
96	Modern School Atlas	1936	90p	£87.50
50	National Fitness (adhesive)	1938	40p	£20.00
50	National Fitness (non-adhesive NZ)	1938	75p	£37.50
50	New Zealand Views	1928	£2.00	£100.00
L1	On The Kitchen Front	1942	—	£1.25
50	Our Empire	1937	£1.00	£50.00
LF110	Photocards "A" (Lancs. Football Teams)	1936	65p	£71.50
LF110	Photocards "B" (N.E. Football Teams)	1936	75p	£81.25
LF110	Photocards "C" (Yorks. Football Teams)	1936	75p	£81.25

ARDATH TOBACCO CO. LTD. — cont.

Qty		Date	Odds	Sets
LF165	Photocards "D" (Scots. Football Teams)	1936	65p	£107.00
LF110	Photocards "E" (Midland Football Teams)	1936	75p	£81.25
LF110	Photocards "F" (Southern Football Teams)	1936	65p	£71.50
LF99	Photocards "Z" (Sport & General Interest)	1936	25p	£25.00
LF11	Photocards "Supplementary"	1936	£2.50	—
LF22	Photocards Group "A" (Sports)	1937	30p	£6.25
LF21/22	Photocards Group "B" (Coronation, Sports)	1937	50p	£10.50
LF21/22	Photocards Group "C" (Lancs. Celebrities)	1937	75p	£15.75
LF22	Photocards Group "D" (Irish Celebrities)	1937	75p	£16.50
LF22	Photocards Group "E" (Films, Sports)	1938	65p	£14.00
LF22	Photocards Group "F" (Films, Sports)	1938	75p	£16.50
LF11	Photocards Group "G" (Cricketers)	1938	£14.00	—
LF66	Photocards Group "GS" (Various)	1938	£1.00	£66.00
LF22	Photocards Group "H" (Films, Sports)	1938	75p	£16.50
LF22	Photocards Group "I" (Films, Various)	1938	95p	£21.00
LF22	Photocards Group "J" (Films, Various)	1939	50p	£11.00
LF22	Photocards Group "K" ("KINGS" Clause)	1939	75p	£16.50
LF22	Photocards Group "K" (No Clause)	1939	75p	£16.50
LF44	Photocards Group "L" (Various)	1939	50p	£22.00
F45	Photocards Group "M" (Films, Various)	1939	65p	£28.00
LF45	Photocards Group "M" ("KINGS" Clause)	1939	65p	£28.00
LF45	Photocards Group "M" (No Clause)	1939	65p	£28.00
F45	Photocards Group "N" (Films)	1939	65p	£28.00
LF45	Photocards Group "N" (Films)	1939	50p	£22.50
LF66	Photocards Views of the World	1938	65p	£42.00
25	Proverbs (1-25)	1936	50p	£12.50
25	Proverbs (26-50)	1936	£1.25	£31.25
L30	Raphael Series	1916	£2.50	£75.00
LF45	Real Photographs Group "O" (Films)	1939	50p	£22.50
F45	Real Photos, 1st Series	1939	80p	£36.00
XF18	Real Photos, 1st Series (Views)	1937	£1.90	—
F54	Real Photos, 2nd Series	1939	80p	£42.50
XF18	Real Photos, 2nd Series	1937	£1.90	—
XF18	Real Photos, 3rd Series (Views)	1937	£1.90	—
XF18	Real Photos, 4th Series	1938	£1.90	—
XF18	Real Photos, 5th Series (Views)	1938	£1.90	—
XF18	Real Photos, 6th Series	1938	£1.90	—
LF44	Real Photos, Series 1—GP1	1939	65p	£28.50
LF44	Real Photos, Series 2—GP2	1939	20p	£8.75
LF44	Real Photos, Series 3—GP3	1939	£1.90	—
LF44	Real Photos, Series 3—CV3 (Views)	1939	65p	—
LF44	Real Photos, Series 4—CV4 (Views)	1939	20p	£8.75
XF36	Real Photos, Series 7	1938	65p	£22.50
XF54	Real Photos, Series 8	1938	50p	£27.00
LF54	Real Photos, Series 9	1938	45p	£24.00
XF54	Real Photos, Series 9	1938	45p	£24.00
LF54	Real Photos, Series 10	1939	45p	£24.00
XF54	Real Photos, Series 10	1939	50p	£27.00
LF54	Real Photos, Series 11	1939	45p	£24.00
XF54	Real Photos, Series 11	1939	65p	£35.00
LF54	Real Photos, Series 12	1939	45p	£24.00
LF54	Real Photos, Series 13	1939	45p	£24.00
LF36	Real Photographs of Famous Landmarks	1939	£2.00	—
XF36	Real Photographs of Famous Landmarks	1939	90p	£32.00

ARDATH TOBACCO CO. LTD.—cont.

Qty		Date	Odds	Sets
LF36	Real Photographs of Modern Aircraft	1939	£1.90	—
XF36	Real Photographs of Modern Aircraft	1939	£1.00	£36.00
L30	Rembrandt Series	1914	£3.00	£90.00
L40	Rembrandt Series (Splendo)	1914	£15.00	£600.00
X30	Rembrandt Series	1914	£4.40	—
L30	Rubens Series	1916	£2.50	£75.00
L30	Rubens Series ("N.Z". At Base)	1916	£12.50	—
L30	Rubens Series (Splendo Cigarettes)	1916	£12.50	—
L30	Rubens Series (Winfred Cigarettes)	1916	£12.50	—
100	Scenes From Big Films	1935	£1.25	—
M100	Scenes From Big Films	1935	£2.20	—
X20	Ships of the Royal Navy (Package)	1953	£9.50	—
50	Silver Jubilee	1935	50p	£25.00
50	Speed Land Sea & Air (State Express)	1935	90p	£45.00
50	Speed Land Sea & Air "(Ardath" —N.Z.)	1935	£1.50	£75.00
X25	Speed Land Sea & Air (Different)	1935	75p	£18.75
50	Sports Champions (title in 1 line)	1935	50p	£25.00
50	Sports Champions (title in 2 lines—N.Z.)	1935	£1.00	£50.00
6	Sportsmen (Double Ace)	1953	£2.50	—
50	Stamps Rare & Interesting	1939	90p	£45.00
50	Swimming Diving and Life-Saving	1937	80p	£40.00
50	Tennis	1938	90p	£45.00
L?	The Beauty of State Express (Circular)	1928	£62.50	—
9	The Office of Chief Whip	1955	£1.90	—
48	Trooping the Colour (Sect.)	1939	£1.25	£60.00
L?	Types of English Manhood (Circular)	1935	£12.50	—
M1	Union Jack Folder	1943	—	£3.75
L30	Velasquez Series	1916	£3.15	£94.50
X30	Velasquez Series	1916	£4.40	—
50	Who is this? (Film Stars)	1936	£1.00	£50.00
X?	Wonderful Handcraft	1935	£15.00	—
X24/25	World Views (2 Printings)	1937	30p	£7.50
50	Your Birthday Tells Your Fortune	1937	45p	£22.50

ASSOCIATED TOBACCO MANUFACTURERS

25	Cinema Stars (5 Brands)	1926	£18.75	—

ATKINSON

30	Army Pictures, Cartoons, etc.	1916	£62.50	—

AVISS BROS. LTD.

40	Naval & Military Phrases	1904	£62.50	—

J. A. BAILEY

40	Naval & Military Phrases	1904	£125.00	—

A. BAKER & CO. LTD.

Qty		Date	Odds	Sets
25	Actresses, 3 Sizes	1901	£20.00	—
L25	Actresses, 3 Sizes (different)	1901	£31.25	—
P?25	Actresses, 3 Sizes (different)	1901	£150.00	—
20	Actresses "BLARM" (Back Design 58mm Long)	1900	£22.00	—
20	Actresses "BLARM" (Back Design 64mm Long)	1900	£20.00	—
10	Actresses "HAGG"	1900	£20.00	£200.00
41	Baker's Tobacconists Shops (Cigar etc. Manufacturers)	1901	£90.00	—
41	Baker's Tobacconists Shops (Try our 3½d Tobaccos)	1901	£150.00	—
25	Beauties of All Nations (Albert Baker)	1898	£12.50	£312.50
25	Beauties of All Nations (A. Baker)	1899	£7.50	£187.50
16	British Royal Family	1902	£37.50	—
20	Cricketers Series	1902	£250.00	—
25	Star Girls	1898	£125.00	—

BAYLEY AND HOLDSWORTH

26	Flag Signalling Code Series	1912	£100.00	—

THOMAS BEAR & SONS LTD.

50	Aeroplanes	1924	£2.50	—
50	Cinema Artistes, Set 2	1936	£2.50	—
50	Cinema Artistes, Set 4	1937	£3.00	—
50	Cinema Stars "BAMT"	1928	£1.50	—
50	Do You Know?	1923	£1.25	£62.50
270	Javanese Series (Blue)	1925	90p	£245.00
100	Javanese Series (Yellow)	1925	£6.25	—
50	Stage and Film Stars	1926	£2.20	—

E. C. BEESTON

30	Army Pictures, Cartoons, etc.	1916	£75.00	—

BELFAST SHIPS STORES

?10	Dickens Characters Burlesqued	1893	£187.50	—

J. & F. BELL LTD.

10	Actresses "HAGG"	1900	£62.50	—
25	Beauties (Scotia Back)	1897	£80.00	—
25	Beauties (Three Bells Back)	1897	£80.00	—
25	Colonial Series	1901	£30.00	£750.00
30	Footballers	1902	£31.25	—
60	Rigsvaabner	1925	£25.00	—
25	Scottish Clan Series	1903	£10.00	£250.00
60	Women of All Nations	1925	£25.00	—

R. BELLWOOD

18	Motor Cycle Series	1913	£75.00	—

RICHARD BENSON LTD.

Qty		Date	Odds	Sets
L24	Old Bristol Series	1925	£2.50	£75.00
X24	Old Bristol Series (Re-Issue)	1946	£1.55	£37.50

BENSON & HEDGES LTD.

1	Advertisement Card, Original Shop	1973	—	95p
48	Ancient & Modern Fire-Fighting Equipment	1947	£2.50	£120.00
L10	B.E.A. Aircraft	1958	£4.40	—
X?25	"Oxford" University Series	1912	£25.00	—

FELIX S. BERLYN

25	Burline Mixture (Golfers Blend) Series	1910	£175.00	—
P25	Burline Mixture (Golfers Blend) Series	1910	£250.00	—

BERRY'S

20	London Views	1904	£125.00	—

BEWLAY & CO.

6	Comic Advertisement Cards (7 Backs)	1909	£162.50	—
P6	Comic Advertisement Cards	1909	£75.00	—
12	War Series (Portraits, Multi-Backed)	1915	£10.00	£120.00
25	War Series (Scenes, Multi-Backed)	1915	£8.75	£220.00

W. O. BIGG & CO.

37	Flags of All Nations (Horizontal Back)	1904	£6.25	—
37	Flags of All Nations (Vertical Back)	1904	£6.25	—
50	Life on Board a Man Of War	1905	£8.00	—

JAS BIGGS & SON

26	Actresses "FROGA A"	1900	£31.25	—
26	Actresses "FROGA B"	1900	£50.00	—
25	Beauties "BOCCA" (Black Back)	1900	£62.50	—
25	Beauties "BOCCA" (Blue Back)	1900	£62.50	—
25	Beauties "CHOAB" (Blue Back)	1902	£62.50	—
50	Beauties "CHOAB" (Black Overprint)	1902	£50.00	—
30	Colonial Troops	1901	£25.00	—
30	Flags & Flags With Soldiers	1903	£21.50	—
25	Star Girls	1900	£125.00	—

J. S. BILLINGHAM

30	Army Pictures, Cartoons, etc.	1916	£62.50	—

R. BINNS

?15	Halifax Town Footballers	1924	£80.00	—

BLANKS CIGARETTES

Qty		Date	Odds	Sets
50	Keystrokes in Break-building	1910	*£125.00*	—

BOCNAL TOBACCO CO.

25	Luminous Silhouettes of Beauty & Charm	1938	£1.50	£37.50
25	Proverbs Up To Date	1938	£1.50	£37.50

ALPHONSE BODE & SON

30	Proverbs	1903	*£125.00*	—

ALEXANDER BOGUSLAVSKY LTD.

P12	Big Events on the Turf	1924	£12.50	£150.00
25	Conan Doyle Characters (black back)	1923	£3.20	£80.00
25	Conan Doyle Characters (green back)	1923	£3.20	£80.00
25	Mythological Gods and Goddesses	1924	80p	£20.00
25	Sports Records (1-25)	1925	50p	£12.50
25	Sports Records 2nd Series (26-50)	1925	50p	£12.50
25	Winners on the Turf (Name No Serifs)	1925	£2.00	£50.00
25	Winners on the Turf (Name With Serifs)	1925	£3.20	—
L25	Winners on the Turf	1925	£3.20	£80.00

R. & E. BOYD LTD.

25	Places of Interest	1938	*£37.50*	—
B25	Places of Interest	1938	*£31.25*	—
L25	Wild Birds at Home	1938	*£31.25*	—

WM. BRADFORD

50	Beauties "CHOAB"	1902	£25.00	—
?25	Beauties, Jersey Lily	1900	*£150.00*	—
20	Boer War Cartoons	1901	*£80.00*	—

THOS. BRANKSTON & CO. LTD.

30	Colonial Troops (Golf Club Mixture)	1901	£25.00	—
30	Colonial Troops (Red Virginia)	1901	£25.00	—
30	Colonial Troops (Sweet as the Rose)	1901	£25.00	—
12	Pretty Girl Series "RASH"	1900	*£150.00*	—

BRIGHAM & CO.

L16	Down The Thames From Henley to Windsor	1912	*£80.00*	—
16	Reading Football Players	1912	*£100.00*	—
X3	Tobacco Growing in Hampshire, England	1912	£9.50	£28.50

BRITANNIA ANONYMOUS SOCIETY

?20	Beauties & Couples	1914	£62.50	—

BRITISH & COLONIAL TOBACCO CO.

25	Armies of the World	1900	*£92.50*	—

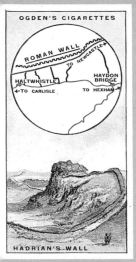

By the Roadside.
Ogden

Time & Money in Different Countries.
Wills. Also Smith, Fry

Famous Buildings.
C.W.S.

Ports and Resorts of the World. Ewbank, Amalgamated Tob.,
B.T., Risca

Features of the World.
Brooke Bond

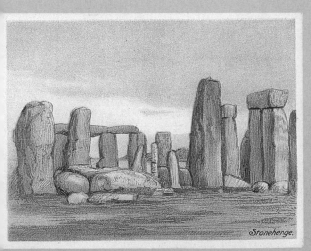

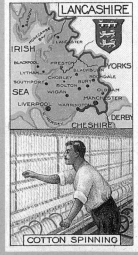

The Nations Shrines.
Player

Counties and Their Industries.
Player

SENSATION CUT PLUG.

Circus Scenes.
Lorillard

Boxing

Pretty Athletes.
Kimball

ALLEN & GINTER'S
CIGARETTES
RICHMOND, VIRGINIA.

Fans of the Period.
Allen & Ginter

MAYO'S CUT PLUG
IS ALWAYS GOOD

For Chewing
and Smoking

P.H.Mayo & Brother
INCOR.
RICHMOND
VA.

SHYLOCK

Shakespeare Characters.
Mayo

OLD POINT
COMFORT

Surf Beauties.
Kinney

BRITISH FASCISTS CIGARETTES

Qty		Date	Odds	Sets
?3	Recruiting Cards	1935	£50.00	—

J. M. BROWN

30	Army Pictures, Cartoons, etc.	1916	£62.50	—

JOHN BRUMFIT

50	The Public Schools Ties Series	1925	£2.50	£125.00

BUCKTROUT & CO. LTD. (Channel Isles)

M416	Around the World/Places of Interest	1924	45p	£187.50
24	Birds of England	1924	£2.50	£60.00
50	Cinema Stars, 1st	1926	£1.20	£62.50
50	Cinema Stars, 2nd	1927	£1.50	£75.00
M50	Football Teams	1928	£1.50	£75.00
L22	Football Teams of the Bailiwick	1927	50p	£11.00
123	Guernsey Footballers (Multi-Backed)	1923	£1.60	£195.00
20	Inventors Series	1924	50p	£10.00
25	Marvels of the Universe Series	1919	£2.00	£50.00
M54	Playing Cards	1930	65p	£35.00
25	Sports & Pastimes	1926	£3.00	£75.00

G. A. BULLOGH

30	Army Pictures, Cartoons, etc.	1916	£62.50	—

BURSTEIN ISAACS & CO. LTD.

50	Famous Prize Fighters (Names in Capitals)	1923	£3.00	£150.00
50	Famous Prize Fighters (Mixed Letters)	1923	£3.00	£150.00
F28	London View Series	1922	£3.15	—

BYRT WOOD & CO.

25	Pretty Girl Series "BAGG"	1900	£100.00	—

CABANA CIGAR CO.

B1	Little Manturios Advertisement Card	1904	—	£175.00

PERCY E. CADLE & CO.

20	Actresses "BLARM"	1900	£25.00	—
26	Actresses "FROGA" (Brown, Printed Back)	1900	£31.25	—
26	Actresses "FROGA" (Brown, Stamped Back) ..	1900	£125.00	—
26	Actresses "FROGA" (Coloured)	1900	£37.50	—
12	Boer War & Boxer Rebellion Sketches	1901	£37.50	—
10	Boer War Generals	1901	£55.00	—
20	Footballers	1904	£25.00	£500.00

CARRERAS LTD.

Qty		Date	Odds	Sets
F24	Actresses and Their Pets (2 Printings)	1926	£3.15	£75.00
50	A Kodak at the Zoo, A Series	1924	50p	£25.00
50	A Kodak at the Zoo, 2nd Series	1925	50p	£25.00
48	Alice in Wonderland (round corners)	1930	50p	£24.00
48	Alice in Wonderland (square corners)	1930	£1.25	£62.50
L48	Alice in Wonderland	1930	55p	£6.50
X1	Alice in Wonderland (Instructions)	1930	—	£5.00
50	Amusing Tricks & How To Do Them...............	1937	40p	£20.00
22	Battle of Waterloo	1934	£1.00	—
L15	Battle of Waterloo	1934	£2.00	—
B1	Battle of Waterloo (Instructions)	1934	—	£4.50
B50	Believe It Or Not	1934	40p	£20.00
50	Birds of the Countryside	1939	50p	£25.00
200	Black Cat Library	1913	£8.15	—
50	Britain's Defences	1938	40p	£20.00
25	British Costumes	1927	90p	£22.50
L25	British Costumes	1927	£1.00	£25.00
F27	British Prime Ministers	1928	80p	£21.50
1	Calendar	1934	—	£18.75
50	Celebrities of British History	1935	50p	£25.00
25	Christie Comedy Girls	1928	£1.25	£31.25
30	Cricketers	1934	£1.90	£57.00
50	Cricketers (A Series of 50, Brown)	1934	£1.75	£87.50
50	Cricketers (A Series of 50, Black)	1934	£25.00	—
F50	Dogs & Friend	1936	20p	£8.75
50	Do You Know?	1939	20p	£7.50
50	Famous Airmen & Airwomen	1936	75p	£37.50
25	Famous Escapes	1926	£1.00	£25.00
L25	Famous Escapes	1926	90p	£22.50
P10	Famous Escapes	1926	£1.55	£15.50
96	Famous Film Stars	1935	50p	£48.00
48	Famous Footballers	1935	40p	£19.50
24	Famous Footballers (25-48 Reprinted)	1935	75p	£18.00
25	Famous Men	1927	£1.00	£25.00
LF24	Famous Naval Men	1929	£1.00	£24.00
X6	Famous Posters (St. Dunstans)	1923	£20.00	—
LF12	Famous Soldiers	1928	£4.40	£53.00
F27	Famous Women	1929	£1.00	£27.00
25	Figures of Fiction	1924	£1.25	£31.25
F54	Film & Stage Beauties	1939	20p	£8.75
LF54	Film and Stage Beauties (2 Printings)	1939	30p	£16.50
LF36	Film and Stage Beauties (2 Printings)	1939	40p	£14.00
XF36	Film and Stage Beauties	1939	65p	£23.50
50	Film Favourites	1938	65p	£32.50
F54	Film Stars, A Series	1937	50p	£27.00
F54	Film Stars, 2nd Series	1938	30p	£16.50
LF54	Film Stars (as 2nd Series)	1938	65p	£35.00
XF36	Film Stars (Different)	1936	£1.75	£63.00
XF36	Film Stars, 2nd Series (Different)	1936	£1.75	£63.00
XF36	Film Stars, 3rd Series	1937	£1.75	£63.00
XF36	Film Stars, 4th Series	1938	£1.75	£63.00
50	Film Stars (By Desmond)	1936	50p	£25.00
72	Film Stars (Oval)	1934	75p	£54.00
F72	Film Stars (Oval) "Real Photos"	1934	£1.25	—

Qty		Date	Odds	Sets
60	Flags of All Nations	Unissued	—	£11.50
28	Flag Dominoes (Unissued)	1926	£6.25	£175.00
K6	Flags & Arms (Circular)	1915	£50.00	—
K6	Flags of the Allies (Shaped)	1915	£37.50	—
K?6	Flags of the Allies (Pin as Mast)	1915	£92.50	—
50	Flowers	1936	25p	£12.50
75	Footballers (Large Titles)	1934	65p	£48.75
75	Footballers (Small Titles)	1934	65p	£48.75
36	Fortune Telling (Card Inset)	1926	25p	£9.00
36	Fortune Telling (Head Inset, Black No.)	1926	20p	£7.20
36	Fortune Telling (Head Inset, Brown No.)	1926	65p	—
L36	Fortune Telling (Card Inset)	1926	20p	£7.20
L36	Fortune Telling (Head Inset)	1926	25p	£9.00
X1	Fortune Telling (Instructions)	1926	—	£5.00
F54	Glamour Girls of Stage and Films	1939	20p	£10.00
LF54	Glamour Girls of Stage and Films	1939	20p	£11.00
LF36	Glamour Girls of Stage and Films	1939	30p	£11.00
XF36	Glamour Girls of Stage and Films	1939	45p	£16.00
B50	Gran-Pop	1934	25p	£12.50
L50	Gran-Pop	1934	30p	£15.00
M16	Guards Series (Sectional)	1970	50p	£8.00
M8	Guards Series (Full Length)	1970	65p	£5.00
M4	Guards Series (Mugs)	1971	65p	£2.50
48	Happy Family	1925	20p	£8.75
L48	Happy Family	1925	20p	£10.00
25	Highwaymen	1924	£1.25	£31.25
50	History of Army Uniforms	1937	75p	£37.50
50	History of Naval Uniforms	1937	65p	£32.50
25	Horses and Hounds	1926	£1.00	£25.00
L20	Horses and Hounds	1926	95p	£19.00
P10	Horses and Hounds	1926	£1.90	£19.00
50	Kings & Queens of England	1935	75p	£37.50
L50	Kings & Queens of England	1935	£1.55	£77.50
L?84	Lace Motifs	1915	£6.25	—
P?12	Lace Motifs (Double Size)	1915	£25.00	—
G?6	Lace Motifs (Quadruple Size)	1915	£37.50	—
F27	Malayan Industries	1929	20p	£5.00
F24	Malayan Scenes	1928	90p	£21.50
LF24	Malayan Scenes	1928	20p	£5.00
7	Millionaire Competition	1971	£1.25	—
K53	Miniature Playing Cards	1934	20p	£8.25
50	Notable M.P.s	1929	45p	£22.50
L50	Notable M.P.s	1929	30p	£15.00
F25	Notable Ships Past & Present	1929	£1.00	£25.00
24	Old Staffordshire Figures	1926	£1.00	£24.00
P12	Old Staffordshire Figures	1926	£2.00	£24.00
L24	Old Staffordshire Figures (Different)	1926	£1.25	£30.00
24	Orchids	1925	30p	£7.25
L24	Orchids	1925	30p	£7.25
P24	Orchids	1925	£1.90	£45.00
50	Our Navy	1937	50p	£25.00
50	Palmistry	1933	20p	£10.00
F27	Paramount Stars	1929	75p	£20.00
25	Picture Puzzle Series	1923	£1.00	£25.00

CARRERAS LTD.—cont.

Qty		Date	Odds	Sets
52	Playing Cards	1926	95p	—
52	Playing Cards & Dominoes (Numbered)	1929	20p	£7.50
52	Playing Cards & Dominoes (Unnumbered)	1929	20p	£9.50
L26	Playing Cards & Dominoes (Numbered)	1929	25p	£6.50
L26	Playing Cards & Dominoes (Unnumbered)	1929	30p	£8.00
48	Popular Footballers	1936	30p	£14.50
72	Popular Personalities (Oval)	1935	50p	£36.00
E12	Premium Silks (Assorted Subjects)	1914	£150.00	—
25	Races Historic & Modern	1927	£1.25	£31.25
L25	Races Historic & Modern	1927	£1.25	£31.25
P12	Races Historic & Modern	1927	£2.50	£30.00
50	Radio & T.V. Favourites	Unissued	£7.50	—
140	Raemaekers War Cartoons (Black Cat)	1916	75p	£105.00
140	Raemaekers War Cartoons (Carreras)	1916	£3.15	—
25	Regalia Series	1925	40p	£10.00
L20	Regalia Series	1925	45p	£9.00
P10	Regalia Series	1925	£1.55	£15.50
L50	Round the World Scenic Models	1925	50p	£25.00
50	School Emblems	1929	40p	£20.00
L40	School Emblems	1929	45p	£18.00
P20	School Emblems	1929	£1.25	£25.00
L216	Sportsman's Guide—Fly Fishing (Canada)	1950	75p	—
48	Tapestry Reproductions of Paintings (Sect.)	1938	40p	£19.50
52	The Greyhound Racing Game	1926	20p	£10.00
L52	The Greyhound Racing Game	1926	20p	£8.75
X1	The Greyhound Racing Game (Instructions)	1926	—	£5.00
B5	The Handy English-French Dictionary	1915	£15.50	—
50	The Nose Game	1927	25p	£12.50
L50	The Nose Game	1927	20p	£10.00
X1	The Nose Game (Instructions)	1927	—	£5.00
50	The Science of Boxing (Black Cat)	1914	£1.25	£62.50
50	The Science of Boxing (Carreras)	1914	£2.50	—
50	Tools and How To Use Them	1935	50p	£25.00
80	Types of London	1919	£1.00	£80.00
F27	Views of London	1929	20p	£5.50
F27	Views of the World	1927	65p	£17.50
M15/20	Wild Animals (Canada)	1985	20p	£3.00
25	Wild Flower Art Series	1923	75p	£18.75
50	Women on War Work	1916	£5.00	£250.00

TURF SLIDES (Cut to Size)

Qty		Date	Odds	Sets
50	British Aircraft	1953	25p	£12.50
50	British Fish	1954	20p	£7.50
50	British Railway Locomotives	1952	45p	£22.50
50	Celebrities of British History	1951	45p	£22.50
50	Famous British Fliers	1956	65p	£32.50
50	Famous Cricketers	1950	£1.60	£80.00
50	Famous Dog Breeds	1952	50p	£25.00
50	Famous Film Stars	1949	50p	£25.00
50	Famous Footballers	1951	75p	£37.50
50	Film Favourites	1948	70p	£35.00
50	Film Stars	1947	60p	£30.00
50	Footballers	1948	70p	£35.00
50	Olympics 1948	1948	75p	£37.50
50	Radio Celebrities	1950	50p	£25.00

CARRERAS LTD.—cont.

Qty		Date	Odds	Sets
50	Sports	1949	50p	£25.00
50	Zoo Animals	1954	20p	£6.25

"BLACK CAT" MODERN ISSUES

50	British Birds	1976	15p	£3.75
50	Flowers All The Year Round	1977	15p	£7.50
50	Kings & Queens of England	1977	15p	£7.50
50	Military Uniforms	1976	15p	£4.50
50	Palmistry	1979	90p	£45.00
50	Sport Fish	1978	15p	£3.75
50	Vintage Cars (with "Filter")	1976	15p	£6.00
50	Vintage Cars (without "Filter")	1976	15p	£4.50

AUSTRALIAN ISSUES

72	Film Stars Series (Smile Away)	1933	£1.90	—
72	Film Stars Series (Standard)	1933	90p	£65.00
72	Football Series	1933	90p	£65.00
24	Personality Series	1933	£1.25	£30.00
72	Personality Series, Film Stars	1933	80p	£57.50
72	Personality Series, Footballers	1933	90p	£65.00

CARRERAS & MARCIANUS

1	Photo Miniatures Folder (3 Printings)	1909	—	£62.50
100	War Series	1915	£50.00	—

CARRICK

12	Military Terms	1900	£50.00	—

P. J. CARROLL & CO.

25	Birds	1939	40p	£10.00
25	British Naval Series	1915	£31.25	—
25	Derby Winners (Black Back)	1914	£62.50	—
25	Derby Winners (Green Back)	1914	£62.50	—
K26	Grand Slam Spelling Bee Cards	1936	£7.50	—
24	Jig Saw Puzzles	1935	£12.50	—
20	Louth—All Ireland Champions	1912	£17.50	—
25	Ship Series	1934	£5.00	£125.00

THE CASKET TOBACCO & CIGARETTE CO. LTD.

?	Cricket Fixture Cards	1905	£250.00	—
1	Cyclists Lighting Up Table	1909	—	£187.50
?	Football Fixture Cards	1909	£150.00	—
?	Road Maps	1909	£187.50	—

S. CAVANDER & CO.

?25	Beauties "PLUMS"	1898	£155.00	—

CAVANDERS LTD.

25	Ancient Chinese	1926	65p	£16.25
25	Ancient Egypt	1928	50p	£12.50
L25	Ancient Egypt (Different)	1928	65p	£16.25

Qty		Date	Odds	Sets
F36	Animal Studies	1936	30p	£11.00
F50	Beauty Spots of Great Britain	1927	20p	£8.00
MF50	Beauty Spots of Great Britain	1927	20p	£9.00
F54	Camera Studies	1926	20p	£7.50
MF56	Camera Studies	1926	20p	£8.75
30	Cinema Stars	1934	75p	£22.50
MS50	Coloured Stereoscopic	1931	30p	£15.00
25	Feathered Friends	1926	£1.50	£37.50
25	Foreign Birds	1926	90p	£22.50
MS50	Glorious Britain	1930	30p	£15.00
25	Little Friends	1924	75p	£18.75
FS72	Peeps into Many Lands, A Series	1927	20p	£12.50
MFS72	Peeps into Many Lands, A Series	1927	25p	£18.00
XFS36	Peeps into Many Lands, A Series	1927	£1.55	£56.00
FS72	Peeps into Many Lands, 2nd Series	1928	20p	£11.00
MFS72	Peeps into Many Lands, 2nd Series	1928	20p	£12.50
FS48	Peeps into Many Lands, 3rd Series	1929	20p	£8.50
MFS48	Peeps into Many Lands, 3rd Series	1929	20p	£9.50
MFS48	Peeps into Many Lands, 3rd (Reprinted)	1929	25p	£12.00
FS48	Peeps into Prehistoric Times, 4th Series	1930	30p	£14.50
MFS48	Peeps into Prehistoric Times, 4th Series	1930	30p	£14.50
F33	Photographs	1935	£1.25	—
L48	Regimental Standards	1923	£8.20	—
25	Reproductions of Celebrated Oil Paintings	1925	65p	£16.25
F108	River Valleys	1926	25p	£25.00
MF108	River Valleys	1926	30p	£31.25
25	School Badges (Dark Blue Back)	1928	40p	£10.00
25	School Badges (Light Blue Back)	1928	40p	£10.00
MF30	The Colonial Series (Large Captions)	1925	30p	£9.00
MF30	The Colonial Series (Small Captions)	1925	30p	£9.00
F54	The Homeland Series (Black Back)	1924	20p	£12.50
F50	The Homeland Series (Blue Back)	1924	65p	£32.50
MF50	The Homeland Series "Hand coloured"	1924	20p	£8.50
MF56	The Homeland Series "Real Photos"	1924	25p	£12.50
MF56	The Homeland Series — uncoloured	1924	25p	£12.50
MF56	The Homeland Series "Reprinted"	1925	30p	£17.50
M25	The Nation's Treasures	1925	40p	£10.00
MF30	Wordsworth's Country	1926	40p	£12.00

R. S. CHALLIS & CO. LTD.

50	Comic Animals	1936	45p	£22.50
?30	Flickits (Fresher Cigarettes)	1936	£31.25	—
36	Wild Birds at Home	1935	40p	£14.00
36	Wild Birds at Home (Baldric deleted)	1935	95p	—

CHAPMAN

30	Army Pictures, Cartoons, etc.	1916	£62.50	—

CHARLESWORTH & AUSTIN

50	Beauties "BOCCA"	1900	£21.50	—
16	British Royal Family	1902	£37.50	—
50	Colonial Troops (Black Back)	1901	£28.00	—

CHARLESWORTH & AUSTIN—cont.

Qty		Date	Odds	Sets
30	Colonial Troops (Brown Back)	1901	£25.00	—
20	Cricketers Series	1902	£250.00	—
30	Flags & Flags with Soldiers	1903	£25.00	—

CHESTERFIELD CIGARETTES

M6	Chesterfield Cocktails	1980	30p	£1.80

A. CHEW & CO.

30	Army Pictures, Cartoons, etc.	1916	£62.50	—

CHING & CO. (Channel Isles)

L24	Around & About in Jersey, 1st Series	1963	20p	£4.75
L24	Around & About in Jersey, 2nd Series	1964	40p	£9.50
25	Do You Know?	1962	—	£2.00
B48	Flowers	1962	65p	£31.25
L24	Jersey Past & Present, 1st Series	1960	—	£2.50
L24	Jersey Past & Present, 2nd Series	1962	—	£3.50
L24	Jersey Past & Present, 3rd Series	1963	—	£2.50
25	Ships and their Workings	1961	—	£2.00
50	Veteran and Vintage Cars	1960	20p	£10.00

W. A. & A. C. CHURCHMAN
36 Page Reference Book—£2.50

24	Actresses, Unicoloured (Blue Printing)	1897	£50.00	—
24	Actresses, Unicoloured (Brown Printing)	1897	£50.00	—
26	Actresses, "FROGA A"	1900	£25.00	—
26	Actresses, "FROGA B"	1900	£31.25	—
M48	Air Raid Precautions	1938	20p	£8.75
25	Army Badges of Rank	1916	£3.75	£93.75
50	Association Footballers, A Series	1938	25p	£12.50
50	Association Footballers, 2nd Series	1939	32p	£16.00
50	A Tour Round The World	1911	£5.00	£250.00
12	Beauties "CERF"	1899	£44.00	£525.00
25	Beauties "CHOAB"	1900	£100.00	—
M?25	Beauties "CHOAB" (Circular)	1900	£312.50	—
25	Beauties "FECKSA"	1903	£75.00	—
25	Beauties "GRACC"	1898	£62.50	—
50	Birds & Eggs	1906	£5.00	£250.00
20	Boer War Cartoons	1901	£87.50	—
41	Boer War Celebrities & Actresses	1901	£15.00	£615.00
20	Boer War Generals "CLAM" (Black)	1901	£31.25	—
20	Boer War Generals "CLAM" (Brown)	1901	£31.25	—
25	Boxing	1922	£2.50	£62.50
50	Boxing Personalities	1938	£1.50	£75.00
50	Boy Scouts, A Series	1916	£4.50	£225.00
50	Boy Scouts, 2nd Series	1916	£4.50	£225.00
50	Boy Scouts, 3rd Series (Blue Back)	1916	£8.25	—
50	Boy Scouts, 3rd Series (Brown Back)	1916	£4.50	£225.00
25	British Film Stars	1934	£1.25	£31.25
54/55	Can You Beat Bogey at St. Andrews?	1934	£1.60	£85.00

W. A. & A. C. CHURCHMAN—cont.

Qty		Date	Odds	Sets
54/55	Can You Beat Bogey (Red Overprint)	1934	£1.60	£85.00
25	Cathedrals & Churches	1924	£1.50	£37.50
X12	Cathedrals & Churches	1924	£8.25	£100.00
50	Celebrated Gateways	1925	£1.75	£87.50
M1	Christmas Greeting Card	1938	—	95p
25	Civic Insignia and Plate	1926	£1.50	£37.50
50	Contract Bridge	1935	30p	£15.00
50	Cricketers	1936	£2.30	£115.00
25	Curious Dwellings	1926	£1.25	£31.25
L12	Curious Dwellings	1926	£3.75	£45.00
25	Curious Signs	1925	£1.50	£37.50
38	Dogs and Fowls	1908	£5.00	£190.00
25	Eastern Proverbs, A Series	1931	40p	£10.00
L12	Eastern Proverbs, A Series	1931	£2.50	£30.00
25	Eastern Proverbs, 2nd Series	1932	40p	£10.00
L12	Eastern Proverbs, 2nd Series	1932	£1.00	£12.00
L12	Eastern Proverbs, 3rd Series	1933	50p	£6.00
L12	Eastern Proverbs, 4th Series	1934	45p	£5.50
50	East Suffolk Churches (Black)	1912	£1.50	£75.00
50	East Suffolk Churches (Sepia)	1917	£1.50	£75.00
50	Empire Railways	1931	£1.75	£87.50
25	Famous Cricket Colours	1928	£2.50	£62.50
50	Famous Golfers	1927	£4.50	£225.00
L12	Famous Golfers, 1st Series	1927	£9.50	—
L12	Famous Golfers, 2nd Series	1928	£9.50	—
25	Famous Railway Trains	1929	£2.00	£50.00
L12	Famous Railway Trains, 1st Series	1929	£3.75	£45.00
L12	Famous Railway Trains, 2nd Series	1929	£3.75	£45.00
50	Fish & Bait	1914	£4.50	£225.00
50	Fishes of the World	1912	£5.00	£250.00
30/50	Fishes of the World	1924	—	£45.00
50	Flags & Funnels of Leading Steamship Lines	1912	£5.00	£250.00
50	Football Club Colours	1909	£6.25	£312.50
50	Footballers (Brown)	1914	£18.00	£900.00
50	Footballers (Coloured)	1914	£7.50	£375.00
52	Frisky	1925	£1.25	£65.00
1	Frisky (Instructions)	1925	—	£3.50
50	History & Development of the British Empire	1934	80p	£40.00
M48	Holidays in Britain (Views & Maps)	1937	20p	£7.50
M48	Holidays in Britain (Views Only)	1938	20p	£7.50
40	Home & Colonial Regiments	1902	£37.50	—
40	Howlers	1937	20p	£6.25
L16	Howlers	1937	40p	£6.50
50	Interesting Buildings	1905	£5.00	£250.00
25	Interesting Door Knockers	1928	£1.75	£43.75
25	Interesting Experiments	1929	£1.00	£25.00
50	In Town To-Night	1938	20p	£6.25
L12	Italian Art Exhibition, 1930, 1st Series	1930	90p	£11.00
L12	Italian Art Exhibition, 1930, 2nd Series	1931	90p	£11.00
50	Kings of Speed	1939	50p	£25.00
50	Landmarks in Railway Progress	1931	£1.90	£95.00
L12	Landmarks in Railway Progress, 1st Series	1932	£3.25	£39.00
L12	Landmarks in Railway Progress, 2nd Series	1932	£3.25	£39.00
50	Lawn Tennis	1928	£1.50	£75.00

W. A. & A. C. CHURCHMAN—cont.

Qty		Date	Odds	Sets
L12	Lawn Tennis	1928	£4.50	£54.00
50	Legends of Britain	1936	65p	£32.50
L12	Legends of Britain	1936	£1.25	£15.00
25	Life in a Liner	1930	90p	£22.50
L12	Life in a Liner	1930	£1.90	£22.75
50	Medals	1910	£5.00	£250.00
50	Men of the Moment in Sport	1928	£1.50	£75.00
L12	Men of the Moment in Sport, 1st Series	1928	£4.50	£54.00
L12	Men of the Moment in Sport, 2nd Series	1928	£4.50	£54.00
M48	Modern Wonders	1938	25p	£12.50
25	Musical Instruments	1924	£1.90	£47.50
25	Nature's Architects	1930	90p	£22.50
L12	Nature's Architects	1930	£2.00	£24.00
D55	Olympic Winners Through the Years	1960	75p	—
50	Phil May Sketches (Gold Flake)	1912	£5.00	£250.00
50	Phil May Sketches (no brand)	1912	£6.25	—
25	Pipes of the World	1927	£1.90	£47.50
50	Prominent Golfers	1931	£5.00	£250.00
L12	Prominent Golfers	1931	£12.50	—
50	Racing Greyhounds	1934	£1.50	£75.00
25	Railway Working, A Series	1926	£2.50	£62.50
L12	Railway Working, A Series	1926	£6.25	£75.00
25	Railway Working, 2nd Series	1927	£1.90	£47.50
L13	Railway Working, 2nd Series	1926	£6.25	£81.25
L12	Railway Working, 3rd Series	1927	£6.25	£75.00
50	Regimental Colours & Cap Badges	1912	£5.00	£250.00
50	Rivers & Broads	1921	£4.40	£220.00
50	Rivers & Broads of Norfolk & Suffolk	1922	£3.75	£187.50
50	Rugby Internationals	1935	90p	£45.00
50	Sectional Cycling Map	1913	£5.00	£250.00
50	Silhouettes of Warships	1915	£6.25	£312.50
50	Sporting Celebrities	1931	£1.50	£75.00
25	Sporting Trophies	1927	£1.50	£37.50
L12	Sporting Trophies	1927	£3.75	£45.00
25	Sports & Games in Many Lands	1929	£1.25	£31.25
25	The Houses of Parliament & Their Story	1931	£1.50	£37.50
25	The Inns of Court	1922	£1.80	£45.00
50	The King's Coronation	1937	20p	£7.50
L15	The King's Coronation	1937	65p	£9.75
M48	The Navy at Work	1937	20p	£6.25
50	The Queen Mary	1936	95p	£47.50
L16	The Queen Mary	1936	£1.50	£24.00
M48	The RAF at Work	1937	50p	£24.00
50	The Story of London	1934	90p	£45.00
L12	The Story of London	1934	£2.15	£26.00
50	The Story of Navigation	1937	20p	£8.00
L12	The Story of Navigation	1937	£1.00	£12.00
D40	The World of Sport	1961	75p	—
36	3 Jovial Golfers	1934	£1.90	£68.50
72	3 Jovial Golfers (Irish Issue)	1934	£3.75	—
50	Treasure Trove	1937	20p	£6.25
L12	Treasure Trove	1937	95p	£11.50
25	Types of British & Colonial Troops	1899	£37.50	—
25	Warriors of All Nations	1929	£2.00	£50.00

W. A. & A. C. CHURCHMAN—cont.

Qty		Date	Odds	Sets
L12	Warriors of All Nations, A Series	1929	£3.15	£38.00
L12	Warriors of All Nations, 2nd Series	1931	£3.15	£38.00
50	Well Known Ties, A Series	1934	50p	£25.00
L12	Well Known Ties, A Series	1934	£1.25	£15.00
50	Well Known Ties, 2nd Series	1935	40p	£20.00
L12	Well Known Ties, 2nd Series	1935	£1.25	£15.00
25	Wembley Exhibition (2 Printings)	1924	£1.75	£43.75
50	West Suffolk Churches	1919	£1.25	£62.50
50	Wild Animals of the World	1907	£5.00	£250.00
M48	Wings Over The Empire	1939	20p	£10.00
50	Wonderful Railway Travel	1937	20p	£10.00
L12	Wonderful Railway Travel	1937	95p	£11.50
50	World Wonders Old and New	Unissued	—	£13.00

OVERSEAS ISSUES (No. I.T.C. Clause)

M48	Air Raid Precautions	1938	£1.25	—
M48	Holidays in Britain (Views & Maps)	1937	£1.25	—
M48	Holidays in Britain (Views only)	1938	£1.25	£62.50
M48	Modern Wonders	1938	£1.25	—
M48	Modern Wonders (Silver Line at Base)	1938	£5.00	—
M48	The Navy at Work	1937	£1.55	£75.00
M48	The R.A.F. at Work	1937	£1.25	—
25	Warriors of all Nations (No Name on Front)	1929	*£6.25*	—
M48	Wings over the Empire	1939	£1.25	—

CIGARETTE COMPANY (Channel Isles)

72	Jersey Footballers (Blue Background)	1910	£3.75	—
50	Jersey Footballers (Grey Background)	1910	£3.75	—
?54	Jersey Footballers (No Frame for Name)	1910	£9.50	—

WM. CLARKE & SON

25	Army Life	1915	£9.00	£225.00
16	Boer War Celebrities	1901	£20.00	£320.00
50	Butterflies & Moths	1912	£6.25	£312.50
30	Cricketer Series	1901	£92.50	—
66	Football Series	1902	£10.50	—
25	Marine Series	1907	£10.00	£250.00
50	Royal Mail	1914	£7.50	£375.00
50	Sporting Terms (Multi-Backed)	1900	£31.25	—
20	Tobacco Leaf Girls	1898	£340.00	—
25	Well Known Sayings	1900	£18.00	£450.00

J. H. CLURE & SON

30	Army Pictures, Cartoons, etc. (No Brands)	1916	*£62.50*	—
30	Army Pictures, Cartoons, etc. (Havana Mixture)	1916	*£62.50*	—
50	War Portraits	1916	*£55.00*	—

J. LOMAX COCKAYNE

50	War Portraits	1916	*£55.00*	—

COHEN WEENEN & CO.

Qty		Date	Odds	Sets
F40	Actresses, Footballers & Jockeys	1901	£35.00	—
26	Actresses "FROGA"	1900	£50.00	—
25	Beauties "BOCCA"	1899	£62.50	—
25	Beauties "GRACC"	1899	£75.00	—
65	Celebrities, Black & White ("250" back)	1900	£3.75	—
25	Celebrities, Black & White ("500" back)	1900	£8.75	—
45	Celebrities, Coloured ("100" back)	1901	£3.25	£145.00
45	Celebrities, Coloured ("250" back)	1901	£7.50	—
76	Celebrities, Coloured ("250", Different)	1901	£3.25	£250.00
30	Celebrities, Gainsborough ("400" back)	1902	£8.75	£262.50
B39	Celebrities, Gainsborough ("250" back)	1902	£31.25	—
B39	Celebrities, Gainsborough (Gold Border)	1902	£31.25	—
M40	Celebrities, Gainsborough (Metal Frame)	1902	£42.50	—
BF?150	Celebrities, Gainsborough	1901	£4.00	—
MF?150	Celebrities, Gainsborough (Metal Frame)	1901	£12.50	—
25	Cricketers	1926	£7.50	£187.50
20	Cricketers, Footballers & Jockeys	1900	£12.50	£312.50
25	Famous Boxers (Black Back)	1912	£7.50	—
25	Famous Boxers (Green Back)	1912	£5.00	£187.50
25	Famous Boxers (Anonymous)	1912	£9.50	—
40	Fiscal Phrases (Copyright Registered)	1902	£8.75	£350.00
40	Fiscal Phrases (No Copyright Clause)	1902	£8.75	£350.00
60	Football Captains	1908	£8.25	£500.00
100	Heroes of Sport	1897	£43.50	—
40	Home & Colonial Regiments ("100" back)	1901	£6.25	£250.00
40	Home & Colonial Regiments ("250" back)	1901	£9.50	£380.00
40	Home & Colonial Regiments (Gold Border)	1901	£95.00	—
20	Interesting Buildings & Views	1902	£7.50	£150.00
20	Interesting Buildings & Views (Gold Surround)	1902	£75.00	—
K52	Miniature Playing Cards (Bandmaster)	1910	£3.25	—
20	Nations (Non Descriptive)	1902	£10.00	£200.00
20	Nations (Descriptive)	1923	£3.75	£75.00
40	Naval & Military Phrases (Blue Back)	1904	£25.00	—
40	Naval & Military Phrases (Red Back)	1906	£15.00	£600.00
40	Naval & Military Phrases (Gold Border)	1906	£75.00	—
50	Owners, Jockeys, Footballers, Cricketers, Series 2	1906	£7.50	£375.00
20	Owners, Jockeys, Footballers, Cricketers, Series 3	1907	£8.25	£165.00
30	Proverbs	1903	£12.50	£375.00
20	Russo Japanese War Series	1902	£12.50	£250.00
25	Silhouettes of Celebrities	1903	£10.00	£250.00
50	Star Artistes	1907	£9.00	£450.00
L16	Victoria Cross Heroes (Silk)	1915	£30.00	—
50	Victoria Cross Heroes (51-100)	1916	£6.25	£312.50
50	Victoria Cross Heroes (51-75, Anonymous)	1916	£9.50	—
50	War Series	1916	£6.25	£312.50
25	War Series (26-50, Anonymous)	1916	£9.50	—
30	Wonders of the World (Green Back)	1908	£6.00	£180.00
30	Wonders of the World (Grey Back)	1923	£2.50	£75.00

T. H. COLLINS

Qty		Date	Odds	Sets
25	Homes of England (Black Front)	1924	£9.50	—
25	Homes of England (Mauve Front)	1924	£4.50	£112.50
25	Sports & Pastimes	1923	£4.50	£112.50

F. COLTON JR.

30	Army Pictures, Cartoons etc., ("Best Brands")	1916	£62.50	—
30	Army Pictures, Cartoons etc., ("Trade Supplied")	1916	£62.50	—
50	War Portraits	1916	£55.00	—

T. W. CONQUEST

30	Army Pictures, Cartoons, etc.	1916	£62.50	

CONTINENTAL CIGARETTE FACTORY

25	Charming Portraits (Firm's Name)	1920	£3.75	—
25	Charming Portraits (Club Mixture, Blue)	1920	£4.50	—
25	Charming Portraits (Club Mixture, Brown)	1920	£6.25	—
25	Charming Portraits (Plain Back)	1920	£3.25	—

COOPER & CO.

25	Boer War Celebrities "STEW" (Alpha)	1901	£100.00	—
25	Boer War Celebrities "STEW" (Gladys)	1901	£100.00	—

CO-OPERATIVE WHOLESALE SOCIETY (C.W.S.)

5	Advertisement Cards	1915	£187.50	—
24	African Types	1936	25p	£6.00
M50	Beauty Spots of Britain	1936	20p	£10.00
50	Boy Scout Badges	1939	45p	£22.50
25	Boy Scout Series	1912	£21.50	—
48	British and Foreign Birds	1938	40p	£19.25
50	British Sports Series (Multi-Backed)	1904	£25.00	—
25	Cooking Recipes	1923	£2.00	£50.00
28	Co-operative Buildings & Works	1909	£10.00	£280.00
24	English Roses	1924	£2.50	£60.00
50	Famous Bridges	1937	50p	£25.00
48	Famous Buildings	1935	40p	£19.25
25	How To Do It	1924	—	£43.75
25	(Anglian Mixture)	1924	£1.75	—
25	(Equity Tobacco)	1924	£1.75	—
25	(Jaycee Brown Flake)	1924	£1.75	—
25	(Raydex Gold Leaf)	1924	£1.75	—
48	Musical Instruments	1934	£2.80	£135.00
25	Parrot Series	1910	£25.00	£625.00
48	Poultry	1927	£3.00	—
48	Railway Engines	1936	£2.25	£110.00
24	Sailing Craft	1935	£1.00	£24.00
18	War Series	1914	£20.00	—
48	Wayside Flowers (Brown Back)	1923	£1.50	£72.00
48	Wayside Flowers (Green Back, Different)	1928	25p	£12.00
48	Wayside Woodland Trees	1924	£1.90	£91.50
24	Western Stars	1957	—	£2.50

COPE BROS. & CO. LTD.

Qty		Date	Odds	Sets
KF?50	Actors & Actresses	1900	£20.00	—
20	Actresses "BLARM" (Plain Backs)	1902	£31.25	—
20	Actresses "BLARM" (Printed Back, 63mm Long)	1902	£31.25	—
20	Actresses "BLARM" (Printed Back, 70mm Long)	1902	£31.25	—
6	Actresses "COPEIS"	1898	£100.00	—
26	Actresses "FROGA"	1900	£75.00	—
F50	Actresses & Beauties	1900	£10.00	£500.00
P?6	Advertisement Cards (Humorous)	1885	£187.50	—
P4	Advertising Postcards	1912	£50.00	—
52	Beauties, Playing Card Inset	1899	£37.50	—
15	Beauties "PAC"	1898	£62.50	—
50	Boats of the World	1912	£8.75	£437.50
25	Boxers (1-25)	1915	£5.00	£125.00
25	Boxers (26-50)	1915	£5.00	£125.00
25	Boxers (51-75)	1915	£5.00	£125.00
25	Boxers (76-100)	1915	£10.00	£250.00
25	Boxers (101-125)	1915	£6.25	£156.00
1	Boxers (New World Champion)	1915	—	£23.00
25	Boxing Lessons	1935	£1.40	£35.00
35	Boy Scouts & Girl Guides	1910	£8.00	£280.00
35	Boy Scouts & Girl Guides (Scandinavian)	1910	£25.00	—
X25	Bridge Problems	1924	£18.75	
25	British Admirals	1915	£8.75	£218.75
50	British Warriors (Black Printing)	1912	£5.00	£250.00
50	British Warriors (Grey Printing)	1912	£7.50	£375.00
25	Castles	1939	50p	£12.50
25	Cathedrals	1939	75p	£18.75
50	Characters From Scott	1900	£8.25	£412.50
20	Chinese Series (1-20)	1903	£9.50	
20	Chinese Series (21-40, Bond of Union)	1903	£9.50	—
20	Chinese Series (21-40, Cope's Courts)	1903	£9.50	—
20	Chinese Series (21-40, Golden Cloud)	1903	£9.50	—
20	Chinese Series (21-40, Golden Magnet)	1903	£9.50	—
20	Chinese Series (21-40, Solace)	1903	£9.50	—
25	Chinese Series (41-65, 2 Printings)	1903	£9.50	—
50	Chinese Series (66-115, Multi-Backed)	1903	£9.50	—
50	Cope's Golfers	1900	£40.00	—
L25	Dickens Character Series	1939	50p	£12.50
50	Dickens Gallery	1900	£7.50	£375.00
50	Dickens Gallery (Solace Back)	1900	£75.00	—
E1	Dickens Gallery Album	1900	—	£110.00
50	Dogs of the World	1912	£7.50	£375.00
50	Dogs of the World (Scandinavian)	1912	£25.00	—
25	Eminent British Regiments Officers Uniforms	1908	£8.75	£218.75
25	Eminent British Regiments (Scandinavian)	1908	£21.50	—
24	Flags, Arms & Types of All Nations (Numbered)	1904	£6.25	£150.00
24	Flags, Arms & Types of All Nations (Unnumbered)	—	£37.50	—
30	Flags of Nations	1903	£10.00	—
30	Flags of Nations (Indian, blue back)	1903	£44.00	—
30	Flags of Nations (plain back)	1903	£8.00	—

COPE BROS. & CO. LTD. — cont.

Qty		Date	Odds	Sets
B50	General Knowledge	1925	£2.50	—
B32	Golf Strokes	1923	£6.50	£210.00
60	Happy Families	1937	90p	£54.00
B50	Household Hints	1925	£1.00	£50.00
X6	Hunting Scenes	1885	£155.00	—
X20	Kenilworth Phrases	1910	£125.00	—
25	Lawn Tennis Strokes	1924	£2.50	£62.50
5	Lawn Tennis Strokes (26-30)	1925	£8.00	—
L50	Modern Dancing	1926	£10.00	—
50	Music Hall Artistes ("Series of 50")	1913	£31.25	—
50	Music Hall Artistes (No Quantity)	1913	£7.50	£375.00
120	Noted Footballers (Clips, 120 Subjects)	1910	£6.25	—
162	Noted Footballers (Clips, 282 Subjects)	1910	£5.00	—
471	Noted Footballers (Clips, 500 Subjects)	1910	£5.00	—
1	Noted Footballers (Clips, Unnumbered)	1910	—	£31.25
195	Noted Footballers (Solace Cigarettes)	1910	£6.25	—
24	Occupations for Women	1897	£62.50	—
X6	Phases of the Moon	1885	£155.00	—
T12	Photo Albums for the Million (Buff)	1902	£12.50	£150.00
T12	Photo Albums for the Million (Green)	1902	£12.50	£150.00
25	Pigeons	1926	£3.00	£75.00
52	Playing Cards (Rounded Corners)	1902	£10.00	—
52	Playing Cards (Squarer Corners)	1902	£10.00	—
30	Scandinavian Actors & Actresses	1910	£37.50	—
50	Shakespeare Gallery	1900	£8.00	£400.00
G14	Smoke Room Booklets	1890	£16.00	—
25	Song Birds	1926	£2.00	£50.00
25	Sports & Pastimes	1925	£2.50	£62.50
L25	The Game of Poker	1936	20p	£5.00
X7	The Seven Ages of Man	1885	£155.00	—
25	The World's Police	1937	£2.30	£57.50
L25	Toy Models — The Country Fair	1925	25p	£6.25
25	Uniforms (Circular Medallion Back)	1898	£25.00	£625.00
25	Uniforms (Square Medallion Back, Narrow)	1898	£20.00	£500.00
25	Uniforms (Square Medallion Back, Wide)	1898	£50.00	—
50	V.C. & D.S.O. Naval & Flying Heroes (Unnumbered)	1916	£5.00	£312.50
25	V.C. & D.S.O. Naval & Flying Heroes (Numbered 51-75)	1916	£6.25	£150.00
20	War Pictures	1915	£8.00	£160.00
25	War Series	1915	£10.00	—
25	Wild Animals & Birds	1907	£15.00	—
25	Wild Animals & Birds (Scandinavian)	1907	£31.25	—

E. CORONEL

25	Types of British & Colonial Troops	1900	£50.00	—

DAVID CORRE & CO.

1	Advertisement Card	1903	£250.00	—
40	Naval & Military Phrases (With Border)	1904	£55.00	—
40	Naval & Military Phrases (No Border)	1904	£55.00	—

JOHN COTTON LTD.

Qty		Date	Odds	Sets
L50	Bridge Hands	1934	£5.00	—
50	Golf Strokes A/B	1936	£5.00	—
50	Golf Strokes C/D	1937	£6.25	—
50	Golf Strokes E/F	1938	£7.50	—
50	Golf Strokes G/H	1939	£40.00	—
50	Golf Strokes I/J	1939	£40.00	—

A. & J. COUDENS LTD.

F60	British Beauty Spots (Numbered)	1923	£1.00	£60.00
F60	British Beauty Spots (Unnumbered)	1923	£1.90	—
F60	British Beauty Spots (Cymax Cigarettes)	1923	£3.75	—
F60	British Beauty Spots (Plain Back Anon)	1923	£3.75	—
F60	Holiday Resorts in East Anglia	1924	90p	£54.00
25	Sports Alphabet	1924	£4.00	£100.00

THE CRAIGMILLAR CREAMERY CO.

M?	Scottish Views	1901	£250.00	—

W. R. DANIEL

30	Colonial Troops (Black Back)	1902	£75.00	—
30	Colonial Troops (Brown Back)	1902	£75.00	—
25	National Flags & Flowers—Girls	1901	£100.00	—

W. T. DAVIES & SONS

?50	Actresses	1902	£62.50	—
30	Aristocrats of the Turf A Series (1-30)	1924	£2.25	£67.50
12	Aristocrats of the Turf (31-42)	1924	£10.00	—
36	Aristocrats of the Turf, 2nd Series	1924	£2.00	£72.00
25	Army Life	1915	£8.75	£218.75
12	Beauties	1903	£31.25	—
25	Boxing	1924	£2.00	£50.00
50	Flags & Funnels of Leading Steamship Lines	1913	£8.25	—
?15	Newport Football Club	1904	£100.00	—
?5	Royal Welsh Fusiliers	1904	£150.00	—

S. H. DAWES

30	Army Pictures, Cartoons, etc.	1916	£62.50	—

J. W. DEWHURST

30	Army Pictures, Cartoons, etc.	1916	£62.50	—

R. I. DEXTER

30	Borough Arms	1900	50p	£15.00

DIANELLOS & VERGOPOULOS

XF?	Views of Cyprus	1926	£30.00	—

GEORGE DOBIE & SON LTD.

Qty		Date	Odds	Sets
M?28	Bridge Problems	1933	*£18.75*	—
M32	Four Square Books (1-32)	1959	65p	£20.50
M32	Four Square Books (33-64)	1960	20p	£6.25
M32	Four Square Books (65-96)	1960	20p	£6.25
25	Weapons of All Ages	1924	£4.40	£110.00

DOBSON'S

8	The European War Series	1917	*£31.25*	—

DOMINION TOBACCO CO. (1929) LTD.

25	Old Ships, 1st Series	1934	£1.00	£25.00
25	Old Ships, 2nd Series	1935	50p	£12.50
25	Old Ships, 3rd Series	1936	50p	£12.50
25	Old Ships, 4th Series	1936	65p	£16.25

JOSEPH W. DOYLE LTD.

F12	Beauties (Series CC.D)	1928	£25.00	—
F12	Beauties (Series CC.E)	1928	£25.00	—
XF18	Children	1928	£9.50	—
F12	Dirt Track Riders (Series CC.A)	1928	*£37.50*	—
F12	Views (Series CC.B)	1928	£25.00	—
F12	Views (Series CC.C)	1928	£25.00	—

DOYLE'S (READING)

?	Merry Miniatures (Booklets)	1924	£75.00	—

MAJOR DRAPKIN & CO.

12	Actresses	1910	£5.00	—
8	Advertisement Cards	1926	£4.50	£36.00
M1	Army Insignia	1915	*£125.00*	—
50	Around Britain	1929	£1.00	£50.00
L50	Around Britain	1929	£2.00	—
50	Around the Mediterranean	1926	£1.00	£50.00
L50	Around the Mediterranean	1926	£2.00	—
F40	Australian and English Test Cricketers	1928	95p	£38.00
?120	Bandmaster Conundrums	1907	£6.25	—
25	British Beauties	1930	£1.90	£47.50
F36	Celebrities of the Great War	1916	45p	£16.00
F34	Celebrities of the Great War (Plain Back)	1916	45p	£15.00
B96	Cinematograph Actors	1913	£7.50	—
15	Dogs and Their Treatment	1924	£3.25	£48.75
L15	Dogs and Their Treatment	1924	£3.75	£56.25
50	Girls of Many Lands	1929	£2.00	—
M50	Girls of Many Lands	1929	25p	£12.50
25	How to Keep Fit (Crayol Cigarettes)	1912	£8.75	£218.75
25	How To Keep Fit (Drapkin Cigarettes)	1912	£8.75	£218.75
54	Life at Whipsnade Zoo	1934	40p	£21.50
50	Limericks	1929	50p	£25.00
F36	National Types of Beauty	1928	50p	£18.00
25	Optical Illusions (Panel 23 x 7mm)	1926	£1.75	£43.75
25	Optical Illusions (Panel 26 x 9mm)	1926	£1.75	£43.75

Although there have been tens of thousands of card sets issued, there are comparatively few books about the hobby. Foremost among the works of reference are those published by the Cartophilic Society. These include a number of books on individual firms, such as Ogden and Wills. Most important however are the four volumes of the "World Tobacco Index" and the three of the "British Trade Index". Each of these builds on the previous volumes, and records new issues, old series that have recently been discovered, and additional subjects to those sets that had been only partially seen. Because it is published annually, our catalogue is often more advanced in its information, and we always welcome news about additions and amendments, which will always be passed on to the Society's research Editor.

A number of dedicated collectors have made their own contributions by compiling lists of a more specialised nature, and we have indeed published many of these ourselves. Among works currently available are three volumes dealing with errors and varieties, one on cricket and two on tennis, a work on tobacco football cards, and a comprehensive list of British silk issues.

There are only three general works now available. These are the well written "Cigarette Card Collecting", the well illustrated "Cigarette Cards & Novelties", and the one we should like to think is a combination of both these features, "The Story of Cigarette Cards". Details of all books that we stock are given in the first few pages of the catalogue.

ERRORS & VARIETIES
BRITISH CIGARETTE CARDS
PART 2

W Bryce Neilson BSc CA

April 1988

MURRAY CARDS

THE STORY OF CIGARETTE CARDS

The Story of
CIGARETTE
CARDS

MARTIN MURRAY

TYPE COLLECTING

TERRY THOMAS

MELKSHAM NUMERAL

There are now many collectors who concentrate on types either exclusively or in addition to their main collections. This involves keeping one or two cards from every series issued. Limitations of space and money make this a good compromise for many people, since they can have a limited goal, yet still providing a sufficient challenge to maintain their interest.

The advent of modern albums has eased one problem for type collectors, since they can now limit themselves to just one card per series, and still be able to see both front and back of that type. Further limitations may also be self-imposed by collecting the issues of just one country, or commodity. One collector 'only' collects one card from each manufacturer, while a lifetime could be spent just in trying to collect the different types issued by the tobacco firm of Wills!

The general collector can also acquire types as a method of identifying those series of which he wishes to obtain complete sets—and those that he wishes to avoid. It is also a useful idea to obtain type cards of all the varieties of one series, so that one can have a complete set of all the pictures and also a specimen of all the different backs that could be found with that front.

RT. HON. H. H. ASQUITH, M.P.

CHURCHMAN'S CIGARETTES.

MRS. L. A. GODFREE.
(GREAT BRITAIN)

STORIES WITHOUT WORDS.

WHO'S THAT CHAP

3

SERIES B.   (7 TO SET)

LICHFIELD

AMOUS OFFICERS

ADM. SIR JOHN JELLICOE.

SINGLETON & COLES
CIGARETTES

H.R.H. PRINCE OF WALES,
Born June 23, 1894.
Promoted Lieutenant,
Royal Navy, 1913.
Joined Grenadier Guards
in 1914.

MAJOR DRAPKIN & CO. —cont.

Qty		Date	Odds	Sets
L25	Optical Illusions	1926	£2.50	£62.50
25	Palmistry	1927	£1.50	£37.50
L25	Palmistry	1927	£1.75	£43.75
48	Photogravure Masterpieces	1915	£7.50	—
25	Puzzle Pictures	1926	£2.00	£50.00
L25	Puzzle Pictures	1926	£2.50	£62.50
M40	Regimental Colours & Badges of the Indian Army (Silk, "BUFFS")	1915	£3.00	—
M40	Regimental Colours & Badges of the Indian Army (Silk, No Brand)	1915	£25.00	—
T25	Soldiers & Their Uniforms (cut-outs)	1914	—	£62.50
T22/25	Soldiers & Their Uniforms (cut-outs)	1914	—	£17.50
T25	Soldiers & Their Uniforms (Crayol)	1914	80p	—
T25	Soldiers & Their Uniforms (Drapkin)	1914	80p	—
F35/36	Sporting Celebrities in Action	1930	90p	£31.50
40	The Game of Sporting Snap	1928	£1.25	£50.00
1	The Greys Advertisement Card	1935	—	£2.00
12	Views of the World	1910	£3.75	—
6/8	Warships	1912	£8.25	£49.50

DRAPKIN & MILLHOFF

?40	Beauties "KEWA" (Eldona Cigarettes)	1899	£92.50	—
?40	Beauties "KEWA" (Explorer Cigarettes)	1889	£92.50	—
25	Boer War Celebrities "PAM" (Multi-Backed)	1901	£21.50	—
30	Colonial Troops (Multi-Backed)	1902	£37.50	—
X?	Pick-Me-Up Paper Inserts	1900	£62.50	—
?25	Pretty Girl Series "BAGG"	1898	£92.50	—

DU MAURIER CIGARETTES

X?50	Advertising Inserts	1931	£4.50	—

J. DUNCAN & CO. LTD.

47/50	Evolution of the Steamship	1925	40p	£18.75
48	Flags, Arms & Types of Nations (Blue)	1911	£25.00	—
48	Flags, Arms & Types of Nations (Green)	1911	£37.50	—
20	Inventors & Their Inventions	1915	£43.00	—
30	Scottish Clans, Arms of Chiefs (Black)	1912	£75.00	—
30	Scottish Clans, Arms of Chiefs (Green)	1912	£15.00	£450.00
L72	Scottish Gems (Coloured)	1912	£10.00	—
L50	Scottish Gems, 2nd Series	1913	£10.00	—
L50	Scottish Gems, 3rd Series	1914	£10.00	—
L50	Scottish Gems (Reprint, Black & White)	1925	45p	£22.50
25	Types of British Soldiers	1910	£37.50	—

GEO. DUNCOMBE

30	Army Pictures, Cartoons, etc.	1916	£62.50	—

ALFRED DUNHILL LTD.

M25	Dunhill King Size Ransom	1985	£1.25	—

EDWARD VII CIGARETTES

40	Home & Colonial Regiments	1901	£187.50	—

EDWARDS, RINGER & CO.

Qty		Date	Odds	Sets
X50	How To Count Cribbage Hands	1908	£62.50	—

EDWARDS RINGER & BIGG

Qty		Date	Odds	Sets
25	Abbeys & Castles (Exmoor Hunt Back)	1912	£6.25	£156.25
25	Abbeys & Castles (New York Back)	1912	£6.25	£156.25
25	Abbeys & Castles (Type Set Back)	1912	£7.50	£187.50
25	Alpine Views (Exmoor Hunt Back)	1912	£6.25	£156.25
25	Alpine Views (New York Back)	1912	£6.25	£156.25
50	A Tour Round the World	1909	£7.50	—
12	Beauties "CERF"	1905	£45.00	—
25	Beauties "FECKSA"	1900	£30.00	—
50	Birds & Eggs	1906	£10.00	—
?25	Boer War Sketches	1901	£95.00	—
25	Boer War Celebrities "STEW"	1901	£37.50	—
25	British Trees & Their Uses	1933	£2.00	£50.00
1	Calendar & Lighting up Table	1899	—	£230.00
1	Calendar	1905	—	£187.50
1	Calendar (Empire Back)	1910	—	£230.00
1	Calendar (New York Back)	1910	—	£230.00
50	Celebrated Bridges	1924	£1.75	£87.50
50	Cinema Stars	1923	75p	£37.50
L25	Cinema Stars	1923	£1.00	£25.00
25	Coast and Country (Exmoor Hunt Back)	1911	£6.25	£156.25
25	Coast and Country (New York Back)	1911	£6.25	£156.25
23	Dogs Series (Exmoor Hunt Back)	1908	£6.25	—
23	Dogs Series (Klondyke Back)	1908	£2.50	£57.50
3	Easter Manoeuvres of our Volunteers	1897	£250.00	—
25	Flags of All Nations (1st Series)	1907	£5.00	—
12	Flags of All Nations (2nd Series)	1907	£5.00	—
37	Flags of All Nations (Exmoor Hunt)	1907	£5.00	—
37	Flags of All Nations (Globe & Flags)	1907	£5.00	—
37	Flags of All Nations (Stag Design)	1907	£5.00	—
37	Flags of All Nations (Vertical Back)	1907	£5.00	—
25	Garden Life	1934	£2.50	£62.50
25	How to Tell Fortunes	1929	£3.20	£80.00
50	Life on Board a Man Of War	1905	£7.50	—
1	Miners Bound for Klondyke	1897	—	£375.00
50	Mining	1925	£1.75	£87.50
25	Musical Instruments	1924	£2.50	£62.50
25	Optical Illusions	1936	£1.90	£47.50
25	Our Pets A series	1926	£1.90	£47.50
25	Our Pets 2nd Series	1926	£2.00	£50.00
25	Past & Present	1928	£3.00	£75.00
10	Portraits of His Majesty the King	1902	£30.00	£300.00
25	Prehistoric Animals	1924	£2.50	£62.50
25	Sports & Games in Many Lands	1935	£2.00	£50.00
56	War Map, Western Front	1916	£8.25	£460.00
54	War Map of the Western Front, Series 2 (Exmoor Hunt Back)	1917	£8.25	—
54	War Map of the Western Front, Series 2 (New York Back)	1917	£8.25	—

S. EISISKI

Qty		Date	Odds	Sets
?20	Actresses "ANGOOD"	1900	£125.00	—
6	Beauties "COPEIS"	1899	£125.00	—
?20	Beauties "FENA" (Printed Back)	1899	£125.00	—
?20	Beauties "FENA" (Rubber Stamped Back)	1899	£125.00	—
?40	Beauties "KEWA" (Birds Eye Back)	1900	£125.00	—
?40	Beauties "KEWA" (New Gold Back)	1900	£125.00	—
?40	Beauties "KEWA" (Rubber Stamped Back)	1900	£125.00	—

R. J. ELLIOTT & CO. LTD.

1	Bulldog Advertisment Card (2 Types)	1910	—	£125.00

EMPIRE TOBACCO CO.

6	Franco British Exhibition	1907	£125.00	—

ENCHANTERESSE EGYPTIAN CIG. CO.

20	Actresses "ANGOOD"	1898	£125.00	—

THE EXPRESS TOBACCO CO. LTD.

M50	How It Is Made (Motor Cars)	1939	£2.20	£110.00

L. & J. FABIAN

F24	The Elite Series (Numbered LLF1-24)	1932	£31.25	—
F?24	The Elite Series (Plain Numerals)	1932	£31.25	—

FAIRWEATHER & SONS

50	Historic Buildings of Scotland	1914	£40.00	£2000.00

W. & F. FAULKNER
12 Page Reference Book — £2.50

26	Actresses "FROGA"	1900	£37.50	—
25	Angling	1929	£3.75	£93.75
12	'Ation Series	1901	£17.50	£210.00
25	Beauties (Coloured)	1898	£50.00	—
49	Beauties "FECKSA"	1901	£15.00	£750.00
16	British Royal Family	1901	£27.50	—
50	Celebrated Bridges	1925	£1.75	£87.50
12	Coster Series	1900	£17.50	£210.00
20	Cricketers Series	1902	£175.00	—
12	Cricket Terms	1899	£43.75	£525.00
12	Football Terms, 1st Series	1900	£17.50	£210.00
12	Football Terms, 2nd Series	1900	£17.50	£210.00
12	Golf Terms	1901	£50.00	£600.00
12	Grenadier Guards	1899	£20.00	£240.00
40	Kings & Queens	1902	£20.00	—
12	Kipling Series	1900	£18.75	—
12	Military Terms, 1st Series	1899	£15.00	£180.00
12	Military Terms, 2nd Series	1899	£15.00	£180.00
12	Nautical Terms, 1st Series (2 Printings)	1900	£15.00	£180.00
12	Nautical Terms, 2nd Series (Grenadier)	1900	£15.00	£180.00

W. & F. FAULKNER—cont.

Qty		Date	Odds	Sets
12	Nautical Terms, 2nd Series (Union Jack)	1900	£17.50	£210.00
25	Old Sporting Prints	1930	£1.90	£47.50
25	Optical Illusions	1935	£1.75	£43.75
90	Our Colonial Troops (Grenadier)	1900	£10.00	£900.00
30	Our Colonial Troops (Grenadier, with			
	Copyright, 1-30)	1900	£18.75	—
60	Our Colonial Troops (Union Jack, 31-90)	1900	£12.50	—
20	Our Gallant Grenadiers	1902	£12.50	£250.00
20	Our Gallant Grenadiers (I.T.C. Clause)	1903	£25.00	—
20	Our Gallant Grenadiers (Numbered 21-40)	1902	£18.75	£375.00
25	Our Pets	1926	£2.50	£62.50
25	Our Pets, 2nd Series	1926	£2.00	£50.00
12	Policemen of the World (Grenadier)	1899	*£125.00*	—
12	Policemen of the World (Nosegay)	1899	£25.00	—
12	Police Terms	1899	£17.50	210.00
25	Prominent Racehorses of the Present Day	1923	£1.90	£47.50
25	Prominent Racehorses of the Present Day,			
	2nd Series	1924	£3.00	£75.00
12	Puzzle Series (Grenadier)	1898	*£90.00*	—
12	Puzzle Series (Nosegay)	1898	£42.50	—
25	South African War Series	1901	£10.00	£240.00
12	Sporting Terms	1900	£21.50	—
12	Street Cries	1902	£18.75	£225.00
12	The Language of Flowers (Grenadier)	1900	£25.00	—
12	The Language of Flowers (Nosegay)	1900	£25.00	—

FIELD FAVORITES CIGARETTES

F?	Footballers	1893	*£187.50*	—

THE FIGARO CIGARETTE

X?12	Caricatures	1880	*£250.00*	—

FINLAY & CO. LTD.

?10	Our Girls	1910	*£125.00*	—
30	World's Aircraft	1912	£42.50	—

FLYNN

26	Beauties "HOL"	1899	*£187.50*	—

C. D. FOTHERGILL

?	Football Shields	1900	*£125.00*	—

FRAENKEL BROS.

?20	Beauties—Don Jorge (2 Printings)	1897	*£155.00*	—
?20	Beauties—"FENA"	1899	£80.00	—
25	Beauties—"GRACC"	1898	*£95.00*	—
24	Beauties—"HUMPS"	1899	*£90.00*	—
26	Music Hall Artistes (Pink Card)	1900	£75.00	—
26	Music Hall Artistes (White Card)	1900	£75.00	—
25	Types of British & Colonial Troops	1900	£55.00	—

FRANKLYN DAVEY & CO.

Qty		Date	Odds	Sets
12	Beauties "CERF"	1905	£45.00	—
50	Birds	1896	£40.00	—
10	Boer War Generals	1901	£80.00	—
25	Boxing	1924	£1.50	£37.50
25	Ceremonial and Court Dress	1915	£7.50	£187.50
50	Children of All Nations	1934	45p	£22.50
1	Comic Dog Folder	1898	—	£187.50
50	Football Club Colours	1909	£8.25	—
50	Historic Events	1924	£1.75	£87.50
25	Hunting	1925	65p	£16.25
50	Modern Dance Steps, A Series	1930	£3.25	£162.50
50	Modern Dance Steps, 2nd Series	1931	50p	£25.00
50	Naval Dress & Badges	1916	£8.25	—
50	Overseas Dominions (Australia)	1923	£3.25	—
25	Star Girls	1901	£125.00	—
10	Types of Smokers	1898	£42.50	£425.00
50	Wild Animals of the World	1902	£8.00	—

A. H. FRANKS & SONS

56	Beauties	1901	£50.00	—
24	Nautical Expressions	1902	£62.50	—
25	Types of British & Colonial Troops	1900	£50.00	—

J. J. FREEMAN & CO.

12	Actresses "FRAN"	1915	£31.25	—
12	Views of the World	1910	£31.25	—

J. R. FREEMAN

33	Football Challenge (3 Printings)	1969	£2.00	—
B12	Manikin Cards	1915	£57.50	—

C. FRYER & SONS LTD.

25	Boer War & General Interest (3 Backs)	1900	£92.50	—
X50	Clan Sketches	1930	£8.00	£400.00
40	Naval & Military Phrases	1904	£42.50	—
?25	Vita Berlin Series	1901	£125.00	—

FRYER & COULTMAN

X12	Almanack	1893	£187.50	—

J. GABRIEL

10	Actresses "HAGG"	1900	£50.00	—
25	Beauties "GRACC"	1898	£100.00	—
20	Cricketers Series	1902	£280.00	—
40	Home & Colonial Regiments	1902	£75.00	—
55	Pretty Girl Series "BAGG"	1898	£62.50	—
25	Types of British & Colonial Troops	1899	£55.00	—

GALA CIGARETTES

1	Stamp Cards	1910	—	£100.00

GALLAHER LTD.

40 Page Reference Book — £2.50

Qty		Date	Odds	Sets
F110	Actors & Actresses	1901	£3.75	—
48	Aeroplanes	1939	45p	£21.50
25	Aesop's Fables ("Series of 25")	1931	75p	£18.75
25	Aesop's Fables ("Series of 50")	1931	75p	£18.75
100	Animals & Birds of Commercial Value	1921	40p	£40.00
48	Army Badges	1939	40p	£19.25
L24	Art Treasures of the World	1930	40p	£9.75
100	Association Football Club Colours	1910	£3.15	£315.00
52	Beauties (Playing Card Inset)	1905	£10.00	£500.00
52	Beauties (No Inset)	1905	£10.00	£500.00
MF48	Beautiful Scotland	1939	50p	£24.00
50	Birds & Eggs (Gallaher Ltd Only Label)	1905	*£31.25*	—
50	Birds & Eggs ("Manufactured By" Label)	1905	£6.25	—
100	Birds Nests & Eggs	1919	£1.00	£100.00
100	Boy Scout Series (Green, Belfast & London)	1911	£1.05	£105.00
86	Boy Scout Series (Green, London & Belfast)	1911	£1.55	—
100	Boy Scout Series (Brown back)	1922	95p	£95.00
48	British Birds	1937	20p	£8.00
100	British Birds by George Rankin	1923	50p	£50.00
100	British Birds by Rankin	1923	*£6.50*	—
75	British Champions of 1923	1924	£1.00	£75.00
50	British Naval Series	1914	£3.20	£160.00
48	Butterflies & Moths	1938	20p	£7.50
25	Champion Animals & Birds of 1923	1924	£1.00	£25.00
48	Champions, A Series (No Captions Front)	1934	25p	£12.00
48	Champions, A Series (Captions on Front)	1934	25p	£12.00
48	Champions, 2nd Series	1935	20p	£9.25
48	Champions of Screen & Stage (Red back)	1934	30p	£15.00
48	Champions of Screen & Stage (Blue Back, Gallaher Cigarettes)	1934	75p	£36.00
48	Champions of Screen & Stage (Blue Back, Gallaher Limited)	1934	65p	£31.50
100	Cinema Stars	1926	£1.00	£100.00
MF48	Coastwise	1938	45p	—
24	Dogs (Caption in block)	1934	40p	£9.75
24	Dogs (Caption in script)	1934	£1.00	£24.00
L24	Dogs (Caption in block)	1934	40p	£9.75
L24	Dogs (Caption in script)	1934	£1.00	£24.00
48	Dogs, A Series	1936	30p	£14.50
48	Dogs, 2nd Series	1938	20p	£9.50
F100	English & Scotch Views	1910	£2.50	£250.00
100	Fables & Their Morals (No. by Caption)	1912	£1.25	£125.00
100	Fables & Their Morals (Thick Numerals)	1922	45p	£45.00
100	Fables & Their Morals (Thin Numerals)	1922	50p	£50.00
100	Famous Cricketers	1926	£1.65	£165.00
48	Famous Film Scenes	1935	40p	£20.00
50	Famous Footballers (Brown Back)	1926	£1.25	£62.50
100	Famous Footballers (Green back)	1925	90p	£90.00
48	Famous Jockeys (Blue Printing)	1936	50p	£24.00
48	Famous Jockeys (Mauve Printing)	1936	£1.00	—
48	Film Episodes	1936	40p	£20.00
48	Film Partners	1935	40p	£20.00
M24	Flags (Silk)	1915	£6.25	—

GALLAHER LTD. — cont.

Qty		Date	Odds	Sets
MF48	Flying	1938	65p	—
50	Footballers (1-50)	1925	£1.00	£50.00
50	Footballers (51-100)	1925	£1.25	£62.50
50	Footballers in Action	1928	£1.20	£60.00
48	Garden Flowers	1938	20p	£7.00
100	How To Do It	1916	£2.50	£250.00
F100	Interesting Views (Black & White)	1923	£1.05	£105.00
F100	Interesting Views (Coloured)	1923	£1.90	£190.00
400	Irish Views Scenery (Numbered on back)	1908	£1.50	—
400	Irish Views Scenery ("Ltd" In Block Letters)	1908	75p	£300.00
F400	Irish View Scenery (Chocolate Fronts)	1910	£1.90	—
F400	Irish View Scenery (Plain Backs)	1910	£2.50	—
F400	Irish View Scenery ("Ltd" In Script)	1910	75p	—
F200	Irish View Scenery (401-600)	1910	£1.55	—
LF48	Island Sporting Celebrities	1938	65p	£31.25
100	Kute Kiddies	1916	£2.50	£250.00
F50	Latest Actresses (Black & White)	1909	£10.00	£500.00
F50	Latest Actresses (Chocolate Fronts)	1909	£14.00	—
50	Lawn Tennis Celebrities	1928	£2.20	£110.00
24	Motor Cars	1934	£2.50	£60.00
48	My Favourite Part	1939	40p	£20.00
MF48	Our Countryside	1938	65p	—
100	Plants of Commercial Value	1917	55p	£55.00
48	Portraits of Famous Stars	1935	50p	£24.00
48	Racing Scenes	1938	25p	£12.00
50	Regimental Colours & Standards	1899	£5.00	£250.00
100	Robinson Crusoe	1928	£1.05	£105.00
50	Royalty Series	1902	£4.50	£225.00
LF48	Scenes from the Empire	1939	20p	£10.00
48	Shots from Famous Films	1935	30p	£15.00
MF24	Shots from the Films	1936	*£1.90*	—
48	Signed Portraits of Famous Stars	1935	£1.00	£48.00
48	Sporting Personalities	1936	20p	£8.25
100	Sports Series	1912	£3.15	£315.00
100	Stage & Variety Celebrities (Multibacked)	1899	£50.00	—
48	Stars of Screen & Stage (Brown back)	1935	£1.00	£48.00
48	Stars of Screen & Stage (Green back)	1935	40p	£20.00
25	The Allies Flags	1914	£3.75	£93.75
100	The Great War Series	1915	£1.75	£175.00
100	The Great War Second Series	1915	£1.90	£190.00
25	The Great War V.C. Heroes, 1st Series	1915	£3.20	£80.00
25	The Great War V.C. Heroes, 2nd Series	1915	£3.00	£75.00
25	The Great War V.C. Heroes, 3rd Series	1915	£3.00	£75.00
25	The Great War V.C. Heroes, 4th Series	1916	£3.00	£75.00
25	The Great War V.C. Heroes, 5th Series	1916	£3.00	£75.00
25	The Great War V.C. Heroes, 6th Series	1917	£3.00	£75.00
25	The Great War V.C. Heroes, 7th Series	1917	£3.00	£75.00
25	The Great War V.C. Heores, 8th Series	1918	£3.00	£75.00
48	The Navy (Gallaher)	1937	25p	£12.00
48	The Navy (Park Drive)	1937	20p	£6.25
100	The Reason Why	1924	45p	£45.00
111	The South African Series	1901	£4.50	£500.00
100	The Zoo Aquarium	1924	80p	£80.00
48	Trains of the World	1937	45p	£21.75

GALLAHER LTD. —cont.

Qty		Date	Odds	Sets
100	Tricks & Puzzles Series (Green back)	1913	£2.80	£280.00
100	Tricks & Puzzles Series (Black back)	1933	50p	£50.00
50	Types of the British Army (Battle Honour)	1897	£7.50	£375.00
50	Types of the British Army (Green back)	1898	£6.25	£312.50
50	Types of the British Army (numbered 1-50, Three Pipe Tobaccos in Brown)	1898	£6.25	£312.50
50	Types of the British Army (numbered 1-50, Now in Three Strengths)	1898	£6.25	£312.50
50	Types of the British Army (numbered 51-100, Three Pipe Tobaccos (2 Printings))	1898	£6.25	£312.50
50	Types of the British Army (numbered 51-100, Now in Three Strengths)	1898	£6.25	£312.50
100	Useful Hints Series	1915	£2.50	£250.00
25	Views in North of Ireland	1912	£36.00	£900.00
50	Votaries of the Weed	1916	£4.40	£220.00
100	Why Is It? (Brown back)	1915	£2.50	£250.00
100	Why Is It? (Green back)	1915	£2.20	£220.00
48	Wild Animals	1937	20p	£7.50
48	Wild Flowers	1939	20p	£8.50
100	Woodland Trees Series	1912	£2.50	£250.00
50	Zoo Tropical Birds, 1st Series	1928	£1.00	£50.00
50	Zoo Tropical Birds, 2nd Series	1929	£1.00	£50.00

GASPA

?20	Our Great Novelists	1930	£37.50	—

SAMUEL GAWITH

X25	The English Lakeland	1926	£15.00	£375.00

F. GENNARI

50	War Portraits	1916	£62.50	—

LOUIS GERARD LTD.

50	Modern Armaments (Numbered)	1938	30p	£15.00
50	Modern Armaments (Unnumbered)	1938	50p	£25.00
24	Screen Favourites (Gerard & Co)....................	1937	£2.20	—
24	Screen Favourites (Gerard Ltd)	1937	£2.20	—
48	Screen Favourites & Dancers	1937	£1.55	£75.00

GLASS & CO. LTD.

20	Actresses "BLARM"	1900	£55.00	—
10	Actresses "HAGG"	1900	£62.50	—
25	Beauties "FECKSA"	1903	£75.00	—
20	Boer War Cartoons	1901	£75.00	—
25	Boer War Celebrities "STEW"	1901	£62.50	—
16	British Royal Family	1901	£55.00	—
20	Cricketers Series	1902	£275.00	—
40	Naval & Military Phrases	1902	£80.00	—
19	Russo Japanese Series	1903	£50.00	—

R. P. GLOAG & CO.

Qty		Date	Odds	Sets
?25	Actresses "ANGLO" (The Challenge Flat)	1896	*£155.00*	—
?25	Actresses "ANGLO" (Citamora)	1896	*£155.00*	—
?50	Beauties "PLUMS" (Black & White, Citamora) .	1896	£80.00	—
?50	Beauties "PLUMS" (Black & White, Challenge Flat)	1896	£80.00	—
?50	Beauties "PLUMS" (Brown, Plain Backs)	1896	*£125.00*	—
?50	Beauties "PLUMS" (Brown, Printed Backs)	1896	*£125.00*	—
40	Home & Colonial Regiments	1900	£40.00	—
30	Proverbs	1901	*£75.00*	—
25	Types of British & Colonial Troops	1900	£50.00	—

THE GLOBE CIGARETTE CO.

25	Actresses — French	1898	£125.00	—

GOLDS LTD.

1	Advertisement Card	1905	*£250.00*	—
18	Motor Cycle Series (Blue Back)	1914	£37.50	—
18	Motor Cycle Series (Grey Back Numbered)	1914	£42.50	—
18	Motor Cycle Series (Grey Back Unnumbered) ...	1914	£50.00	—
L?15	Prints from Noted Pictures	1908	*£100.00*	—

T. P. & R. GOODBODY

20	Actresses "ANGOOD"	1898	*£125.00*	—
?50	Beauties "KEWA" (Mauve Back)	1898	*£90.00*	—
?50	Beauties "KEWA" (Red Back)	1898	*£90.00*	—
25	Boer War Celebrities (Multi-Backed)	1901	£25.00	—
16	Boer War Celebrities (Complete Frame, Multi-Backed)	1900	£25.00	—
16	Boer War Celebrities (No Vertical Lines, Multi-Backed)	1900	£31.25	—
16	Boer War Celebrities (With Vertical Lines, Only 2 Horizontal, Multi-Backed)	1900	£31.25	—
50	Colonial Forces (Black Back)	1900	£55.00	—
50	Colonial Forces (Brown Back)	1900	£55.00	—
B50	Colonial Forces	1900	*£125.00*	—
?50	Dogs (Multi-Backed)	1903	*£62.50*	—
26	Eminent Actresses	1900	£40.00	£1000.00
20	Irish Scenery (Donore Castle Cigarettes)	1905	£37.50	—
20	Irish Scenery (Furze Blossom Cigarettes)	1905	£37.50	—
20	Irish Scenery (Primrose Cigarettes)	1905	£37.50	—
20	Irish Scenery (Royal Wave Cigarettes)	1905	£37.50	—
20	Irish Scenery (Straight Cut Cigarettes)	1905	£37.50	—
?25	Pretty Girl Series "BAGG" (Grey Back)	1898	*£90.00*	—
?25	Pretty Girl Series "BAGG" (Mauve Back)	1898	*£90.00*	—
?25	Pretty Girl Series "BAGG" (Red Back)	1898	*£90.00*	—
?25	Pretty Girl Series "BAGG" (No Brands)	1898	*£90.00*	—
50	Questions & Answers in Natural History	1924	£2.00	£100.00
25	Sports & Pastimes	1925	£4.40	£110.00
25	Types of Soldiers	1914	£42.50	—
20	War Pictures	1915	£18.75	£375.00
12	With the Flag to Pretoria	1901	£80.00	—

GORDON'S

| ?4 | Billiards .... | 1912 | £150.00 | — |

GRAVESON

| 30 | Army Pictures, Cartoons, etc. (3 Backs) .... | 1916 | £62.50 | — |

FRED GRAY

| 25 | Types of British Soldiers .... | 1914 | £80.00 | — |

GRIFFITHS BROS.

| XF18 | Children .... | 1928 | £62.50 | — |

GUERNSEY TOBACCO CO. (Channel Isles)

49	And When Did You Last See Your Father?	1936	£1.00	£50.00
K52	Miniature Playing Cards	1933	75p	—
48	The Laughing Cavalier (Sect)	1935	£1.00	£50.00
48	The Toast (Sect, Black Back)	1935	£1.00	£50.00
48	The Toast (Sect, Green Back)	1935	£6.25	—

HARRIS & SONS

26	Beauties ''HOL''	1900	£25.00	—
30	Colonial Troops	1901	£75.00	—
25	Star Girls	1899	£155.00	—

JAS. H. HARRISON

| 18 | Motor Cycle Series .... | 1914 | £55.00 | — |

HARVEY & DAVEY

50	Birds & Eggs	1905	£3.00	£150.00
35	Chinese & South African Series	1901	£105.00	—
30	Colonial Troops	1902	£62.50	—
25	Types of British & Colonial Troops	1901	£75.00	—

W. HEATON

| ?6 | Birkby Views .... | 1912 | £125.00 | — |

HENLY & WATKINS LTD.

| 25 | Ancient Egyptian Gods (Plain back) .... | 1924 | £2.00 | £50.00 |
| 25 | Ancient Egyptian Gods (Printed back) .... | 1924 | £2.50 | £62.50 |

HIGNETT BROS & CO.

50	Actors Natural & Character Studies	1938	50p	£25.00
26	Actresses ''FROGA''	1900	£42.50	—
25	Actresses, Photogravure	1900	£20.00	—
28	Actresses, PILPI I	1901	£16.00	£450.00
F50	Actresses, PILPI II	1901	£10.00	£500.00
P1	Advertisement Card, Calendar Back	1884	—	£312.50
P8	Advertisement Cards (6 Brands)	1890	£250.00	—

HIGNETT BROS. & CO. — cont.

Qty		Date	Odds	Sets
50	A.F.C. Nicknames	1933	£2.00	—
50	Air Raid Precautions	1939	50p	£25.00
60	Animal Pictures	1899	£25.00	—
50	Arms & Armour	1924	£2.00	£100.00
25	Beauties ''CHOAB''	1900	*£100.00*	—
50	Beauties, Gravure (Cavalier Cigarettes)	1898	£55.00	—
50	Beauties, Gravure (Golden Butterfly)	1898	£55.00	—
BF50	Beauties (Chess Cigarettes) (Set 1)	1927	75p	£37.50
BF50	Beauties (No Brand)	1927	90p	£45.00
BF50	Beauties (Chess Cigarettes) (Set 2)	1927	75p	£37.50
50	British Birds & Their Eggs	1938	£1.25	£62.50
50	Broadcasting	1935	£1.50	—
20	Cabinet 1900	1900	£62.50	—
25	Cathedrals & Churches	1909	£3.15	£78.75
50	Celebrated Old Inns	1925	£2.20	£110.00
50	Champions of 1936	1936	£1.50	£75.00
25	Common Objects of the Sea-Shore	1924	£1.90	£47.50
25	Company Drill	1915	£3.00	£75.00
50	Coronation Procession	1937	£1.55	—
50	Dogs	1936	£1.25	£62.50
50	Football Caricatures	1935	£1.50	—
50	Football Club Captains	1936	£1.55	—
25	Greetings of the World	1907	£2.00	£50.00
25	Historical London	1926	£2.00	£50.00
50	How to Swim	1935	50p	£25.00
50	Interesting Buildings	1905	£4.40	£220.00
25	International Caps and Badges	1924	£2.50	£62.50
25	Life In Pond & Stream	1925	£2.00	£50.00
40	Medals	1900	£20.00	—
25	Military Portraits	1914	£3.60	£90.00
50	Modern Railways	1936	£1.55	—
25	Modern Statesmen (Butterfly Cigarettes)	1906	£4.40	£110.00
25	Modern Statesmen (Pioneer Cigarettes)	1906	£4.40	£110.00
20	Music Hall Artistes	1898	£42.50	—
50	Ocean Greyhounds	1938	£1.00	£50.00
M1	Oracle Butterfly (Several Printings)	1898	—	£75.00
25	Panama Canal	1914	£5.00	£125.00
12	Pretty Girl Series ''RASH''	1900	£42.50	—
50	Prominent Cricketers of 1938	1938	£2.00	£100.00
50	Prominent Racehorses of 1933	1933	£1.50	£75.00
G1	Riddle Folder	1893	—	*£150.00*
50	Sea Adventure	1939	25p	£12.50
25	Ships, Flags & Cap Badges, A Series	1926	£2.25	£56.25
25	Ships, Flags & Cap Badges, 2nd Series	1927	£3.00	£75.00
50	Shots from the Films	1936	£1.25	£62.50
25	The Prince of Wales Empire Tour	1924	£2.00	£50.00
50	Trick Billiards	1934	£2.00	—
25	Turnpikes	1927	£1.90	£47.50
P?	Uniforms & Armies of Countries	1890	*£250.00*	—
25	V.C. Heroes	1901	£37.50	£937.50
20	Yachts (Black back)	1898	£50.00	—
20	Yachts (White back)	1898	£57.50	—
50	Zoo Studies	1937	75p	£37.50

R. & J. HILL LTD.
28 Page Reference Book — £2.50

Qty		Date	Odds	Sets
25	Actresses — Belle of New York (39mm Wide) ...	1899	£17.50	£437.50
25	Actresses — Belle of New York (41mm Wide) ...	1899	£18.75	£468.75
20	Actresses — Chocolate (Hill Cigarettes)	1917	£15.00	—
20	Actresses — Chocolate (Hill Tobaccos)	1917	£15.00	—
20	Actresses — Chocolate (Plain Back)	1917	£15.00	—
30	Actresses — Continental (Whisky Back)	1906	£15.00	—
30	Actresses — Continental (Seven Wonders)	1906	£12.50	£375.00
30	Actresses — Continental (Plain Back)	1906	£15.00	—
26	Actresses "FROGA"	1900	£42.50	—
?16	Actresses "HAGG" (High Class Cigarettes)	1900	£31.25	—
?16	Actresses "HAGG" (Stockrider)	1900	£31.25	—
20	Animal Series (Crowfoot Cigarettes)	1909	£20.00	—
20	Animal Series (Hill's)	1909	£21.50	—
20	Animal Series (Anonymous, Cigarettes Back) ...	1909	£17.50	—
20	Animal Series (Anonymous, Space at Base)	1909	£17.50	—
20	Animal Series (Anonymous, Plain Back)	1909	£17.50	—
F25	Artistas Teatrais Portuguesos	1924	£31.25	—
25	Aviation Series (Hill Cigarettes)	1934	£1.40	£35.00
25	Aviation Series (Gold Flake Honeydew)	1934	£1.90	—
?15	Battleships (Printed Backs)	1908	£125.00	—
?15	Battleships (Plain Backs)	1908	£37.50	—
25	Battleships & Crests	1901	£12.50	£312.50
12	Boer War Generals	1901	£30.00	£360.00
20	Breeds of Dogs (Archer's M.F.H.)	1914	£15.00	—
20	Breeds of Dogs (Badminton)	1914	£15.00	—
20	Breeds of Dogs (Spinet Tobacco)	1914	£15.00	—
20	Breeds of Dogs (Verbena Mixture)	1914	£15.00	—
L30	Britain's Stately Homes (Silk)	1917	£3.15	£94.50
?50	British Navy Series	1902	£21.50	—
L40	Canvas Masterpieces, Series 1 (Badminton)	1916	£1.25	£50.00
L40	Canvas Masterpieces, Series 1 (Spinet)	1916	£1.90	£76.00
L40	Canvas Masterpieces, Series 2 (Silk)	1916	£1.90	£76.00
X10	Canvas Masterpieces, Series 2 (Silk)	1916	£1.90	—
50	Caricatures of Famous Cricketers	1926	£1.90	£95.00
L50	Caricatures of Famous Cricketers	1926	£1.00	£50.00
?	Celebrated Pictures	1905	£125.00	—
50	Celebrities of Sport (Hill Cigarettes)	1939	£1.25	£62.50
50	Celebrities of Sport (Gold Flake)	1939	£2.00	—
P4/5	Chinese Pottery & Porcelain (Silk)	1915	50p	£2.00
X11	Chinese Pottery & Porcelain 2 (Silk)	1915	£4.40	—
10	Chinese Series	1912	£50.00	—
35	Cinema Celebrities (Spinet House)	1936	45p	£15.75
35	Cinema Celebrities (Anonymous)	1936	45p	£15.75
30	Colonial Troops (Leading Lines)	1901	£20.00	£600.00
30	Colonial Troops (Perfection Vide Dress)	1901	£20.00	£600.00
50	Colonial Troops (Sweet American)	1901	£20.00	£1000.00
40	Crystal Palace Souvenir Cards (Matt)	1937	80p	£32.00
40	Crystal Palace Souvenir Cards (Varnished)	1937	80p	£32.00
48	Decorations & Medals (Hill Back)	1940	£1.25	£60.00
48	Decorations & Medals (Gold Flake)	1940	£2.50	—
F48	Famous Cinema Celebrities (Spinet)	1931	£2.50	—
F48	Famous Cinema Celebrities (No Brand)	1931	£2.50	—
LF48	Famous Cinema Celebrities, Series A (Kadi)	1931	£3.15	

R. & J. HILL LTD.—cont.

Qty		Date	Odds	Sets
LF48	Famous Cinema Celebrities, Series A (No Brand)	1931	£3.15	—
F50	Famous Cinema Celebrities, Series C (Devon) ..	1932	*£5.00*	—
F50	Famous Cinema Celebrities, Series C (Toucan) .	1932	*£5.00*	—
F50	Famous Cinema Celebrities, Series C (No Brand)	1932	£2.50	—
LF50	Famous Cinema Celebrities, Series D (Kadi)	1932	£2.50	—
LF50	Famous Cinema Celebrities, Series D (No Brand)	1932	£2.50	—
28	Famous Cricketers Series (Blue back)	1912	£44.00	—
28	Famous Cricketers Series (Red back)	1912	£44.00	—
40	Famous Cricketers	1923	£3.15	£125.00
50	Famous Cricketers, including the S. African Team	1925	£2.50	£125.00
L50	Famous Cricketers, including the S. African Team	1925	£3.15	£157.50
50	Famous Dog Breeds	1952	£5.00	—
L30	Famous Engravings, Series XI	1910	£3.75	£112.50
40	Famous Film Stars	1938	65p	£26.00
40	Famous Film Stars (Arabic Text)	1938	80p	£32.00
20	Famous Footballers Series	1912	£10.00	£200.00
50	Famous Footballers (Brown)	1923	£1.55	£77.50
50	Famous Footballers (Coloured, Archer)	1939	£1.25	—
50	Famous Footballers (With Address)	1939	£1.00	£50.00
25	Famous Footballers (51-75)	1939	£1.50	£37.50
25	Famous Pictures (Fine Art Cigarettes)	1913	£3.15	£78.75
25	Famous Pictures (Cigarette Series)	1913	£3.15	£78.75
50	Famous Ships (Matt)	1940	40p	£20.00
50	Famous Ships (Varnished)	1940	30p	£15.00
48	Film Stars and Celebrity Dancers	1935	£1.25	£60.00
30	Flags & Flags with Soldiers	1901	£20.00	—
24	Flags, Arms & Types of Nations	1910	£8.75	£210.00
20	Football Captain Series (Large Print)	1906	£18.75	—
20	Football Captain Series (Small Print)	1906	£17.50	—
20	Fragments From France (Coloured)	1916	£17.50	—
10	Fragments From France (Buff)	1916	£20.00	£200.00
10	Fragments From France (Black & White)	1916	£62.50	—
L23	Great War Leaders, Series 10 (Silk)	1917	£4.40	£95.00
50	Historic Places From Dickens' Classics	1926	50p	£25.00
L50	Historic Places From Dickens' Classics	1926	45p	£22.50
50	Holiday Resorts (Brown Back)	1925	£1.00	—
50	Holiday Resorts (Green Back)	1925	50p	£25.00
L50	Holiday Resorts (Brown Back)	1925	£1.25	—
L50	Holiday Resorts (Green Back)	1925	65p	£32.50
20	Inventors & Their Inventions (1-20)	1907	£3.75	£75.00
20	Inventors & Their Inventions (Plain Back)	1934	95p	£19.00
20	Inventors & Their Inventions Series (21-40)	1908	£6.25	£125.00
15	Japanese Series (Black & White)	1904	£37.50	—
15	Japanese Series (Black & White Lind Back)	1904	*£95.00*	—
15	Japanese Series (Coloured, Blue Panel)	1904	*£90.00*	—
15	Japanese Series (Coloured, Red Panel)	1904	£50.00	—
20	Lighthouse Series (No Frame Line)	1903	£31.25	£625.00
30	Lighthouse Series (With Frame Line)	1903	£30.00	£900.00
50	Magical Puzzles	1938	90p	£45.00

R. & J. HILL LTD.—cont.

Qty		Date	Odds	Sets
50	Modern Beauties	1939	65p	£32.50
30	Music Hall Celebrities—Past & Present	1930	£1.00	£30.00
L30	Music Hall Celebrities—Past & Present	1930	£1.00	£30.00
20	National Flag Series (Printed Black)	1914	£6.25	£125.00
20	National Flag Series (Plain Back)	1914	£6.25	£125.00
30	Nature Pictures	1930	£1.00	£30.00
30	Nautical Songs	1937	50p	£15.00
B25	Naval Series (Unnumbered)	1901	£37.50	—
30	Naval Series (Numbered 21-50)	1902	£10.00	—
30	Our Empire Series	1929	20p	£6.00
L30	Our Empire Series	1929	20p	£6.00
M30	Popular Footballers, Series A	1935	£1.50	£45.00
M20	Popular Footballers, Series B	1935	£1.50	£30.00
20	Prince of Wales Series	1911	£10.00	£200.00
L?15	Prints From Noted Pictures	1908	*£95.00*	—
50	Public Schools and Colleges	1923	50p	£25.00
L50	Public Schools and Colleges	1923	50p	£25.00
75	Public Schools and Colleges	1923	65p	£48.75
L75	Public Schools and Colleges	1923	75p	£56.25
50	Puzzle Series	1937	50p	£25.00
42	Real Photographs, Set 1 (Space at Back)	1930	£1.90	—
F42	Real Photographs, Set 1 (Space at Back)	1930	£1.90	
42	Real Photographs, Set 1 (London Idol)	1930	£1.90	—
F42	Real Photographs, Set 1 (London Idol)	1930	£1.90	—
F42	Real Photographs, Set 2	1930	£1.90	—
20	Rhymes	1904	£22.00	£440.00
F50	Scenes from the Films	1934	£1.90	£95.00
40	Scenes from the Films	1938	30p	£12.00
35	Scientific Inventions and Discoveries	1929	75p	£26.25
35	Scientific Inventions and Discoveries (Coloured)	1929	65p	£22.75
L35	Scientific Inventions and Discoveries (Coloured)	1929	75p	£26.25
F50	Sports	1934	£2.50	—
F50	Sports Series (As Above)	1934	£5.00	—
F50	Sports Series (As Above, No Title)	1934	£6.25	—
30	Statuary, Set 1 (Matt Front)	1898	£25.00	—
30	Statuary, Set 1 (Varnished)	1898	£10.00	—
30	Statuary Set 1 (Brown Front)	1898	*£62.50*	—
30	Statuary, Set 2	1899	£7.50	£225.00
25	Statuary, Set 3 (Black Panel)	1898	£18.75	—
25	Statuary, Set 3 (Grey Panel)	1898	£45.00	—
25	Statuary, Set 3 (White Panel)	1898	£18.75	—
X1	Sunripe Twins Bookmark	1925	—	£10.50
30	The All Blacks	1924	£3.15	£94.50
50	The Railway Centenary	1925	£1.00	£50.00
L50	The Railway Centenary (Brown Back)	1925	£1.00	£50.00
L50	The Railway Centenary (Grey Back)	1925	£2.50	—
25	The Railway Centenary, 2nd Series	1925	£1.25	£31.25
L25	The Railway Centenary, 2nd Series	1925	£1.25	£31.25
25	The River Thames (1-25)	1924	£1.25	£31.25
25	The River Thames (26-50)	1924	£1.00	£25.00
L50	The River Thames (Green Back)	1924	90p	45.00
100	Transfers	1935	£4.40	—

R. & J. HILL LTD.—cont.

Qty		Date	Odds	Sets
20	Types of the British Army (Badminton)	1914	£25.00	—
20	Types of the British Army (Verbena)	1914	£25.00	—
LF48	Views of Interest, 1st Series (Spinet)	1938	20p	£10.00
LF48	Views of Interest, 1st Series (Sunripe)	1938	20p	£8.25
LF48	Views of Interest, 2nd Series	1938	20p	£8.25
LF48	Views of Interest, 3rd Series	1939	20p	£9.00
LF48	Views of Interest, 4th Series	1939	30p	£14.50
LF48	Views of Interest, 5th Series	1939	30p	£14.50
LF48	Views of Interest—Canada	1940	25p	£12.00
LF48	Views of Interest—India	1940	£2.50	£120.00
50	Views of London	1925	65p	£32.50
L50	Views of London	1925	75p	£37.50
L50	Views of the River Thames (Green and Black)	1924	90p	£45.00
25	War Series	1915	£10.00	£250.00
50	Who's Who in British Films	1927	75p	£37.50
L50	Who's Who in British Films	1927	90p	£45.00
84	Wireless Telephony	1923	95p	£80.00
L20	Wireless Telephony—Broadcasting Series	1923	£2.00	£40.00
25	World's Masterpieces, 2nd Series	1914	£1.90	£47.50
50	Zoological Series	1924	65p	£32.50
L50	Zoological Series	1924	75p	£37.50

L. HIRST & SON

T25	Soldiers & Their Uniforms (Cut-Outs)	1914	£125.00	—

J. W. HOBSON

18	Motor Cycle Series	1914	£62.50	—

HOCKINGS BAZAAR, PORTHCAWL

30	Army Pictures, Cartoons, etc.	1916	£62.50	—

J. & T. HODGE

?5	Britain's Naval Crests	1896	£187.50	—
16	British Royal Family	1901	£125.00	—
?20	Scottish Views (Size 74 x 39mm)	1898	£100.00	—
?20	Scottish Views (Size 80 x 45mm)	1898	£100.00	—

HOOK OF HOLLAND CIGARETTES

?15	Footballers	1900	£150.00	—

HUDDEN & CO.

26	Actresses "FROGA"	1900	£50.00	—
25	Beauties "CHOAB"	1901	£42.50	—
20	Beauties, Crown Seal	1898	£105.00	—
24	Beauties "HUMPS" (Blue Back)	1899	£55.00	—
24	Beauties "HUMPS" (Orange Back)	1899	£50.00	—
24	Beauties "HUMPS" (Type Set Back)	1899	£187.50	—
?12	Comic Phrases	1900	£90.00	—
25	Famous Boxers	1927	£20.00	—
25	Flags of All Nations	1904	£15.00	£375.00
48	Japanese Playing Cards (Dandy Dot)	1900	£105.00	—

HUDDEN & CO.—cont.

Qty		Date	Odds	Sets
48	Japanese Playing Cards (Hudden Cigarettes)	1900	*£80.00*	—
18	Pretty Girl Series "RASH"	1900	£62.50	—
50	Public Schools & Colleges	1924	£1.75	£87.50
25	Soldiers of the Century	1903	£37.50	£937.50
25	Sports & Pastimes	1926	£50.00	—
25	Star Girls	1900	£62.50	—
25	Types of Smokers	1903	£37.50	£937.50

HUDSON'S

25	Beauties "BOCCA"	1900	*£187.50*	—

HUNTER

?12	Footballers	1910	*£187.50*	—

JAMES ILLINGWORTH LTD.

MF48	Beautiful Scotland	1939	75p	—
M25	Cavalry	1924	£4.40	£110.00
MF48	Coastwise	1938	75p	£36.00
25	Comicartoons of Sport	1927	£4.40	£110.00
MF48	Flying	1938	80p	—
25	Motor Car Bonnets	1925	£5.00	£125.00
25	Old Hostels	1926	£5.00	£125.00
MF48	Our Countryside	1938	75p	£36.00
MF24	Shots from the Films	1937	£1.90	—
?10	Views from the English Lakes	1895	*£125.00*	

IMPERIAL TOBACCO CO. LTD.

50	British Birds	1909	£3.75	£187.50
X1	Coronation Folder	1902	—	£75.00

INGRAMS (Eastleigh)

30	Army Pictures, Cartoons etc.	1916	*£75.00*	—

INTERNATIONAL TOBACCO CO. LTD.

28	Domino Cards	1938	20p	£5.50
D50	Famous Buildings & Monuments, Series A. (International Tobacco Co. Ltd)	1934	65p	£32.50
D50	Famous Buildings & Monuments, Series A. (International Tobacco (Overseas) Ltd)	1934	95p	—
D50	Famous Buildings & Monuments, Series B	1934	£1.00	—
100	Film Favourites (Black Backs)	1937	£1.00	—
100	Film Favourites (Brown Backs)	1937	£1.00	—
D100	Gentlemen! The King! (Black Back)	1938	20p	£15.00
D100	Gentlemen! The King (Blue Back)	1938	30p	—
50	International Code of Signals	1934	20p	£10.00
48	.Screen Lovers (Summit)	Unissued	£1.75	£84.00

The main problem regarding the storage of cigarette cards lies in the effort to strike a balance between being able to maintain them in as good condition as possible and yet being able to examine them. If the reader is simply an investor there is no problem—he can wrap each set carefully in paper, put it into a box, and thence into a bank vault. But the only way to enjoy cigarette cards is to look at them. The modern method is to house cards in transparent pages, which can accommodate most sizes of cards and can be stored in loose leaf binders. The entire card may be viewed, both back and front, yet will not deteriorate through sticky fingers or spilt coffee. Care should be taken to use a page made from a suitable material— there are on the market now many apparently cheap pages which contain large amounts of plasticiser, a substance which could adversely affect certain cards. Full details of our own Nostalgia and Hendon albums are given on pages 16 and 17 of this book.

Another method of storage which is becoming more popular is to mount cards in frames, which can then be hung on a suitable wall. Several framing systems are now available which hold the cards in position without harming them, and enable the backs to be examined, as well as accommodating complete sets of 50 cards.

This huge Company was founded on 2nd Novemebr 1901 in order to combat the spreading influence in Britain of the American Tobacco Co. The founder members were headed by Wills, and included such well known card issuers as Player, Smith, Hignett and Lambert & Butler. During the next few years they were to acquire a number of other well known companies such as Churchman and Faulkner. However their most important acquisitions were those of Ogden at the conclusion of the Tobacco war, and Mardon Son & Hall, the printers who became responsible for the production of most of their cigarette cards.

The formation date is most important to cartophilists, because from that time onward the card issues of the constituent firms bore the message "Branch of the Imperial Tobacco Co. (of Great Britain and Northern Ireland) Ltd." in addition to the individual firm's name. Because, for example, there are two printings of Wills Locomotives and Faulkner Our Gallant Grenadiers, one with and one without the "I.T.C. clause" as it is popularly known, it is safe to say that each of these was issued around 1901-2; or that Vanity Fair came a little earlier and Borough Arms a little later.

Cards issued abroad (including the Channel Islands) which mentioned the I.T.C. member's names did NOT include the I.T.C. clause, since they were always issued by the British American Tobacco Co. which was partly owned by I.T.C.

A cartophilic consequence of the formation of the I.T.C. was the practice of issuing identical card series under several of the firm's, or indeed by B.A.T. Hence Garden Life was issued by Edwards Ringer & Bigg, Lambert & Butler and Wills; Angling by Faulkner, Mitchell and B.A.T.; Boy Scouts by Churchman, Ogden and I.T.C. (Canada). It is always likely that series issued by I.T.C. firms with the same series title will be the same basic set, such as Air Raid Precautions by Churchman, Hignett, Mitchell, Ogden and Wills.

PETER JACKSON

Qty		Date	Odds	Sets
F28	Beautiful Scotland	1939	75p	£21.00
MF48	Beautiful Scotland	1939	75p	£36.00
F28	Coastwise	1938	75p	£21.00
MF48	Coastwise	1938	95p	—
F28	Famous Film Stars	1935	£1.90	£53.00
F27	Famous Films	1934	£1.90	£51.25
F28	Film Scenes	1936	£1.75	£50.00
LF28	Film Scenes (Different)	1936	£2.50	£70.00
F28	Flying	1938	£2.50	£70.00
MF48	Flying	1938	£2.50	—
D100	Gentlemen! The King			
	(Overprinted on Black International)	1938	95p	—
	(Overprinted on Blue International)	1938	95p	—
	(Reprinted with Jackson Name)	1938	75p	—
	(Reprinted on Paper)	1938	65p	£65.00
F28	Life in the Navy	1937	£1.25	£35.00
LF28	Life in the Navy (Different)	1937	£1.75	£50.00
F28	Our Countryside	1938	75p	£21.00
MF48	Our Countryside	1938	95p	—
F28	Shots from the Films	1937	£1.25	£35.00
MF24	Shots from the Films	1937	£1.90	£45.00
D250	Speed Through the Ages (Mixed Sizes)	1937	25p	£62.50
F28	Stars in Famous Films	1934	£2.00	£56.00
D150	The Pageant of Kingship (P. Jackson Ltd.)	1937	25p	£37.50
D150	The Pageant of Kingship (P. Jackson Overseas Ltd)	1937	40p	£60.00

JACOBI BROS. & CO. LTD.

?50	Boer War Celebrities "JASAS"	1901	£100.00	—

JAMES & CO. (B'HAM) LTD.

M20	Arms of Countries	1915	£90.00	—

JAMES'S

?50	Pretty Girl Series "BAGG"	1898	£150.00	—

JERSEY TOBACCO CO. LTD. (Channel Isles)

K53	Miniature Playing Cards	1933	75p	—

SOCIETE JOB

25	British Lighthouses	1925	£3.75	£93.75
B48	Cinema Stars (Numbered)	1926	£6.25	—
B48	Cinema Stars (Unnumbered)	1926	40p	£32.50
48	Cinema Stars (Numbered)	1926	£2.50	—
48	Cinema Stars (Unnumbered)	1926	£2.50	—
25	Dogs	1911	£15.00	£375.00
25	Liners	1912	£25.00	—
K53	Miniature Playing Cards	1926	£6.25	—
25	Orders of Chivalry	1924	£2.00	£50.00
25	Orders of Chivalry, 2nd Series	1927	£2.00	£3.00

SOCIETE JOB—cont.

Qty		Date	Odds	Sets
3	Orders of Chivalry (Unnumbered)	1927	£5.00	£15.00
25	Racehorses	1909	£15.00	£375.00

GERMAN ISSUES

X70	Sport in Zehn Bildern	1930	£2.50	—

J. B. JOHNSON & CO.

25	National Flags, Flowers & Girls	1901	£125.00	—

JOHNSTON'S

?	Views	1910	£125.00	—

JONES BROS.

14/18	Spurs Footballers	1912	£4.40	£70.00

A. I. JONES & CO. LTD.

B1	Advertisement Card	1901	—	£312.50
12	Nautical Terms	1905	£37.50	£450.00

ALEX JONES & CO.

20	Actresses "ANGOOD" (Brown Front)	1898	£125.00	—
20	Actresses "ANGOOD" (Green Front)	1898	£125.00	—
1	Diamond Jubilee 1897	1897	—	£112.50

A. S. JONES

30	Army Pictures, Cartoons, etc.	1916	£62.50	—

T. E. JONES & CO.

12	Conundrums	1900	£125.00	—
50	Flags of All Nations	1899	£80.00	—
?50	Footballers	1900	£100.00	—
16	Well-known Proverbs	1900	£125.00	—

C. H. JORDEN LTD.

F12	Celebrities of the Great War	1915	£62.50	—

J. & E. KENNEDY

25	Beauties "FECKSA"	1902	£37.50	—

RICHARD KENNEDY

P?25	Army & Navy Cartoons	1906	£90.00	—
50	War Portraits	1916	£62.50	—

KINNEAR LTD.

13	Actresses	1899	£100.00	—
B1	A Gentleman in Kharki	1900	—	£50.00
15	Australian Cricket Team	1897	£165.00	—

KINNEAR LTD. — cont.

Qty		Date	Odds	Sets
?25	Cricketers	1898	£312.50	—
X1	Cricket Fixture Folder	1903	—	£400.00
25	Footballers & Club Colours	1898	£80.00	—
12	Jockeys, Set 1	1898	£31.25	£375.00
1	Jockeys, Tod Sloane	1898	—	£62.50
25	Jockeys (Different, Large Captions)	1898	£62.50	—
25	Jockeys (Different, Small Captions)	1898	£55.00	—
2	Prominent Personages	1902	£187.50	—
13	Royalty	1897	£37.50	£487.50
L1	The Four Generations	1900	—	£150.00
K?25	Views	1898	£187.50	—

B. KRIEGSFELD & CO.

1	Advertisement Card	1900	—	£312.50
50	Beauties "KEWA" (Matt Front)	1898	£75.00	—
50	Beauties "KEWA" (Semi Glossy Front)	1898	£125.00	—
?10	Celebrities (Horizontal Back)	1901	£125.00	—
?10	Celebrities (Vertical Back)	1901	£125.00	—
50	Flags of All Nations	1899	£55.00	—
50	Phrases & Advertisements	1900	£62.50	—

A. KUIT LTD.

K?12	Arms of Cambridge Colleges	1914	£62.50	—
K?12	Arms of Companies	1914	£62.50	—
F30	British Beauties (Oval)	1914	£42.50	—
F?50	Crosmedo Bijou Cards	1915	£100.00	—
25	Principal Streets of British Cities	1915	£90.00	—
F50	Types of Beauty	1914	£90.00	—

L. & Y. TOB. MFG. CO.

26	Actresses "FROGA"	1900	£155.00	—

LAMBERT & BUTLER
32 Page Reference Book — £2.50

10	Actresses & their Autographs (narrow)	1898	£90.00	—
10	Actresses & their Autographs (wide)	1898	£105.00	—
20	Actresses "BLARM"	1900	£20.00	£400.00
50	Admirals	1900	—	£750.00
50	(Bird's Eye)	1900	£15.00	—
50	(Flaked Gold Leaf Honeydew)	1900	£15.00	—
50	(May Blossom)	1900	£15.00	—
50	(Viking)	1900	£15.00	—
1	Advertisement Card	1898	—	£312.50
50	Aeroplane Markings	1937	80p	£40.00
25	A History of Aviation (Brown Front)	1933	£1.50	£37.50
25	A History of Aviation (Green Front)	1932	£1.00	£25.00
40	Arms of Kings & Queens of England	1906	£3.00	£120.00
25	Aviation	1915	£2.00	£50.00
26	Beauties "HOL" (Flaked Gold Leaf)	1899	£28.00	—
26	Beauties "HOL" (Log Cabin)	1899	£28.00	—
26	Beauties "HOL" (May Blossom)	1899	£28.00	—

LAMBERT & BUTLER—cont.

Qty		Date	Odds	Sets
26	Beauties "HOL" (Viking Navy Cut)	1899	£28.00	—
50	Birds & Eggs	1906	£2.25	£112.50
?25	Boer War & Boxer Rebellion—Sketches	1901	£25.00	—
20	Boer War Generals "CLAM" (Black Back)	1901	£25.00	—
20	Boer War Generals "CLAM" (Brown Back)	1901	£25.00	—
10	Boer War Generals "FLAC"	1901	£28.50	—
25	British Trees & Their Uses	1927	£1.25	£31.25
1	Colonel Baden-Powell, King of Scouts	1901	—	£312.50
25	Common Fallacies	1928	£1.50	£37.50
50	Conundrums (Blue Back)	1901	£17.50	—
50	Conundrums (Green Back)	1901	£12.50	
12	Coronation Robes	1902	£15.50	£185.00
25	Dance Band Leaders	1936	£2.50	£62.50
28	Dominoes (Packets)	1955	£1.25	
50	Empire Air Routes	1936	£1.00	£50.00
25	Famous British Airmen & Airwomen	1935	65p	£16.25
25	Fauna of Rhodesia	1929	75p	£18.75
50	Find Your Way (Drury Lane in Address)	1932	95p	£47.50
50	Find Your Way (Without Drury Lane)	1932	95p	£47.50
50	Find Your Way (Red Overprint)	1932	95p	£47.50
1	Find Your Way Joker Card	1932	—	£8.00
50	Footballers 1930-1	1931	£1.90	£95.00
25	Garden Life	1930	75p	£18.75
25	Hints & Tips for Motorists	1929	£2.50	£62.50
50	Horsemanship	1938	£1.00	£50.00
25	How Motor Cars Work	1931	£1.50	£37.50
50	Interesting Customs & Traditions of the Navy, Army & Air Force	1939	65p	£32.50
25	Interesting Musical Instruments	1929	£2.25	£56.25
50	Interesting Sidelights on the Work of the G.P.O.	1939	65p	£32.50
20	International Yachts	1902	£40.00	—
25	Japanese Series	1904	£6.00	£150.00
4	Jockeys (no Frame)	1902	£27.50	£110.00
10	Jockeys (with Frame)	1902	£27.50	£275.00
50	Keep Fit	1937	45p	£22.50
25	London Characters	1934	£1.50	£37.50
25	Motor Car Radiators	1928	£3.75	£93.75
25	Motor Cars, A Series (Green Back)	1922	£1.90	£47.50
25	Motor Cars, 2nd Series (26-50)	1923	£1.90	£47.50
50	Motor Cars, 3rd Series	1926	£2.25	£112.50
25	Motor Cars (Grey Back)	1934	£2.00	£50.00
50	Motor Cycles	1923	£2.50	£125.00
50	Motor Index Marks	1926	£1.55	£77.50
25	Motors	1908	£20.00	£500.00
25	Naval Portraits (Series of 25)	1914	£3.00	£75.00
50	Naval Portraits (Series of 50)	1915	£3.00	£150.00
25	Pirates & Highwaymen	1926	60p	£15.00
25	Rhodesian Series	1928	£1.00	£25.00
50	The Thames From Lechlade to London (Large Numerals)	1907	£5.00	—
50	The Thames From Lechlade to London (Small Numerals)	1907	£4.40	£220.00
25	Third Rhodesian Series	1930	50p	£12.50

LAMBERT & BUTLER — cont.

Qty		Date	Odds	Sets
4	Types of the British Army & Navy (Black Specialities Back)	1897	£50.00	£200.00
4	Types of the British Army & Navy (Brown Specialities Back)	1897	£50.00	£200.00
4	Types of the British Army & Navy (Viking)	1897	£60.00	—
PF?	Warships	1910	£25.00	—
25	Waverley Series	1904	£8.75	£218.75
25	Winter Sports	1914	£2.00	£50.00
25	Wireless Telegraphy	1909	£3.75	£93.75
25	Wonders of Nature	1924	50p	£12.50
25	World's Locomotives (Series of 25)	1912	£3.15	£78.75
50	World's Locomotives (Series of 50)	1912	£3.75	£187.50
25	World's Locomotives (Additional)	1913	£3.75	£93.75

OVERSEAS ISSUES

Qty		Date	Odds	Sets
50	Actors & Actresses "WALP"	1908	£2.50	—
250	Actresses "ALWICS" (Firm's Name)	1908	£2.50	—
250	Actresses "ALWICS" (Scout Cigarettes)	1908	£2.50	—
250	Actresses "ALWICS" (Black Front)	1908	£6.25	—
250	Actresses "ALWICS" (Mauve Front, 3 Backs)	1908	£12.50	—
250	Actresses "ALWICS" (Red Border)	1908	£12.50	—
50	Beauties "LAWHA" (Scout Cigarettes)	1908	£2.50	—
50	Beauties "LAWHA" (No Brand, 3 Backs)	1908	£2.50	—
83	Danske Byvaabner	1912	£10.00	—
26	Etchings (Dogs)	1928	£18.75	—
L26	Etchings (Dogs)	1928	£25.00	—
25	Flag Girls of All Nations	1910	£8.75	£218.75
F50	Homeland Events	1925	£1.00	£50.00
?1	Indian Women (Blue Front)	1910	£37.50	—
?1	Indian Women (Red Front)	1910	£37.50	—
25	London Characters	1934	£10.00	—
F50	London Zoo	1924	£1.00	£50.00
50	Merchant Ships of the World	1924	£1.55	£77.50
30	Music Hall Celebrities	1906	£2.50	—
F50	Popular Film Stars (Title in 1 Line)	1925	90p	£45.00
F50	Popular Film Stars (Title in 2 Lines)	1925	80p	£40.00
F50	Popular Film Stars (Varsity Cigarettes)	1925	£1.50	—
100	Royalty Notabilities & Events 1900-2	1902	£9.20	—
100	Russo Japanese Series	1903	£3.75	£375.00
F50	The Royal Family at Home and Abroad	1928	75p	£37.50
F50	The World of Sport	1928	90p	£45.00
F50	Types of Modern Beauty	1927	75p	£37.50
F50	Who's Who in Sport (1926)	1926	90p	£45.00

LAMBKIN BROS.

Qty		Date	Odds	Sets
36	Country Scenes (Series 1-6)	1924	£4.40	—
L36	Country Scenes (Series 7-12)	1926	£5.00	—
L?9	Irish Views (Plain Back)	1925	£18.75	—
L?6	Lily of Killarney Views	1925	£62.50	—

C. & J. LAW

Qty		Date	Odds	Sets
25	Types of British Soldiers	1914	£20.00	£500.00
50	War Portraits	1915	£62.50	—

R. J. LEA LTD.

Qty		Date	Odds	Sets
2	Advertisement Cards	1913	£187.50	—
B12	Butterflies & Moths (Silk)	1924	£2.00	£24.00
L12	Butterflies & Moths (Silk)	1924	£2.00	£24.00
P6	Butterflies & Moths (Silk)	1924	£2.50	£15.00
12	Chairman Puzzles	1910	£150.00	—
70	Cigarette Transfers (Locomotives)	1916	£5.00	£350.00
25	Civilians of Countries Fighting with the Allies	1914	£8.75	£218.75
F48	Coronation Souvenir (Glossy, Lea Back)	1937	30p	£15.00
F48	Coronation Souvenir (Glossy, Successors)	1937	25p	£12.50
48	Coronation Souvenir (Matt, Lea Back)	1937	45p	£22.00
F48	Coronation Souvenir (Matt, Successors)	1937	30p	£15.00
LF48	Coronation Souvenir	1937	50p	£25.00
25	Dogs (1-25)	1923	£3.15	£78.75
25	Dogs (26-50)	1923	£4.40	—
25	English Birds (Glossy)	1922	£2.00	£50.00
25	English Birds (Matt)	1922	£3.15	
F54	Famous Film Stars	1939	95p	£51.50
F48	Famous Racehorses of 1926	1927	£1.55	£74.50
MF48	Famous Racehorses of 1926	1927	£2.20	£106.00
F48	Famous Views (Glossy)	1936	20p	£10.00
48	Famous Views (Matt)	1936	45p	£22.00
MF48	Famous Views	1936	45p	£22.00
F36	Film Stars, 1st Series	1934	£1.75	£62.50
F36	Film Stars, 2nd Series	1934	£1.55	£56.00
25	Fish	1926	£1.25	£31.25
50	Flowers to Grow—The Best Perennials	1913	£3.00	£150.00
F48	Girls from the Shows (Glossy)	1935	£1.25	£60.00
48	Girls from the Shows (Matt)	1935	£1.55	£74.50
50	Miniatures (No Border)	1912	£2.20	£110.00
50	Miniatures (Gold Border)	1912	£2.20	£110.00
50	Miniatures (51-100)	1912	£2.00	£100.00
46/50	Modern Miniatures	1913	95p	£43.75
12	More Lea's Smokers (Green Border)	1906	£62.50	—
12	More Lea's Smokers (Red Frame)	1906	£80.00	
P24	Old English Pottery & Porcelain	1912	£5.00	£120.00
50	Old English Pottery & Porcelain	1912	£1.50	£75.00
50	Old Pottery & Porcelain, 2nd (Chairman)	1912	£1.25	£62.50
50	Old Pottery & Porcelain, 2nd (Recorder)	1912	£4.40	
50	Old Pottery & Porcelain, 3rd (Chairman)	1912	£1.25	£62.50
50	Old Pottery & Porcelain, 3rd (Recorder)	1912	£4.40	—
50	Old Pottery & Porcelain, 4th Series	1913	£1.25	£62.50
50	Old Pottery & Porcelain, 5th Series	1913	£1.25	£62.50
54	Old Pottery (Silk)	1914	80p	£55.00
72	Old Pottery (Silk, Different)	1914	80p	£62.50
F54	Radio Stars (Glossy)	1935	£1.50	£81.00
54	Radio Stars (Matt)	1935	£1.55	
100	Regimental Crests & Badges (Silk)	1923	£1.00	£100.00
50	Roses	1924	80p	£40.00
50	Ships of the World	1925	£1.50	£75.00
25	The Evolution of the Royal Navy	1925	£1.50	£37.50
25	War Pictures	1915	£3.50	£87.50
25	War Portraits	1915	£4.40	£110.00
F48	Wonders of the World (Glossy)	1938	30p	£14.50

R. J. LEA LTD.—cont.

Qty		Date	Odds	Sets
48	Wonders of the World (Matt)	1938	50p	£25.00
MF48	Wonders of the World	1938	45p	£22.00

ALFRED L. LEAVER

B12	Manikin Cards	1915	£50.00	—

J. LEES

20	Northampton Town Football Club	1912	£62.50	—

LEON DE CUBA CIGARS

30	Colonial Troops	1902	£90.00	—

A. LEWIS & CO. (WESTMINSTER) LTD.

52	Horoscopes	1938	75p	£39.00

H. C. LLOYD & SONS LTD.

28	Academy Gems (Green Front, Multi Backs)	1902	£42.50	—
28	(Mauve Front, Multi-Backs)	1902	£42.50	—
28	(Orange Front, Multi-Backs)	1902	£42.50	—
26	Actresses & Boer War Celebrities	1901	£37.50	—
B18	Devon Footballers (With Frame Line)	1902	£100.00	—
B40	Devon Footballers & Boer War Celebrities	1902	£40.00	—
25	Star Girls (Different Printings)	1899	£155.00	—
L36	War Pictures	1914	£95.00	—

RICHARD LLOYD & SONS

20	Actresses, Celebrities & Yachts	1900	£80.00	—
25	Atlantic Records	1936	£1.50	£37.50
25	Boer War Celebrities	1899	£30.00	—
F27	Cinema Stars (1-27)	1935	£4.40	—
F27	Cinema Stars (28-54)	1935	50p	£13.50
F27	Cinema Stars, 3rd Series (55-81)	1936	£4.40	—
25	Cinema Stars (Matt)	1937	75p	£18.75
25	Famous Cricketers Puzzle Series	1930	£3.75	£93.75
96	National Types, Costumes & Flags	1900	£27.50	—
25	Old English Inns	1923	£1.00	£25.00
25	Old Inns, Series 2	1924	£2.00	£50.00
50	Old Inns	1924	75p	£37.50
10	Scenes From San Toy	1905	£8.15	£81.50
25	Tricks & Puzzles	1935	40p	£10.00
25	Types of Horses	1926	£2.00	£50.00
25	Zoo Series	1926	75p	£18.75

LUSBY LTD.

25	Scenes from Circus Life	1902	£100.00	—

HUGH McCALL

Qty		Date	Odds	Sets
1	RAF Recruiting Card	1924	£125.00	—

D. & J. MACDONALD

Qty		Date	Odds	Sets
10	Actresses "MUTA"	1901	£100.00	—
L?	Cricket & Football Teams (Tontine)	1902	£155.00	—
L?	Cricket & Football Teams (Winning Team)	1902	£125.00	—
25	Cricketers	1902	£250.00	—
L1	Yorkshire County Team	1900	—	£460.00

MACKENZIE & CO.

Qty		Date	Odds	Sets
F50	Music Hall Artistes	1902	£15.00	£750.00
50	The Zoo	1910	£18.75	—
50	Victorian Art Pictures	1910	£15.00	—

WM. McKINNELL

Qty		Date	Odds	Sets
20	The European War Series	1915	£50.00	—
50	War Portraits	1916	£62.50	—

MACNAUGHTON JENKINS & CO. LTD.

Qty		Date	Odds	Sets
B50	Castles of Ireland—Ancient & Modern	1924	£2.50	£125.00
50	Various Uses of Rubber	1924	£1.90	£95.00

A. McTAVISH

Qty		Date	Odds	Sets
30	Army Pictures, Cartoons, etc	1916	£62.50	—

McWATTIE & SONS

Qty		Date	Odds	Sets
30	Army Pictures, Cartoons, etc.	1916	£62.50	—

THE MANXLAND TOBACCO CO.

Qty		Date	Odds	Sets
?	Views of the Isle of Man (Matt)	1900	£187.50	—
?	Views of the Isle of Man (Varnished)	1900	£187.50	—

MARCOVITCH & CO.

Qty		Date	Odds	Sets
F18	Beauties (Plain Back)	1932	50p	£9.00
7	The Story in Red and White	1955	£2.50	—
L7	The Story in Red and White	1955	£1.90	£13.50

MARCUS'S

Qty		Date	Odds	Sets
?25	Cricketers	1897	£312.50	—
25	Footballers & Club Colours	1898	£87.50	—
L1	The Four Generations	1900	—	£187.50

MARKHAM

Qty		Date	Odds	Sets
M?25	Views of Bridgwater	1906	£87.50	—

MARSUMA CO.

Qty		Date	Odds	Sets
50	Famous Golfers & Their Strokes	1914	£18.75	£937.50

C. MARTIN

Qty		Date	Odds	Sets
30	Army Pictures, Cartoons etc.	1916	*£62.50*	—

MARTINS LTD.

1	Arf A Mo Kaiser!	1915	—	£50.00
D?12	Carlyle Series (Different Printings)	1923	*£81.25*	—
P?750	The Performer Tobacco Fund Photographs	1916	£5.00	—
25	V.C. Heroes	1916	£18.75	£468.75

MASCOT CIGARETTES

?20	British Views	1925	*£43.75*	—

R. MASON & CO.

30	Colonial Troops	1902	£50.00	—
40	Naval & Military Phrases (No Border)	1904	£42.50	—
40	Naval & Military Phrases (White Border)	1904	£42.50	—

JUSTUS VAN MAURIK

X12	Views of Holland	1915	*£100.00*	—

MAY QUEEN VIRGINIA CIGARETTES

M10/12	Interesting Pictures	—	50p	£5.00

MENTORS LTD.

32	Views of Ireland	1912	£7.50	—

J. MILLHOFF & CO. LTD.

F54	Antique Pottery	1927	75p	£40.00
MF56	Antique Pottery	1927	75p	£42.00
30	Art Treasures	1927	65p	£19.50
L50	Art Treasures	1926	45p	£22.50
L25	Art Treasures, 2nd Series (51-75)	1928	75p	£18.75
25	British Orders Of Chivalry & Valour	1939	£1.00	£25.00
M20	De Reszke Rilette Pictures	1925	£2.50	—
M25	De Reszke Rilette Pictures	1925	£2.50	—
M30	De Reszke Rilette Pictures	1925	£2.50	—
M42	De Reszke Rilette Pictures	1925	£1.90	£80.00
M43	De Reszke Rilette Pictures	1925	£2.50	—
M56	De Reszke Rilette Pictures	1925	£2.50	—
M74	De Reszke Rilette Pictures	1925	£2.50	—
L25	England Historic & Picturesque (1-25)	1928	75p	£18.75
L25	England Historic & Picturesque, 2nd Series	1928	75p	£18.75
F27	Famous Golfers	1928	£5.65	£152.50
F27	Famous Test Cricketers	1928	£3.15	£85.00
MF27	Famous Test Cricketers	1928	£3.15	£85.00
P24	Film Stars	1934	*£6.25*	—
M25	Gallery Pictures	1929	90p	£22.50
50	Geographia Map Series (Sect.)	1931	£1.25	£62.50
F36	In The Public Eye	1930	95p	£34.25

J. MILLHOFF & CO. LTD.—cont.

Qty		Date	Odds	Sets
1	Jigsaw Advertisement Card (3 Types)	1933	—	£9.40
25	Men of Genius	1924	£3.15	£78.75
L25	Picturesque Old England	1931	75p	£18.75
F27	Real Photographs, A Series (Glossy)	1931	25p	£6.75
F27	Real Photographs, A Series (Matt)	1931	45p	£12.25
F27	Real Photographs, 2nd Series	1931	25p	£6.75
F27	Real Photographs, 3rd Series	1932	25p	£6.75
F27	Real Photographs, 4th Series	1932	30p	£8.00
F27	Real Photographs, 5th Series	1933	30p	£8.00
F27	Real Photographs, 6th Series	1933	30p	£8.00
25	Reproductions of Celebrated Oil Paintings	1928	£1.00	£25.00
L25	Roses	1927	£1.50	£37.50
M?6	Theatre Advertisement Cards (Multi-Backed)	1905	£75.00	—
X?6	Theatre Advertisement Cards (Multi-Packed).....	1905	£92.50	—
F54	The Homeland Series	1933	20p	£10.75
MF56	The Homeland Series	1933	20p	£11.25
50	Things to Make	1935	40p	£20.00
50	What the Stars Say	1934	30p	£15.00
F36	Zoological Studies	1929	20p	£7.25

DUTCH ISSUES

Qty		Date	Odds	Sets
L40	Film Series 1	1924	£6.25	—
L60	Film Series 1 (2 Printings)	1924	£6.25	—
L60	Film Series 2	1925	£6.25	—
L25	Film Series 3	1925	£6.25	—
MF105	Film Series 4	1926	£5.00	—
MF206	Film Series 4	1926	£5.00	—
F?70	Sports Series	1925	£15.00	—

MIRANDA LTD.

Qty		Date	Odds	Sets
20	Dogs	1925	£4.40	—
25	Sports and Pastimes	1925	£3.60	£90.00

STEPHEN MITCHELL

Qty		Date	Odds	Sets
51	Actors & Actresses "FROGA" (Coloured)	1899	£15.50	—
26	Actors & Actresses "FROGA B" (Brown)	1899	£15.50	—
26	Actors & Actresses "FROGA C" (Brown)	1899	£15.50	—
50	Actors & Actresses "FROGA D" (Brown)	1899	£15.00	£750.00
1	Advertisement Card	1900	—	£312.50
50	A Gallery of 1934	1935	£1.20	£60.00
50	A Gallery of 1935	1935	£1.00	£50.00
50	Air Raid Precautions	1938	75p	£37.50
30	A Model Army	1932	90p	£27.00
25	Angling	1928	£3.15	£78.75
50	Arms & Armour	1916	£3.15	£157.50
25	Army Ribbons & Buttons	1916	£3.15	£78.75
50	A Road Map of Scotland (Small Numeral)	1933	£1.25	£62.50
50	A Road Map of Scotland (Large Numeral)	1933	£1.25	£62.50
50	A Road Map of Scotland (Red Overprint)	1933	£1.55	—
1	A Road Map of Scotland (Substitute)	1933	—	£7.50
25	Boxer Rebellion—Sketches	1901	£20.00	—
25	British Warships (1-25)	1915	£5.00	£125.00
25	British Warships, 2nd Series (26-50)	1915	£5.00	£125.00
50	Clan Tartans, A Series	1927	£1.25	£62.50
25	Clan Tartans, 2nd Series	1927	50p	£12.50

STEPHEN MITCHELL—cont.

Qty		Date	Odds	Sets
25	Empire Exhibition, Scotland 1938	1938	40p	£10.00
25	Famous Crosses	1923	40p	£10.00
50	Famous Scots	1933	50p	£25.00
50	First Aid	1938	65p	£32.50
P3	Glasgow International Exhibition 1901	1901	£50.00	—
50	Humorous Drawings	1924	£1.55	£77.50
50	Interesting Buildings	1905	£5.00	—
40	London Ceremonials	1928	£1.00	£40.00
25	Medals	1916	£3.75	£93.75
25	Money	1913	£3.75	£93.75
25	Old Sporting Prints	1930	80p	£20.00
50	Our Empire	1937	30p	£15.00
25	Regimental Crests & Collar Badges	1900	£10.00	£250.00
70	River & Coastal Steamers	1925	£1.90	£133.00
50	Scotland's Story	1929	£1.75	£87.50
25	Scottish Clan Series	1903	£8.75	£218.75
50	Scottish Footballers	1934	£1.25	£62.50
50	Scottish Football Snaps	1935	£1.25	£62.50
25	Seals	1911	£3.75	£93.75
25	Sports	1907	£8.75	£218.75
25	Stars of Screen & History	1939	£1.00	£25.00
25	Statues & Monuments	1914	£3.75	£93.75
50	The World of Tomorrow	1936	65p	£32.50
25	Village Models	1925	£1.50	£37.50
L25	Village Models	1925	£3.00	£75.00
25	Village Models, 2nd Series	1925	£1.75	£43.75
25	Village Models, 2nd (Not Inscribed 2nd)	1925	£2.00	—
L25	Village Models, 2nd Series	1925	£3.00	£75.00
50	Wonderful Century	1937	40p	£20.00

MOORGATE TOBACCO CO. LTD.

D30	The New Elizabethan Age (Matt)	1953	£2.50	—
D30	The New Elizabethan Age (Varnished)	1953	£1.75	£52.50

B. MORRIS & SONS LTD.

30	Actresses (Black & White)	1898	£1.00	£45.00
26	Actresses "FROGA A" (Borneo Queen)	1899	£25.00	—
26	(Gold Seals)	1899	£25.00	—
26	(Morris Cigarettes)	1899	£25.00	—
26	(Tommy Atkins)	1899	£62.50	—
L26	Actresses "FROGA B"	1899	£250.00	—
1	Advertisement Card	1900	—	£250.00
6	Agriculture in the Orient	1910	£5.00	£30.00
50	Animals at the Zoo (Blue Back)	1924	50p	£25.00
50	Animals at the Zoo (Grey Back)	1924	65p	£32.50
6	Architectural Monuments	1910	£5.00	£30.00
35	At the London Zoo Aquarium	1928	30p	£10.50
25	Australian Cricketers	1925	£2.00	£50.00
M24	Battleship Crests (Silk)	1915	£21.50	—
50	Beauties "CHOAB" (Gold Flake Honeydew)	1900	£34.00	—
50	(Golden Virginia)	1900	£34.00	—
50	(Levant Favourites)	1900	£34.00	—
50	(Reina Regenta)	1900	£34.00	—

B. MORRIS & SONS LTD.—cont.

Qty		Date	Odds	Sets
50	Beauties Collotype (Multi-Backed)	1897	*£100.00*	—
21	Beauties "MOM" (Borneo Queen)	1899	£25.00	—
21	(Gold Seals)	1899	£25.00	—
21	(Morris Cigarettes)	1899	£25.00	—
21	(Tommy Atkins)	1899	£75.00	—
20	Boer War 1900	1900	£31.25	£625.00
25	Boer War Celebrities "PAM"	1901	£21.50	—
25	Captain Blood	1937	65p	£16.25
L25	English & Foreign Birds (Silk)	1915	£3.15	—
L25	English Flowers (Silk, Panel Cigarettes)	1915	£2.50	£62.50
L25	English Flowers ("Cruel" Silk)	1915	£3.75	—
L25	English Flowers (Silk, No Brand)	1915	£3.75	—
L50	English Flowers (Silk)	1915	£3.00	£150.00
50	Film Star Series	1923	£2.00	£100.00
25	Golf Strokes Series	1923	£2.50	£62.50
12	Horoscopes	1936	30p	£3.75
25	How Films Are Made	1934	65p	£16.25
50	How to Sketch	1929	80p	£40.00
20	London Views (American Gold)	1904	£25.00	—
20	(Borneo Queen)	1904	£25.00	
20	(Gold Flake)	1904	£25.00	—
20	(Reina Regenta)	1904	£25.00	—
25	Marvels of the Universe Series	1912	£3.00	£75.00
25	Measurement of Time	1924	90p	£22.50
25	Motor Series	1922	£2.50	£62.50
50	National & Colonial Arms	1917	£5.00	£250.00
25	Racing Greyhounds	1939	80p	£20.00
L25	Regimental Colours (Silk)	1916	£2.00	£50.00
G4	Regimental Colours (Silk)	1916	*£50.00*	
6	Schools in Foreign Countries	1910	£6.25	£37.50
24	Shadowgraphs	1925	£1.75	£42.00
6	Strange Vessels	1910	£6.25	£37.50
6	The Ice Breaker	1910	£6.25	£37.50
25	The Queen's Dolls House	1925	£2.00	£50.00
13	Treasure Island	1924	50p	£6.50
50	Victory Signs Series	1928	30p	£15.00
25	War Celebrities	1916	£4.40	£110.00
25	War Pictures	1916	£6.25	£156.25
25	Wax Art Series	1931	30p	£7.50
25	Whipsnade Zoo	1932	30p	£7.50
25	Wireless Series	1923	£2.50	£62.50

PHILIP MORRIS & CO. LTD.

50	British Views	1924	£2.00	£100.00
L50	British Views	1924	£2.50	—
T108	Classic Collection	1987	£1.25	—
M72	Motormania	1986	£1.25	—

P. MOUAT & CO.

30	Colonial Troops	1902	*£105.00*	—

MOUSTAFA LTD.

Qty		Date	Odds	Sets
F50	Camera Studies (Printed Backs)	1923	£2.50	—
F50	Camera Studies (Plain Backs)	1923	£2.50	—
25	Cinema Stars	1924	£3.75	—
40	Leo Chambers Dogs Heads	1924	£2.00	£80.00
25	Pictures of World Interest	1923	£2.50	£62.50
F25	Real Photos	1925	30p	£7.50

MUNRO

30	Colonial Troops	1902	£125.00	—

B. MURATTI SONS & CO. LTD.

Qty		Date	Odds	Sets
P?25	Actresses, Collotype	1899	£100.00	—
26	Actresses "FROGA" (Cigarette Connoisseur)	1899	£17.50	£450.00
26	Actresses "FROGA" (Zinnia)	1899	£22.50	—
P?50	Actresses & Beauties, (Horizontal Back)	1899	£125.00	—
P?50	Actresses & Beauties (Vertical Back)	1899	£125.00	—
P?50	Actresses & Beauties (Stamped Back)	1899	£125.00	—
P?50	Actresses & Beauties (Plain Back)	1899	£125.00	—
X?30	Advertisement Cards	1900	£250.00	—
F24	Australian Racehorses	1931	65p	£15.00
50	Beauties "CHOAB" (Black Back)	1900	£37.50	—
50	Beauties "CHOAB" (Green Back)	1900	£37.50	—
L50	Beautiful Women	1900	£75.00	—
20	Boer War Generals "CLAM"	1900	£28.00	—
X?	Book Postcard Series	1902	£62.50	—
B15	Caricatures (Specialities)	1903	£20.00	£300.00
B15	Caricatures (Vassos)	1903	£42.50	—
B15	Caricatures (Vassos Blanked Out)	1903	£42.50	—
B15	Caricatures (Zinnia, Black)	1903	£22.00	£300.00
B15	Caricatures (Zinnia, Brown)	1903	£22.00	—
L35	Crowned Heads	1912	£12.50	—
53	Japanese Series (Printed Back)	1904	£12.50	—
53	Japanese Series (Plain Back)	1904	£10.50	—
XF?	Midget Post Card Series (Glossy)	1902	£6.25	—
X?	Midget Post Card Series (Matt)	1902	£6.25	—
X?	Queens Postcard Series	1902	£7.50	—
19	Russo Japanese Series	1904	£10.00	£190.00
25	Star Girls	1899	£125.00	—
50	Views of Jersey (Printed Back)	1913	£15.00	—
50	Views of Jersey (Plain Back)	1913	£12.50	—
25	War Series I	1916	£18.75	—
25	War Series II	1917	£10.00	£250.00

SILK ISSUES

Qty		Date	Odds	Sets
L40	Canvas Masterpieces, Series M—Large Globe	1916	£5.00	—
L40	Canvas Masterpieces, Series M—Small Globe	1916	£2.00	£80.00
P16	Canvas Masterpieces, Series P	1916	£9.40	—
M24	Flags, Series A (26-49)	1914	£3.15	£75.00
P3	Flags, Series A (1-3)	1914	£8.15	—
L1	Flags, Series B (No. 19)	1914	—	£9.40
M25	Flags, Series C (20-44)	1914	£3.15	£78.75
P18	Flags, Series C (1-18)	1914	£8.15	—
P3	Flags, Series D (45-47)	1914	£8.15	—

B. MURATTI SONS & CO. LTD.—cont.

Qty		Date	Odds	Sets
M25	Flags, Series E (48-72)	1914	£3.15	£78.75
P6	Flags, Series F (73-78)	1914	£6.25	—
P18	Great War Leaders, Series P	1916	£10.00	—
M25	Regimental Badges, Series A	1915	£3.75	£93.75
L48	Regimental Badges, Series B	1915	£5.00	—
L15	Regimental Badges, Series B (Different, 4-18)	1915	£5.00	—
L16	Regimental Badges, Series G (79-94)	1915	£7.50	—
L25	Regimental Colours, Series CB	1915	£8.15	—
M72	Regimental Colours, Series RB	1915	£5.00	—

GERMAN ISSUES

X216	Brennpunkte des Deutschen Sports 1	1935	55p	£125.00
X288	Brennpunkte des Deutschen Sports 2	1936	75p	—
X216	Brennpunkte des Deutschen Sports 3	1936	55p	£125.00
?30	Cinema Stars Serie No.2	1932	£3.75	—

MURRAY, SONS & CO.

20	Actresses "BLARM"	1902	£75.00	—
F22	Bathing Beauties	1929	£4.40	—
40	Bathing Belles	1939	20p	£5.75
15	Chess & Draughts Problems	1910	£42.50	—
F22	Cinema Scenes	1929	£4.40	—
20	Cricketers (Series H, Black Front)	1912	£55.00	—
20	Cricketers (Series H, Brown Front)	1912	£87.50	—
25	Crossword Puzzles	1923	£50.00	—
F26	Dancers	1929	£4.40	—
F25	Dancing Girls (Belfast, Ireland)	1929	£2.00	£50.00
F25	Dancing Girls (London & Belfast)	1929	£2.00	£50.00
F26	Dancing Girls ("Series of 26")	1930	£2.20	—
25	Famous Works of Art	1910	£15.50	—
B16	Flags (Silk)	1910	£18.75	—
X3	Flags & Arms (Silk)	1910	£62.50	—
34	Footballers, Series H	1912	£15.50	—
104	Footballers Series J	1913	£15.50	—
?25	Football Colours (Shaped, Maple Cigarettes)	1905	£37.50	—
?25	Football Colours (Shaped, Murray Cigarettes)	1905	£37.50	—
25	Football Rules	1911	£20.00	£500.00
25	High Class Works of Art	1909	£18.75	—
20	Holidays by the L.M.S.	1927	£8.15	£163.00
20	Inventors Series	1924	£3.15	£63.00
25	Irish Scenery (Hall Mark Cigarettes)	1905	£20.00	—
25	Irish Scenery (Pineapple Cigarettes)	1905	£20.00	—
25	Irish Scenery (Special Crown Cigarettes)	1905	£20.00	—
25	Irish Scenery (Straight Cut Cigarettes)	1905	£20.00	—
25	Irish Scenery (Yachtsman Cigarettes)	1905	£20.00	—
31	Orders of Chivalry (Silk)	1925	£15.00	—
25	Polo Pictures	1910	£18.75	£468.75
50	Prominent Politicians (Two Strengths)	1909	£2.00	£100.00
50	Prominent Politicians (Without "In Two Strengths")	1909	£15.00	—
50	Puzzle Series	1929	£3.15	—
B25	Regimental Badges (Silk)	1910	£15.50	—
50	Stage and Film Stars	1926	£2.00	£100.00
25	Steamships	1939	65p	£16.25

MURRAY, SONS & CO.—cont.

Qty		Date	Odds	Sets
50	The Story of Ships	1940	20p	£6.25
25	Types of Aeroplanes	1929	75p	£18.75
20	Types of Dogs	1924	£3.75	£75.00
35	War Series K	1915	£20.00	£700.00
25	War Series L	1916	£1.90	£62.50

H. J. NATHAN

40	Comic Military & Naval Pictures (No Border)	1904	£50.00	—
40	Comic Military & Naval Pictures (White Border)	1904	£50.00	—

JAMES NELSON

?20	Beauties "FENA"	1899	£150.00	—

EDWD. J. NEWBEGIN

F50	Actors & Actresses	1901	£40.00	—
10	Actresses "HAGG"	1900	£125.00	—
20	Cricketers Series	1902	£275.00	—
1	Mabel Love Advertisement Card (3 Colours)	1900	—	£312.50
19	Russo Japanese Series	1904	£100.00	—
16	Well-known Proverbs	1900	£85.00	—
24	Well-known Songs	1900	£85.00	—

W. H. NEWMAN LTD.

18	Motor Cycle Series	1914	£62.50	—

THE NEW MOSLEM CIG. CO. LTD.

30	Proverbs	1903	£62.50	—

THOS. NICHOLLS & CO.

50	Orders of Chivalry	1916	£3.75	£187.50

THE NILMA TOBACCO COY.

40	Home & Colonial Regiments	1903	£62.50	—
30	Proverbs	1903	£62.50	—

M. E. NOTARAS LTD.

B24	Chinese Scenes	1925	25p	£6.00
F36	National Types of Beauty	1925	50p	£18.00

OGDENS LTD.
244 Page Illustrated Reference Book (With Guinea Gold)—£12.50

25	ABC of Sport	1927	£1.90	£47.50
50	Actors, Natural & Character Studies	1938	60p	£30.00
25	Actresses (No Glycerine, Black Front)	1895	£80.00	—
25	Actresses (No Glycerine, Brown Front)	1895	£80.00	—
?100	Actresses, Collotype (Mauve Stamped Back)	1894	£37.50	—
?100	Actresses, Collotype (Red Stamped Back)	1894	£45.00	—

Qty		Date	Odds	Sets
?100	Actresses, Collotype (Printed Back)	1894	£37.50	—
50	Actresses, Green Gravure	1898	£7.50	£375.00
?1	Actresses, Green, Green Border	1898	*£187.50*	—
50	Actresses, Tabs Type, Red Tint	1902	£25.00	—
?210	Actresses, Woodburytype	1894	£31.25	—
F?573	Actresses, Guinea Gold Type	1900	£1.90	—
50	A.F.C. Nicknames	1933	£2.00	£100.00
50	Air Raid Precautions	1938	30p	£15.00
50	Applied Electricity	1928	80p	£40.00
192	Army Crests and Mottoes	1902	£3.75	£720.00
36	Australian Test Cricketers	1928	£2.50	£90.00
28	Beauties "BOCCA"	1899	£20.00	£560.00
50	Beauties "CHOAB"	1899	£21.50	—
26	Beauties "HOL" (Blue Printed Back)	1899	£15.00	£390.00
26	Beauties "HOL" (Rubber Stamped Back)	1899	*£95.00*	—
66	Beauties, Green Net Back (Black & White)	1901	£9.40	£625.00
100	Beauties, Green Net Back (Coloured)	1901	£18.75	—
52	Beauties, P/C Inset	1899	£25.00	£1300.00
26	Beauties, As P/C Inset	1899	£31.25	—
52	Beauties & Military, P/C Inset	1898	£25.00	£1300.00
F50	Beauty Series (Unnumbered)	1900	£50.00	—
F50	Beauty Series (Numbered)	1900	£1.90	£95.00
50	Billiards by Tom Newman	1928	£1.00	£50.00
50	Birds Eggs	1908	£1.25	£62.50
50	Birds Eggs (Cut-Outs)	1923	50p	£25.00
F?141	Boer War & General Interest	1901	£2.20	—
LF?50	Boer War & General Interest	1901	*£25.00*	—
50	Boxers	1915	£3.75	£187.50
25	Boxing	1914	£3.15	£78.75
50	Boy Scouts (Blue Back)	1911	£1.90	£95.00
50	Boy Scouts (Green Back)	1911	£3.15	£157.50
50	Boy Scouts, 2nd Series (Blue Back)	1912	£1.90	£95.00
50	Boy Scouts, 2nd Series (Green Back)	1912	£3.15	£157.50
50	Boy Scouts, 3rd Series (Blue Back)	1912	£1.90	£95.00
50	Boy Scouts, 3rd Series (Green Back)	1912	£3.15	£157.50
50	Boy Scouts, 4th Series	1913	£2.00	£100.00
25	Boy Scouts, 5th Series	1914	£2.00	£50.00
50	Boy Scouts (Different)	1929	90p	£45.00
50	British Birds	1905	£1.25	£62.50
50	British Birds, 2nd Series	1909	£1.50	£75.00
50	British Birds (Cut-Outs)	1923	40p	£20.00
50	British Birds & Their Eggs	1939	£1.25	£62.50
50	British Costumes From 100 B.C. to 1904	1905	£5.00	£250.00
50	Broadcasting	1935	75p	£37.50
50	By the Roadside	1932	75p	£37.50
44	Captains of Association Football Clubs & Colours	1926	£1.75	£77.00
50	Cathedrals & Abbeys	1936	75p	£37.50
50	Champions of 1936	1937	75p	£37.50
50	Children of All Nations	1924	40p	£20.00
50	Club Badges	1914	£3.75	£187.50
50	Colour in Nature	1932	65p	£32.50
25	Comic Pictures	1897	*£250.00*	—
50	Construction of Railway Trains	1930	£1.60	£80.00

PLAYER'S CIGARETTES

ARMY VETERINARY CORPS,
1908

Uniforms of the Territorial Army.
Player

"ARF A 'MO' KAISER!"

Arf A Mo Kaiser!
Martin

THOMSON & PORTEOUS

ITS A LONG, LONG WAY
TO TIPPERARY.

COPYRIGHT
DOBSON, MOLLE & Cº LTᴰ EDINBURGH & LONDON.   Nº 5.

The European War
Series. Thomson &
Porteus. Also many
other tobacco & trade

PROPELLED WEAPONS

TORPEDO

Propelled Weapons.
Amalgamated Tobacco

COMPANY DRILL SERIES Nº 9.
A COLUMN OR CLOSE COLUMN FORMING LINE OUTWARDS IN THE SAME DIRECTION.
(Infantry Training Section 843ii.)

ORDERS:-
Company Commander :-
LINE OUTWARDS: ONE PLATOON TO THE RIGHT
REMAINDER, FORM-FOURS: OUTWARDS:
QUICK-MARCH.
Platoon Commanders :- Nºˢ 2.3.4
Halt :- Right (or left) turn (on gaining
position in line.)

ORIGINAL POSITION IN BLACK.
MOVEMENTS & NEW FORMATIONS IN RED.
For notes see other side.

Company Drill.
Hignett

Player's Cigarettes.

MON·DROIT

H.M.S.
VICTORY.

Ships' Figureheads.
Player

France.

Officer of Artillery,
Review Order.

Soldiers & Sailors.
Wills

PLAYER'S CIGARETTES.

1ST CLASS PETTY OFFICER, 1855.

History of Naval Dress.
Player

Australian Footballers.
Schuh

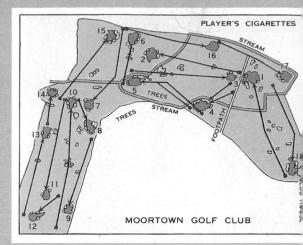

Championship Golf Courses.
Player

Winners on the Turf.
Boguslavsky

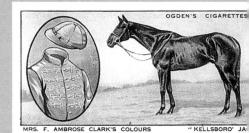

Prominent Racehorses of 1933.
Ogden. Also Hignett

Cricketers Series.
Pattreiouex

Champions.
Goodwin

Football Caricatures.
Hignett. Also Ogden

OGDENS LTD.—cont.

Qty		Date	Odds	Sets
50	Coronation Procession (Sect.)	1937	80p	£40.00
12	Cricket & Football—Women (Gold Medal)	1896	£215.00	—
12	Cricket & Football—Women (Cox Back)	1896	£280.00	—
12	Cricket & Football—Women (Otto De Rose)	1896	£315.00	—
50	Cricketers & Sportsmen	1898	£56.25	—
50	Cricket 1926	1926	£1.75	£87.50
25	Derby Entrants 1926	1926	£1.80	£45.00
50	Derby Entrants 1928	1928	£1.25	£62.50
50	Derby Entrants 1929	1929	£1.50	£75.00
50	Dogs	1936	£1.25	£62.50
55	Dominoes	1909	£1.15	£63.25
112	Dominoes—Actress & Beauty Backs	1900	£20.00	—
25	Famous Dirt Track Riders	1929	£2.50	£62.50
50	Famous Footballers	1908	£2.30	£115.00
50	Famous Rugby Players	1926	£1.25	£62.50
50	Flags & Funnels of Steamship Lines	1906	£3.15	£157.50
50	Football Caricatures	1935	£1.25	£62.50
43	Football Club Badges (Shaped)	1910	£4.40	—
50	Football Club Captains	1936	£1.00	£50.00
51	Football Club Colours	1906	£2.30	£117.00
50	Foreign Birds	1924	50p	£25.00
50	Fowls Pigeons & Dogs	1904	£2.25	£112.50
25	Greyhound Racing, 1st Series	1927	£2.50	£62.50
25	Greyhound Racing, 2nd Series	1928	£2.50	£62.50
1	History of the Union Jack (Folder)	1900	—	£165.00
50	How to Swim	1935	30p	£15.00
50	Infantry Training	1915	£1.65	£82.50
50	Jockey and Owners Colours	1927	£1.65	£82.50
50	Jockeys 1930	1930	£1.75	£87.50
50	Leaders of Men	1924	£1.25	£62.50
MF3	Liners (Guinea Gold Type)	1901	£125.00	—
P6	Liners (6 Brands)	1902	£87.50	—
25	Marvels of Motion	1928	£1.50	£37.50
K52	Miniature Playing Cards (Actresses)	1900	£3.15	—
K102	Miniature Playing Cards (Beauty Backs)	1900	£3.15	—
K52	Miniature Playing Cards (Coolie No Border)	1904	£2.00	£104.00
K52	Miniature Playing Cards (Coolie White Border)	1904	£3.15	—
K52	Miniature Playing Cards (Tabs)	1909	£2.50	£130.00
50	Modern British Pottery	1925	65p	£32.50
50	Modern Railways	1936	£1.50	£75.00
50	Modern War Weapons	1915	£2.20	£110.00
25	Modes of Conveyance	1927	£1.90	£47.50
50	Motor Races 1931	1931	£1.75	£87.50
50	Ocean Greyhounds	1938	70p	£35.00
25	Optical Illusions	1923	£1.75	£43.75
50	Orders of Chivalry	1907	£2.50	£125.00
25	Owners Racing Colours & Jockeys (Green Back)	1914	£2.50	£62.50
50	Owners Racing Colours & Jockeys (Blue Back)	1906	£2.00	£100.00
25	Picturesque People of the Empire	1927	£1.00	£25.00
50	Picturesque Villages	1936	75p	£37.50
25	Poultry (Ogdens On Front) (1-25)	1915	£2.00	£50.00
25	Poultry (No Ogdens On Front) (1-25)	1915	£2.50	£62.50
25	Poultry, 2nd Series (26-50)	1916	£2.00	£50.00

OGDENS LTD. — cont.

Qty		Date	Odds	Sets
25	Poultry Alphabet	1924	£1.60	£40.00
25	Poultry Rearing & Management, 1st Series	1922	£1.50	£37.50
25	Poultry Rearing & Management, 2nd Series	1923	£1.50	£37.50
50	Prominent Cricketers of 1938	1938	£1.00	£50.00
50	Prominent Racehorses of 1933	1934	£1.25	£62.50
50	Pugilists & Wrestlers, A Series (1-50)	1908	£2.00	£100.00
25	Pugilists & Wrestlers, 2nd Series (51-75)	1909	£2.50	£62.50
50	Pugilists in Action	1928	£1.20	£60.00
50	Racehorses	1907	£2.30	£115.00
50	Racing Pigeons	1931	£1.80	£90.00
25	Records of the World	1908	£2.00	£50.00
50	Royal Mail	1909	£3.15	£157.50
50	Sea Adventure	1939	20p	£8.75
50	Sectional Cycling Map	1910	£2.00	£100.00
50	Shakespeare Series (Numbered)	1905	£10.00	£500.00
50	Shakespeare Series (Unnumbered)	1905	£9.40	£470.00
50	Shots from the Films	1936	£1.00	£50.00
25	Sights of London	1923	£1.00	£25.00
50	Smugglers and Smuggling	1932	£1.00	£50.00
50	Soldiers of the King (Grey Captions)	1909	£3.75	£187.50
25	Soldiers of the King (Brown Captions)	1909	£5.00	£125.00
P36	Sporting & Other Girls	1898	*£312.50*	—
50	Steeplechase Celebrities	1931	£1.40	£70.00
50	Steeplechase Trainers and Owners Colours	1927	£1.40	£70.00
50	Swimming Diving and Life Saving	1931	65p	£32.50
25	Swiss Views 1-25	1910	£2.50	£62.50
25	Swiss Views 26-50	1910	£4.40	£110.00
50	The Blue Riband of the Atlantic	1929	£1.70	£85.00
50	The Story of Sand	1935	65p	£32.50
25	Trainers and Owners Colours, 1st Series	1925	£1.40	£35.00
25	Trainers and Owners Colours, 2nd Series	1926	£1.75	£43.75
50	Trick Billiards	1934	90p	£45.00
50	Turf Personalities	1929	£1.75	£87.50
48	Victoria Cross Heroes	1901	£10.00	£500.00
25	Whaling	1927	£2.00	£50.00
50	Yachts & Motor Boats	1930	£1.55	£77.50
50	Zoo Studies	1937	40p	£20.00

GUINEA GOLD PHOTOGRAPHIC ISSUES

Qty		Date	Odds	Sets
LF1	Actresses Base C	1899	—	£32.50
F375	Actresses Base D	1900	90p	—
MF54	Actresses Base D (Medium Size)	1900	£8.15	—
F270	Actresses Base D	1900	£1.05	—
F40	Actresses Base E	1900	£2.50	£100.00
F638	Actresses Base I	1899	80p	—
F23	Actresses Base I (¾ White Frame)	1899	£2.50	—
LF21	Actresses Base I	1899	£37.50	—
F30	Actresses Base J	1899	£3.15	—
F238	Actresses Base K	1899	£1.90	—
F216	Actresses Base L	1899	£1.90	—
F113	Actresses & Miscellaneous Base I	1900	90p	£102.50
F2974	Actresses & Miscellaneous Base M	1900	75p	—
LF403	Actresses & Miscellaneous Base M	1900	£1.05	—
F58	Boer War & Actresses Base F	1901	75p	£43.50
F186	Boer War & Miscellaneous Base D	1901	65p	—

OGDENS LTD. —cont.

Qty		Date	Odds	Sets
LF153	Boer War & Miscellaneous Base D	1900	95p	—
F321	Continental Actresses Base B	1899	£1.90	—
LF71	Continental Actresses Base B	1899	£12.50	—
F11	Cricketers Base I	1901	£9.40	£103.50
F50	Cricketers Base M (Set 1)	1899	£12.50	—
F27	Cricketers Base M (Set 2)	1899	£18.75	—
F57	Cyclists Base M	1899	£4.40	—
F58	Denumbered Group Base D	1900	£1.90	—
LF50	Denumbered Group Base D	1900	£2.50	—
F176	Footballers Base M	1899	£5.00	—
F320	General Interest (White Panel) Base D	1900	75p	£240.00
F200	General Interest Numbered 1-200	1899	30p	£60.00
F300	General Interest Numbered 201-500	1900	80p	—
F395	General Interest Numbered 501-898	1900	75p	£300.00
F180	General Interest Numbered 899-1098	1901	£1.25	—
F50	General Interest Numbered 1099-1148	1901	£1.00	—
F18	Golf Base I	1901	£12.50	£225.00
F14	London Street Scenes Base I	1901	£2.00	£28.00
F400	New Series 1	1902	75p	£300.00
F400	New Series B	1902	90p	£360.00
F300	New Series C	1902	65p	£195.00
F46	Pantomime & Theatre Artistes Base D	1899	£3.15	—
LF45	Pantomime & Theatre Artistes Base D	1899	£3.75	—
F50	Pantomime & Theatre Artistes Base M	1899	£3.75	—
F60/62	Politicians, Base D	1900	80p	£48.00
F3	Royalty Base M	1899	£2.00	£6.00
F32	Turner Paintings Base I	1901	£1.00	£32.00
F10	Views & Scenes Abroad Base I	1901	90p	£9.00

TABS TYPE ISSUES

Qty		Date	Odds	Sets
75	Actresses (numbered 126-200)	1900	£9.40	—
200	Actresses (Plain Back)	1900	£2.00	—
200	Actresses & Foreign Views	1900	£1.55	—
1	General de Wet	1901	—	£3.15
1	General Interest (Unnumbered)	1901	—	£4.40
?36	General Interest (No Labour Clause)	1900	£21.50	—
150	General Interest A Series	1901	50p	£137.50
200	General Interest B Series	1901	50p	£162.50
200	General Interest C Series (1-200)	1902	50p	£100.00
100	General Interest C Series (201-300)	1902	£1.90	—
50	General Interest C Series (301-350)	1902	65p	£32.50
200	General Interest D Series	1902	50p	£100.00
120	General Interest E Series	1902	80p	£96.00
320	General Interest F Series (1-320)	1902	75p	£240.00
99	General Interest F Series (321-420)	1902	£2.20	—
120	General Interest (1-120)	1902	80p	£96.00
196	General Interest (Item 95)	1902	65p	£127.50
100	General Interest (Item 96)	1902	65p	£65.00
100	General Interest (Item 97-1)	1902	£1.00	£100.00
21	General Interest (Item 97-2, Cricket)	1902	£3.75	£78.75
25	General Interest (Item 97-2, Fotball)	1902	£1.90	£47.50
15	General Interest (Item 97-2, Golf)	1902	£8.00	£120.00
139	General Interest (Item 97-2, Various)	1902	75p	£105.00
?110	General Interest (Oblong Back)	1902	£10.50	—
17	Heroes of the Ring	1901	£3.75	—

Qty		Date	Odds	Sets
1	H.M. The Queen	1901	—	£3.15
2	H.R.H. The Prince of Wales	1901	£3.15	—
14	Imperial Interest	1901	75p	£10.50
106	Imperial or International Interest	1901	65p	£70.00
3	International Interest	1901	£1.25	£3.75
14	International Interest or a Prominent British Officer	1901	65p	£9.25
71	Leading Artistes of the Day (Name in Black)	1901	90p	£64.00
	(Name in Black, No Labour Clause)	1901	£18.75	—
25	Leading Artistes of the Day (Name in White, Printed Back)	1901	£12.50	—
	(Name in White, Plain Back)	1901	£12.50	—
	(No Name)	1901	£12.50	—
?75	Leading Artistes of the Day (Non Descriptive, Printed Back)	1901	£10.00	—
	(Non Descriptive, Plain Back)	1901	£10.00	—
22	Leading Athletes	1901	£1.75	£38.50
15	Leading Favourites of the Turf	1901	£2.50	£37.50
54	Leading Generals at the War	1901	65p	—
25	Leading Generals at the War (Different)	1901	75p	—
25	Leading Generals at the War (No "Tabs")	1901	£1.25	—
47	Leading Generals at the War (Non-Descriptive)	1901	75p	—
25	Leading Generals at the War (Lucky Star)	1901	£3.75	—
25	("Guinea Gold" Rubber Stamped)	1901	£6.25	—
2	Members of Parliament	1901	£2.50	£5.00
11	Notable Coursing Dogs	1901	£4.40	—
12	Our Leading Cricketers	1901	£10.00	£120.00
17	Our Leading Footballers	1901	£3.15	—
37	Prominent British Officers	1901	75p	£27.75
50	Stage Artistes & Celebrities	1900	£1.90	£95.00
1	The Yacht "Columbia"	1901	—	£5.00
1	The Yacht "Shamrock"	1901	—	£5.00

AUSTRALIAN ISSUES TABS TYPE

Qty		Date	Odds	Sets
1	Christian de Wet	1901	—	£7.50
1	Corporal G. E. Nurse, V.C.	1901	—	£7.50
14	English Cricketer Series	1901	£37.50	—
400	General Interest (Numbered)	1901	£2.50	—
100	General Interest (Unnumbered)	1901	£4.40	—
1	Imperial Interest	1901	—	£7.50
27	Imperial or International Interest	1901	£5.00	—
64	International Interest	1901	£6.25	—
1	Lady Sarah Wilson	1901	—	£7.50
39	Leading Generals at the War	1901	£5.00	—
13	Prominent British Officers	1901	£6.25	—

OTHER OVERSEAS ISSUES

Qty		Date	Odds	Sets
51	Actresses, Black & White (Polo)	1906	£2.50	—
?10	Actresses, Black & White (Polo, Small Pictures, Numbered)	1906	£12.50	—
?10	Actresses, Black & White (Polo, Small Pictures, Unnumbered)	1906	£12.50	—
30	Actresses, Brown (Polo, 3 Printings)	1908	£2.00	£60.00

OGDENS LTD.—cont.

Qty		Date	Odds	Sets
17	Animals (Polo)	1916	£10.00	—
60	Animals (Ruler)	1912	£2.20	£132.00
60	Animals (Tabs, With Captions)	1912	£2.20	£132.00
50	Animals (Tabs, No Captions)	1912	£2.50	£125.00
50	Aviation Series (Tabs, Ogden at Base)	1912	£4.40	—
50	Aviation Series (Tabs, Ogden England)	1912	£4.40	—
45	Beauties—Picture Hats (Polo)	1911	£5.00	—
50	Best Dogs of Their Breed (Polo Blue with Eastern Characters)	1916	£6.25	—
50	Best Dogs of their Breed (Polo Blue without Eastern Characters)	1916	£6.25	—
50	Best Dogs of Their Breed (Polo Pink)	1916	£6.25	—
52	Birds of Brilliant Plumage (Frame Line)	1914	£2.50	£130.00
52	Birds of Brilliant Plumage (No Frame, 2 Printings)	1914	£2.50	£130.00
25	British Trees & Their Uses (Guinea Gold)	1927	£1.50	£37.50
25	China's Ancient Warriors (Ruler)	1913	£3.75	£93.75
25	Famous Railway Trains (Guinea Gold)	1928	£2.00	£50.00
20	Flowers (Polo Packet 49mm Long, with Eastern Characters)	1915	£5.00	—
20	Flowers (Polo Packet 49mm Long, no Eastern Characters)	1915	£5.00	—
20	Flowers (Polo Packet 46mm Long)	1915	£5.00	—
25	Indian Women (Polo, Apple Green Border)	1919	£4.40	£110.00
25	Indian Women (Polo, Emerald Green)	1919	£4.40	£110.00
30	Music Hall Celebrities (Polo)	1911	£4.40	£132.00
50	Music Hall Celebrities (Tabs)	1911	£4.40	—
52	Playing Cards (Polo)	1922	£10.00	—
50	Riders of the World (Polo, Reg. No. 1294)	1911	£3.15	£157.50
50	Riders of the World (Polo, No "Reg. No.")	1911	£3.15	£157.50
50	Riders of the World (Polo, Cigarettes Uneven)	1911	£3.15	£157.50
50	Russo Japanese Series	1904	£18.75	—
36	Ships & Their Pennants (Polo)	1911	£5.00	—
32	Transport of the World (Polo)	1917	£5.00	—

THE ORLANDO CIGARETTE & CIGAR CO.

40	Home & Colonial Regiments	1901	£187.50	—

W. T. OSBORNE & CO.

40	Naval & Military Phrases (White Border)	1904	£37.50	—
40	Naval & Military Phrases (No Border)	1904	£37.50	—

OSBORNE TOBACCO CO.

50	Modern Aircraft (Blue Front)	1952	—	£7.50
50	Modern Aircraft (Brown Front)	1952	—	£12.50

PALMER & CO.

B12	Manikin Cards	1915	£62.50	—

J. A. PATTREIOUEX LTD.

Qty		Date	Odds	Sets
EARLY PHOTOGRAPHIC ISSUES				
F96	Animals (CA1-96)	1926	80p	—
LF50	Animals & Scenes (Unnumbered)	1924	95p	—
LF50	Animals & Scenes (1-50)	1925	95p	—
F192	Animals & Scenes (250-441 Junior Member)	1925	80p	—
F192	Animals & Scenes (250-441 Titled)	1925	80p	—
F96	Animals & Scenes (3 Brands, 346-441)	1925	80p	—
F96	Animals & Scenes (CC1-96)	1926	80p	—
LF50	Animals & Scenes (I1-50)	1927	95p	—
F96	Animals & Scenes (JS1-96A)	1928	80p	—
LF100	Animal Studies (A42-141)	1925	80p	—
LF50	Animal Studies (A151-200)	1925	80p	—
LF30	Beauties (JM1-30)	1928	£1.90	—
LF50	British & Egyptian Scenes (CM1-50A)	1927	95p	—
LF50	British Empire Exhibition (JM1-50B)	1928	£1.25	£62.50
XF100	Cathedrals, Abbeys & Castles (SJ1-100)	1928	£1.75	—
LF30	Child Studies (JM No. 1-30)	1928	£3.15	—
F96	Famous Cricketers (C1-96, Plain Back)	1926	£35.00	—
F96	Famous Cricketers (C1-96, Printed Back)	1926	£35.00	—
F191	Famous Footballers (F1-191)	1927	£4.40	—
LF50	Famous Statues (JCM1-50C)	1928	£1.25	£62.50
F96	Footballers (FA1-96)	1927	£3.15	—
F96	Footballers (FB1-96)	1928	£3.15	—
F96	Footballers (FC1-96)	1928	£2.50	—
LF48	Football Teams (F192-239)	1927	£7.50	—
F96	Natives & Scenes (1-96B)	1926	80p	—
F36	Natives & Scenes (1-36B) (As Above)	1926	80p	—
F96	Natives & Scenes (Numbered CB1-CB96)	1926	80p	—
F96	Natives & Scenes (Numbered 1-96)	1926	80p	—
F96	Natives & Scenes (JS1-96) (As Above)	1926	80p	—
F96	Overseas Scenes (1-96C)	1926	80p	—
LF50	Overseas Scenes (CM1-50B)	1926	95p	—
LF50	Overseas Scenes (JM1-50B) (As Above)	1928	95p	£47.50
LF50	Overseas Scenes (CM1-50S)	1927	95p	£47.50
LF50	Overseas Scenes (S101-150) (As Above)	1929	95p	£47.50
F96	Overseas Scenes (1-96D)	1927	80p	—
LF50	Overseas Scenes (1-50E)	1928	95p	£47.50
LF50	Overseas Scenes (1-50F)	1928	95p	£47.50
LF50	Overseas Scenes (JM1-50A)	1928	95p	£47.50
LF50	Scenes (201-250)	1925	95p	£47.50
LF50	Scenes (G1-50)	1927	£1.25	—
LF50	Scenes (1-50H, Grey Back)	1927	95p	£47.50
LF50	Scenes (1-50H, Brown Back)	1927	95p	—
LF50	Scenes (JCM1-50D, with Firm's Name)	1927	95p	£47.50
LF50	Scenes (JCM1-50D, Junior Member No.10 2 Sizes)	1927	95p	—
LF100	Scenes (S1-100)	1928	95p	—
LF4	Scenes (V1-4)	1928	£3.75	—
OTHER ISSUES				
F28	Beautiful Scotland	1939	65p	£18.25
MF48	Beautiful Scotland	1939	20p	£8.00
MF48	Britain from the Air	1939	20p	£8.00
50	British Empire Exhibition Series	1929	£1.75	£87.50

J. A. PATTREIOUEX LTD. — cont.

Qty		Date	Odds	Sets
MF48	British Railways	1938	30p	£14.50
50	Builders of the British Empire	1929	£2.20	£110.00
50	Celebrities in Sport	1930	£2.20	£110.00
F28	Coastwise	1939	65p	£18.25
MF48	Coastwise	1939	20p	£8.00
75	Cricketers Series	1928	£6.25	—
50	Dirt Track Riders	1929	£6.25	—
F54	Dirt Track Riders (Descriptive)	1930	£8.15	—
F54	Dirt Track Riders (Non Descriptive)	1930	£18.75	—
PF54	Dirt Track Riders (Premium Issue)	1930	£125.00	—
MF48	Dogs	1939	20p	£9.00
30	Drawing Made Easy	1930	£2.00	£60.00
F28	Flying	1938	£1.25	£35.00
MF48	Flying	1938	30p	£15.00
F78	Footballers in Action	1934	£1.90	£150.00
100	Footballers Series (Brown Captions)	1927	£4.40	—
50	Footballers Series (Blue Captions)	1927	£5.00	—
MF48	Holiday Haunts by the Sea	1938	20p	£9.00
X24	Jackpot Jigsaws	1969	65p	—
25	King Lud Problems	1936	£10.00	—
26	Maritime Flags	1931	£7.50	—
F28	Our Countryside	1938	65p	£18.25
MF48	Our Countryside	1938	20p	£8.00
25	Photos of Football Stars	1929	£18.75	—
50	Railway Posters by Famous Artists	1930	£5.00	£250.00
F54	Real Photographs of London	1936	£1.55	£83.75
F28	Shots from the Films	1938	£1.25	£35.00
MF48	Sights of Britain	1936	20p	£6.00
MF48	Sights of Britain, 2nd Series (2 Printings)	1936	20p	£5.50
MF48	Sights of Britain, 3rd Series	1937	20p	£6.75
MF48	Sights of London, 1st Series	1935	20p	£15.00
MF12	Sights of London — Supplementary Series	1935	50p	£6.00
F54	Sporting Celebrities	1935	£1.90	£102.50
MF96	Sporting Events and Stars	1935	50p	£48.00
50	Sports Trophies	1931	£1.90	£95.00
MF48	The Bridges of Britain	1938	20p	£8.00
52	The English & Welsh Counties	1928	£1.55	£80.00
MF48	The Navy (2 Printings)	1937	20p	£8.75
B24	Treasure Isle	1968	£1.25	—
F51	Views	1933	£1.00	£50.00
F54	Views of Britain	1937	£1.50	£81.00
MF48	Winter Scenes	1937	20p	£6.75

W. PEPPERDY

30	Army Pictures, Cartoons, etc.	1916	£62.50	—

M. PEZARO & SON

25	Armies of the World (Cake Walk)	1900	£87.50	—
25	Armies of the World (Nestor)	1900	£87.50	—
?25	Song Titles Illustrated	1900	£112.50	—

GODFREY PHILLIPS LTD.
40 Page Reference Book—£2.50

Qty		Date	Odds	Sets
50	Actresses (Oval)	1916	£5.00	£250.00
50	Actresses (Oval, Anonymous)	1916	£3.75	£187.50
25	Actresses, C Series (Ball of Beauty)	1900	*£80.00*	—
25	Actresses, C Series (Carriage)	1900	£27.50	—
25	Actresses, C Series (Derby)	1900	*£75.00*	—
25	Actresses, C Series (Horseshoe)	1900	£25.00	—
25	Actresses, C Series (Teapot)	1900	*£80.00*	—
25	Actresses, C Series (Volunteer)	1900	*£75.00*	—
2	Advertisement Cards	1934	£8.75	£17.50
50	Aircraft	1938	80p	£40.00
54	Aircraft Series No. 1 (Matt)	1938	30p	£16.00
54	Aircraft Series No. 1 (Varnished)	1938	£2.50	—
54	Aircraft Series No. 1 (Millhoff Back)	1938	£2.50	—
40	Animal Series	1903	£5.00	£200.00
M30	Animal Studies	1936	20p	£6.00
50	Annuals	1939	20p	£8.00
L25	Arms of the English Sees	1924	£3.75	£93.75
48	A Selection of BDV Wonderful Gifts	1930	80p	£38.50
48	A Selection of BDV Wonderful Gifts	1931	80p	£38.50
48	A Selection of BDV Wonderful Gifts	1932	80p	£38.50
24	Beauties ''HUMPS''	1898	£55.00	—
24	Beauties ''HUMPS'' (Plums Front)	1898	*£187.50*	—
30	Beauties, Nymphs	1896	£62.50	—
?50	Beauties, Plums (Black & White Front)	1897	*£125.00*	—
50	Beauties, Plums (Green Front)	1897	£42.50	—
50	Beauties, Plums (Plum Front)	1897	£42.50	—
25	Beauties (Numbered 801-825)	1902	£8.50	£212.50
30	Beauties, Oval (Plain Back)	1914	£1.65	£49.50
44	Beauties of To-day	1937	90p	£39.50
50	Beauties of To-day	1938	50p	£25.00
36	Beauties of To-day, 2nd Series	1940	40p	£14.50
F54	Beauties of To-day	1939	80p	£43.25
LF36	Beauties of To-day	1938	£2.20	£79.50
LF36	Beauties of To-day (Different Subjects)	1938	£3.75	—
XF36	Beauties of To-day (Unnumbered)	1937	£1.25	£45.00
XF36	Beauties of To-day, 2nd Series	1938	90p	£32.50
XF36	Beauties of To-day, 3rd Series	1938	65p	£23.50
XF36	Beauties of To-day, 4th Series	1938	65p	£23.50
XF36	Beauties of To-day, 5th Series	1938	40p	£14.50
XF36	Beauties of To-day, 6th Series	1939	40p	£14.50
XF36	Beauties of To-day, 7th Series	1939	40p	£14.50
XF36	Beauties of To-day (B.D V. Back)	1939	20p	£7.25
36	Beauties of the World	1931	£1.05	£37.50
36	Beauties of the World Series No. 2	1933	£1.05	£37.50
50	Beautiful Women (I.F. Series)	1908	£8.00	£400.00
50	Beautiful Women (W.I. Series)	1908	£8.00	£400.00
L50	Beautiful Women	1908	£15.50	—
P30	Beauty Spots of the Homeland	1938	20p	£6.00
50	Bird Painting	1938	20p	£8.75
25	Boxer Rebellion	1904	£20.00	—
50	British Beauties (Photogravure)	1916	£5.00	£250.00
K76	British Beauties	1916	£2.50	£190.00
F54	British Beauties (1-54)	1914	£2.00	£108.00

Qty		Date	Odds	Sets
F54	British Beauties (55-108, Glossy)	1915	£2.00	£108.00
54	British Beauties (55-108, Matt)	1914	£2.00	—
108	British Beauties (Plain Back, Brown)	1914	£3.15	—
108	British Beauties (Plain Back, Sepia)	1914	2.80	—
50	British Birds and Their Eggs	1936	50p	£25.00
30	British Butterflies, No. 1 Issue	1911	£3.75	£112.50
25	British Butterflies	1927	50p	£12.50
25	British Butterflies (Transfers)	1936	50p	£12.50
25	British Orders of Chivalry & Valour	1939	£1.00	£25.00
25	British Warships	1915	£5.00	£125.00
L25	British Warships	1915	£31.25	—
F80	British Warships	1916	£10.50	—
50	Busts of Famous People (Brown Back)	1907	*£21.50*	—
50	Busts of Famous People (Green Back)	1907	£5.00	£250.00
50	Busts of Famous People (Pale Green)	1907	£15.50	—
M36	Characters Come to Life	1938	20p	£7.25
?25	Children's Stories (Booklets)	1924	*£30.00*	—
25	Chinese Series (English Text)	1910	£5.00	£125.00
25	Chinese Series (Volunteer Cigarettes)	1910	£6.25	£156.25
G?6	Chinese Series	1910	*£50.00*	—
M25	Cinema Stars (Circular)	1924	£1.75	£43.75
F52	Cinema Stars (Set 1)	1923	£2.00	£104.00
30	Cinema Stars (Brown)	1924	£1.75	£52.50
30	Cinema Stars (Black & White)	1925	£1.00	£30.00
32	Cinema Stars (Black & White)	1930	£1.00	£32.00
32	Cinema Stars (Brown, Hand Coloured)	1934	95p	£30.50
30	Cinema Stars (Plain Back)	1935	45p	£13.50
50	Colonial Toops	1902	£20.00	—
50	Coronation of Their Majesties	1937	20p	£7.50
M36	Coronation of Their Majesties	1937	20p	£5.50
P24	Coronation of Their Majesties (Postcards)	1937	£1.00	£24.00
P24	Coronation of Their Majesties (Non-Postcard)	1937	£3.75	—
KF198	Cricketers (Pinnace)	1924	£5.00	—
F192	Cricketers (Brown Back)	1924	£6.25	—
LF25	Cricketers (Brown Back)	1924	£16.00	—
LF?100	Cricketers (Pinnace)	1924	£31.25	—
PF?223	Cricketers (Premium Issue)	1924	£25.00	—
1	Cricket Fixture Card	1936	—	£3.75
25	Derby Winners & Jockeys	1923	£2.50	£62.50
30	Eggs, Nests & Birds (Numbered)	1912	£4.40	£132.00
30	Eggs, Nests & Birds (Unnumbered)	1912	£5.00	£150.00
25	Empire Industries	1927	75p	£18.75
49/50	Evolution of the British Navy	1930	75p	£37.50
25	Famous Boys	1924	£1.90	£47.50
32	Famous Cricketers	1926	£3.75	£120.00
25	Famous Crowns	1938	20p	£5.00
50	Famous Footballers	1936	80p	£40.00
M36	Famous Love Scenes	1939	20p	£7.25
50	Famous Minors	1936	20p	£8.00
P26	Famous Paintings	1936	£1.00	£26.00
25	Feathered Friends	1928	£1.00	£25.00
50	Film Favourites	1934	25p	£12.50
50	Film Stars	1934	24p	£12.00
P24	Film Stars (Series of Cards, Postcard)	1934	75p	£18.00

GODFREY PHILLIPS LTD. — cont.

Qty		Date	Odds	Sets
P24	Film Stars (Series of Cards, Non-Postcard)	1934	£2.50	—
P24	Film Stars, (Series of 24 Cards, Postcard)	1934	£1.25	£30.00
P24	Film Stars (Series of 24 Cards, Non-Postcard) ..	1934	£2.50	—
P24	Film Stars, 2nd (25-48 Postcard Backs)	1934	£2.50	£60.00
P24	Film Stars, 2nd (25-48, Non-Postcard)	1934	£3.75	—
50	First Aid	1923	95p	£47.50
25	First Aid Series	1914	£5.00	£125.00
25	Fish	1924	£1.90	£47.50
M30	Flower Studies	1937	20p	£5.00
P30	Flower Studies	1937	30p	£9.00
KF112	Footballers (Brown Oval Back)	1922	£2.50	—
KF400	Footballers (Black Oval Back)	1923	95p	—
KF?517	Footballers (Double Frame Line Back)	1923	95p	—
KF940	Footballers (1-940, Address "Photo")	1923	65p	—
KF?179	Footballers (941-1109, Address "Photo")	1923	£1.25	—
KF940	Footballers (1-940, Address "Pinnace")	1923	65p	—
KF1522	Footballers (941-2462, Address "Pinnace")	1923	£1.25	—
LF?400	Footballers (Oval Design Back)	1923	£2.20	—
LF?1100	Footballers (Double Frame Line Back)	1923	£2.20	—
LF?2462	Footballers (Single Frame Line Back)	1923	£2.20	—
PF2462	Footballers (Premium Issue)	1923	£6.25	—
GF?	Football Teams (Premium Issue)	1923	£62.50	—
P1	Franco British Exhibition	1908	—	£16.00
P30	Garden Studies	1938	20p	£5.50
13	General Interest	1896	£37.50	£500.00
90	Guinea Gold Series (Numbered, Glossy)	1902	£3.45	£312.50
90	Guinea Gold Series (Numbered, Matt)	1902	£3.45	£312.50
100	Guinea Gold Series	1902	£4.40	£440.00
161	Guinea Gold Series (Different)	1902	£3.45	£555.00
100	Guinea Gold Series (Brown)	1902	£8.15	—
25	Home Pets	1924	£1.65	£41.25
25	How to Build a Two Valve Set	1929	£1.50	£37.50
25	How To Do It Series	1913	£6.25	£156.25
25	How to Make a Valve Amplifier	1924	£1.90	£47.50
25	How to Make Your Own Wireless Set	1923	£1.25	£31.25
25	Indian Series	1908	£12.50	£312.50
54	In the Public Eye	1935	20p	£8.75
50	International Caps	1936	65p	£32.50
35/37	Kings & Queens of England	1925	£1.50	£52.50
25	Lawn Tennis	1930	£1.50	£37.50
K52	Miniature Playing Cards (Red back)	1906	£90.00	—
K53	Miniature Playing Cards (Blue Design)	1934	45p	£23.75
K53	Miniature Playing Cards (Buff, 3 Types)	1932	45p	£23.75
K53	Miniature Playing Cards (White)	1933	50p	—
K53	Miniature Playing Cards (Yellow)	1933	50p	—
25	Model Railways	1927	£1.90	£47.50
30	Morse Signalling	1916	£6.25	£187.50
50	Motor Cars at a Glance	1924	£2.50	£125.00
20	Novelty Series	1924	£7.50	£150.00
25	Old Favourites	1924	£1.00	£25.00
M36	Old Masters	1939	25p	£9.00
36	Olympic Champions, Amsterdam 1928	1928	£1.00	£36.00
25	Optical Illusions	1927	£1.50	£37.50
36	Our Dogs	1939	90p	£32.50

GODFREY PHILLIPS LTD. —cont.

Qty		Date	Odds	Sets
M30	Our Dogs	1939	30p	£9.00
P30	Our Dogs	1939	£3.00	£90.00
M48	Our Favourites	1935	20p	£7.00
P30	Our Glorious Empire	1939	30p	£9.00
M30	Our Puppies	1936	25p	£7.50
P30	Our Puppies	1936	£1.25	£37.50
25	Personalities of To-day	1932	£1.25	£31.25
25	Popular Superstitions	1930	£1.00	£25.00
25	Prizes for Needlework	1925	£1.90	£47.50
25	Railway Engines	1934	£1.90	£47.50
KF27	Real Photo Series (War Leaders)	1916	£6.25	£168.75
1	Real Stamp Card	1928	—	80p
25	Red Indians	1927	£1.75	£43.75
20	Russo Japanese War Series	1905	£125.00	—
25	School Badges	1927	75p	£18.75
48	Screen Stars A (Embossed)	1936	50p	£24.00
48	Screen Stars A (Not Embossed)	1936	£1.00	£48.00
48	Screen Stars B (Different)	1936	50p	£24.00
30	Semaphore Signalling	1916	£6.25	£187.50
25	Ships and their Flags	1924	£2.00	£50.00
M36	Ships that have Made History	1938	20p	£6.25
M48	Shots from the Films	1934	20p	£8.50
50	Soccer Stars	1936	65p	£32.50
36	Soldiers of The King (Adhesive)	1939	£1.25	—
36	Soldiers of The King (Non-Adhesive)	1939	40p	£14.50
M20	Special Jubilee Year Series	1925	20p	£4.00
P12	Special Jubilee Year Series	1935	£1.55	£18.75
30	Speed Champions	1930	£1.15	£34.50
36	Sporting Champions	1929	£1.05	£37.75
25	Sporting Series	1910	£15.00	—
25	Sports	1923	£2.50	£62.50
50	Sportsmen—Spot the Winner	1937	45p	£22.50
50	Sportsmen—Spot the Winner (Back Inverted)	1937	20p	£9.00
35	Stage & Cinema Beauties A	1933	80p	£28.00
35	Stage & Cinema Beauties B (Different)	1933	65p	£22.75
50	Stage & Cinema Beauties (Different)	1935	80p	£40.00
54	Stars of the Screen	1934	80p	£43.25
48	Stars of the Screen (Embossed)	1936	40p	£19.25
48	Stars of the Screen (Not Embossed)	1936	40p	£19.25
X16	Stars of the Screen (Strips of 3)	1936	£1.25	£20.00
25	Statues & Monuments (Brown Back)	1907	£37.50	—
25	Statues & Monuments (Green, Patent)	1907	£7.50	£187.50
25	Statues & Monuments (Green, Prov. Patent)	1907	£7.50	£187.50
25	Territorial Series (Motors Back)	1908	£18.00	£450.00
25	The 1924 Cabinet	1924	£1.50	£37.50
48	The "Old Country"	1935	40p	£19.25
50	This Mechanized Age, 1st (Adhesive)	1936	20p	£8.00
50	This Mechanized Age, 1st (Non-Adhesive)	1936	25p	£12.50
50	This Mechanized Age, 2nd Series	1937	20p	£10.00
25	Types of British & Colonial Troops	1899	£37.50	—
25	Types of British Soldiers (M651-M675)	1900	£15.00	£375.00
F63	War Photos	1916	£7.50	£472.50
X20	Wrestling Holds	1930	£21.50	—
XS30	Zoo Studies—Come to Life Series	1939	90p	£27.00

Qty		Date	Odds	Sets
X1	Zoo Studies Viewer	1939	—	£3.15

BDV PACKAGE ISSUES

Qty		Date	Odds	Sets
17	Boxers	1932	£2.00	—
53	Cricketers	1932	£5.00	—
67	Film Stars	1932	£1.25	—
132	Footballers	1932	£1.75	—
19	Jockeys	1932	£1.75	—
21	Speedway Riders	1932	£5.00	—
38	Sportsmen	1932	£2.00	—

"SPORTS" PACKAGE ISSUES

Qty		Date	Odds	Sets
50	All Sports 1st	1948	£2.50	—
25	All Sports 2nd	1949	£2.50	—
25	All Sports 3rd	1953	£2.50	—
25	All Sports 4th	1954	£2.50	—
25	Cricketers 1st	1948	£5.00	—
25	Cricketers 2nd	1951	£5.00	—
25	Footballers 1st	1948	£2.50	—
50	Footballers 2nd	1950	£2.50	—
25	Footballers 3rd	1951	£2.50	—
25	Jockeys	1952	£2.50	—
25	Radio Stars	1949	£1.90	—
25	Rugby & Association Footballers	1952	£2.50	—

OVERSEAS ISSUES

Qty		Date	Odds	Sets
50	Animal Studies	1930	£1.25	£62.50
50	Annuals	1939	80p	£40.00
X32	Australian Birds (Cartons)	1968	—	£7.50
X24	Australian Scenes (Cartons)	1965	—	£7.50
50	Australian Sporting Celebrities	1932	£1.75	£87.50
X32	Australian Wild Flowers (Cartons)	1967	—	£7.50
50	Film Stars	1934	£1.25	£62.50
E16	Gemstones (Cartons)	1970	—	£5.00
50	Stars of British Films (B.D.V.)	1934	£1.25	£62.50
50	Stars of British Films (De Reszke)	1934	£1.25	£62.50
50	Stars of British Films (Greys)	1934	£1.25	£62.50
50	Stars of British Films (No Brand)	1934	£1.25	£62.50
38	Test Cricketers (B.D.V.)	1932	£1.65	£62.75
38	Test Cricketers (Greys)	1932	£1.65	£62.75
38	Test Cricketers (No Brand)	1932	£1.90	£72.25
X32	The Barrier Reef (Cartons)	1968	—	£4.50
50	Victorian Footballers (B.D.V.)	1933	£1.25	—
50	Victorian Footballers (Greys)	1933	£1.25	—
50	Victorian Footballers (No Brand)	1933	£1.25	—
75	Victorian Footballers	1933	£1.25	—
50	Victorian League and Association Footballers	1934	£1.55	—
100	Who's Who in Australian Sport	1933	£1.55	£155.00

SILK ISSUES

Qty		Date	Odds	Sets
M62	Arms of Countries & Territories	1912	£3.15	—
B32	Beauties — Modern Paintings	1910	£9.40	—
P32	Beauties — Modern Paintings	1910	£37.50	—
B100	Birds	1920	£1.90	—
M12	Birds of the Tropics	1913	£9.40	—

Qty		Date	Odds	Sets
L12	Birds of the Tropics	1913	£10.50	—
P12	Birds of the Tropics	1913	£15.50	—
X24	British Admirals	1916	£4.40	£105.00
D50	British Butterflies & Moths	1922	£2.50	—
M108	British Naval Crests (Anon, Blue Nos.)	1915	£1.05	—
M9	British Naval Crests (Anon, Brown Nos.)	1915	£3.15	—
M108	British Naval Crests (B.D.V.)	1915	£1.25	—
B23	Butterflies	1911	£8.15	—
B47	Ceramic Art	1925	90p	£42.25
M47	Ceramic Art	1925	75p	£35.00
L47	Ceramic Art	1925	£1.55	—
B65	Clan Tartans	1922	95p	
M65	Clan Tartans (B.D.V.)	1922	75p	£50.00
M49	Clan Tartans (Anon)	1922	95p	£46.50
L56	Clan Tartans	1922	£2.50	—
P12	Clan Tartans	1922	£3.75	£45.00
M108	Colonial Army Badges	1913	£1.05	£110.00
M17	County Cricket Badges (Anon)	1921	£10.00	—
M17	County Cricket Badges (B.D.V.)	1921	£10.00	—
M108	Crests & Badges of the British Army (Anon, Numbered)	1914	65p	£70.00
M108	Crests & Badges of the British Army (Anon, Unnumbered)	1914	80p	£86.50
M108	Crests & Badges of the British Army (B.D.V.)	1914	65p	£70.00
L108	Crests & Badges of the British Army (Anon)	1914	£1.00	—
L108	Crests & Badges of the British Army (B.D.V.)	1914	£1.25	—
M143	Flags, Set 4-1 (Short)	1913	75p	—
M119	Flags, Set 4-2 (Short, Renumbered)	1913	65p	—
M114	Flags, Set 4-3 (Short, Renumbered)	1913	65p	—
L142	Flags, Set 4 (Long)	1913	£1.50	—
M24	Flags, Set 5 (With Caption)	1913	75p	£18.00
M12	Flags, Set 5 (No Caption)	1913	95p	£11.50
G8	Flags, Set 5	1913	£12.50	—
M18	Flags, Set 6	1913	75p	£13.50
M20	Flags, Set 7	1913	80p	£16.00
M50	Flags, 5th Series	1914	£1.50	£75.00
M120	Flags, 7th Series	1914	65p	£78.00
L120	Flags, 10th Series	1915	75p	—
M120	Flags, 12th Series	1915	65p	—
L65	Flags, 15th Series	1916	95p	—
L64	Flags, 16th Series	1916	95p	£60.00
M132	Flags, 20th Series (B.D.V. Brown)	1917	65p	—
M?48	Flags, 20th Series (B.D.V. Orange)	1917	£1.90	—
M126	Flags, 25th Series	1917	65p	—
L63	Flags, 25th Series	1917	£2.50	—
M112	Flags, 26th Series (B.D.V. Brown)	1918	65p	—
M?38	Flags, 26th Series (B.D.V. Blue)	1918	£3.15	—
M70	Flags, 28th Series	1918	65p	£45.00
P18	Flags, Set 13	1914	£1.50	£27.00
G23	Flags, Set 13 (Anon)	1914	£1.50	£34.50
G27	Flags, Set 13 (B.D.V.)	1914	£1.50	£40.50
M21	Football Colours (Anon)	1920	£4.40	—
M86	Football Colours (B.D.V.)	1920	£3.75	—
P78	Football Colours	1920	£3.15	—

Qty		Date	Odds	Sets
M126	G.P. Territorial Badges	1913	£1.25	—
L25	Great War Leaders (Sepia)	1915	£3.75	£93.75
M3	Great War Leaders & Celebrities (Anon)	1916	£5.00	£15.00
M4	Great War Leaders & Celebrities (B.D.V.)	1916	£5.00	£20.00
L3	Great War Leaders & Celebrities (Anon)	1916	£5.00	£15.00
L2	Great War Leaders & Celebrities (B.D.V.)	1916	£5.00	£10.00
P18	Great War Leaders & Celebrities (B.D.V.)	1916	£3.75	—
G29	Great War Leaders & Celebrities (Anon)	1916	£3.15	—
G45	Great War Leaders & Celebrities (B.D.V.)	1916	£3.15	—
52	Great War Leaders & Warships	1914	£5.00	—
B25	Heraldic Series	1924	90p	—
M25	Heraldic Series	1924	90p	£22.50
L25	Heraldic Series	1924	£2.50	—
P12	Heraldic Series	1924	£3.75	£45.00
M26	House Flags	1915	£6.25	—
M10	Irish Patriots	1919	£10.50	—
X10	Irish Patriots	1919	£10.50	—
P10	Irish Patriots	1919	£15.50	—
M1	Irish Republican Stamp	1925	—	£1.25
M1	Let 'Em All Come	1920	—	£9.40
?	Miniature Rugs	1924	£3.75	—
M54	Naval Badges of Rank & Military Headdress	1917	£5.00	—
G1	Nelson's Signal at Trafalgar	1921	—	£37.50
G40	Old Masters, Set 1	1911	£25.00	£1000.00
G20	Old Masters, Set 2 (Anon)	1912	£3.75	£75.00
G20	Old Masters, Set 2 (B.D.V.)	1912	£3.15	£63.00
M85	Old Masters, Set 3 (Anon)	1912	£2.20	—
M40	Old Masters, Set 3 (B.D.V.)	1912	£2.50	—
M120	Old Masters, Set 4	1913	£1.55	£186.00
M20	Old Masters, Set 5 (Anon, Unnumbered)	1915	£2.50	—
M20	Old Masters, Set 5 (Anon, 101-120)	1915	£1.25	—
M60	Old Masters, Set 5 (B.D.V. 1-60)	1915	95p	—
M20	Old Masters, Set 5 (B.D.V. 101-120)	1915	£1.25	£25.00
B50	Old Masters, Set 6	1924	95p	—
M50	Old Masters, Set 7 (301-350)	1916	£1.90	—
M50	Orders of Chivalry (Anon)	1920	£1.75	—
M24	Orders of Chivalry (B.D.V., 1-24)	1914	£1.25	£30.00
M24	Orders of Chivalry (GP401-424)	1914	£1.55	—
M25	Pilot & Signal Flags (Anon)	1921	£1.90	—
M25	Pilot & Signal Flags (B.D.V.)	1921	£1.50	£37.50
L72	Regimental Colours	1914	£3.15	—
M50	Regimental Colours, Series 12	1918	£1.55	£77.50
M120	Regimental Colours & Crests (Anon)	1915	80p	—
M120	Regimental Colours & Crests (B.D.V.)	1915	80p	—
G120	Regimental Colours & Crests (Anon)	1915	£4.40	—
G120	Regimental Colours & Crests (B.D.V.)	1915	£3.75	—
M10	Religious Pictures	1911	£15.50	—
X10	Religious Pictures	1911	£15.50	—
G10	Religious Pictures	1911	£25.00	—
B1	The Allies Flags	1915	—	£7.50
G2	The Allies Flags (Anon)	1915	£7.50	—
G2	The Allies Flags (B.D.V.)	1915	£7.50	—
M75	Town & City Arms	1918	£1.55	—
L75	Town & City Arms	1918	£1.55	—

GODFREY PHILLIPS LTD. — cont.

Qty		Date	Odds	Sets
M25	Victoria Cross Heroes I	1915	£8.75	—
M25	Victoria Cross Heroes II (With Flags)	1915	£10.00	—
M90	War Pictures	1915	£5.00	—

JOHN PLAYER & SONS
44 Page Reference Book — £2.50

Qty		Date	Odds	Sets
25	Actors & Actresses	1898	£20.00	£500.00
50	Actresses	1897	£20.00	£1000.00
6/7	Advertisement Cards (Navy Cut Back)	1894	£250.00	—
4/5	Advertisement Cards (Testimonial Back)	1894	£250.00	—
1	Advertisement Card — Sailor	1929	—	£3.15
L1	Advertisement Card — Sailor	1929	—	£15.50
L1	Advertisement Card — Wants List	1936	—	80p
P6	Advertisement Postcards	1906	£62.50	—
50	Aeroplanes (Eire)	1935	£1.00	£50.00
50	Aeroplanes (Civil)	1935	40p	£20.00
50	Aircraft of the Royal Air Force	1938	50p	£25.00
X10	Allied Cavalry	1914	£6.25	£62.50
L24	A Nature Calendar	1930	£2.50	£60.00
50	Animals of the Countryside	1939	20p	£7.50
50	Animals of the Countryside (Eire)	1939	65p	—
L25	Aquarium Studies	1932	£1.50	£37.50
L25	Architectural Beauties	1927	£1.75	£43.75
50	Arms & Armour (Blue Back)	1909	£1.90	£95.00
50	Army Corps & Divisional Signs (1-50, 2 Printings)	1924	20p	£7.50
100	Army Corps & Divisional Signs, 2nd (51.501)	1925	20p	£20.00
25	Army Life	1910	£1.00	£25.00
X12	Artillery in Action	1917	£3.15	£37.75
50	A Sectional Map of Ireland	1932	£1.75	£87.50
50	Association Cup Winners	1930	80p	£40.00
50	Aviary & Cage Birds	1933	50p	£25.00
50	Aviary & Cage Birds (Transfers)	1933	30p	£15.00
L25	Aviary & Cage Birds	1935	£1.75	£43.75
50	Badges & Flags of British Regiments (Green)	1903	£1.55	£77.50
50	Badges & Flags of British Regiments (Brown Back, Numbered)	1904	£1.55	£77.50
50	Badges & Flags of British Regiments (Brown Back, Unnumbered)	1904	£2.00	£100.00
50	Birds & Their Young	1937	20p	£7.50
50	Birds & Their Young (Eire) (Adhesive)	1937	65p	—
50	Birds & Their Young (Eire) (Non-Adhesive)	1937	75p	—
25	Birds & Their Young (Non-Adhesive)	Unissued	20p	£3.00
25	Birds & Their Young, 2nd (Non-Adhesive)	Unissued	20p	£3.00
K1	Bookmark (Calendar back)	1902	—	£95.00
CF10	Bookmarks (Authors)	1900	£50.00	£500.00
25	Boxing (Eire)	1934	£3.00	£75.00
50	Boy Scout & Girl Guide	1933	20p	£10.00
50	Boy Scout & Girl Guide (Transfers)	1933	25p	£12.50
L25	British Butterflies	1934	£2.50	£62.50
50	British Empire Series	1904	95p	£47.50
25	British Livestock	1915	£1.00	£25.00
X25	British Livestock (Blue Back)	1923	£1.50	£37.50

JOHN PLAYER & SONS—cont.

Qty		Date	Odds	Sets
X25	British Livestock (Brown Back)	1916	£2.00	£50.00
L25	British Naval Craft	1939	40p	£10.00
X20	British Pedigree Stock	1925	£1.70	£34.00
L25	British Regalia	1937	90p	£22.50
50	Butterflies	1932	75p	£37.50
50	Butterflies (Transfers)	1932	30p	£15.00
50	Butterflies & Moths	1904	£1.25	£62.50
25	Bygone Beauties	1914	90p	£22.50
X10	Bygone Beauties	1916	£3.75	£37.50
G?30	Cabinet Size Pictures			
	(Brown Front, Printed Back)	1899	£75.00	—
	(Brown Front, Plain Back)	1899	£75.00	—
	(Green Front, Printed Back)	1899	£75.00	—
	(Green Front, Plain Back)	1899	£75.00	—
20	Castles & Abbeys (No Border)	1895	£25.00	£500.00
20	Castles & Abbeys (White Border)	1895	£21.50	£430.00
L24	Cats	1936	£5.00	£120.00
50	Celebrated Bridges	1903	£2.00	£100.00
50	Celebrated Gateways	1909	95p	£47.50
25	Ceremonial and Court Dress	1911	£1.25	£31.25
L25	Championship Golf Courses	1936	£5.00	£125.00
25	Characters from Dickens, A Series (1-25)	1912	£1.50	£37.50
25	Characters from Dickens, 2nd Series (26-50)	1912	£1.50	£37.50
50	Characters from Dickens (Re-issue)	1923	£1.00	£50.00
X10	Characters from Dickens	1914	£4.40	£44.00
L25	Characters from Fiction	1933	£1.75	£43.75
25	Characters from Thackeray	1913	£1.00	£25.00
50	Cities of the World	1900	£3.15	£157.50
L20	Clocks—Old & New	1928	£3.75	£75.00
25	Colonial & Indian Army Badges	1917	75p	£18.75
50	Coronation Series—Ceremonial Dress	1937	20p	£8.75
25	Counties and Their Industries (Numbered)	1914	75p	£18.75
25	Counties and Their Industries (Unnumbered)	1914	80p	£20.00
50	Countries Arms & Flags (Thick Card)	1905	50p	£25.00
50	Countries Arms & Flags (Thin Card)	1912	50p	£25.00
50	Country Seats and Arms (1-50)	1909	50p	£25.00
50	Country Seats and Arms, 2nd (51-100)	1910	50p	£25.00
50	Country Seats and Arms, 3rd (101-150)	1910	50p	£25.00
L25	Country Sports	1930	£3.00	£75.00
50	Cricketers 1930	1930	95p	£47.50
50	Cricketers 1934	1934	50p	£25.00
50	Cricketers 1938	1938	30p	£15.00
50	Cricketers, Caricatures by "RIP"	1926	95p	£47.50
25	Cries of London, A Series	1913	£1.50	£37.50
X10	Cries of London, A Series	1912	£3.75	£37.50
X10	Cries of London, 2nd Series	1914	£2.80	£28.00
25	Cries of London, 2nd Series (Blue Back)	1916	75p	£18.75
25	Cries of London, 2nd Series (Black Back)	1916	£2.50	—
50	Curious Beaks	1929	20p	£10.00
50	Cycling	1939	40p	£20.00
50	Cycling (Eire) (Adhesive)	1939	75p	—
50	Cycling (Eire) (Non-Adhesive)	1939	75p	—
50	Dandies	1932	20p	£9.00
L25	Dandies	1932	£1.40	£35.00

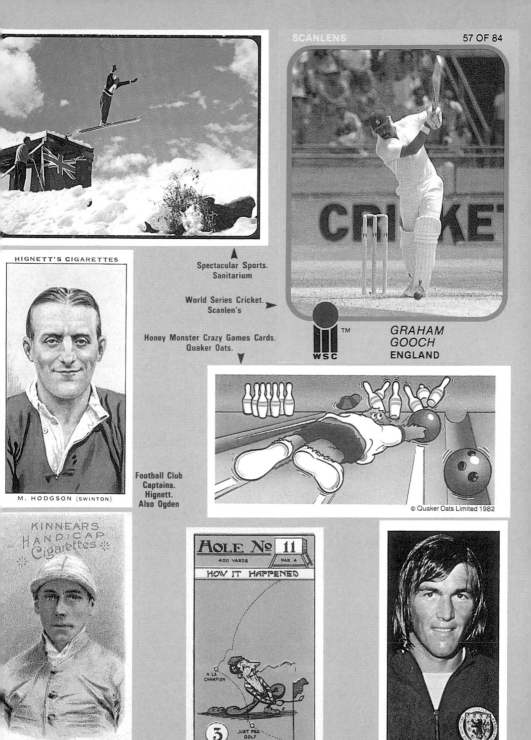

Spectacular Sports.
Sanitarium

World Series Cricket.
Scanlen's

Honey Monster Crazy Games Cards.
Quaker Oats.

HIGNETT'S CIGARETTES

M. HODGSON (SWINTON)

GRAHAM
GOOCH
ENGLAND

© Quaker Oats Limited 1982

Football Club
Captains.
Hignett.
Also Ogden

KINNEARS
HANDICAP
Cigarettes

A. NIGHTINGAL.
LORD WM. BENTINCK'S COLORS

Jockeys. Kinnear

HOLE No 11
400 YARDS PAR 4
HOW IT HAPPENED

A LA
CHAMPION

JUST PRO.
GOLF

3 STROKES

Smokers Golf Cards. I.T.C. Canada

World Cup Stars. Bassett

Nations.
Cohen Weenen

14. CHIPPEWAY BRAVE.

Types of North American Indians.
B.A.T.

A. BRAHMIN

Races of Mankind.
Wills (Overseas)

Everyday Phrases by Tom Browne.
Player

Wisecracks. Barratt

F. & J. SMITH'S CIGARETTES.

"DOES YOUR POETRY PAY?"
WELL, IT JUST KEEPS
THE WOLF FROM THE DOOR."
"I SUPPOSE YOU READ IT TO HIM!"

Phil May Sketches. Smith.
Also Churchman, Fry

WHAT HAS A HEAD
AND A TAIL BUT
NO BODY?

Happy Howlers.
Primrose

A. LONG SHOT (Before Match).
Young Lady (first acquaintance
with Polo) "I wish you would
begin. I am so anxious to see the
ponies kick the ball about!"
[*She hails from great football county.*]

Jokes.
A.T.C., Sniders & Abrahams

JOHN PLAYER & SONS — cont.

Qty		Date	Odds	Sets
50	Decorations & Medals	Unissued	£1.75	£87.50
50	Derby and Grand National Winners	1933	£1.25	£62.50
50	Derby and Grand National Winners (Transfers)	1933	30p	£15.00
50	Dogs (Scenic Background)	1925	65p	£32.50
X12	Dogs (Scenic Background)	1924	£2.00	£24.00
50	Dogs, by Wardle (Full Length)	1931	40p	£20.00
50	Dogs, by Wardle (Transfers)	1931	30p	£15.00
L25	Dogs, by Wardle (Full Length)	1933	£1.65	£41.25
50	Dogs, by Wardle (Heads)	1929	65p	£32.50
L20	Dogs, by Wardle, A Series (Heads)	1926	£1.70	£34.00
L20	Dogs, by Wardle, 2nd Series (Heads)	1928	£1.65	£33.00
25	Dogs, by Wardle, A Series (Eire) (Heads)	1927	£1.50	£37.50
25	Dogs, by Wardle, 2nd Series (Eire) (Heads)	1929	£1.50	£37.50
50	Dogs Heads by Biegel	Unissued	25p	£12.50
L25	Dogs (Heads)	Unissued	75p	£18.75
50	Dogs' Heads (Silver Background, Eire)	1940	£2.20	£110.00
50	Drum Banners & Cap Badges (2 Printings)	1924	50p	£25.00
25	Egyptian Kings & Queens and Classical Deities	1912	90p	£22.50
X10	Egyptian Sketches	1915	£3.15	£31.50
25	England's Military Heroes (Narrow)	1898	£27.50	—
25	England's Military Heroes (Wide)	1898	£37.50	—
25	England's Military Heroes (Narrow, Plain Backs)	1898	£27.50	—
25	England's Military Heroes (Wide, Plain Backs)	1898	£37.50	
25	England's Naval Heroes (Non-Descriptive, Narrow)	1897	£21.00	£525.00
25	England's Naval Heroes (Non-Descriptive, Wide)	1897	£34.00	—
25	England's Naval Heroes (Descriptive, Narrow)	1898	£21.00	£525.00
25	England's Naval Heroes (Descriptive, Wide)	1898	£34.00	—
25	Everyday Phrases by Tom Browne	1900	£12.50	£312.50
L25	Fables of Aesop	1927	£1.90	£47.50
20	Famous Authors & Poets (Narrow)	1900	£17.50	£350.00
20	Famous Authors & Poets (Wide)	1900	£25.00	£500.00
L25	Famous Beauties	1937	£1.25	£31.25
50	Famous Irish Bred Horses	1936	£2.20	£110.00
50	Famous Irish Greyhounds	1935	£3.00	—
X10	Famous Paintings	1913	£2.80	£28.00
50	Film Stars	1934	75p	£37.50
50	Film Stars, Second Series	1934	50p	£25.00
50	Film Stars, Second Series (Eire)	1934	£1.25	—
50	Film Stars, Third Series	1938	40p	£20.00
L25	Film Stars	1934	£2.00	£50.00
L25	Film Stars (Eire)	1934	*£5.00*	—
50	Firefighting Appliances	1930	£1.00	£50.00
50	Fishes of the World	1903	£1.50	£75.00
50	Flags of the League of Nations	1928	20p	£10.00
50	Football Caricatures by "MAC"	1927	40p	£20.00
50	Footballers, Caricatures by "RIP"	1926	40p	£20.00
50	Footballers 1928	1928	45p	£22.50
25	Footballers 1928-9, 2nd Series	1929	30p	£7.50
50	Fresh-Water Fishes (Pink Back)	1933	50p	£25.00
50	Fresh-Water Fishes (White Back)	1934	90p	£45.00

JOHN PLAYER & SONS—cont.

Qty		Date	Odds	Sets
L25	Fresh-Water Fishes	1935	£2.00	£50.00
L25	Fresh-Water Fishes (Eire, Non-Adhesive)	1935	£5.00	—
25	From Plantation to Smoker	1926	20p	£4.50
50	Gallery of Beauty Series	1896	£20.00	£1000.00
5	Alternative Subjects	1896	£43.75	—
50	Game Birds and Wild Fowl	1927	75p	£37.50
L25	Game Birds and Wild Fowl	1928	£2.50	£62.50
25	Gems of British Scenery	1917	40p	£10.00
50	Gilbert and Sullivan, A Series	1925	75p	£37.50
X25	Gilbert and Sullivan, A Series	1926	£2.50	£62.50
50	Gilbert and Sullivan, 2nd Series	1927	65p	£32.50
L25	Gilbert and Sullivan, 2nd Series	1928	£2.50	£62.50
L25	Golf	1939	£6.00	£150.00
25	Hidden Beauties	1929	20p	£4.25
25	Highland Clans	1907	£1.75	£43.75
50	Hints on Association Football	1934	25p	£12.50
X10	Historic Ships	1910	£3.45	£34.50
50	History of Naval Dress	1930	50p	£25.00
L25	History of Naval Dress	1929	£1.50	£37.50
50	International Air Liners	1936	20p	£10.00
50	International Air Liners (Eire)	1936	65p	—
25	Irish Place Names, A Series	1927	£1.50	£37.50
25	Irish Place Names, 2nd Series	1929	£1.50	£37.50
M5	Jubilee Issue	1960	90p	£4.50
50	Kings & Queens of England	1935	75p	£37.50
L50	Kings & Queens of England	1935	£1.55	£77.50
50	Life on Board a Man of War—1805 & 1905	1905	£1.50	£75.00
25	Live Stock	1925	£2.50	£62.50
50	Military Head-Dress	1931	65p	£32.50
50	Military Series	1900	£15.00	£750.00
50	Military Uniforms of the British Empire Overseas	1938	45p	£22.50
25	Miniatures	1923	25p	£6.25
50	Modern Naval Craft	1939	25p	£12.50
50	Modern Naval Craft (Eire)	1939	65p	£32.50
50	Motor Cars, A Series	1936	75p	£37.50
50	Motor Cars (Eire), A Series	1936	£1.25	£62.50
50	Motor Cars, 2nd Series	1937	65p	£32.50
L20	Mount Everest	1925	£1.90	£38.00
25	Napoleon	1916	75p	£18.75
50	National Flags and Arms	1936	20p	£7.50
50	National Flags and Arms (Eire)	1936	65p	—
50	Natural History	1924	20p	£10.00
X12	Natural History	1924	90p	£11.00
X12	Natural History, 2nd Series	1924	90p	£11.00
50	Nature Series	1909	90p	£45.00
X10	Nature Series (Birds)	1908	£8.15	£81.50
X10	Nature Series (Mammals)	1913	£3.45	£34.50
50	Old England's Defenders	1898	£15.00	£750.00
L25	Old Hunting Prints	1938	£2.00	£60.00
L25	Old Naval Prints	1936	£1.90	£47.50
X25	Old Sporting Prints	1924	£1.90	£47.50
L25	Picturesque Bridges	1929	£2.00	£50.00
L25	Picturesque Cottages	1929	£2.00	£50.00

JOHN PLAYER & SONS—cont.

Qty		Date	Odds	Sets
L25	Picturesque London	1931	£2.50	£62.50
25	Players Past & Present	1916	50p	£12.50
25	Polar Exploration, A Series	1915	£1.00	£25.00
25	Polar Exploration, 2nd Series	1916	90p	£22.50
L25	Portals of the Past	1930	£1.75	£43.75
50	Poultry	1931	65p	£32.50
50	Poultry (Transfers)	1931	30p	£15.00
25	Products of the World	1908	40p	£10.00
50	Products of the World (Different)	1928	20p	£7.50
25	Racehorses	1926	£3.75	£93.75
40	Racing Caricatures	1925	50p	£20.00
L25	Racing Yachts	1938	£2.50	£62.50
50	R.A.F. Badges (No Motto)	1937	30p	£15.00
50	R.A.F. Badges (With Motto)	1937	30p	£15.00
50	Regimental Colours & Cap Badges (Regulars)	1907	65p	£32.50
50	Regimental Colours & Cap Badges (Territorials, Blue Back)	1910	75p	£37.50
50	Regimental Colours & Cap Badges (Territorials, Brown Back)	1910	65p	£32.50
50	Regimental Standards and Cap Badges	1930	50p	£25.00
50	Regimental Uniforms (Blue)	1912	£1.25	£62.50
50	Regimental Uniforms (Brown)	1914	£1.25	£62.50
X10	Regimental Uniforms (Different)	1914	£5.65	£56.50
50	Regimental Uniforms, 2nd Series (51-100)	1913	90p	£45.00
50	Riders of the World	1905	£1.25	£62.50
P30	Rulers & Views	1902	£75.00	—
50	Sea Fishes	1935	20p	£9.00
50	Sea Fishes (Eire)	1935	65p	—
50	Screen Celebrities (Eire)	1938	£1.00	—
25	Shakespearean Series	1917	50p	£12.50
L20	Ship-Models	1926	£2.25	£45.00
50	Shipping	Unissued	—	£56.25
25	Ships' Figure-Heads (2 Printings)	1912	75p	£18.75
L25	Ships' Figure-Heads	1931	£1.25	£31.25
L8	Snap Cards	1930	£6.25	£50.00
50	Speedway Riders	1937	75p	£37.50
S150	Stereoscopic Series	1904	*£62.50*	—
50	Straight Line Caricatures	1926	30p	£15.00
25	Struggle for Existence (2 Printings)	1923	20p	£4.25
50	Tennis	1936	35p	£17.50
116	The Corsair Game (Eire)	1965	75p	—
L25	The Nation's Shrines	1929	£1.75	£43.75
X1	The Royal Family	1937	—	£1.90
P6	The Royal Family	1901	£37.50	£225.00
25	Those Pearls of Heaven	1916	40p	£10.00
66	Transvaal Series	1902	£4.40	—
L25	Treasures of Britain	1931	£1.50	£37.50
25	Treasures of Ireland	1930	£1.50	£37.50
L25	Types of Horses	1939	£2.00	£50.00
50	Uniforms of the Territorial Army	1939	45p	£22.50
50	Useful Plants & Fruits	1902	£1.25	£62.50
25	Victoria Cross	1914	90p	£22.50
90	War Decorations & Medals	1927	45p	£40.00
50	Wild Animals' Heads	1931	25p	£12.50

JOHN PLAYER & SONS—cont.

Qty		Date	Odds	Sets
25	Wild Animals' Heads (Transfers)	1931	£1.25	—
50	Wild Animals' Heads (Transfers, "Series of 50")	1927	30p	£15.00
L25	Wild Animals (Heads), A Series	1932	£1.25	£31.25
L25	Wild Animals (Heads), 2nd Series	1932	£1.25	£31.25
45	Wild Animals of the World (Narrow) (No Ltd) ...	1901	£4.40	—
45	Wild Animals of the World (Narrow) (With Ltd)	1901	£4.40	—
45	Wild Animals of the World (Narrow) (Branch) ...	1901	£6.25	—
50	Wild Animals of the World (Wide) (No Ltd)	1901	£2.00	£100.00
50	Wild Animals of the World (Wide) (With Ltd) ...	1901	£2.00	£100.00
50	Wild Animals of the World (Wide) (Branch)	1901	£3.75	—
50	Wild Birds	1932	20p	£7.50
50	Wild Birds (Transfers)	1932	30p	£15.00
L25	Wild Birds	1934	£1.75	£43.75
L25	Wildfowl	1937	£2.00	£50.00
50	Wonders of the Deep	1904	£1.25	£62.50
25	Wonders of the World (Blue Back)	1916	50p	£12.50
25	Wonders of the World (Grey Back, Eire)	1926	90p	£22.50
X10	Wooden Walls	1908	£4.40	£44.00
25	Wrestling & Ju-Jitsu (Blue Back)	1913	65p	£16.25
25	Wrestling & Ju-Jitsu (Grey Back, Eire)	1925	£1.00	£25.00
26	Your Initials (Transfers)	1932	40p	£10.00
L25	Zoo Babies	1938	30p	£7.50

OVERSEAS ISSUES

Qty		Date	Odds	Sets
50	Aeroplane Series	1926	£1.50	£75.00
50	Aircraft of the Royal Air Force	1938	75p	£37.50
50	Animals of the Countryside	1939	50p	£25.00
50	Arms & Armour (Grey Back)	1926	£2.20	£110.00
F50	Beauties	1925	£1.00	£50.00
BF50	Beauties (Coloured)	1925	£1.25	£62.50
F50	Beauties, 2nd Series	1925	£1.00	£50.00
50	Birds & Their Young	1937	50p	£25.00
52	Birds of Brilliant Plumage	1927	£2.80	—
25	"Bonzo" Dogs	1923	£2.50	£62.50
50	Boy Scouts	1924	£1.55	£77.50
L25	British Live Stock	1924	£5.00	£125.00
50	Butterflies (Girls)	1928	£3.75	£187.50
50	Coronation Series—Ceremonial Dress	1937	50p	£25.00
50	Cricketers 1938	1938	£1.00	£50.00
50	Cycling	1939	50p	£25.00
25	Dogs (Heads)	1927	75p	£18.75
32	Drum Horses	1911	£5.00	—
L25	Famous Beauties	1937	£1.50	—
50	Film Stars, Third Series	1938	75p	—
25	Flag Girls of all Nations	1908	£5.00	—
L25	Golf	1939	£5.65	£141.25
50	Household Hints	1928	75p	£37.50
50	International Air Liners	1936	50p	£25.00
50	Lawn Tennis	1928	£1.55	£77.50
50	Leaders of Men	1925	£1.25	£62.50
50	Military Uniforms of the British Empire Overseas (Adhesive)	1938	75p	£37.50
50	Military Uniforms of the British Empire Overseas (Non-Adhesive)	1938	90p	£45.00

JOHN PLAYER & SONS — cont.

Qty		Date	Odds	Sets
50	Modern Naval Craft	1939	50p	£25.00
50	Motor Cars, A Series	1936	£1.25	£62.50
50	Motor Cars, 2nd Series	1937	£1.25	£62.50
50	National Flags and Arms	1936	50p	£25.00
L25	Old Hunting Prints	1938	£2.50	£62.50
M22	Old Masters	1966	90p	—
L25	Old Naval Prints	1936	£2.25	£56.25
48	Pictures of the East	1931	£1.50	£75.00
25	Picturesque People of the Empire	1938	£1.75	£43.75
B53	Playing Cards	1929	95p	—
50	Pugilists in Action	1928	£1.60	£80.00
L25	Racing Yachts	1938	£3.00	—
50	R.A.F. Badges	1937	60p	£30.00
50	Railway Working	1926	£1.25	£62.50
50	Sea Fishes	1935	50p	£25.00
50	Ships' Flags & Cap Badges	1930	£1.00	£50.00
50	Signalling Series	1926	£1.00	£50.00
F50	The Royal Family at Home & Abroad	1927	£1.25	—
L25	Types of Horses	1939	£2.50	—
25	Whaling	1930	£1.50	£37.50
L25	Zoo Babies	1937	£1.50	—

MODERN ISSUES (DONCELLA)

Qty		Date	Odds	Sets
T32	Britain's Endangered Wildlife	1984	20p	£5.00
T30	Britain's Nocturnal Wildlife	1987	20p	£5.50
T30	Britain's Wild Flowers	1986	20p	£5.50
T32	British Butterflies	1984	20p	£6.25
T30	British Mammals	1983	20p	£4.25
T32	Country Houses and Castles	1981	20p	£4.25
T24	Golden Age of Flying	1977	20p	£4.25
T1	Golden Age of Flying Completion Offer	1978	—	£1.25
T24	Golden Age of Motoring	1975	25p	£6.00
T24	Golden Age of Motoring Completion Offer	1976	£2.20	£53.00
T24	Golden Age of Sail	1978	20p	£4.25
T1	Golden Age of Sail Completion Offer	1979	—	£1.25
T24	Golden Age of Steam	1976	20p	£5.00
T1	Golden Age of Steam Completion Offer	1977	—	£1.55
T24	History of the V.C.	1980	40p	£9.50
T1	History of the V.C. Completion Offer	1980	—	£2.50
T24	Napoleonic Uniforms	1980	20p	£5.00
T1	Napoleonic Uniforms Completion Offer	1980	—	£1.90
T30	The Living Ocean	1985	20p	£5.50

MODERN ISSUES (GRANDEE)

Qty		Date	Odds	Sets
T30	African Wildlife	1990	20p	£5.50
T32	Britain's Endangered Wildlife	1984	20p	£6.25
T30	Britain's Nocturnal Wildlife	1987	25p	£7.50
T30	Britain's Wayside Wildlife	1988	25p	—
T30	Britain's Wild Flowers	1986	25p	£7.50
T32	British Birds	1980	25p	£8.00
T32	British Butterflies	1983	20p	£6.00
T30	British Mammals (Imperial Tobacco Ltd)	1982	20p	£6.00
T30	British Mammals (Imperial Group PLC)	1983	20p	£6.00
T28	Famous M.G. Marques	1981	25p	£7.00
T7	Limericks	1977	£6.25	—
T30	The Living Ocean	1985	25p	£7.50

Qty		Date	Odds	Sets
T25	Top Dogs	1979	50p	£12.50
T6	World of Gardening	1976	£6.25	—

MODERN ISSUES (TOM THUMB)

L30	Britain's Maritime History	1989	20p	£5.50
L32	Exploration of Space	1982	20p	£6.25
L30	History of Britain's Railways	1987	25p	£7.50
L30	History of British Aviation	1988	20p	£6.00
L30	History of Motor Racing (Imp. Tob. Ltd.)	1986	£1.55	—
L30	History of Motor Racing (Imp. Group PLC.)	1986	25p	£8.00
L32	Myths & Legends	1981	65p	£21.00
L32	Wonders of the Ancient World	1984	25p	£8.00
L30	Wonders of the Modern World	1985	25p	£8.00

MODERN ISSUES (OTHER)

?44	Black Jack	1984	£1.25	—
M?44	Black Jack	1984	50p	—
T?44	Black Jack	1984	50p	—
?	Cash Derby	1985	£1.25	—
B?	Cash Derby	1985	£1.25	—
M?	Cash Derby	1985	50p	—
T8	Panama Puzzles	1976	£5.00	—
T?	Player Clues	1987	50p	—
T?63	Player Games (Green)	1983	50p	—
T?29	Player Games (Yellow)	1983	75p	—
T?62	Player Games (Orange)	1984	50p	—
T?106	Player Games (Silver)	1984	50p	—
T?	Player Games (Yellow)	1984	75p	—
T?127	Player Quiz (Green)	1985	65p	—
T?	Player Quiz (Blue)	1986	65p	—
T?	Player Quiz (Red)	1986	65p	—
T6	Play Ladbroke Spot Ball	1975	£5.00	—
T6	Play Panama Spot Six	1977	£5.00	—
T4	Recordbreakers	1976	65p	—
T50	Super Cars (35 x 90mm)	1987	65p	—
T50	Super Cars (47 x 90mm)	1987	65p	—
60	Super Deal	1984	£1.25	—
M60	Super Deal	1984	65p	—
T60	Super Deal (35 x 90mm)	1984	£1.25	—
T60	Super Deal (47 x 90mm)	1984	65p	—
T108	Super Year 88 (35 x 90mm)	1988	£1.25	—
T108	Super Year 88 (47 x 90mm)	1988	65p	—
152	World Tour	1986	£1.25	—
M153	World Tour	1986	65p	—
T152	World Tour (35 x 90mm)	1986	£1.25	—
T152	World Tour (47 x 90mm)	1986	65p	—

JAMES PLAYFAIR & CO.

25	How To Keep Fit	1912	£30.00	£750.00

PREMIER TOBACCO MFRS. LTD.

48	Eminent Stage & Screen Personalities	1936	£1.25	£60.00
K52	Miniature Playing Cards	1935	£6.25	—

PREMIER TOBACCO MFRS. LTD.—cont.

Qty		Date	Odds	Sets
50	Stage & Screen Personalities (Brown)	1936	£1.55	—
100	Stage & Screen Personalities (Grey)	1936	£1.00	£100.00

PRITCHARD & BURTON

Qty		Date	Odds	Sets
51	Actors & Actresses "FROGA" (Blue Back)	1899	£15.00	—
51	Actors & Actresses "FROGA" (Grey Back)	1899	£37.50	—
15	Beauties "PAC"	1899	£50.00	—
20	Boer War Cartoons	1900	£75.00	—
30	Flags & Flags with Soldiers (Draped)	1902	£12.50	£375.00
15	Flags & Flags with Soldiers (Different Back)	1902	£18.75	—
15	Flags & Flags with Soldiers (Undraped)	1902	£17.50	—
25	Holiday Resorts & Views	1902	£15.00	£375.00
40	Home & Colonial Regiments	1901	£42.50	—
25	Royalty Series	1902	£18.75	£468.75
25	South African Series	1901	£15.00	£375.00
25	Star Girls	1900	*£105.00*	—

G. PRUDHOE

Qty		Date	Odds	Sets
30	Army Pictures, Cartoons, etc.	1916	*£62.50*	—

Q.V. CIGARS

Qty		Date	Odds	Sets
B?10	Barnum & Bailey's Circus Performers	1900	*£125.00*	—

JAS. QUINTON LTD.

Qty		Date	Odds	Sets
26	Actresses "FROGA"	1899	£125.00	—

RAY & CO. LTD.

Qty		Date	Odds	Sets
K6	Flags of the Allies (Shaped)	1916	*£50.00*	—
25	War Series (1-25)	1915	£10.00	—
75	War Series (26-100)	1915	£7.50	—
24	War Series (101-124)	1916	£17.50	—

RAYMOND REVIEWBAR

Qty		Date	Odds	Sets
BF25	Striptease Artistes	1960	£8.75	—

RECORD CIGARETTE & TOBACCO CO.

Qty		Date	Odds	Sets
X36	The Talkie Cigarette Card (Record Cigarette Co.)	1934	£30.00	—
X36	The Talkie Cigarette Card (Record Tobacco Co.)	1934	£30.00	—

REDFORD & CO.

Qty		Date	Odds	Sets
20	Actresses "BLARM"	1900	*£55.00*	—
25	Armies of the World	1901	£42.50	—
25	Beauties "GRACC"	1899	*£80.00*	—
30	Colonial Troops	1902	£42.50	—
24	Nautical Expressions	1900	*£62.50*	—
40	Naval & Military Phrases	1904	£42.50	—
25	Picture Series	1906	£50.00	—

REDFORD & CO.—cont.

Qty		Date	Odds	Sets
25	Sports & Pastimes	1906	£55.00	—
50	Stage Artistes of the Day	1908	£12.50	£625.00

RELIANCE TOBACCO MFG. CO.

24	British Birds	1934	£3.75	—
35	Famous Stars	1934	£3.45	£120.00

A. S. RICHARDSON

B12	Manikin Cards	1915	£62.50	—

RICHMOND CAVENDISH CO. LTD.

26	Actresses "FROGA"	1900	£25.00	—
28	Actresses "PILPI I"	1902	£12.50	£350.00
F50	Actresses "PILPI II"	1903	£8.00	£400.00
?179	Actresses, Gravure (Back Top-Bottom)	1904	£5.00	—
50	Actresses, Gravure (Back Bottom-Top)	1904	£5.00	—
14	Beauties "AMBS" (12 Backs)	1899	£37.50	—
52	Beauties P/C Inset	1897	£42.50	—
28	Chinese Actors & Actresses	1923	£3.50	£98.00
F50	Cinema Stars	1927	£2.00	—
40	Medals	1900	£15.00	£600.00
20	Music Hall Artistes	1901	£31.25	£625.00
12	Pretty Girl Series "RASH"	1899	£31.25	£375.00
20	Yachts (Black Back)	1900	£50.00	—
20	Yachts (White Back)	1900	£55.00	—

ROBERTS & SONS

26	Actresses "FROGA"	1899	£50.00	—
25	Armies of the World (Plain Back)	1900	£40.00	—
25	Armies of the World (Printed Back)	1900	£42.50	—
M50	Beautiful Women	1898	£155.00	—
50	Beauties "CHOAB" (Black Back)	1900	£62.50	—
50	Beauties "CHOAB" (Blue Back)	1900	£62.50	—
50	Colonial Troops	1902	£37.50	—
B28	Dominoes	1905	£50.00	—
K52	Miniature Playing Cards (Blue)	1905	£50.00	—
K52	Miniature Playing Cards (Pink)	1905	£50.00	—
K52	Miniature Playing Cards (Yellow)	1905	£50.00	—
24	Nautical Expressions (Navy Cut Cigarettes)	1902	£50.00	—
24	Nautical Expressions (Without Navy Cut)	1902	£50.00	—
70	Stories Without Words	1904	£42.50	—
25	Types of British & Colonial Troops	1900	£40.00	—

ROBINSON & BARNSDALE LTD.

B25	Actresses, Colin Campbell	1898	£105.00	—
?14	Actresses, Cupola	1898	£125.00	—
1	Advertisement Card, Colin Campbell	1897	—	£100.00
?13	Beauties, Collotype (Black Backs)	1895	£125.00	—
?13	Beauties, Collotype (Red Backs "NANA")	1895	£125.00	—
?13	Beauties, Collotype (Red, Golden Beauties)	1895	£125.00	—
B?20	Beauties, Highest Honors (Viginia)	1895	£155.00	—
B?20	Beauties, Highest Honors (Virginia)	1895	£155.00	—

E. ROBINSON & SONS

Qty		Date	Odds	Sets
10	Beauties (10 Brands)	1897	£42.50	—
?50	Derbyshire and the Peak	1903	*£87.50*	—
25	Egyptian Studies	1914	£17.50	—
25	King Lud Problems	1934	£15.00	—
6	Medals & Decorations	1902	*£112.50*	—
40	Nature Studies	1914	£17.50	—
25	Regimental Mascots	1916	£50.00	—
25	Wild Flowers	1915	£15.00	—

ROMAN STAR CIGARS

Qty		Date	Odds	Sets
26	Actresses "FROGA"	1899	*£100.00*	—
24	Beauties "BOCCA"	1899	£100.00	—

ROTHMANS LTD.

Qty		Date	Odds	Sets
40	Beauties of the Cinema	1939	80p	£32.00
L24	Beauties of the Cinema (Circular, Matt)	1939	£2.50	£60.00
L24	Beauties of the Cinema (Varnished)	1939	£2.50	£60.00
X25	Canterbury Bankstown District Rugby League Football Club (New Zealand)	1980	*£3.15*	—
24	Cinema Stars	1925	50p	£12.50
L25	Cinema Stars	1925	65p	£16.25
P30	Country Living Cards	1974	—	£8.75
28	Dominoes	1986	*£1.25*	—
L50	International Football Stars	1984	*15p*	—
?40	Know Africa	1970	£1.25	—
?80	Know Your Language	1970	£1.25	—
36	Landmarks in Empire History	1936	75p	£27.00
?	Lucky Charms (Metal)	1930	*£2.50*	—
50	Modern Inventions	1935	75p	£37.50
LF54	New Zealand	1933	65p	£35.00
24	Prominent Screen Favourites	1934	65p	£15.50
F50	Punch Jokes	1935	30p	£15.00
5	Rare and Historic Banknotes	1970	£1.50	£7.50

WM. RUDDELL LTD.

Qty		Date	Odds	Sets
?	Couplet Cards	1924	*£9.40*	—
25	Grand Opera Series	1924	£6.25	£156.25
25	Rod & Gun	1924	£5.00	£125.00
50	Songs That Will Live Forever	1924	£2.50	£125.00

I. RUTTER & CO.

Qty		Date	Odds	Sets
15	Actresses (Printed Back)	1900	£42.50	—
15	Actresses (Rubber Stamped Back)	1900	*£55.00*	—
15	Actresses (Plain Back)	1900	£18.75	—
1	Advertisement Card	1899	—	*£312.50*
7	Boer War Celebrities	1901	£42.50	£300.00
7	Boer War Celebrities (Plain Back)	1901	£18.75	—
54	Comic Phrases	1905	£15.00	£800.00
20	Cricketers Series	1902	£187.50	—
30	Flags & Flags with Soldiers	1901	£20.00	£600.00
24	Girls, Flags & Arms of Countries	1900	£31.25	£750.00

I. RUTTER & CO.—cont.

Qty		Date	Odds	Sets
25	Proverbs (Green Seal)	1904	£37.50	—
25	Proverbs (Red Seal)	1904	£37.50	—
25	Shadowgraphs	1903	£31.25	—

S.D.V. TOBACCO CO. LTD.

16	British Royal Family	1901	*£155.00*	—

SACCONE & SPEED

F55	Beauties	1912	*£5.00*	—
F55	Beauties (Red Overprint)	1912	£4.40	—

ST. PETERSBURG CIGARETTE CO. LTD.

?	Footballers	1904	*£175.00*	—

SALMON & GLUCKSTEIN LTD.

X1	Advertisement Card (Snake Charmer)	1897	—	*£375.00*
15	Billiard Terms (Large Numerals)	1905	£42.50	—
15	Billiard Terms (Small Numerals)	1905	£42.50	—
12	British Queens	1902	£37.50	£450.00
X30	Castles, Abbeys & Houses (Brown Back)	1906	£15.00	£450.00
X30	Castles, Abbeys & Houses (Red Back)	1906	£20.00	—
32	Characters From Dickens	1903	£22.00	£685.00
25	Coronation Series	1911	£7.50	£187.50
L25	Famous Pictures (Brown)	1912	£8.75	£218.75
L25	Famous Pictures (Green, Different)	1912	£6.00	£150.00
6	Her Most Gracious Majesty Queen Victoria	1897	£43.75	£262.50
40	Heroes of the Transvaal War	1901	£9.00	£550.00
25	Magical Series	1923	£3.15	£78.75
30	Music Hall Celebrities	1902	£40.00	—
25	Occupations	1898	£312.00	—
20	Owners & Jockeys Series	1900	£42.50	—
L50	Pottery Types (Silk, Numbered Front & Back)	1916	£3.15	£157.50
L50	Pottery Types (Silk, Numbered Backs Only)	1916	£3.15	£157.50
6	Pretty Girl Series "RASH"	1900	£55.00	—
22	Shakespearian Series (Frame on Back)	1902	£21.00	£460.00
22	Shakespearian Series (No Frame on Back)	1902	£31.25	—
25	Star Girls (Brown Back)	1899	£105.00	—
25	Star Girls (Red Back)	1899	£105.00	—
50	The Great White City	1908	£10.00	£500.00
48	The Post in Various Countries	1900	£20.00	£960.00
25	Traditions of the Army & Navy (Large No.)	1917	£7.50	£187.50
25	Traditions of the Army & Navy (Small No.)	1917	£8.75	£218.75
25	Wireless Explained	1923	£3.75	£93.75

W. SANDORIDES & CO. LTD.

25	Aquarium Studies From The London Zoo (Large Numerals)	1925	£2.50	£62.50
25	Aquarium Studies From The London Zoo (Small Numerals)	1925	£2.50	£62.50
L25	Aquarium Studies From The London Zoo	1925	£2.50	£62.50

W. SANDORIDES & CO. LTD.—cont.

Qty		Date	Odds	Sets
25	Cinema Celebrities	1924	£2.00	£50.00
X25	Cinema Celebrities	1924	£3.75	—
25	Cinema Stars (With Firm's Name)	1924	£5.00	—
25	Cinema Stars (Big Gun)	1924	£6.25	—
25	Cinema Stars (Lucana)	1924	£5.00	—
X25	Cinema Stars (Big Gun)	1924	£1.75	£43.75
X25	Cinema Stars (Lucana 66)	1924	£6.25	—
X25	Cinema Stars (Sandorides)	1924	£2.00	£50.00
50	Famous Racecourses	1926	£1.90	£95.00
L50	Famous Racecourses	1926	£2.50	£125.00
50	Famous Racehorses	1923	£1.50	£75.00
50	Famous Racehorses (Big Gun Label)	1923	£9.40	—
25	Sports & Pastimes	1924	£10.00	—

SANSOM'S CIGAR STORES

?	London Views	1905	£155.00	—

NICHOLAS SARONY & CO.

25	A Day On The Airway	1928	75p	£18.75
L25	A Day On The Airway	1928	90p	£22.50
50	Around The Mediterranean	1926	65p	£32.50
L50	Around The Mediterranean	1926	75p	£37.50
?	Boer War Scenes	1901	£187.50	—
100	Celebrities and Their Autographs (2 Printings)	1923	40p	£40.00
L100	Celebrities and Their Autographs (2 Printings)	1923	45p	£45.00
50	Cinema Stars	1933	75p	£37.50
P38	Cinema Stars	1930	£7.50	—
P42	Cinema Stars, 2nd Series	1930	£3.75	—
P50	Cinema Stars, 3rd Series	1930	£3.75	—
P42	Cinema Stars, 4th Series	1930	£3.75	—
P25	Cinema Stars, 5th Series	1930	£3.75	£93.75
25	Cinema Studies	1929	65p	£16.25
F54	Life at Whipsnade Zoo	1934	40p	£21.50
50	Links with the Past	1925	20p	£10.00
L50	Links with the Past	1925	20p	£10.00
25	Links with the Past (Australia)	1926	40p	—
L25	Links with the Past (Australia)	1926	45p	—
25	Links with the Past (New Zealand)	1926	40p	£10.00
L25	Links with the Past (New Zealand)	1926	30p	£7.50
L25	Links with Past (Presentation Issue)	1926	£1.25	—
25	Museum Series	1927	25p	£6.25
L25	Museum Series	1927	25p	£6.25
L25	Museum Series (Australia)	1927	40p	—
25	Museum Series (New Zealand)	1927	40p	£10.00
L25	Museum Series (New Zealand)	1927	40p	—
L25	Museum Series (Presentation Issue)	1927	50p	£12.50
F36	National Types of Beauty	1928	25p	£9.00
MF36	National Types of Beauty	1928	25p	£9.00
15	Origin of Games	1923	£2.00	£30.00
L15	Origin of Games	1923	£2.25	£33.75
50	Saronicks	1929	20p	£8.75
M50	Saronicks	1929	20p	£8.75
50	Ships of all Ages	1929	30p	£15.00

NICHOLAS SARONY & CO.—cont.

Qty		Date	Odds	Sets
M50	Ships of all Ages	1929	30p	£15.00
25	Tennis Strokes	1923	£1.75	£43.75

T. S. SAUNT

30	Army Pictures, Cartoons, Etc.	1916	£62.50	—

SCOTTISH C.W.S.

25	Burns (Large Numeral)	1924	65p	£16.25
25	Burns (Small Numeral)	1924	£1.90	£47.50
25	Burns (Plain Back)	1924	£3.75	—
20	Dogs	1925	£8.15	—
25	Dwellings of all Nations (Large Numeral)	1924	£1.50	£37.50
25	Dwellings of all Nations (Small Numeral)	1924	£3.15	£78.75
25	Dwellings of all Nations (Plain Back)	1924	£5.00	—
L25	Famous Pictures	1924	£5.00	—
L25	Famous Pictures—Glasgow Galleries (Adhesive)	1927	£1.00	£25.00
L25	Famous Pictures—Glasgow Galleries (Non-Adhesive)	1927	£1.75	£43.75
L25	Famous Pictures—London Galleries (Adhesive)	1927	£1.00	£25.00
L25	Famous Pictures—London Galleries (Non-Adhesive)	1927	£1.75	£43.75
50	Feathered Favourites (Adhesive)	1926	£1.00	£50.00
50	Feathered Favourites (Non-Adhesive, Grey Border)	1926	£1.50	£75.00
50	Feathered Favourites (Non-Adhesive, White Border)	1926	£1.50	£75.00
25	Racial Types	1925	£6.25	£156.25
50	Triumphs of Engineering (Brown Border)	1926	£1.55	£77.50
50	Triumphs of Engineering (White Border)	1926	£1.55	£77.50
50	Wireless	1924	£2.25	£112.50

SELBY

B12	Manikin Cards	1915	£62.50	—

SHARPE & SNOWDEN

?	Views of England	1905	£125.00	—
?	Views of London	1905	£125.00	—

W. J. SHEPHERD

25	Beauties "FECKSA"	1901	£80.00	—

SHORTS

L?13	House Views (Numbered)	1924	£31.25	—
L6	House Views (Unnumbered)	1924	£31.25	—

SIMONETS LTD. (Channel Isles)

MF36	Beautiful Women	1928	£3.45	£125.00
F24	Cinema Scenes Series	1926	£4.40	—

SIMONETS LTD. (Channel Isles) — cont.

Qty		Date	Odds	Sets
F27	Famous Actors & Actresses	1929	£3.00	£81.00
50	Local Footballers	1925	£2.50	£125.00
25	Picture Series	1925	£3.15	—
F27	Sporting Celebrities	1929	£4.40	—
LF50	Views of Jersey (Plain Back)	1926	£1.55	—

JOHN SINCLAIR LTD.

Qty		Date	Odds	Sets
B?65	Actresses	1902	*£50.00*	—
F48	Birds (Numbered)	1924	£1.55	£74.50
F48	Birds ("Specimen Cigarette Card")	1924	£4.40	—
LF50	Birds	1924	£3.75	—
50	British Sea Dogs	1928	£3.00	£150.00
F54	Champion Dogs, A Series	1938	30p	£16.00
LF52	Champion Dogs, A Series	1938	40p	£20.00
F54	Champion Dogs, 2nd Series	1939	£1.90	£102.50
LF52	Champion Dogs, 2nd Series	1939	£2.25	—
F50	English & Scottish Football Stars	1935	65p	£32.50
F54	Film Stars (Series of 54 Real Photos)	1934	£1.00	£54.00
F54	Film Stars (Series of Real Photos)	1937	90p	£48.50
F54	Film Stars (55-108)	1937	75p	£40.00
M12	Flags (Numbered, Silk, 25-36)	1914	£12.50	—
M24	Flags (Unnumbered Silk, Blue Captions)	1914	£7.50	—
M24	Flags (Unnumbered, Silk, Myrtle Green)	1914	£6.25	—
M24	Flags (Unnumbered, Silk, Olive Green)	1914	£6.25	—
M25	Flags (Unnumbered, Silk, Grey Captions)	1914	£9.40	—
M24	Flags (Unnumbered, Silk, Red Captions)	1914	£7.50	—
M50	Flags, 4th Series (Silk)	1914	£5.00	—
M50	Flags, 5th Series (Silk)	1914	£5.00	—
D50	Flags, 6th Series (Silk)	1914	£6.25	—
G10	Flags, 7th Series (Silk)	1914	*£42.50*	—
F96	Flowers & Plants (Numbered)	1924	£1.50	£144.00
F96	Flowers & Plants ("Specimen Cigarette Card")	1924	£4.40	—
F50	Football Favourites	1906	£50.00	—
4	North Country Celebrities	1904	£50.00	—
F?81	Northern Gems	1902	£50.00	—
50	Picture Puzzles & Riddles Series	1916	£18.75	—
F54	Radio Favourites	1935	£1.00	£54.00
L50	Regimental Badges (Silk)	1915	£4.40	—
D24	Regimental Colours (Silk) (38-61)	1914	£12.50	—
K53	Rubicon Cards (Miniature P/C)	1934	£5.00	—
K53	Rubicon Cards (Red Overprint)	1934	£6.25	—
G1	The Allies Flags (No. 37, Silk)	1915	—	*£31.25*
50	Trick Series	1916	£18.75	—
50	Well Known Footballers — N.E. Counties	1938	40p	£20.00
50	Well Known Footballers — Scottish	1938	50p	£25.00
50	World's Coinage	1914	£15.00	£750.00

ROBERT SINCLAIR TOBACCO CO. LTD.

Qty		Date	Odds	Sets
X4	Battleships & Crests (Silk)	1915	£43.75	—
10	Billiards, 1st Set	1928	£4.40	£44.00
15	Billiards, 2nd Set	1928	£5.00	£75.00
3	Billiards, 3rd Set	1928	£6.25	—
28	Dominoes	1902	*£42.50*	—

ROBERT SINCLAIR TOBACCO CO. LTD.—cont.

Qty		Date	Odds	Sets
M10	Flags (Silk)	1915	£25.00	—
?5	Footballers (Black & White on Card)	1900	£187.50	—
?2	Footballers (Mauve on Paper)	1900	£187.50	—
P6	Great War Area (Silk)	1915	£37.50	—
M10	Great War Heroes (Silk)	1915	£31.25	—
12	Policemen of the World	1899	£125.00	—
X1	Red Cross Nurse (Silk)	1915	—	£43.75
M5	Regimental Badges (Silk)	1915	£25.00	—
12	The Smiler Series	1924	£4.40	£53.00
L12	The Smiler Series	1924	£7.50	£90.00

J. SINFIELD

24	Beauties "HUMPS"	1899	£187.50	—

SINGLETON & COLE LTD.

50	Atlantic Liners	1910	£15.00	£750.00
25	Bonzo Series	1928	£3.75	£93.75
50	Celebrities—Boer War Period	1901	£15.00	£750.00
110	Crests & Badges of The British Army (Silk)	1915	£3.75	—
35	Famous Boxers (Numbered)	1930	£6.25	—
35	Famous Boxers (Unnumbered)	1930	£18.75	—
25	Famous Film Stars	1930	£6.25	—
35	Famous Officers	1915	£12.50	£625.00
35	Famous Officers (Hero Series)	1915	£125.00	—
50	Footballers	1905	£50.00	—
40	Kings & Queens	1902	£15.00	£600.00
B12	Manikin Cards	1915	£62.50	—
25	Maxims of Success (Orange Border)	1906	£21.50	—
25	Maxims of Success (Yellow Border)	1906	£125.00	—
10	Orient Line (Anonymous, 5 Ports on Back)	1904	£37.50	—
10	Orient Line (Anonymous, 11 Ports on Back)	1904	£37.50	—
8	Orient Royal Mail Line (Firm's Name)	1904	£37.50	£300.00
8	Orient Pacific Line (Anonymous)	1904	£50.00	—
25	The Wallace-Jones Keep Fit System	1910	£17.50	—

F. & J. SMITH
36 Page Illustrated Reference Book—£2.50

24	Advertisement Cards	1897	£175.00	£4200.00
50	A Tour Round The World (Postcard Back)	1904	£37.50	—
50	A Tour Round The World (Script Backs)	1904	£20.00	£1000.00
50	A Tour Round The World (Descriptive, Multi-Backed)	1906	£6.25	£312.50
50	Battlefields of Great Britain (15 Backs)	1913	£10.00	£500.00
25	Boer War Series (Black & White)	1901	£50.00	—
50	Boer War Series (Coloured)	1901	£20.00	£1000.00
50	Champions of Sport (Blue Back)	1902	£50.00	—
50	Champions of Sport (Red Multi-Backed)	1902	£45.00	—
25	Cinema Stars (8 Brands)	1920	£5.00	£125.00
50	Cricketers (1-50)	1912	£10.00	£500.00
20	Cricketers, 2nd Series (51-70)	1912	£25.00	£500.00
50'	Derby Winners	1913	£8.75	£437.50
50	Famous Explorers	1911	£8.15	£407.50

F. & J. SMITH—cont.

Qty		Date	Odds	Sets
50	Football Club Records	1917	£8.15	£407.50
50	Football Club Records (Different)	1922	£7.50	£375.00
120	Footballers (Brown Back)	1906	£18.75	—
100	Footballers (Blue Back, No Series Title)	1908	£7.50	£750.00
150	Footballers (Titled, Dark Blue Backs)	1912	£6.25	£937.50
150	Footballers (Titled, Light Blue Backs)	1912	£6.25	£937.50
50	Fowls, Pigeons & Dogs	1908	£6.25	£312.50
25	Holiday Resorts	1925	£5.00	£125.00
50	Medals (Numbered, Smith Multi-Backed)	1902	£6.25	£312.50
50	Medals (Numbered, Imperial Tob. Co., Multi-Backed)	1903	£30.00	—
50	Medals (Numbered, Imperial Tobacco Company Multi-Backed)	1906	£7.50	£375.00
20	Medals (Unnumbered)	1905	£10.00	£200.00
G1	Medal Album (Printed)	1902	—	£125.00
50	Nations of the World	1923	£4.40	£220.00
50	Naval Dress & Badges (Descriptive Multi-Backed)	1911	£7.50	£375.00
50	Naval Dress & Badges (Non-Descriptive, Multi Backed)	1914	£7.50	£375.00
50	Phil May Sketches (Brown, 4 Brands)	1924	£3.75	£187.50
50	Phil May Sketches (Grey Multi-Backed)	1908	£6.25	£312.50
25	Prominent Rugby Players	1924	£7.50	£187.50
40	Races of Mankind (No Title, Multi-Backed)	1900	£52.50	—
40	Races of Mankind (Titled, Multi-Backed)	1900	£40.00	—
25	Shadowgraphs (7 Brands)	1915	£3.60	£90.00
25	War Incidents, A Series	1914	£4.00	£100.00
25	War Incidents, 2nd Series	1915	£4.00	£100.00

SNELL & CO.

25	Boer War Celebrities ''STEW''	1901	£125.00	—

SOROKO

6	Jubilee Series	1935	£18.75	—
L6	Jubilee Series	1935	£18.75	—

S. E. SOUTHGATE & SON

25	Types of British & Colonial Troops	1900	£90.00	—

SOUTH WALES TOB. MFG. CO. LTD.

30	Army Pictures, Cartoons, etc.	1915	£62.50	—
100	Game of Numbers	1912	£50.00	—
25	Views of London	1912	£17.50	—

T. SPALTON

30	Army Pictures, Cartoons, etc.	1916	£62.50	—

SPIRO VALLERI & CO.

?15	Noted Footballers	1905	£187.50	—

G. STANDLEY

Qty		Date	Odds	Sets
B12	Manikin Cards	1915	£62.50	—

STAPLETON

B12	Manikin Cards	1915	£62.50	—

STAR OF THE WORLD

20	Boer War Cartoons	1901	£75.00	—
?50	Boer War Celebrities "JASAS"	1901	£100.00	—
30	Colonial Troops	1901	£62.50	—

H. STEVENS & CO.

20	Dogs	1923	£6.25	—
25	Zoo Series	1926	£4.40	—

A. STEVENSON

50	War Portraits	1916	£62.50	—

ALBERT STOCKWELL

30	Army Pictures, Cartoons, etc.	1916	£62.50	—

STRATHMORE TOBACCO CO.

M25	British Aircraft	1938	£1.00	£25.00

SWEET ALVA CIGARETTES

?50	Boer War Celebrities "JASAS"	1901	£75.00	—

T.S.S.

24	Nautical Expressions	1900	£62.50	—

TADDY & CO.
32 Page Reference Book—£2.50

72	Actresses, Collotype	1897	£81.00	—
25	Actresses with Flowers	1899	£70.00	£1750.00
37	Admirals & Generals—The War (2 Backs)	1914	£10.00	£625.00
25	Admirals & Generals—The War (S. Africa)	1914	£30.00	£750.00
25	Autographs	1912	£13.00	£325.00
20	Boer Leaders	1901	£14.00	£280.00
50	British Medals & Decorations, Series 2			
	(Steel Blue Back)	1912	£8.00	£400.00
	(Black Back)	1912	£25.00	—
50	British Medals & Ribbons	1912	£8.00	£400.00
20	Clowns & Circus Artistes	—	£625.00	—
30	Coronation Series	1902	£17.50	£525.00
238	County Cricketers	1907	£31.50	—
50	Dogs	1900	£18.00	£900.00
5	English Royalty	1897	£440.00	—
25	Famous Actors/Famous Actresses	1903	£12.00	£300.00
50	Famous Horses and Cattle	1912	£87.50	—

CODE NAMES

When cigarette cards first became popular in this country the most prolific subjects were actresses and militaria—since virtually all cigarette smokers were men! In the golden age around the turn of the century many manufacturers including many of the largest issued some of the same sets as their competitors. In order to distinguish the many similar series a coding system has been developed for series of Actresses and Boer War subjects that in general do not have a series title of their own. This is based on the first letter (or letters) of the names of some of the leading issuers of the particular set.

Thus Beauties PAC were issued by Pritchard & Burton, Adkin and Cope, and Beauties HOL by Harris, Ogden & Lambert & Butler. Actresses HAGG were issued by Hill, Anonymous, Gabriel and Glass (as well as Baker and Bell), while Boer War Celebrities CLAM, is taken from Churchman, Lambert & Butler, Anonymous and Muratti. The most popular of this set must surely have been Actresses FROGA which includes four sets all similar in appearance and was issued by more than 25 different companies, including Dunn's Hats in Britain, and tobacco issuers in Canada and India.

It is fortunate that so many of the series had an anonymous version, allowing the frequent use of the letter 'A', and hence some sort of pronounceable acronyms.

As a general rule in British issues Actress series are those in which the subject's name is printed, while the unidentified ladies are known as Beauties.

BRAND ISSUES

A brand issue is a card which bears the name of the cigarette with which it was inserted, but not the name of the issuing firm. This does not normally present a problem to compilers of catalogues and other lists, since most brand names have been registered, so that they cannot be used by a competitor—just as "Nostalgia" is a registered brand name for plastic albums!

Whenever possible we have listed brand issues under the name of the firm. This often enables us to bring together alternative printings of the same set, such as Hill Aviation and Decorations & Medals, each of which was issued either with the Hill name at the base or just advertising Gold Flake Honeydew. Similarly, under B. Morris there will be found four printings of Beauties CHOAB, 2 of which do not mention the firm's name.

One difficulty that occurs is that one Company may take over another, and inherit brand names. Hence Honest Long Cut was used by Duke and then the American Tobacco Co., which also took over brands such as Kinney's Sweet Caporal and Lorillard's Red Cross.

The most difficult problem however concerns groups of Companies which may use the same brand name under a different firm in different countries. Thus the Phillips Group used "Greys" as a U.K.T.C. brand in Britain, but as a Phillips brand in Australia. Similarly, Flag Cigarettes was used by Wills in Asia and U.T.C. in South Africa.

In the Catalogue on Pages 18-20 there appears an Index of brands with the name of the issuing firm (or firms), and the catalogue section in which they are listed. Names will only appear in the index when the firm's name does NOT appear AS WELL AS the brand on the card. When the issuer of the brand is not known, such as Field Favorite Cigarettes, the brand will not appear in the Index, and the set will be listed in the normal alphabetic order in the catalogue.

In a similar way to cigarette cards, there may also be brand issues of chocolates, periodicals etc. These have their own index at the beginning of section 3 of the Catalogue.

TADDY & CO.—cont.

Qty		Date	Odds	Sets
25	Famous Jockeys (No Frame)	1910	£21.50	£537.50
25	Famous Jockeys (With Frame)	1910	£17.50	£437.50
50	Footballers (New Zealand)	1900	£55.00	—
25	Heraldry Series	1911	£12.00	£300.00
25	Honours & Ribbons	1915	£14.00	£350.00
10	Klondyke Series	1900	£50.00	£500.00
60	Leading M.L.A.'s (South Africa)	1900	*£400.00*	—
25	Natives of the World	1899	£40.00	£1000.00
25	Orders of Chivalry	1911	£14.00	£350.00
25	Orders of Chivalry, 2nd Series	1912	£19.00	£475.00
595	Prominent Footballers (No Footnote)	1907	£6.00	—
400	Prominent Footballers (With Footnote)	1908	£7.00	—
?350	Prominent Footballers (London Mixture)	1913	£20.00	—
20	Royalty, Actresses & Soldiers	1898	£160.00	—
25	Royalty Series	1903	£15.00	£375.00
25	Russo Japanese War (1-25)	1904	£11.00	£275.00
25	Russo Japanese War (26-50)	1904	£16.00	£400.00
15	South African Cricket Team, 1907	1907	£46.00	£690.00
26	South African Football Team, 1906-7	1906	£17.50	£450.00
25	Sports & Pastimes	1912	£14.00	£350.00
25	Territorial Regiments	1908	£15.00	£375.00
25	Thames Series	1903	£30.00	£750.00
20	Victoria Cross Heroes (1-20)	1901	£42.50	£850.00
20	Victoria Cross Heroes (21-40)	1901	£37.50	£750.00
20	VC Heroes—Boer War (41-60)	1902	£12.00	£240.00
20	VC Heroes—Boer War (61-80)	1902	£12.00	£240.00
20	VC Heroes—Boer War (81-100)	1902	£14.00	£280.00
25	Victoria Cross Heroes (101-125)	1904	£40.00	—
2	Wrestlers	1908	£215.00	£430.00

TADDY & CO. (RE-REGISTERED)
(No Connection with Original Company)

Qty		Date	Odds	Sets
8	Advertisement Cards	1980	30p	£2.40
26	Motor Cars (Clown Cigarettes)	1980	—	£4.00
26	Motor Cars (Myrtle Grove Cigarettes)	1980	—	£5.00
26	Railway Locomotives (Clown Cigarettes)	1980	—	£2.50
26	Railway Locomotives (Myrtle Grove Cigarettes)	1980	—	£2.50

W. & M. TAYLOR

Qty		Date	Odds	Sets
8	The European War Series (Bendigo Cigarettes)	1915	£37.50	—
8	The European War Series (Tipperary	1915	£37.50	—
25	War Series (Bendigo Cigarettes)	1915	£20.00	—
25	War Series (Tipperary Cigarettes)	1915	£12.50	£312.50

TAYLOR WOOD

Qty		Date	Odds	Sets
18	Motor Cycle Series	1914	*£62.50*	—

TEOFANI & CO. LTD.

Qty		Date	Odds	Sets
25	Aquarium Studies From The London Zoo	1925	£9.00	—
50	Cinema Celebrities (Broadway Novelties)	1926	£2.50	—

TEOFANI & CO. LTD. — cont.

Qty		Date	Odds	Sets
50	Cinema Celebrities (Anonymous)	1926	£2.50	—
25	Cinema Stars (Blue Band Cigarettes)	1924	£6.25	—
25	Cinema Stars ("Favourites" Printed)	1924	£6.25	—
25	Cinema Stars ("Favourites" Stamped)	1924	£6.25	—
25	Cinema Stars (Three Star Cigarettes)	1924	£6.25	—
25	Cinema Stars (Three Star Magnums)	1924	£6.25	—
X25	Cinema Stars	1924	£4.40	—
25	Famous Boxers	1925	£4.40	—
F32	Famous British Ships & Officers	1934	£1.90	£60.00
50	Famous Racehorses	1923	£7.50	—
12	Film Actors & Actresses (Plain Back)	1936	25p	£3.00
20	Great Inventors	1924	£3.75	£75.00
20	Head-Dress of all Nations (Plain Back)	1926	£9.00	£180.00
LF50	Icelandic Employees	1926	£4.40	—
12	London Views (Plain Back)	1936	20p	£2.50
48	Modern Movie Stars & Cinema Celebrities	1934	40p	£19.25
50	Natives in Costume (Plain Back)	1926	£10.00	—
24	Past & Present "A" — The Army (No Frame)	1938	75p	£18.00
24	Past & Present "A" (Frame Line on Back)	1938	£1.00	£24.00
24	Past & Present "B" — Weapons of War	1938	30p	£7.25
4	Past & Present "C" — Transport	1939	£3.15	£12.50
50	Public Schools & Colleges	1923	£2.80	£140.00
50	Ships and their Flags	1925	£2.00	£100.00
25	Sports & Pastimes (Plain Back)	1924	£3.00	£75.00
25	Sports & Pastimes (Printed Back)	1924	£10.00	—
22	Teofani Gems	1925	£1.90	—
28	Teofani Gems	1925	65p	—
36	Teofani Gems	1925	£1.90	—
48	Transport Then & Now	1939	25p	£12.00
50	Views of London	1925	£1.90	—
F36	Views of the British Empire	1927	80p	£29.00
24	Well Known Racehorses	1923	£4.40	—
50	Worlds Smokers (Plain Back)	1926	£10.00	£500.00
50	Zoological Studies	1924	£3.15	—
L50	Zoological Studies	1924	£6.25	—

TETLEY & SONS

1	The Allies	1915	£187.50	—
50	War Portraits	1916	£55.00	—
25	World's Coinage	1914	£42.50	—

THEMANS & CO.

?10	Anecdotes & Riddles	1913	£175.00	—
55	Dominoes	1913	£75.00	—
18	Motor Cycle Series	1914	£62.50	—
50	War Portraits	1915	£40.00	—
14	War Posters	1916	£125.00	—

SILK ISSUES (MAINLY ANONYMOUS)

M10	Crests of Warships (Series B4)	1914	£6.25	—
L2	Crests of Warships (Series C4)	1914	£9.40	—
M48	Film Stars (Series B6)	1914	£6.25	—
P14	Film Stars (Series D6)	1914	£6.25	—

THEMANS & CO. —cont.

Qty		Date	Odds	Sets
M10	Flags (Series B1)	1914	£6.25	—
M12	Flags (Series B2)	1914	£6.25	—
L4	Flags (Series C1)	1914	£9.40	—
L4	Flags (Series C2)	1914	£9.40	—
P1	Flags (Series D1)	1914	£12.50	—
P1	Flags (Series D2)	1914	£12.50	—
M12	Regimental Badges (Series B3)	1914	£6.25	—
L4	Regimental Badges (Series C3)	1914	£9.40	—
P1	Regimental Badges (Series D3)	1914	£12.50	—
M12	Views of Blackpool (Series B5)	1914	*£18.75*	—
X7	Views of Blackpool (Series D5)	1914	*£18.75*	—

THOMSON & PORTEOUS

50	Arms of British Towns	1905	£10.00	£500.00
25	Boer War Celebrities "STEW"	1901	£42.50	—
25	Shadowgraphs	1902	£31.25	—
20	The European War Series	1915	£9.50	£190.00
41	V.C. Heroes (Firm's Name at Bottom)	1916	£8.50	£350.00
41	V.C. Heroes (Firm's Name at Top)	1916	£25.00	—

TOM NODDY

P12	Children of the Year Series	1904	*£31.25*	—

TOPSY CIGARETTES

F?10	Actresses	1896	*£155.00*	—

TURKISH MONOPOLY CIGARETTE CO. LTD.

X?12	Boer War Scenes	1901	£100.00	—

UNITED KINGDOM TOBACCO CO. LTD.

50	Aircraft	1933	75p	£37.50
P48	Beautiful Britain, A Series	1929	£1.00	£48.00
P48	Beautiful Britain, 2nd Series	1929	£1.00	£48.00
25	British Orders of Chivalry & Valour (2 Printings)	1936	75p	£18.75
24	Chinese Scenes	1933	25p	£6.25
32	Cinema Stars	1933	95p	£30.00
50	Cinema Stars (with Firm's Name)	1934	90p	£45.00
50	Cinema Stars (Anonymous)	1934	90p	£45.00
36	Officers Full Dress	1936	90p	£32.50
?50	Soldiers (Metal)	1935	£10.00	—
36	Soldiers of the King	1937	90p	£32.50

UNITED SERVICES MFG. CO. LTD.

50	Ancient Warriors	1938	80p	£40.00
25	Ancient Warriors	1957	£2.50	—
50	Bathing Belles	1939	30p	£15.00
100	Interesting Personalities	1935	£1.55	£155.00
50	Popular Footballers	1936	£2.20	£110.00
50	Popular Screen Stars	1937	£2.00	£100.00

UNITED TOBACCONISTS ASSOCIATION LTD.

Qty		Date	Odds	Sets
10	Actresses "MUTA"	1901	*£125.00*	—
12	Pretty Girl Series "RASH"	1900	*£125.00*	—

WALKERS TOBACCO CO. LTD. (W.T.C.)

60	British Beauty Spots	1924	*£12.50*	—
28	Dominoes (Old Monk)	1908	*£50.00*	—
28	Dominoes (W.T.C.)	1924	£3.15	—
F30/32	Film Stars (Tatleys)	1936	£1.00	£30.00
F48	Film Stars (Walkers)	1935	£3.15	—

WALTERS TOBACCO CO. LTD.

L6	Angling Information	1939	95p	£5.75

E. T. WATERMAN

30	Army Pictures, Cartoons, etc.	1916	*£62.50*	—

WEBB & RASSELL

50	War Portraits	1916	*£62.50*	

HENRY WELFARE & CO.

?25	Prominent Politicians	1912	£62.50	—

WESTMINSTER TOBACCO CO. LTD.

F36	Australia, 1st Series	1932	20p	£6.25
F36	Australia, 2nd Series (Plain Back)	1933	20p	£5.00
F48	British Royal and Ancient Buildings (Unnumbered)	1925	65p	£31.25
F48	British Royal and Ancient Buildings (Numbered)	1925	50p	£24.00
F48	British Royal Ancient Buildings, 2nd Series	1926	20p	£10.00
F36	Canada, 1st Series	1926	45p	£16.00
F36	Canada, 2nd Series	1928	45p	£16.00
F48	Indian Empire, 1st Series	1925	20p	£10.00
F48	Indian Empire, 2nd Series	1926	20p	£10.00
F36	New Zealand, 1st Series	1928	25p	£9.00
F36	New Zealand, 2nd Series	1929	20p	£5.00
F36	South Africa, 1st Series	1928	40p	£14.50
F36	South Africa, 2nd Series	1928	40p	£14.50

OVERSEAS ISSUES

L?200	Adamson's Oplevelser	1926	£15.00	—
MF50	Beauties	1924	£2.50	—
MF100	Beautiful Women	1915	£1.90	—
M50	Birds, Beasts & Fishes	1923	£2.00	£100.00
B100	British Beauties (Hand Coloured)	1915	£2.50	—
B102	British Beauties (Uncoloured)	1915	*£3.15*	—
F48	British Royal and Ancient Buildings	1925	75p	£36.00
B50	Butterflies & Moths	1920	£2.00	—
F36	Canada, 1st Series	1926	75p	—
F36	Canada, 2nd Series	1928	75p	—
30	Celebrated Actresses	1921	£4.40	£132.00

WESTMINSTER TOBACCO CO. LTD.—cont.

Qty		Date	Odds	Sets
X25	Champion Dogs	1934	£2.50	£62.50
100	Cinema Artistes (Green Back)	1928	£2.00	—
50	Cinema Artistes (Grey Back)	1931	£2.00	—
48	Cinema Celebrities (C)	1935	£2.20	—
F50	Cinema Stars	1927	£1.90	—
MF50	Cinema Stars (Coloured)	1926	£2.20	—
MF50	Cinema Stars (Uncoloured)	1930	£2.20	—
B27	Dancing Girls	1917	£4.40	£120.00
50	Do You Know?	1922	£1.90	—
24	Fairy Tales (Booklets)	1926	£3.75	—
M100	Famous Beauties (Blue Caption)	1916	£1.90	—
M100	Famous Beauties (Brown Caption)	1916	£1.55	£155.00
MF52	Film Favourites (Coloured)	1927	£2.50	—
MF52	Film Favourites (Uncoloured)	1927	£2.20	—
M50	Film Personalities	1931	£2.50	—
M50	Garden Flowers of the World	1917	£2.00	£100.00
M50	Garden Flowers of the World (Silk)	1913	£3.75	£187.50
F48	Indian Empire, 1st Series	1925	75p	—
F48	Indian Empire, 2nd Series	1926	75p	—
MF50	Islenzkar Eimskipamyndir	1931	£2.00	£100.00
MF50	Islenzkar Landslagsmyndir	1928	£1.75	£87.50
MF50	Islenzkar Landslagsmyndir Nr 2	1929	£1.75	£87.50
40	Merrie England Studies	1914	£5.00	—
X24	Miniature Rugs	1924	£15.00	—
36	Modern Beauties	1938	£2.50	—
MF52	Movie Stars	1925	£2.20	—
F36	New Zealand, 1st Series	1928	75p	—
F36	New Zealand, 2nd Series	1929	75p	—
53	Playing Cards (P.O. Box 78)	1934	£1.90	—
53	Playing Cards (Special Blend)	1934	£1.90	—
M55	Playing Cards (Blue Back)	1934	£1.55	—
M55	Playing Cards (Red Back)	1934	£1.55	—
F50	Popular Film Stars	1926	£2.50	—
L?200	Skjeggen's Oplevelser	1926	£15.00	—
F36	South Africa, 1st Series	1928	95p	—
F36	South Africa, 2nd Series	1928	95p	—
M49	South Africa Succulents	1937	20p	£8.75
M100	Stage & Cinema Stars (Black Caption)	1921	£1.90	—
M100	Stage & Cinema Stars (Grey Caption)	1921	£1.00	£100.00
MF50	Stars of Filmland (Firm in Brown)	1927	£2.20	—
MF50	Stars of Filmland (Firm in White)	1927	£2.50	—
50	Steamships of the World	1920	£5.00	—
40	The Great War Celebrities	1914	£5.00	—
50	The World of Tomorrow	1938	65p	£32.50
M50	Uniforms of all Ages	1917	£7.50	—
F50	Views of Malaya	1930	£4.40	£220.00
25	Wireless (Several Printings)	1923	£3.75	£93.75
M50	Women of Nations	1922	£3.15	£157.50

WHALE & COMPANY

?12	Conundrums	1900	£112.50	—

M. WHITE & CO.

20	Actresses "BLARM"	1900	£105.00	—

WHITFIELD'S

Qty		Date	Odds	Sets
30	Army Pictures, Cartoons etc.	1916	*£62.50*	—

WHITFORD & SONS

20	Inventors	1924	£37.50	—

WHOLESALE TOBACCO CO.

25	Armies of the World	1903	£62.50	—
40	Army Pictures (Home & Colonial Regiments)	1902	*£80.00*	—

P. WHYTE

30	Army Pictures, Cartoons, etc.	1916	*£62.50*	—

W. WILLIAMS & CO.

30	Aristocrats of the Turf, A Series	1924	£5.00	—
36	Aristocrats of the Turf, 2nd Series	1924	*£12.50*	—
25	Boer War Celebrities "STEW"	1901	£50.00	—
25	Boxing	1923	£5.00	—
50	Interesting Buildings	1912	£10.50	—
12	Views of Chester	1912	£21.00	£250.00
12	Views of Chester, 2nd Series (As It Was)	1913	£22.00	£264.00

W. D. & H. O. WILLS LTD.

200 Pages Illustrated Reference Book—£7.50

?	Actresses (Typeset Back)	1895	*£375.00*	—
52	Actresses (Brown Back, P/C Inset)	1898	£12.50	£650.00
52	Actresses (Grey Back, P/C Inset)	1897	£13.75	£718.75
52	Actresses (Grey Back, No Inset)	1897	£15.00	—
25	Actresses, Collotype (Wills', Brands Back)	1894	£62.50	—
25	Actresses, Collotype (Wills', No Brands)	1894	£62.50	—
50	Actresses & Celebrities Collotype (Wills's Four Brands on Back)	1894	£80.00	—
50	Actresses & Celebrities Collotype (Wills's Export Manufacturers Back)	1894	£80.00	—
1	Advertisement Card (Serving Maid)	1890	—	*£500.00*
4	Advertisement Cards (Cigarette Packets)	1891	*£625.00*	—
11	Advertisement Cards (Tobacco Packings)	1891	£500.00	—
3	Advertisement Cards (Showcards, 7 Brands)	1893	£250.00	—
6	Advertisement Cards (Showcards)	1893	£250.00	—
1	Advertisement Card—Three Castles	1965	—	65p
L1	Advertisement Card—Wants List	1935	—	35p
P4	Advertisement Postcards	1902	£80.00	—
50	Air Raid Precautions	1938	20p	£10.00
40	Air Raid Precautions (Eire)	1938	65p	£26.00
50	Allied Army Leaders	1917	£1.00	£50.00
50	Alpine Flowers	1913	50p	£25.00
49	And When Did You Last See Your Father? (Sect.)	1932	65p	£31.75
50	Animals & Birds (Descriptive)	1900	£15.00	£750.00
50	Animals & Birds in Fancy Costume	1896	£40.00	£2000.00
48	Animalloys (Sect.)	1934	20p	£7.50
L25	Animals and Their Furs	1929	£1.50	£37.50

W. D. & H. O. WILLS LTD. — cont.

Qty		Date	Odds	Sets
50	Arms of Companies	1913	45p	£22.50
50	Arms of Foreign Cities (2 Printings)	1912	50p	£25.00
L42	Arms of Oxford & Cambridge Colleges	1922	£1.00	£42.00
L25	Arms of Public Schools, 1st Series	1933	£1.25	£31.25
L25	Arms of Public Schools, 2nd Series	1934	£1.25	£31.25
50	Arms of the Bishopric	1907	65p	£32.50
50	Arms of the British Empire	1910	45p	£22.50
L25	Arms of the British Empire, 1st Series	1933	£1.25	£31.25
L25	Arms of the British Empire, 2nd Series	1933	£1.25	£31.25
L25	Arms of Universities	1923	£1.00	£25.00
50	Association Footballers (Frame on Back)	1935	50p	£25.00
50	Association Footballers (No Frame on Back)	1939	60p	£30.00
50	Association Footballers (Eire)	1939	75p	—
L25	Auction Bridge	1926	£1.75	£43.75
50	Aviation	1910	£1.00	£50.00
?17	Beauties, Collotype (Firefly)	1894	*£90.00*	—
?17	Beauties, Collotype (Wills Cigarettes)	1894	*£90.00*	—
?112	Beauties Actresses & Children	1894	*£87.50*	—
K52	Beauties, Playing Card Inset	1896	£21.50	—
52	Beauties, Playing Card Inset	1897	£14.00	£728.00
10	(Alternative Subjects)	1897	£32.50	—
?	Beauties (No Inset, Scroll Back)	1897	*£125.00*	—
?	Beauties (No Inset, Type Set Back)	1897	*£156.25*	—
?	Beauties, Girl Studies	1895	*£425.00*	—
L25	Beautiful Homes	1930	£1.50	£37.50
48	Between Two Fires (Sect.)	1930	20p	£8.75
50	Billiards	1909	£1.00	£50.00
K9	Boer War Medallions (6 Brands)	1900	£55.00	—
50	Borough Arms (Scroll Back, Numbered)	1903	£8.50	£425.00
50	Borough Arms (Scroll Back, Unnumbered)	1903	75p	£37.50
50	Borough Arms (1-50 Descriptive)	1904	75p	£37.50
50	Borough Arms Second Edition (1-50)	1906	50p	£25.00
50	Borough Arms, 2nd Series (51-100)	1904	45p	£22.50
50	Borough Arms Second Edition (51-100)	1906	45p	£22.50
50	Borough Arms, 3rd Series (101-150 Red)	1905	50p	£25.00
50	Borough Arms, 3rd Series (101-150 Grey)	1905	65p	£32.50
50	Borough Arms Second Edition (101-150)	1906	45p	£22.50
50	Borough Arms, 4th Series (151-200)	1905	45p	£22.50
24	Britain's Part in the War	1917	65p	£15.50
50	British Birds	1915	75p	£37.50
50	British Butterflies	1927	45p	£22.50
L25	British Castles	1925	£1.50	£37.50
1	British Commanders of the Transvaal War (Booklet)	1900	—	£62.50
L25	British School of Painting	1927	£1.00	£25.00
M48	British Sporting Personalities	1937	40p	£19.25
50	Builders of the Empire	1898	£5.00	£250.00
L40	Butterflies & Moths	1938	50p	£20.00
1	Calendar for 1911	1910	—	£10.00
1	Calendar 1912	1911	—	£5.00
L25	Cathedrals	1933	£1.50	£37.50
L25	Celebrated Pictures (2 Printings)	1916	£1.50	£37.50
L25	Celebrated Pictures, 2nd Series	1916	£1.90	£47.50
50	Celebrated Ships	1911	75p	£37.50
25	Cinema Stars, 1st Series	1928	£1.00	£25.00

Qty		Date	Odds	Sets
25	Cinema Stars, 2nd Series	1928	75p	£18.75
50	Cinema Stars, 3rd Series	1931	£1.00	£50.00
P12	Cities of Britain	1929	£5.50	£66.00
25	Conundrums (No Album Clause)	1898	£6.25	£156.25
25	Conundrums (With Album Clause)	1898	£5.00	£125.00
60	Coronation Series (Narrow Arrows)	1902	£4.40	£264.00
60	Coronation Series (Wide Arrows)	1902	£3.75	£225.00
50	Cricketers	1896	£50.00	£2500.00
25	Cricketer Series 1901 (Plain Background)	1901	£18.75	£468.75
50	Cricketer Series 1901 (Vignettes)	1901	£15.00	£750.00
25	Cricketers (WILLS'S)	1908	£4.40	£110.00
50	Cricketers (WILLS's)	1908	£3.75	£187.50
50	Cricketers, 1928	1928	80p	£40.00
50	Cricketers, 2nd Series	1929	75p	£37.50
50	Dogs	1937	30p	£15.00
50	Dogs (Eire)	1937	90p	£45.00
L25	Dogs, A Series	1914	£2.50	£62.50
L25	Dogs, 2nd Series	1915	£2.50	£62.50
50	Double Meaning	1898	£7.50	£375.00
52	Double Meaning (P/C Inset)	1898	£8.15	£425.00
50	Do You Know, A Series	1922	25p	£12.50
50	Do You Know, 2nd Series	1924	20p	£7.50
50	Do You Know, 3rd Series	1926	20p	£9.25
50	Do You Know, 4th Series	1933	25p	£12.50
50	Engineering Wonders	1927	25p	£12.50
50	English Period Costumes	1929	65p	£32.50
L25	English Period Costumes	1927	£2.00	£50.00
L40	Famous British Authors	1937	75p	£30.00
L30	Famous British Liners, A Series	1934	£2.80	£84.00
L30	Famous British Liners, 2nd Series	1935	£1.90	£57.00
L25	Famous Golfers	1930	£8.75	£218.75
50	Famous Inventions	1915	65p	£32.50
50	First Aid (No Album Clause)	1913	75p	£37.50
50	First Aid (With Album Clause)	1913	75p	£37.50
50	Fish & Bait	1910	£1.00	£50.00
25	Flags of the Empire, A Series	1926	65p	£16.25
25	Flags of the Empire, 2nd Series	1929	65p	£16.25
50	Flower Culture in Pots	1925	25p	£12.50
L30	Flowering Shrubs	1934	75p	£22.50
50	Flowering Trees & Shrubs	1924	40p	£20.00
66	Football Series	1902	£4.40	£290.00
50	Garden Flowers	1933	30p	£15.00
50	Garden Flowers by Sudell	1939	20p	£6.25
50	Garden Flowers by Sudell (Eire)	1939	25p	£12.50
L40	Garden Flowers—New Varieties, A Series	1938	25p	£10.00
L40	Garden Flowers—New Varieties 2nd Series	1939	20p	£6.25
50	Garden Hints	1938	20p	£5.50
50	Garden Hints (Eire)	1938	20p	£10.00
50	Gardening Hints	1923	20p	£7.50
50	Garden Life	1914	40p	£20.00
50	Gems of Belgian Architecture	1915	45p	£22.50
50	Gems of French Architecture	1916	90p	£45.00
F50	Gems of Italian Architecture (Repro.)	—	—	£25.00
50	Gems of Russian Architecture	1917	45p	£22.50

Qty		Date	Odds	Sets
L25	Golfing	1924	£5.00	£125.00
X32	Happy Families	1939	—	£125.00
L25	Heraldic Signs & Their Origin	1925	£1.50	£37.50
50	Historic Events	1912	75p	£37.50
F54	Homeland Events	1932	20p	£9.00
50	Household Hints	1927	20p	£8.75
50	Household Hints, 2nd Series	1930	25p	£12.50
50	Household Hints (Different)	1936	20p	£5.50
50	Household Hints (Eire)	1936	20p	£10.00
50	Hurlers (Eire)	1927	80p	£40.00
2	Indian Series	1900	£187.50	—
P12	Industries of Britain	1930	£5.50	£66.00
25	Irish Beauty-Spots	1924	£3.15	£78.75
25	Irish Holiday Resorts	1924	£3.15	£78.75
50	Irish Industries (Ask your Retailer...)	1937	65p	£32.50
50	Irish Industries (This Surface...)	1937	£2.50	—
25	Irish Rugby Internationals	1926	£5.00	£125.00
50	Irish Sportsmen	1936	£2.25	£112.50
50	Japanese Series	1900	£32.00	£1600.00
50	Kings & Queens (Short Card, Brown Back)	1898	£8.75	£437.50
50	Kings & Queens (Short Card, Grey Back)	1898	£3.75	£187.50
50/51	Kings & Queens (Long, "WILLS" At Base)	1902	£4.40	£220.00
50	Kings & Queens (Long, "WILLS" At Top)	1902	£9.40	—
L25	Lawn Tennis, 1931	1931	£3.75	£93.75
50	Life in the Hedgerow	Unissued	40p	£20.00
50	Life in the Royal Navy	1939	20p	£7.50
50	Life in the Treetops	1925	20p	£8.75
50	Locomotives & Rolling Stock (No Clause)	1901	£4.40	£220.00
7	Additional Subjects	1902	£16.00	£124.00
50	Locomotives & Rolling Stock (ITC Clause)	1902	£5.00	£250.00
50	Lucky Charms	1923	20p	£8.75
100	Maori Series (White Borders)	1900	£75.00	—
50	Maori Series (Green Borders)	1900	£75.00	—
3	Maori Series (Green Borders, Numbered Top Left)	1900	£125.00	—
4	Maori Series (Green Borders, Unnumbered)	1900	£125.00	—
50	Medals	1906	£1.90	£95.00
50	Merchant Ships of the World	1924	65p	£32.50
50	Military Motors (Not Passed by Censor)	1916	£1.00	£50.00
50	Military Motors (Passed by Censor)	1916	£1.00	£50.00
52	Miniature Playing Cards (Blue Back, Numbered, 4 Printings)	1931	40p	£20.00
52	Miniature Playing Cards (Blue Back, Unnumbered)	1931	40p	£20.00
52	Miniature Playing Cards (Blue Back, Red Overprint)	1931	40p	£20.00
52	Miniature Playing Cards (3 Pink Backs)	1931	50p	£26.00
52	Miniature Playing Cards (Eire, 7 Backs)	1931	95p	—
50	Mining	1916	50p	£25.00
L25	Modern Architecture	1931	£1.00	£25.00
L30	Modern British Sculpture	1928	95p	£28.50
48	Mother & Son (Sect.)	1931	20p	£8.75
50	Musical Celebrities	1912	£1.75	£87.50
50	Musical Celebrities, 2nd Series	1914	£2.50	£125.00
8	(Original Subjects)	1914	£155.00	—

W. D. & H. O. WILLS LTD.—cont.

Qty		Date	Odds	Sets
25	National Costumes	1895	£155.00	—
?	National Types	1893	*£375.00*	—
50	Naval Dress & Badges	1909	£1.55	£77.50
50	Nelson Series	1905	£2.20	£110.00
50	Old English Garden Flowers	1910	50p	£25.00
50	Old English Garden Flowers, Second Series	1913	50p	£25.00
L25	Old Furniture, 1st Series	1923	£2.50	£62.50
L25	Old Furniture, 2nd Series	1924	£2.50	£62.50
L40	Old Inns, A Series	1936	£1.55	£62.00
L40	Old Inns, Second Series	1939	95p	£38.00
L25	Old London	1929	£2.50	£62.50
L30	Old Pottery & Porcelain	1934	80p	£24.00
L25	Old Silver	1924	£2.00	£50.00
L25	Old Sundials	1928	£1.75	£43.75
20	Our Gallant Grenadiers	1902	£25.00	£500.00
50	Our King & Queen	1937	20p	£7.50
50	Overseas Dominions (Australia)	1915	40p	£20.00
50	Overseas Dominions (Canada)	1914	40p	£20.00
50	Physical Culture	1914	50p	£25.00
25	Pond & Aquarium, 1st Series …Unissued		—	£5.65
25	Pond & Aquarium, 2nd Series …Unissued		—	£7.00
50	Portraits of European Royalty (1-50)	1908	75p	£37.50
50	Portraits of European Royalty (51-100)	1908	£1.00	£50.00
L25	Public Schools	1927	£2.00	£50.00
L25	Punch Cartoons, 1st Series	1916	£2.50	£62.50
L25	Punch Cartoons, 2nd Series	1917	£12.50	£312.50
L40	Racehorses & Jockeys 1938	1939	£1.00	£40.00
50	Radio Celebrities, A Series	1934	40p	£20.00
50	Radio Celebrities, A Series (Eire)	1934	75p	—
50	Radio Celebrities, 2nd Series	1934	30p	£15.00
50	Radio Celebrities, 2nd Series (Eire)	1934	75p	—
50	Railway Engines	1924	75p	£37.50
50	Railway Engines (Adhesive)	1936	65p	£32.50
50	Railway Engines (Eire)	1936	£1.25	—
50	Railway Equipment	1938	20p	£7.50
50	Railway Locomotives	1930	80p	£40.00
12	Recruiting Posters	1915	£5.00	£60.00
L25	Rigs of Ships	1929	£2.50	£62.50
50	Romance of the Heavens	1928	25p	£12.50
50	Roses, A Series (1-50)	1912	60p	£30.00
50	Roses, Second Series (51-100)	1913	50p	£25.00
50	Roses (Different)	1926	40p	£20.00
L40	Roses (Different)	1936	50p	£20.00
M48	Round Europe	1936	20p	£9.50
50	Rugby Internationals	1929	75p	£37.50
50	Safety First	1934	50p	£25.00
50	Safety First (Eire)	1934	95p	—
50	School Arms	1906	45p	£22.50
50	School Arms (With "Series of 50")	1906	*£12.50*	—
50	Seaside Resorts (Mixed Backs)	1899	—	£375.00
50	(Best Birds Eye)	1899	£7.50	—
50	(Capstan)	1899	£7.50	—
50	(Gold Flake)	1899	£7.50	—
50	(Three Castles)	1899	£7.50	—

W. D. & H. O. WILLS LTD. — cont.

Qty		Date	Odds	Sets
50	Seaside Resorts (Traveller)	1899	£7.50	—
50	(Westward Ho)	1899	£7.50	—
40	Shannon Electric Power Scheme (Eire)	1931	£1.05	£42.00
25	Ships (Three Castles Back)	1895	£25.00	£625.00
25	Ships (No "WILLS" On Front)	1895	£25.00	£625.00
50	Ships (With "WILLS" On Front)	1896	£15.00	£750.00
100	Ships (Brownish Card)	1897	£15.00	£1500.00
50	Ships' Badges	1925	25p	£12.50
50	Signalling Series	1911	50p	£25.00
50	Soldiers & Sailors (Blue Back)	1894	£37.50	£1875.00
50	Soldiers & Sailors (Grey Back)	1894	£37.50	£1875.00
100	Soldiers of the World (Ltd. Back)	1895	£5.65	£565.00
	Soldiers of the World (No Ltd. On Back)	1895	£5.00	£500.00
52	Soldiers of the World (P/C Inset)	1896	£18.75	£975.00
100	South African Personalities, Collotype (4 Different Printings)	1901	£75.00	—
50	Speed	1930	90p	£45.00
50	Speed (Different)	1938	20p	£8.75
50	Speed (Eire)	1938	50p	£25.00
50	Sports of all Nations (Multi-Backed)	1901	£6.25	£312.50
50	Strange Craft	1931	65p	£32.50
48	The Boyhood of Raleigh (Sect.)	1931	20p	£10.00
P12	The British Empire	1929	£5.50	£66.00
50	The Coronation Series	1911	75p	£37.50
L40	The King's Art Treasures	1938	20p	£7.50
48	The Laughing Cavalier (Sect., 2 Backs)	1931	20p	£10.00
48	The Laughing Cavalier (Sect. Eire)	1931	£1.55	—
50	The Life of H.M. King Edward VIII	Unissued	£15.00	—
50	The Reign of King George V	1935	30p	£15.00
50	The Sea Shore	1938	20p	£7.00
50	The Sea Shore (Eire)	1938	50p	£25.00
48	The Toast (Sect.)	1931	20p	£8.25
48	The Toast (Sect., Eire)	1931	£1.55	—
25	The World's Dreadnoughts	1910	£1.50	£37.50
50	Time & Money in Different Countries	1908	£1.00	£50.00
50	Transvaal Series (Black Border)	1901	£7.50	—
66	Transvaal Series (White Border)	1901	£1.50	£99.00
66	Transvaal Series (Non Descriptive)	1902	£4.40	£300.00
L40	Trees	1937	45p	£18.00
L25	University Hoods & Gowns	1926	£2.00	£50.00
50	Vanity Fair Series (Unnumbered)	1902	£3.75	£187.50
50	Vanity Fair, 1st Series	1902	£3.75	£187.50
50	Vanity Fair, 2nd Series	1902	£3.75	£187.50
50	Waterloo	Unissued	£87.50	—
50	Wild Animals of the World (Green Scroll Back)	1900	£3.75	£187.50
15	Wild Animals of the World (Grey Descriptive Back)	1902	£25.00	£375.00
52	Wild Animals of the World (P/C Inset)	1900	£10.00	£500.00
50	Wild Flowers, (2 Printings)	1923	30p	£15.00
50	Wild Flowers, A Series (Adhesive)	1936	20p	£8.25
50	Wild Flowers (Eire)	1936	45p	£22.50
50	Wild Flowers, 2nd Series	1937	20p	£6.25
50	Wild Flowers, 2nd Series (Eire)	1937	45p	£22.50
50	Wonders of the Past	1926	30p	£15.00

W. D. & H. O. WILLS LTD. — cont.

Qty		Date	Odds	Sets
50	Wonders of the Sea	1928	30p	£15.00

MODERN ISSUES (EMBASSY)

Qty		Date	Odds	Sets
56	Caribbean Treasure Cruise	1985	£1.25	—
M56	Caribbean Treasure Cruise	1985	65p	—
T48	Familiar Phrases	1986	80p	—
L30	History of Britain's Railways	1987	95p	—
L30	History of Motor Racing	1987	95p	—
T5	Pica Punchline	1984	95p	—
L144	Punch Lines	1983	40p	—
T288	Punch Lines	1983	40p	—
T48	Ring The Changes	1985	65p	£31.25
56	Showhouse (33 x 60mm)	1988	£1.25	—
56	Showhouse (35 x 80mm)	1988	50p	—
M56	Showhouse (47 x 68mm)	1988	£1.25	
M56	Showhouse (47 x 80mm)	1988	50p	—
T56	Showhouse (47 x 90mm)	1988	50p	—
T10	Spot The Shot	1986	£1.90	—
?	Wheel of Fortune	1988	£1.25	—
M?	Wheel of Fortune	1988	50p	—
56	Wonders of the World	1986	90p	—
M56	Wonders of the World	1986	65p	£36.50
T56	Wonders of the World	1986	40p	£22.50
M36	World of Firearms	1982	20p	£3.75
M36	World of Speed	1981	20p	£3.75

AUSTRALIAN ISSUES

Qty		Date	Odds	Sets
100	Actresses (Capstan)	1903	£2.20	—
100	Actresses (Vice Regal)	1903	£2.20	—
1	Advertisement Card (Capstan)	1902	—	£150.00
60	Animals (Cut-Outs, Specialities)	1916	75p	£45.00
60	Animals (Cut-Outs, Havelock)	1916	£1.55	—
50	Arms & Armour (Capstan, "ALSO OBTAINABLE")	1910	£1.25	£62.50
50	Arms & Armour (Capstan, No Extra Words)	1910	£1.25	£62.50
50	Arms & Armour (Vice Regal)	1910	£1.25	£62.50
50	Arms & Armour (Havelock)	1910	£2.50	—
50	Arms of the British Empire (Specialities)	1910	65p	£32.50
50	Arms of the British Empire (Havelock)	1910	£1.50	
M50	Arms of the British Empire (Silk)	1910	£2.50	£125.00
50	A Tour Round the World (Blue Caption)	1907	£2.00	£100.00
50	A Tour Round the World (Mauve Caption)	1907	£2.00	£100.00
25	Australian & English Cricketers (Numbered)	1903	£10.00	£250.00
25	Australian & English Cricketers (Blue Border, Capstan)	1909	£10.00	£250.00
	(Blue Border, Vice Regal)	1909	£10.00	£250.00
	(Red Border, Capstan)	1909	£10.00	£250.00
	(Red Border, Vice Regal)	1909	£10.00	£250.00
59	Australian & English Cricketers, Titled	1911	—	£590.00
50	Capstan, "SERIES OF 50"	1911	£10.00	—
50	Capstan, "SERIES OF "	1911	£10.00	—
9	51-59, Capstan, "SERIES OF 59"	1911	£10.00	—
50	Vice Regal, "SERIES OF 50"	1911	£10.00	—
50	Vice Regal, "SERIES OF "	1911	£10.00	—
9	51-59, Vice Regal, "SERIES OF 59"	1911	£10.00	—
50	Havelock	1911	£31.25	—

Qty		Date	Odds	Sets
60	Australian & South African Cricketers	1910	—	£600.00
60	Light Background, Blue Border	1910	£10.00	—
60	Light Background, Red Border	1910	£10.00	—
24	Dark Background, Blue Border, Capstan	1910	£12.50	—
24	Dark Background, Blue Border, Vice Regal	1910	£12.50	—
24	Dark Background, Red Border, Capstan	1910	£12.50	—
24	Dark Background, Red Border, Vice Regal	1910	£12.50	—
60	Light Background, Havelock	1910	£31.25	—
M50	Australian Butterflies (Silk)	1914	£2.50	£125.00
40/47	Australian Club Cricketers	1905	—	£600.00
40	Blue Back, with State	1905	£15.00	—
40	Blue Back, No State	1905	£15.00	—
40	Green Back	1905	£15.00	—
39/47	Blue Back, Brown Frame Line	1905	£18.75	—
MF100	Australian Scenic Series	1925	65p	£65.00
50	Australian Wild Flowers (Specialities)	1913	50p	£25.00
50	Australian Wild Flowers (Havelock)	1913	£1.25	—
75	Aviation (Black Back, Capstan)	1910	95p	£71.25
75	Aviation (Black Back, Vice Regal)	1910	95p	£71.25
75	Aviation (Black Back, Havelock)	1910	£1.90	—
75	Aviation (Green Back, Capstan)	1910	£1.25	—
75	Aviation (Green Back, Vice Regal)	1910	£1.25	—
75	Aviation (Green Back, Havelock)	1910	£2.20	—
85	Aviation (Capstan)	1910	£1.25	£106.25
85	Aviation (Vice Regal)	1910	£1.25	£106.25
50	Best Dogs of Their Breed (Specialities)	1914	£2.50	£125.00
50	Best Dogs of Their Breed (Havelock)	1914	£4.40	—
M50	Birds and Animals of Australia (Silk)	1915	£2.50	£125.00
100	Birds of Australasia (Green, Capstan)	1912	75p	£75.00
100	Birds of Australasia (Green, Vice Regal)	1912	75p	£75.00
100	Birds of Australasia (Green, Havelock)	1912	£1.90	—
100	Birds of Australasia (Yellow Back)	1912	65p	£65.00
100	Birds of Australasia (Yellow, Havelock)	1912	£1.90	—
50	Britain's Defenders (1-50)	1914	80p	£40.00
50	Britain's Defenders (Havelock)	1914	£1.90	£95.00
8	Britain's Defenders (51-8)	1914	£6.25	—
50	British Empire Series (Capstan)	1912	50p	£25.00
50	British Empire Series (Vice Regal)	1912	50p	£25.00
50	British Empire Series (Havelock)	1912	£1.25	£62.50
M68	Crests and Colours of Australian Universities Colleges and Schools	1929	45p	£30.50
M50	Crests and Colours of Australian Universities Colleges & Schools (Silk)	1929	£2.50	£125.00
M1	Crests and Colours of Australian Schools (Silk, Unnumbered)	1929	—	£18.75
50	Cricketer Series (Grey Scroll Back, No Frame) ..	1901	£80.00	—
25	Cricketer Series (Grey Scroll Back, Fancy Frame)	1902	£75.00	—
F63	Cricketers (Plain Back)	1926	£6.25	£395.00
F40/48	Cricket Season, 1928-29	1929	£1.90	£76.00
L20	Dogs, A Series (Three Castles & Vice Regal) ...	1927	£1.90	—

W. D. & H. O. WILLS LTD. — cont.

Qty		Date	Odds	Sets
L20	Dogs (World Renowned, Album Clause)	1927	£1.90	—
L20	Dogs (World Renowned, No Album Clause)	1927	£1.90	—
L20	Dogs, 2nd Series	1928	£1.90	—
L25	English Period Costumes	1929	£1.25	£31.25
100	Famous Film Stars	1930	50p	£50.00
M100	Famous Film Stars	1933	90p	—
MF100	Famous Film Stars	1933	£1.90	—
B20	Fiestas (Cartons)	1968	65p	—
50	Fish of Australasia (Capstan)	1912	50p	£25.00
50	Fish of Australasia (Vice Regal)	1912	50p	£25.00
50	Fish of Australasia (Havelock)	1912	£1.25	—
50	Flag Girls of all Nations	1908	—	£75.00
50	Capstan, Small Captions	1908	£1.50	—
25	Capstan, Large Captions	1908	£2.50	—
50	Vice Regal, Small Captions	1908	£1.50	—
25	Vice Regal, Large Captions	1908	£2.50	—
8	Flags (Shaped, Metal, 4 Printings)	1915	£6.25	—
M13	Flags (Lace)	1916	£3.75	£48.75
28	Flags of the Allies (Silk, Capitals)	1915	£1.55	£43.50
23	Flags of the Allies (Silk, Small Letter)	1915	£1.75	£40.00
25	Flags of the Empire	1926	£5.00	—
28	Football Club Colours & Flags (Capstan)	1913	£2.50	—
28	Football Club Colours & Flags (Havelock)	1913	£3.75	—
200	Footballers 1933	1933	40p	£80.00
M200	Footballers 1933	1933	65p	—
?6	Footballers (Shaped)	1910	£50.00	—
?	Football Pennants (Shaped, Capstan)	1905	£31.25	—
?	Football Pennants (Shaped, Havelock)	1905	£31.25	—
50	Girls of all Nations (Capstan)	1908	£1.90	£95.00
50	Girls of all Nations (Vice Regal)	1908	£1.90	£95.00
X?	Havelock Comics	1904	£62.50	—
50	Historic Events (Specialities)	1913	75p	£37.50
50	Historic Events (Havelock)	1913	£1.50	£75.00
L25	History of Naval Dress	1929	£15.00	—
50	Horses of Today (Capstan)	1906	£1.55	£77.50
50	Horses of Today (Vice Regal)	1906	£1.55	£77.50
50	Horses of Today (Havelock)	1906	£3.15	—
50	Interesting Buildings	1905	£1.55	£77.50
5	Islands of the Pacific	1917	£150.00	—
38	Kings & Queens of England (Silk)	1910	£3.75	£142.50
45	Melbourne Cup Winners	1906	£4.40	—
40	Merrie England Studies	1916	£4.40	£176.00
50	Modern War Weapons (Specialities)	1915	£1.25	£62.50
50	Modern War Weapons (Havelock)	1915	£2.50	—
50	Past & Present Champions (Cigarettes)	1908	£3.75	—
50	Past & Present Champions (Tobacco)	1908	£3.15	£157.50
M50	Popular Flowers (Silk, Large Packets)	1913	£3.15	—
M50	Popular Flowers (Silk, 1/- Packets)	1913	£3.15	£157.50
L70	Practical Wireless	1923	£3.15	—
50	Prominent Australian & English Cricketers (1-50)	1907	£8.75	£562.50
23	Prominent Australian & English Cricketers (51-73, Grey Captions)	1907	£10.00	£230.00

W. D. & H. O. WILLS LTD.—cont.

Qty		Date	Odds	Sets
8	Prominent Australian & English Cricketers (66-73, Red Captions)	1907	£12.50	£100.00
10	Recruiting Posters (Anon Back)	1915	£5.00	£50.00
50	Riders of the World	1913	£1.25	£62.50
50	Riders of the World (Havelock)	1913	£2.50	—
50	Royal Mail (Capstan)	1913	£2.50	£125.00
50	Royal Mail (Vice Regal)	1913	£2.50	£125.00
50	Royal Mail (Anonymous Printed Back)	1913	£3.75	—
50	Royal Mail (Anonymous Plain Back)	1913	£5.00	—
50	Royal Mail (Havelock, 2 Printings)	1913	£3.75	—
50	Signalling Series (Capstan)	1912	75p	£37.50
50	Signalling Series (Vice Regal)	1912	75p	£37.50
50	Signalling Series (Havelock)	1912	£1.55	£77.50
39/40	Sketches in Black & White	1905	£1.90	£75.00
?39/40	Sketches (White on Black)	1905	£62.50	—
50	Soldiers of the World	1902	£5.00	£250.00
25	Sporting Terms (Capstan)	1905	£7.50	—
25	Sporting Terms (Vice Regal)	1905	£7.50	—
50	Sports of the World	1917	£2.50	—
50	Stage & Music Hall Celebrities (Capstan)	1904	£2.20	£110.00
50	Stage & Music Hall Celebrities (Vice Regal)	1904	£2.20	—
50	Stage & Music Hall Celebrities (Havelock)	1904	£3.75	—
50	Stage & Music Hall Celebrities (Square Frame)	1904	£2.50	—
L25	The Nation's Shrines	1928	£1.00	£25.00
25	The World's Dreadnoughts (Capstan)	1910	£1.25	£31.25
25	The World's Dreadnoughts (Vice Regal)	1910	£1.25	£31.25
50	Time & Money in Different Countries			
50	Capstan	1908	£1.00	£50.00
50	Vice Regal, Album Clause	1908	£1.00	£50.00
50	Vice Regal, No Album Clause	1908	£1.00	£50.00
50	Havelock	1908	£2.00	£100.00
50	Types of the British Army (Capstan, 3 Printings)	1912	£1.55	£77.50
50	Types of the British Army (Vice Regal, 3 Printings)	1912	£1.55	£77.50
50	Types of the Commonwealth Forces (Capstan, 2 Printings)	1910	£1.90	£95.00
50	Types of the Commonwealth Forces (Vice Regal, 2 Printings)	1910	£1.90	£95.00
50	Types of the Commonwealth Forces (Havelock)	1910	£3.75	—
P1	Union Jack (Silk)	1915	—	£15.50
25	United States Warships (Capstan)	1911	£1.90	£47.50
25	United States Warships (Vice Regal)	1911	£1.90	£47.50
25	United States Warships (Havelock)	1911	£3.15	—
25	Victoria Cross Heroes (Specalities)	1915	£1.50	£37.50
25	Victoria Cross Heroes (Havelock)	1915	£3.15	£78.75
29	Victorian Football Pennants			
	(Capstan, Multi Backed)	1910	£2.20	—
	(Vice Regal, Multi Backed)	1910	£2.20	—
	(Havelock, Multi Backed)	1910	£3.75	—
FS165	Views of the World (Capstan)	1908	65p	—
FS165	Views of the World (Vice Regal)	1908	65p	—

Qty		Date	Odds	Sets
50	War Incidents, A Series (Specialities)	1915	80p	£40.00
50	War Incidents, A Series (Havelock)	1915	£1.55	—
50	War Incidents, 2nd Series (Specialities)	1915	80p	£40.00
50	War Incidents, 2nd Series (Havelock)	1915	£1.90	—
L67	War Medals (Silk)	1916	£2.50	£167.50
50	War Pictures (Specialities)	1915	80p	£40.00
50	War Pictures (Havelock)	1915	£1.90	£95.00
50	Wild Animals (Heads)	1934	40p	£20.00
M25	Wild Animals (Heads)	1934	90p	£22.50
50	Wild Animals of the World	1906	£3.75	£187.50
LF50	Zoological Series	1922	£1.55	—

BRAND ISSUES

(A) Autocar Cigarettes

40	Chinese Trades	1905	£5.00	—

(B) Flag Cigarettes

67	International Footballers, 1909-1910	1910	£5.00	—
50	Jiu Jitsu	1911	£3.75	—
50	Types of the British Army	1912	£4.40	—

(C) Four Aces Cigarettes

52	Birds of Brilliant Plumage (P/C Inset)	1924	£2.00	£104.00
75	Film Favourites	1928	£1.00	£75.00
25	Modes of Conveyance	1928	£1.50	£37.50
50	Stage & Film Stars (Numbered)	1926	£1.25	£62.50
50	Stage & Film Stars (Unnumbered)	1926	£1.50	£75.00
F52	Stars of the Cinema	1926	£2.50	—

(D) Pirate Cigarettes

G?	Advertisement Cards	1910	£50.00	—
?100	Baseball Series	1912	£31.25	—
52	Birds of Brilliant Plumage (P/C Inset, Frame Line)	1914	£3.15	£165.00
52	Birds of Brilliant Plumage (P/C Inset, No Frame)	1914	£2.50	£125.00
100	China's Ancient Warriors (Multi-Backed)	1911	95p	£95.00
28	Chinese Actors & Actresses	1907	£2.00	£56.00
50	Chinese Beauties (Multi-Backed)	1907	£1.00	£50.00
50	Chinese Costumes	1928	£2.50	—
P25	Chinese Pagodas	1911	£25.00	—
50	Chinese Proverbs (Brown, 2 Backs)	1928	£1.00	£50.00
50	Chinese Proverbs (Coloured, 3 Backs)	1914	£1.00	£50.00
33	Houses of Parliament	1914	80p	£26.75
50	Products of the World	1913	£1.00	£50.00

(E) Purple Mountain Cigarettes

20	Flowers (Numbered)	1914	£9.40	—
100	Flowers (Unnumbered)	1915	£7.50	—
25	Roses (Wills on Front)	1912	£4.40	£110.00
25	Roses (Without Wills on Front)	1912	£4.40	£110.00

(F) Ruby Queen Cigarettes

30	Birds & Animals (2 Backs)	1911	£2.00	£60.00
50	Birds of the East (Multi-Backs/Fronts)	1912	£1.00	£50.00
30	Chinese Children's Games (2 Backs)	1911	£1.75	—

MULTI-BACKS

There are many instances in the enlarged catalogue when a set by one issuer is noted as occurring in more than one back. For example, each card in Wills Seaside Resorts can be found with six different brands advertised, while in the case of Smith Battlefields of Great Britain each number can have no less than 15 different advertisements!

In addition to these varieties there are also many series, particularly among the earlier issues, where there are different backs, but not every front may be found with every back. These are known as multi-backs. A good example of this is the Wills set Sports of all Nations, which like Seaside Resorts also has six advertisements; however in this case each number only occurs with two different brands, and these run in distinct groups of numbers. The issues of Smith are also an excellent source of multi-backed series, with many series including

Champions of Sport, Medals and Phil May Sketches featuring prominently. Indeed the Smith issues are so complicated that it has been necessary to publish a separate Reference Book detailing all the varieties known.

In the catalogue we now show when a series is multi-backed, but without indicating all the options available; this would have been too complicated, especially for a series such as Adkin Pretty Girl Series RASH, with its 50 different backs! Most type collectors would probably wish to obtain one of each of these multi-backs, and full information is normally to be found in the Cartophilic Society's Reference Books.

One additional term worth remembering is "vari-backed". This is used when there are different advertisements on the back, but where each front can be found with one back only.

DISSIMILAR SERIES

When a firm decides to issue a new set of cards it may have undertaken some market research, but it will never be certain how successful it may become. If the response is positive it may then produce an extra set, which would normally be distinguished as 2nd or continuation series. In the case of Lea's Pottery or Ogden Boy Scouts this extended to five series. Sometimes when a subject appeared popular, different aspects would be covered by sets with different titles, as in the case of Player with their aircraft sets and Ogden with its racing series.

Sometimes a popular series was extended by producing it in different sizes. Apart from the better known multi sized sets such as those of International T.C. and Jackson, there are examples where the small and large cards depict different subjects. These include Wills English Period Costumes, Baker Actresses and Carreras Old Staffordshire Figures.

Another quite complicated situation can occur when a Company decides to issue a completely new series under the same title as an earlier set. Wills were very fond of this, with two or more series titled Wild Flowers, Association Footballers, Garden Flowers and Speed.

Ogden too issued a later set of Boy Scouts some years after its first five, but its newer series of Bird's Eggs and British Birds were easily distinguishable by being cut-outs!

Finally, there is a group of series which are not quite the same. There are series where the pictures have been re-drawn, and show minor differences. These include two sets by Gallaher—Boy Scouts and the first series of Champions; also half the set of Carreras Famous Footballers and Huntley & Palmer's Sports.

WHITSTABLE WHELKER

W. D. & H. O. WILLS LTD.—cont.

Qty		Date	Odds	Sets
50	Chinese Proverbs	1927	£1.50	—
50	Chinese Transport (2 Backs)	1914	£1.90	—

(G) Scissors Cigarettes

Qty		Date	Odds	Sets
50	Actresses (Black & White)	1904	£6.25	—
50	Actresses (Four Colour Surround)	1904	£5.00	—
30	Actresses (Green Surround)	1905	£2.50	£75.00
30	Actresses (Mauve Surround)	1916	£1.25	£37.50
30	Actresses (Orange Surround)	1916	£1.90	£57.00
30	Actresses (Purple Brown, Brown Back)	1908	£1.90	£57.00
30	Actresses (Purple Brown, Red Back)	1908	£1.25	£37.50
30	Actresses (Purple Brown, Long Card)	1909	£1.55	£46.50
25	Army Life	1914	£1.50	£37.50
30	Beauties (Green Surround)	1921	£3.75	—
52	Beauties (P/C Inset—Lattice Back)	1911	£2.50	£125.00
52	Beauties (P/C Inset—No Lattice Back)	1911	£3.75	—
52	Beauties (P/C Inset—No Packets)	1911	*£12.50*	—
32	Beauties (Picture Hat)	1914	£2.00	£64.00
40	Beauties (Brown Tint)	1913	£1.25	£50.00
30	Beauties & Children	1910	£1.90	£65.00
36	Boxers	1911	£4.40	£158.50
50	Britain's Defenders (Green Back)	1914	£1.00	£50.00
50	Britain's Defenders (Red Back & Front)	1914	95p	£47.50
50	Britain's Defenders (Red Back, Blue Front)	1914	95p	£47.50
43	British Army Boxers Series	1913	£3.75	£160.00
25	Cinema Stars	1916	£1.90	£47.50
F50	Cinema Stars	1926	*£3.15*	—
27	Dancing Girls (Series of 27)	1915	£1.90	£51.50
27/28	Dancing Girls (Series of 28)	1915	£2.00	£54.00
25	Derby Day Series	1914	£4.40	£110.00
25	Derby Day Series A (No Series Title)	1914	£6.25	—
32	Drum Horses (Horizontal Back)	1909	£4.40	£140.00
32	Drum Horses (Vertical Back)	1909	£6.25	—
50	Famous Footballers	1914	£4.40	£220.00
25	Flag Girls of all Nations (Numbered)	1908	£6.25	—
25	Flag Girls of all Nations (Unnumbered)	1908	£9.00	—
50	Football Club Colours	1907	£4.40	£220.00
25	Governors-General of India	1912	£5.00	£125.00
30	Heroic Deeds	1913	£1.90	£57.00
50	Indian Regiments Series	1912	£5.00	£250.00
67	International Footballers, 1909-1910	1910	£5.00	£335.00
50	Jiu Jitsu	1910	£4.40	£220.00
53	Jockeys & Owners Colours (P/C Inset)	1914	£5.00	£265.00
25	Military Portraits	1917	£3.15	£78.75
50	Music Hall Celebrities	1911	£5.00	—
K52	Playing Cards	1906	£10.00	—
25	Puzzle Series (Green, United Service Backs)	1910	£4.40	—
25	Puzzle Series (Yellow, United Service Backs)	1910	£4.40	—
50	Regimental Colours & Cap Badges	1907	£1.00	£50.00
33	Regimental Pets	1911	£4.40	£145.00
30	Sporting Girls	1913	£5.00	£150.00
50	Types of the British Army	1908	£3.75	£187.50
25	Victoria Cross Heroes	1915	£1.90	£47.50
50	War Incidents	1915	£1.25	£62.50
30	What It Means	1916	£1.00	£30.00

W. D. & H. O. WILLS LTD.—cont.

Qty		Date	Odds	Sets
F50	"Zoo"	1927	£3.15	—

(H) United Service Cigarettes

50	Arms & Armour	1910	£2.20	£110.00
32	Drum Horses	1909	£4.40	£145.00
25	Flag Girls of all Nations	1908	£1.90	£47.50
67	International Footballers, 1909-1910	1910	£5.00	—
	Puzzle Series—See Scissors Cigarettes			
50	Regimental Colours & Cap Badges (Blue Back)	1907	90p	£45.00
50	Regimental Colours & Cap Badges (Red Back)	1907	£1.00	£50.00

(I) Wild Woodbine Cigarettes

50	British Army Uniforms	1909	£4.40	£220.00

CHANNEL ISLAND ISSUES

50	Air Raid Precautions	1938	45p	£22.50
50	Association Footballers	1935	50p	£25.00
50	Dogs	1937	50p	£25.00
50	Garden Flowers by Sudell	1939	30p	£15.00
50	Garden Hints	1938	30p	£15.00
50	Household Hints	1936	30p	£15.00
50	Life in the Royal Navy	1939	30p	£15.00
50	Our King & Queen	1937	40p	£20.00
50	Railway Equipment	1938	30p	£15.00
50	Speed	1938	30p	£15.00
50	The Sea Shore	1938	30p	£15.00
50	Wild Flowers, A Series	1936	30p	£15.00
50	Wild Flowers, 2nd Series	1937	30p	£15.00

NEW ZEALAND ISSUES

F50	A Sporting Holiday in New Zealand	1928	40p	£20.00
LF50	A Sporting Holiday in New Zealand (Different)	1928	60p	£30.00
F50	Beautiful New Zealand	1928	20p	£8.75
50	Birds, Beasts and Fishes	1924	30p	£15.00
F48	British Royal and Ancient Buildings	1925	25p	£12.50
45	British Rugby Players	1930	£1.15	£51.75
50	Children of all Nations	1925	30p	£15.00
50	Coaches and Coaching Days	1925	80p	£40.00
50	Dogs	1926	50p	£25.00
F25	English Cricketers	1926	£1.50	£37.50
26	Etchings (Dogs)	1925	65p	£17.00
L26	Etchings (Dogs)	1925	£1.00	£26.00
50	Famous Inventions	1926	50p	£25.00
L25	Heraldic Signs & Their Origin	1925	£1.00	£25.00
F50	Homeland Events	1927	20p	£8.75
50	Household Hints (Wills at Top Back)	1927	20p	£8.75
50	Household Hints (Scroll at Top Back)	1927	£1.25	—
50	Lighthouses	1926	60p	£30.00
50	Merchant Ships of the World	1925	60p	£30.00
48	Motor Cars	1923	£1.00	£50.00
F50	Motor Cars	1926	75p	£37.50
50	Motor Cycles	1926	£1.90	£95.00
50	New Zealand Birds	1925	45p	£22.50

Qty		Date	Odds	Sets
F50	New Zealand—Early Scenes & Maori Life	1926	20p	£10.00
F50	New Zealand Footballers	1927	20p	£10.00
50	New Zealand Racehorses	1928	50p	£50.00
50	N.Z. Butterflies, Moths & Beetles	1925	45p	£22.50
25	Past & Present	1929	75p	£18.75
25	Picturesque People of the Empire	1928	50p	£12.50
25	Pirates & Highwaymen	1925	40p	£10.00
50	Products of the World	1929	20p	£10.00
50	Railway Engines	1925	60p	£30.00
50	Railway Working	1927	£1.25	£62.50
50	Regimental Standards and Cap Badges	1928	40p	£20.00
50	Riders of the World	1931	50p	£25.00
50	Romance of the Heavens	1928	£1.25	—
50	Safety First	1935	50p	£25.00
F50	Ships and Shipping	1928	20p	£10.00
50	Ships' Badges	1925	65p	£32.50
F50	The Royal Family at Home and Abroad	1927	40p	£20.00
F50	The Royal Navy	1929	£1.00	£50.00
F50	Units of the British Army and R.A.F.	1928	20p	£10.00
50	U.S.S. Co's. Steamers	1930	£1.55	—
50	V.C.'s	1926	90p	£45.00
25	Village Models Series	1925	75p	£18.75
L25	Village Models Series	1925	£3.75	—
50	Warships	1926	90p	£45.00
25	Wonders of the World	1926	40p	£10.00
F50	"Zoo"	1926	20p	£8.75

OTHER OVERSEAS ISSUES

Qty		Date	Odds	Sets
50	Actors & Actresses "WALP" (Black)	1905	£1.90	—
50	Actors & Actresses "WALP" (Flesh Tint)	1905	£1.90	£95.00
250	Actresses "ALWICS" (Black & Red Front)	1905	£1.00	£250.00
250	Actresses "ALWICS" (All Red Front)	1905	£1.90	—
250	Actresses "ALWICS" (All Black Front)	1905	£1.90	—
250	Actresses "ALWICS" (No Address on Back)	1905	£1.90	—
25	Actresses, Tabs Type (101-125)	1902	£10.00	£250.00
50	Actresses, Four Colour Surround (Matt)	1904	£1.90	£95.00
50	Actresses, Four Colour Surround (Varnished)	1904	£1.90	£95.00
50	Aeroplanes	1926	£1.90	—
50	Animals & Birds (With Series Title)	1912	£3.15	£157.50
50	Animals & Birds (No Series Title)	1909	£3.15	£157.50
50	Arms of the British Empire	1911	75p	£37.50
50	Art Photogravures—Set 1	1912	45p	£22.50
B50	Art Photogravures—Set 1	1912	50p	£25.00
50	Art Photogravures—Set 2	1913	45p	£22.50
50	Aviation Series (Wills on Back)	1911	£1.90	£95.00
50	Aviation Series (Anon. Back, Album Clause)	1911	£1.90	£95.00
50	Aviation Series (Anon. Back, No Clause)	1911	£1.90	£95.00
50	Beauties "LAWHA" (Red Tinted)	1905	£1.25	£62.50
40	Beauties (Brown Tinted)	1913	£2.20	—
52	Beauties (P/C Inset)	1911	£4.40	—
32	Beauties—Picture Hats	1914	£4.40	£141.00
M72	Beauties	1923	£10.00	—
BF50	Beauties (Hand Coloured)	1925	£2.20	—
F25	Beauties	1925	£2.50	—
F50	Beauties, 2nd Series	1925	£2.50	—

W. D. & H. O. WILLS LTD.—cont.

Qty		Date	Odds	Sets
52	Birds of Brilliant Plumage (P/C Inset)	1914	£3.75	£187.50
36	Boxers	1911	£4.40	£158.50
50	Britain's Defenders	1914	£1.50	£75.00
101	British Beauties	1915	£1.55	£156.50
50	British Costumes From 100 BC to 1904	1905	£50.00	—
50	Chateaux	1925	£3.15	£157.50
50	Conundrums	1903	£8.00	£400.00
25	Derby Day Series	1914	£5.00	—
32	Drum Horses	1909	£4.40	£140.00
26	Etchings (Gold Flake Cigarettes)	1925	£4.40	—
26	Etchings (Dutch Text, Frame on Back)	1925	£5.00	—
26	Etchings (Dutch Text, No Frame Line)	1925	£5.00	—
50	Famous Footballers	1914	£5.00	—
25	Flag Girls of all Nations	1908	£1.75	£43.75
126	Flags & Ensigns	1904	80p	£100.00
6	Flags of the Allies (Shaped)	1915	£9.40	£56.50
50	Girls of all Nations	1908	£2.20	—
32	Houses of Parliament	1912	£1.55	£50.00
50	Indian Regiments Series	1912	£6.25	—
24	Merveilles Du Monde	1927	£5.00	—
M25	Miniatures (Metal)	1914	£37.50	£937.50
F48	Movie Stars	1927	£2.50	—
50	National Flags and Arms	1936	£1.25	—
FS50	Nature Studies	1928	£1.25	—
25	Police of the World	1910	£6.25	£156.50
25	Products of the World	1913	£1.50	£37.50
50	Races of Mankind	1911	£10.00	£500.00
100	Royalty, Notabilities & Events, 1900-2	1902	£1.55	£155.00
27	Rulers of the World	1911	£5.00	£135.00
100	Russo Japanese Series (Black Front, 2 Printings)	1905	£1.15	£115.00
50	Russo Japanese Series (Red Front)	1905	£6.25	—
LF48	Scenes From The Empire	1939	£1.50	—
30	Semaphore Signalling	1910	£2.00	£60.00
36	Ships & Their Pennants	1913	£4.40	—
75	Soldiers of the World	1903	£7.50	—
F52	Stars of the Cinema	1926	£3.75	—
25	The Evolution of the British Navy	1915	£2.00	£50.00
25	The World's Dreadnoughts	1910	£1.50	£37.50
50	Wild Animals of the World (Star, Circle & Leaves)	1906	£6.25	—

WILSON & CO.

50	War Portraits	1916	£62.50	—

W. WILSON

30	Army Pictures, Cartoons, etc.	1916	£62.50	—

A. & M. WIX

D250	Cinema Cavalcade	1940	40p	£100.00
D250	Cinema Cavalcade, Volume 2	1940	40p	£100.00
100	Film Favourites	1930	£1.55	—
100	Film Favourites, 2nd Series	1931	£1.55	—

A. & M. WIX—cont.

Qty		Date	Odds	Sets
100	Film Favourites, 3rd Series	1932	65p	£65.00
L?23	Maxims of Max (Package Issue)	1952	£6.25	—
X100	Men of Destiny	1934	£1.25	£125.00
D250	Speed—Through the Ages (English Text)	1938	25p	£62.50
D250	Speed—Through the Ages (2 Languages)	1938	25p	—
D250	This Age of Power & Wonder	1935	25p	£62.50

J. WIX & SONS LTD.

Qty		Date	Odds	Sets
F?	Animals	1928	£31.25	—
P80	Bridge Favours & Place Cards	1937	£10.00	—
P50	Bridge Hands	1937	£10.00	—
L48	British Empire Flags (Silk)	1934	50p	£24.00
L48	British Empire Flags (Printed in U.S.A.)	1934	50p	£24.00
50	Builders of the Empire	1937	20p	£10.00
42	Card Tricks	1938	£2.50	—
M42	Card Tricks	1938	£2.50	—
50	Coronation (Kensitas)	1937	20p	£8.00
50	Coronation (Wix)	1937	20p	£8.00
L50	Henry	1935	40p	£20.00
P25	Henry	1935	£2.00	£50.00
L50	Henry, 2nd Series (No Album Price)	1936	£1.25	
L50	Henry, 2nd Series (With Album Price)	1936	75p	£37.50
P25	Henry, 2nd Series	1936	£2.00	£50.00
L50	Henry, 3rd Series	1936	30p	£15.00
L50	Henry, 4th Series	1936	30p	£15.00
L50	Henry, 5th Series	1937	30p	£15.00
L101	Jenkynisms, 1st Series (Yellow)	1932	75p	—
L50	Jenkynisms, 2nd Series (Yellow)	1932	75p	—
L30	Jenkynisms, 3rd Series (Yellow)	1932	75p	—
L1	Jenkynisms, 4th Series (Yellow)	1932	—	£1.90
8	Jenkynisms (Red Borders, Unnumbered)	1931	£2.50	
?44	Jenkynisms (Red Borders, Numbered)	1931	£2.50	—
?30	Jenkynisms (Red Borders, Series B)	1931	£2.50	—
?19	Jenkynisms (Red Borders, Series C)	1931	£2.50	—
?34	Jenkynisms (Red Borders, Series D)	1931	£2.50	—
?3	Jenkynisms (Red Borders, Series E)	1931	£5.00	—
6	Jenkynisms (Red Borders, Vertical)	1931	£4.40	—
L46	Jenkynisms (Red Borders, Unnumbered)	1931	£2.50	—
?L44	Jenkynisms (Red Borders, Numbered)	1931	£2.50	—
?L30	Jenkynisms (Red Borders, Series B)	1931	£2.50	—
?L19	Jenkynisms (Red Borders, Series C)	1931	£2.50	—
?L34	Jenkynisms (Red Borders, Series D)	1931	£2.50	—
?L3	Jenkynisms (Red Borders, Series E)	1931	£5.00	—
L6	Jenkynisms (Red Borders, Vertical)	1931	£4.40	—
P96	Ken-Cards	1969	25p	£24.00
60	Kensitas Flowers (Silk, Plain Back)	1933	£2.00	£120.00
60	Kensitas Flowers (Silk, 3 Printed Backs)	1933	£2.00	£120.00
L60	Kensitas Flowers (Silk, Plain Back)	1933	£3.00	£180.00
L60	Kensitas Flowers (Silk, 3 Printed Backs)	1933	£3.00	£180.00
P30	Kensitas Flowers (Silk, Plain Backs)	1933	£30.00	—
P30	Kensitas Flowers (Silk, 3 Printed Backs)	1933	£30.00	£900.00
40	Kensitas Flowers 2nd Series (Silk)	1934	£3.25	£240.00
L40	Kensitas Flowers 2nd Series (Silk)	1934	£4.50	£325.00

J. WIX & SONS LTD.—cont.

Qty		Date	Odds	Sets
25	Love Scenes From Famous Films, 1st Series	1932	£2.00	£50.00
L25	Love Scenes From Famous Films, 1st Series	1932	£2.00	£50.00
P25	Love Scenes From Famous Films, 1st Series	1932	£3.15	—
19/25	Love Scenes From Famous Films, 2nd Series ...	1932	£2.00	£40.00
L19/25	Love Scenes From Famous Films, 2nd Series ...	1932	£2.50	—
P19/25	Love Scenes From Famous Films, 2nd Series ...	1932	£6.25	—
K53	Miniature Playing Cards (Blue Scroll)	1938	20p	£8.25
K53	Miniature Playing Cards (Red Scroll)	1938	20p	£8.25
K53	Miniature Playing Cards (Revenge)	1938	20p	£10.00
K53	Miniature Playing Cards (Victory)	1938	20p	£10.00
L60	National Flags (Silk)	1934	50p	£37.50
F24	Royal Tour in New Zealand	1928	£8.15	—
25	Scenes From Famous Films, 3rd Series	1932	£2.00	£50.00
P25	Scenes From Famous Films, 3rd Series	1932	£5.00	—

T. WOOD & SON

30	Army Pictures, Cartoons, etc.	1916	£62.50	—

WOOD BROS.

28	Dominoes	1910	£50.00	—

JOHN J. WOODS

?	Views of London	1905	£125.00	—

W. H. & J. WOODS LTD.

25	Aesop's Fables	1932	£1.25	£31.25
F50	Modern Motor Cars	1936	£2.80	£140.00
25	Romance of the Royal Mail	1931	75p	£18.75
25	Types of Volunteer & Yeomanry	1902	£20.00	£500.00

J. & E. WOOLF

50	Beauties "KEWA"	1898	£187.00	—

M. H. WOOLLER

25	Beauties "BOCCA"	1899	£187.00	—

T. E. YEOMANS & SONS LTD.

M72	Beauties	1900	£125.00	—
50	War Portraits	1916	£62.50	—

JOHN YOUNG & SONS LTD.

12	Naval Skits	1904	£125.00	—
12	Russo Japanese Series	1904	£62.50	—

A. ZICALIOTTI

1	Milly-Totty Advertisement Card	1900	—	£312.50

Part 2

OVERSEAS TOBACCO
MANUFACTURERS

AFRICAN TOBACCO MANUFACTURERS (S. Africa)

Qty		Date	Odds	Sets
L29	All Blacks South African Tour, 1928	1928	£8.00	—
60	Animals	1922	£3.00	—
MF48	British Aircraft	1926	£3.00	—
50	Chinese Transport	1923	£3.00	—
MF48	Cinema Artistes	1926	£2.50	—
50	Cinema Stars "OMBI"	1923	£1.50	—
50	Cinema Stars "OMBI", 2nd Series	1923	£1.50	—
B50	Famous & Beautiful Women	1938	£1.25	—
L50	Famous & Beautiful Women	1938	£1.00	£50.00
33	Houses of Parliament	1923	£5.00	—
?60	Miniatures	1924	£5.00	—
MF48	National Costumes	1926	£2.50	—
53	Playing Cards (MP)	1929	£1.25	—
53	Playing Cards (OK)	1929	£1.25	—
53	Playing Cards (Scots)	1929	£1.25	—
MF48	Popular Dogs	1926	£3.00	—
B100	Postage Stamps—Rarest Varieties	1930	£1.00	£100.00
B80	Prominent N. Z. & Australian Rugby Players & Springbok 1937 Touring Team	1937	£1.00	—
L80	Prominent N. Z. & Australian Rugby Players & Springbok 1937 Touring Team	1937	£1.00	£80.00
29	S.A. Rugby Football Team 1912-13	1912	£15.00	—
L30	Some Beautiful Roses (Silk)	1928	£6.25	£187.50
B132	S.A. Members of Legislative Assembly	1919	£20.00	—
25	The Arcadia Fair	1923	£6.25	—
25	The Racecourse	1923	£6.25	—
B100	The World of Sport	1939	£1.25	—
L100	The World of Sport	1939	£1.25	—
L25	Types of British Birds (Silk)	1928	£6.25	£150.00
L20	Types of British Butterflies (Silk)	1928	£7.50	—
L25	Types of Railway Engines (Silk)	1928	£18.75	—
L25	Types of Sea Shells (Silk)	1928	£9.25	—

ALLEN TOBACCO CO. (U.S.A.)

Qty		Date	Odds	Sets
X250	Views & Art Studies	1912	£3.00	—

ALLEN & GINTER (U.S.A.)

Qty		Date	Odds	Sets
50	American Editors	1887	£17.50	£875.00
X50	American Editors	1887	£21.50	—
50	Arms of all Nations	1887	£15.00	£750.00
50	Birds of America	1888	£8.75	£437.50
X50	Birds of America	1890	£16.50	£825.00
50	Birds of the Tropics	1889	£8.75	£437.50
X50	Birds of the Tropics	1889	£18.75	· —
50	Celebrated American Indian Chiefs	1888	£12.50	£625.00
50	City Flags	1888	£8.00	£400.00
50	Fans of the Period	1889	£17.50	£875.00
50	Fish from American Waters	1889	£8.75	£437.50
X50	Fish from American Waters	1889	£18.75	
48	Flags of All Nations	1887	£5.00	£240.00
50	Flags of All Nations, 2nd Series	1890	£6.25	£312.50
47	Flags of the States and Territories	1888	£8.00	£376.00
50	Fruits	1891	£15.00	£750.00

ALLEN & GINTER (U.S.A.)—cont.

Qty		Date	Odds	Sets
50	Game Birds	1889	£8.75	£437.50
X50	Game Birds	1889	£18.75	—
50	General Government & State Capitol Buildings .	1889	£8.75	£437.50
50	Great Generals	1886	£20.00	—
50	Natives in Costume	1886	£20.00	—
50	Naval Flags	1887	£9.00	£450.00
50	Parasol Drill	1888	£16.25	£812.50
F?	Photographic Cards (Many Types)	1885	£1.50	—
50	Pirates of the Spanish Main	1888	£20.00	—
50	Prize & Game Chickens	1892	£11.25	£562.50
50	Quadrupeds	1890	£9.00	£450.00
X50	Quadrupeds	1890	£18.75	—
50	Racing Colors of the World (No Border)	1888	£15.00	—
50	Racing Colors of the World (White Border)	1888	£12.50	£625.00
50	Song Birds of the World	1890	£8.75	£437.50
X50	Song Birds of the World	1890	£18.75	—
X50	The American Indian	1888	£20.00	£1000.00
50	The World's Beauties	1888	£15.00	£750.00
50	The World's Beauties, 2nd Series	1888	£15.00	£750.00
50	The World's Champions	1888	£10.00	—
50	The World's Champions, 2nd Series	1889	£12.50	—
X50	The World's Champions, 2nd Series	1889	£25.00	—
50	The World's Decorations	1890	£9.00	£450.00
X50	The World's Decorations	1890	£18.50	£925.00
50	The World's Racers	1888	£15.00	—
50	Types of All Nations	1889	£15.00	£750.00
50	Wild Animals of the World	1888	£10.00	£500.00
50	World's Dudes	1889	£15.00	£750.00
50	World's Smokers	1888	£11.25	£562.50
50	World's Sovereigns	1889	£18.50	£925.00

"SPECIAL ISSUES" (U.S.A. & Britain)

Qty		Date	Odds	Sets
F?150	Actresses, Celebrities & Children, Gold Borders	1887	£40.00	—
?25	Actresses, Collotype	1887	£62.50	—
20	Children, Gold Background, Set 1	1887	£62.50	—
20	Children, Gold Background, Set 1 (Holborn)	1887	£125.00	—
50	Children, Gold Background, Set 2, Plain Back	1887	£62.50	—
30	Children, Gold Background, Set 3	1887	£62.50	—
?	Sepia-Litho Series	1887	£50.00	—
9	Women Baseball Players (2 Types)	1887	£50.00	—
?	Woodburytype Series	1887	£50.00	—

PRINTED ALBUMS (EXCHANGED FOR COUPONS)

		Date	Odds	Sets
	American Editors	1887	—	£85.00
	Birds of America	1888	—	£55.00
	Birds of the Tropics	1889	—	£65.00
	Celebrated American Indian Chiefs	1888	—	£95.00
	City Flags	1888	—	£55.00
	Decorations of the Principal Orders	1890	—	£55.00
	Fish from American Waters	1889	—	£55.00
	Flags of All Nations	1890	—	£65.00
	Game Birds	1889	—	£50.00
	General Government & State Capitol Buildings of the United States	1889	—	£55.00

ALLEN & GINTER (U.S.A.)—cont.

Qty		Date	Odds	Sets
	George Washington	1889	—	£65.00
	Napoleon	1889	—	£65.00
	Our Navy	1889	—	£65.00
	Paris Exhibition 1889	1889	—	£65.00
	Quadrupeds	1890	—	£80.00
	Racing Colors of the World	1888	—	£80.00
	Song Birds of the World	1890	—	£50.00
	With the Poets in Smokeland	1890	—	£50.00
	World's Beauties, 1st Series	1888	—	£75.00
	World's Beauties, 2nd Series	1888	—	£75.00
	World's Champions, 1st Series	1888	—	*£275.00*
	World's Champions, 2nd Series	1889	—	*£275.00*
	World's Inventors	1888	—	£70.00
	World's Racers	1888	—	£95.00

AMERICAN CIGARETTE CO. (China)

Qty		Date	Odds	Sets
10	Admirals & Generals	1900	£40.00	—
25	Beauties (Black Back)	1902	£15.00	—
?25	Beauties (Green Back)	1901	£15.00	—
53	Beauties, Playing Card Inset	1901	£37.50	—
?	Chinese Girls	1900	*£50.00*	—
50	Flowers	1902	£10.00	£500.00

AMERICAN EAGLE TOBACCO CO. (U.S.A.)

Qty		Date	Odds	Sets
?25	Actresses, Blue Frame (Double 5)	1886	£43.00	—
?20	Actresses, Brown Front	1886	£50.00	—
36	Flags of All Nations	1890	£25.00	—
36	Flags of States	1890	£25.00	—
50	Occupations for Women	1892	£35.00	—
F?	Photographic Cards	1886	£3.75	—
LF?	Photographic Cards	1886	£7.50	—
23	Presidents of U.S.	1890	£37.50	—

AMERICAN TOBACCO CO. (U.S.A.)

EARLY ISSUES

Qty		Date	Odds	Sets
F100	Actresses (Black Back)	1901	£1.50	—
F300	Actresses (Blue Back, 2 Types)	1901	£1.50	—
44	Australian Parliament	1901	£3.00	£132.00
25	Battle Scenes	1901	£6.25	£156.25
177	Beauties (Typeset Back)	1901	£1.50	—
350	Beauties (Old Gold Back)	1901	£1.25	—
101	Beauties (Label Back)	1901	£1.75	—
?500	Beauties (Green Net Back)	1901	£1.25	—
?75	Beauties (Blue Net Back)	1901	£6.25	—
24	Beauties (Plain Back, Carton)	1901	£2.50	£60.00
25	Beauties, Black Background	1900	£6.25	£156.25
25	Beauties, Blue Frame Line	1900	£15.00	—
25	Beauties, Curtain Background	1900	£5.00	£125.00
28	Beauties, Domino Girls (2 Types)	1895	£15.00	£420.00
25	Beauties, Flower Girls (2 Types)	1900	£5.00	£125.00
25	Beauties, Flowers Inset	1900	£4.00	£100.00
25	Beauties, International Code of Signals, 1st	1900	£4.00	£100.00
25	Beauties, International Code of Signals, 2nd	1900	£5.00	£125.00

Qty		Date	Odds	Sets
50	Beauties, Marine & Universe Girls	1900	*£15.00*	—
25	Beauties, Numbered (2 Types)	1900	£12.50	—
25	Beauties, Orange Framelines	1900	£20.00	—
25	Beauties, Palette Girls	1900	£6.25	£156.25
25	Beauties, Palette Girls (Red Border)	1900	*£30.00*	—
F?	Beauties, Photographic	1894	*£12.50*	—
52	Beauties, Playing Card Inset, Set 1	1900	£6.25	
52	Beauties, Playing Card Inset, Set 2	1900	£5.00	£260.00
53	Beauties, Playing Card Superimposed	1900	£6.25	£330.00
25	Beauties, Star Girls (2 Types)	1900	£10.50	—
25	Beauties, Star Series	1900	£10.00	—
25	Beauties, Stippled Background	1900	£6.25	£156.25
100	Beauties, Thick Borders	1895	*£18.75*	—
25	Boer War, Series A (3 Types)	1901	£3.00	£75.00
22	Boer War, Series B	1901	£4.25	£93.50
L47	Boer War Celebrities (Kimball)	1901	£18.75	
L10	Boer War Celebrities Rutan	1901	£25.00	—
50	Butterflies	1895	£15.00	—
32	Celebrities	1900	£3.75	£120.00
25	Chinese Girls	1900	£8.00	—
1	Columbian & Other Postage Stamps	1895	—	£7.50
25	Comic Scenes	1901	£6.25	£156.25
50	Congress of Beauty, World's Fair	1893	£15.00	—
25	Constellation Girls	1894	£18.75	—
25	Dancers	1895	£8.00	—
50	Dancing Women	1895	£10.00	—
50	Fancy Bathers	1895	£10.00	—
25	Fish From American Waters (Green Net)	1900	£5.00	£125.00
50	Fish From American Waters (List Back)	1895	£8.00	—
28	Flags, Dominoes Superimposed (Carton)	1900	£3.00	£84.00
50	Flags of All Nations	1895	£6.25	
50	Heroes of The Spanish American War (Carton)	1900	£3.75	£187.50
?36	Japanese Girls	1900	*£30.00*	—
50	Jokes	1906	*£12.50*	—
25	Military Uniforms, A	1894	£10.00	—
25	Military Uniforms, B	1896	£8.75	£218.75
27	Military Uniforms, C (Green Net Back)	1900	£3.75	£100.00
27	Military Uniforms, C (Typeset Back)	1900	£5.00	£135.00
25	Military Uniforms, D	1900	£8.75	£218.75
50	Musical Instruments	1895	£10.00	—
50	National Flags & Arms (Green Net Back)	1895	£7.50	—
50	National Flags & Arms (Typeset Back)	1895	£7.50	—
25	National Flags & Flower-Girls	1900	£15.00	—
25	Old Ships, 1st Series	1900	£3.00	£75.00
25	Old Ships, 2nd Series	1900	£5.00	£125.00
50	Savage & Semi Barbarous Chiefs & Rulers	1895	£15.00	—
25	Songs A (2 Types)	1900	£8.00	—
25	Songs B	1900	£8.00	—
25	Songs C, 1st Group	1900	£5.00	£125.00
25	Songs C, 2nd Group	1900	£8.00	—
25	Songs D	1900	£4.25	£100.00
27	Songs E	1900	£7.50	—
25	Songs F	1900	£7.50	—
25	Songs G	1900	£5.00	£125.00

Qty		Date	Odds	Sets
25	Songs H	1900	£10.50	£262.50
25	Songs I	1900	£15.50	—
F150	Views	1901	£1.50	—

LATER ISSUES

Qty		Date	Odds	Sets
L50	Actors	1907	£2.50	—
L50	Actresses "Between The Acts"	1902	£5.00	—
G25	Actressess "Turkish Trophies" (Premiums)	1902	£10.00	£250.00
B85	Actress Series	1904	£4.25	—
L80	Animals	1912	90p	£72.00
L25	Arctic Scenes	1916	£1.75	£43.75
M15	Art Gallery Pictures	1915	£3.00	—
50	Art Reproductions	1904	£3.75	—
21	Art Series (Grand Duke)	1902	£10.00	—
P10	Artistic Pictures	1910	*£7.50*	—
18	Ask Dad	1905	*£9.25*	—
L50	Assorted Standard Bearers of Different Countries	1910	£3.75	—
B25	Auto-Drivers	1908	£7.50	£187.50
M50	Automobile Series	1908	£6.25	£312.50
L50	Baseball Folders	1907	*£10.00*	—
M121	Baseball Series (T204)	1907	*£10.00*	—
208	Baseball Series (T205, Gold Borders)	1907	*£9.25*	—
522	Baseball Series (T206, White Borders)	1907	*£8.75*	—
200	Baseball Series (T207, Brown Background)	1911	*£12.50*	—
?578	Baseball Series (T210, Red Borders)	1907	*£12.50*	—
75	Baseball Series (T211, Southern Association)	1907	*£15.50*	—
376	Baseball Series (T212, "Obak")	1907	*£10.00*	—
180	Baseball Series (T213, "Coupon")	1907	*£15.00*	—
?90	Baseball Series (T214, Victory Tobacco)	1907	*£15.00*	—
159	Baseball Series (T215, Red Cross)	1907	*£12.50*	—
L76	Baseball Triple Folders	1907	*£16.00*	—
50	Bird Series (Gold Border)	1912	£1.25	£62.50
50	Bird Series (White Border)	1912	£1.25	£62.50
30	Bird Series (Fancy Gold Frame)	1911	£1.50	£45.00
M361	Birthday Horoscopes	1910	£1.25	—
P80	Bridge Favors & Place Cards	1938	£3.00	—
P100	Bridge Game Hands	1938	£4.25	—
M24	British Buildings	1937	£1.75	£42.00
M42	British Sovereigns	1939	£1.50	£63.00
M50	Butterfly Series	1908	£2.00	—
L153	Champion Athlete & Prizefighter Series	1910	£1.50	—
X50	Champion Athlete & Prizefighter Series (Prizefighters Only)	1910	£3.00	—
L50	Champion Pugilists	1908	£5.00	—
X100	Champion Women Swimmers	1906	£4.25	—
M150	College Series	1914	80p	£120.00
G25	College Series (Premiums)	1904	£8.75	£218.75
M50	Costumes and Scenery for All Countries of The World	1912	£2.50	£125.00
X49	Cowboy Series	1914	£3.00	£150.00
M?50	Cross Stitch	1906	£7.50	—
L?17	Embarrassing/Emotional Moments	1906	*£12.50*	—
M50	Emblem Series	1908	£1.50	£75.00
L100	Fable Series	1913	£1.25	£125.00

Qty		Date	Odds	Sets
PF?53	Famous Baseball Players, American Athletic Champions & Photoplay Stars	1910	*£9.00*	—
100	Fish Series	1909	£1.25	£125.00
200	Flags of All Nations Series	1909	£1.00	£200.00
L100	Flags of All Nations Series (Red Cross)	1904	*£5.00*	—
50	Foreign Stamp Series A	1906	£3.75	—
L505	Fortune Series	1907	£1.00	—
G12	Hamilton King Girls (1-12, Sketches)	1902	£12.50	—
G12	Hamilton King Girls (13-24, Girls)	1902	£10.00	—
G12	Hamilton King Girls (25-36, Bathing Girls)	1902	£10.00	—
G25	Hamilton King Girls (37-61, Period Gowns)	1902	£10.00	—
G25	Hamilton King Girls (62-86, Flag Girls)	1902	£10.00	—
G25	Hamilton King Girls (1-25)	1913	£10.00	—
L?3	Helmar Girls	1902	*£28.00*	—
M79	Henry	1937	£1.00	£79.00
X50	Heroes of History	1912	£2.50	—
M50	Historic Homes	1913	£1.50	£75.00
X24/25	Historical Events Series	1911	£2.50	£60.00
M25	Hudson-Fulton Series	1908	£3.00	—
45	Imitation Cigar Bands	1909	£1.75	—
L50	Indian Life in The "60's"	1914	£3.00	£150.00
L221	Jig Saw Puzzle Pictures	1910	£3.00	—
L50	Lighthouse Series	1912	£2.30	£115.00
X50	Men of History 2nd Series	1912	£2.50	—
B100	Military Series (White Borders)	1908	£3.00	
50	Military Series (Gold Borders)	1908	£3.75	—
50	Military Series (Recruit)	1908	£3.00	—
50	Movie Stars	1915	£1.75	—
L100	Movie Stars	1915	£2.00	—
M25	Moving Pictures (Flip Books)	1910	*£12.50*	—
B15	Moving Picture Stars Series	1915	*£15.00*	—
X50	Murad Post Card Series	1905	£5.00	—
100	Mutt & Jeff Series (Black & White)	1908	£2.50	—
?183	Mutt & Jeff Series (Coloured)	1908	£3.00	—
F16	National League & American League Teams	1910	*£18.75*	—
G126	Prominent Baseball Players & Athletes (Premium)	1911	*£20.00*	—
50	Pugilistic Subjects	1908	£8.00	—
X18	Puzzle Picture Series	1904	*£9.25*	—
L200	Riddle Series	1907	£1.50	—
X?60	Royal Bengal Souvenir Cards	1906	£3.75	—
M150	Seals of the United States & Coats of Arms	1912	£1.00	£150.00
L25	Series of Champions	1906	£10.00	—
X50	Sights & Scenes of The World	1912	£2.00	£100.00
X50	Silhouettes	1908	£3.75	—
L25	Song Bird Series	1905	*£6.25*	—
50	Sports Champions	1908	£8.75	—
45	Stage Stars (Transfers)	1910	*£5.00*	—
B25	State Girl Series	1910	£3.75	—
L50	Theatres Old and New Series	1912	£2.50	—
L?100	The World's Best Short Stories	1910	£9.25	—
L25	The World's Greatest Explorers	1914	£2.00	£50.00
L50	Toast Series (Sultan)	1910	*£3.75*	—
M550	Toast Series (Mogul)	1910	£1.00	—

AMERICAN TOBACCO CO. (U.S.A.)—cont.

Qty		Date	Odds	Sets
X25	Toasts	1910	£7.50	—
50	Types of Nations Series	1912	£1.50	£75.00
M25	Up To Date Baseball Comics	1908	£8.75	—
L26	Up To Date Comics	1908	£4.25	—
250	Up To Date War Pictures	1916	£1.00	—
F?500	World Scenes & Portraits	1910	£1.50	—
X50	World's Champion Athletes	1909	£6.25	—

SILK ISSUES

Qty		Date	Odds	Sets
M111	Actresses	1910	£3.00	—
X2	Actresses	1910	£37.50	£67.50
L15	Animals	1910	£4.50	£67.50
P250	Athlete and College Seal	1910	£3.00	—
G250	Athlete and College Seal	1910	£3.75	—
B?12	Automobile Pennants	1910	£40.00	—
M?100	Baseball—Actress Series	1910	£4.25	—
M125	Baseball Players	1910	£12.50	—
G25	Baseball Players	1910	£18.75	—
M25	Bathing Beach Girls	1910	£6.25	£150.00
G6	Bathing Girls	1910	£10.00	£60.00
X50	Birds, Set 1	1910	£3.75	—
B26	Birds, Set 2	1910	£3.75	—
B30	Birds, Set 3	1910	£3.75	—
L20	Birds in Flight	1910	£4.25	£85.00
L25	Breeds of Dogs	1910	£6.25	—
L10	Breeds of Fowls	1910	£6.25	—
P6	Butterflies	1910	£10.00	£60.00
L25	Butterflies & Moths, Set 1	1910	£2.50	—
L50	Butterflies & Moths, Set 2	1910	£2.50	—
L25	Butterflies & Moths, Set 3	1910	£3.00	—
B77	City Seals	1910	£2.50	—
G50	College Flag, Seal, Song, Yell	1910	£4.25	—
T26	College Pennants	1910	£4.25	—
B145	College Seals	1910	£1.75	—
G?7	College Yells	1910	£12.50	—
L10	Comics	1910	£6.25	£62.50
M25	Domestic Animals' Heads	1910	£4.25	£106.25
G6	Domestic Animals' Heads	1910	£10.00	£60.00
M50	Emblem Series	1910	£3.75	—
L15	Famous Queens	1910	£6.25	—
L11	Feminine Types	1910	£6.25	£68.75
D322	Flags & Arms (Woven)	1910	£1.75	—
P24	Flag Girls of all Nations	1910	£5.00	—
G24	Flag Girls of all Nations	1910	£6.25	—
X50	Flowers, Set 1	1910	£3.75	—
M25	Flowers, Set 2	1910	£3.75	—
L50	Flowers, Set 2	1910	£4.25	—
L52	Flowers, Set 3	1910	£3.75	—
L10	Fruits	1910	£5.00	£50.00
G5	Generals	1910	£50.00	—
M10	Girls (Portrait in Circle)	1910	£18.75	—
L10	Girls (Portrait in Circle)	1910	£31.25	—
G10	Girls (Portrait in Circle)	1910	£42.50	—
G?50	Hatbands	1910	£9.25	—
M50	Indian Portraits	1910	£3.75	—

AMERICAN TOBACCO CO. (U.S.A.)—cont.

Qty		Date	Odds	Sets
G6	Indian Portraits	1910	£12.50	—
L25	Indian Portraits & Scenes	1910	£5.00	—
P10	Indian Portraits & Scenes	1910	£8.75	—
G12	King Girls	1910	*£7.50*	—
G20	Kink Series	1910	*£37.50*	—
B51	Military & Lodge Medals	1910	£3.00	£150.00
L?5	Miniature National Flags	1910	*£18.75*	—
L10	Mottoes & Quotations	1910	£5.00	£50.00
L25	National Arms (Silko)	1910	£2.50	—
B42	National Arms (Woven)	1910	£3.00	£126.00
L154	National Flags	1910	£1.50	—
G?150	National Flags (Many Styles)	1910	£2.50	—
L25	National Flags & Arms	1910	£1.75	—
X40	National Flags & Arms	1910	£1.75	—
P53	National Flags & Arms (Many Styles)	1910	£2.50	—
X27	National Flags, Song & Flower	1910	£3.75	—
P20	National Flags, Song & Flower	1910	£3.75	—
G17	National Flags, Song & Flower	1910	£5.00	—
M50	Orders & Military Medals	1910	*£5.00*	—
B24	Presidents of U.S.	1910	£4.25	—
P24	Ruler With National Arms	1910	£8.00	—
P10	Rulers of The Balkans & Italy	1910	£9.25	£92.50
L120	Silk National Flags	1910	£1.25	—
M36	State Flags	1910	£3.00	—
B?11	State Flowers	1910	*£6.25*	—
M25	State Flowers	1910	£5.00	—
L25	State Girl & Flower	1910	£5.00	—
M50	State Maps & Maps of Territories	1910	£5.00	—
M48	State Seals	1910	£3.00	—
X?75	Twelth Night Miscellany	1910	£7.50	—
M25	Women of Ancient Egypt	1910	£6.25	—
L10	Zira Girls	1910	£6.25	£62.50

BLANKET ISSUES

Qty		Date	Odds	Sets
P?	Animal Pelts	1908	£4.25	—
G90	Baseball Players	1908	*£12.50*	—
P?	Butterflies	1908	£2.00	—
G?	Butterflies	1908	£2.50	—
P135	College Athlete, Pennant, Seals	1908	£1.75	—
G10	College Pennants	1908	*£3.75*	—
G53	College Seals	1908	£1.50	—
X?	Conventional Rug Designs	1908	£2.00	—
P?	Conventional Rug Designs	1908	£2.50	—
G?	Conventional Rug Designs	1908	£2.75	—
X5	Domestic Pets	1908	£5.00	—
P?	Miniature Indian Blankets	1908	£1.50	—
G?	Miniature Indian Blankets	1908	£1.50	—
E6	National Arms	1908	£2.50	—
P45	National Flags	1908	£1.00	—
G71	National Flags	1908	£1.00	—
E31	National Flags	1908	£1.50	—
G?	National Flags and Arms	1908	£1.75	—
X9	Nursery Rhymes	1908	*£5.00*	—
X13	Soldiers	1908	£8.00	—

AMERICAN TOBACCO CO. (U.S.A.)—cont.

Qty		Date	Odds	Sets
LEATHER ISSUES				
B15	Breeds of Dogs	1908	£5.00	—
X97	College Building, Shield, Etc.	1908	£2.50	—
P19	College Buildings	1908	£2.50	—
M14	College Fraternity Seals	1908	*£4.25*	—
M159	College Pennants	1908	£1.00	—
M112	College Pennants (Shaped)	1908	£1.50	—
X23	College Pennant, Yell, Emblem	1908	£3.00	—
M144	College Seals	1908	£1.00	—
M122	College Seals (Shaped)	1908	£1.50	—
M29	College Seals (Card Suit Shaped)	1908	£2.50	—
M19	Comic Designs	1908	£2.50	—
B23	Flowers	1908	£3.00	—
B9	Girls	1908	£3.75	—
M26	Girls (Alphabet Background)	1908	£4.25	—
M94	Mottoes & Quotations	1908	£2.20	—
M5	Movie Film Personalities	1908	*£6.25*	—
M21	National Flags	1908	*£3.00*	—
M45	Nursery Rhymes Illustrated	1908	£3.75	—
M56	State Seals	1908	£1.00	—
M18	State Seals (Pennant Shaped)	1908	£1.50	—
CELLULOID BUTTONS & PINS				
K245	Actresses	1901	£2.00	—
K152	Baseball Players	1901	*£10.00*	—
K8	Boer War Leaders	1901	£45.00	—
K362	Comic Pictures	1901	£2.50	—
K425	Comic Sayings	1901	£2.50	—
K14	Cricketers	1901	£87.50	—
K125	Flags	1901	£1.75	—
K48	Girls' Heads	1901	*£5.00*	—
K25	Jockeys	1901	*£6.25*	—
K48	State Arms	1901	£1.75	—
K187	Yellow Kid Designs	1901	*£5.00*	—

A.T.C. OF NEW SOUTH WALES (Australia)

Qty		Date	Odds	Sets
25	Beauties, Group 1	1902	£6.25	£156.25
25	Beauties, Group 2	1902	£7.50	£187.50

A.T.C. OF VICTORIA LTD. (Australia)

Qty		Date	Odds	Sets
100	Beauties	1902	£8.00	—

ATLAM CIGARETTE FACTORY (Malta)

Qty		Date	Odds	Sets
150	Beauties	1924	*£3.00*	—
B65	Beauties	1924	£1.75	—
B519	Celebrities	1924	£1.00	£500.00
L50	Views of Malta	1924	*£3.00*	—
B128	Views of The World	1924	*£3.00*	—

BANNER TOBACCO CO. (U.S.A.)

Qty		Date	Odds	Sets
X25	Beauties	1890	£20.00	—

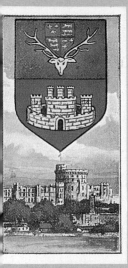

Heraldry of Famous Places.
Reddings

HENRY I.
BORN:1068. CROWNED:AUG.5.1100.
DIED: DEC. 1135. AGE 67.

Kings & Queens of England.
Godfrey Phillips

DRUM HORSE OF THE
3rd. (PRINCE OF WALES'S) Dragoon Guards.

Drum Horses.
Player, B.A.T., Wills

The Coronation Series.
Wills

CEYLON

Flags of All Nations.
Carreras

HONOURS & RIBBONS Nº 10.

Roberts' Star.

Honours & Ribbons.
Taddy

GIRDING ON THE SWORD

Coronation of Their Majesties.
Godfrey Phillips

Decorations and Medals.
Hill

Champions of Screen & Stage.
Gallaher

Film Stars (By Desmond).
Carreras

BETTE DAVIS

Screen Stars.
Abdulla

This Age of Power & Wonder.
A. & M. Wix

Burns.
Scottish C.W.S.

Beauties.
Richmond Cavendish

British Beauties.
Kuit, Phillips

Beauties, Green Net Back.
Ogden

AUG. BECK & CO. (U.S.A.)

Qty		Date	Odds	Sets
24	Actors & Actresses	1885	£50.00	—
?	Beauties—Burdick 488	1888	£44.00	—
25	National Dances	1889	£50.00	—
F?	Photographic Cards	1886	£4.00	—
?	Picture Cards	1888	£45.00	—
24	Presidents of U.S.A.	1890	£44.00	—
?	State Seals	1887	£50.00	—

DE BEER & CO. (Australia)

20	Admirals & Warships of U.S.A.	1908	£32.50	—
?14	Caricatures of Cyclists	1908	£40.00	—

BOOKER TOBACCO CO. (U.S.A.)

35	Indian Series	1906	£32.50	—
?20	U.S. Battleships	1906	£28.00	—

NICOLA BOSIOS (Malta)

?39	Opera Singers	1920	£25.00	—

BRITISH AMERICAN TOBACCO CO. LTD. (B.A.T)

336 Page Illustrated Tobacco War & B.A.T. Book—£12.50

(1) SERIES WITH FIRM'S NAME

30	Actrices	1905	£5.00	—
48	A Famous Picture Series, The Toast (Sect.)	1931	£1.75	—
BF50	Beauties	1925	£1.00	—
BF40	Beauties	1925	£1.00	—
25	Beauties, Art Series	1903	£6.25	—
25	Beauties, Black Background	1903	£6.25	£156.25
25	Beauties, Blossom Girls	1903	£28.00	—
25	Beauties, Flower Girls	1903	£5.00	£125.00
25	Beauties, Fruit Girls	1903	£8.75	£218.75
25	Beauties, Girls in Costumes	1903	£7.50	£187.50
20	Beauties, Group 1	1903	£6.25	£125.00
25	Beauties, Lantern Girls	1903	£5.00	£125.00
50	Beauties, Marine & Universe Girls	1903	£6.25	£312.50
25	Beauties, Numbered	1903	£15.00	—
25	Beauties, Palette Girls	1903	£6.25	£156.25
25	Beauties, Palette Girls (Red Border)	1903	£10.00	—
53	Beauties, Playing Card Superimposed	1903	£5.00	—
24	Beauties, Smoke Girls	1903	£10.50	£250.00
25	Beauties, Star Girls	1903	£10.00	—
25	Beauties, Stippled Background	1903	£5.00	£125.00
25	Beauties, Water Girls	1903	£5.00	£125.00
32	Beauties of Old China	1933	£1.75	—
M50	Birds, Beasts & Fishes	1934	£1.25	—
50	Buildings	1905	£6.25	—
25	Chinese Girls "A"	1904	£6.25	—
25	Chinese Girls "B"	1904	£6.25	—
25	Chinese Girls "C"	1904	£6.25	—
25	Chinese Girls "D"	1904	£6.25	—
25	Chinese Girls "E"	1904	£6.25	—
25	Chinese Girls "F1"	1904	£6.25	—

Qty		Date	Odds	Sets
25	Chinese Girls "F2"	1904	£6.25	—
50	Chinese Girls "F3"	1904	£6.25	—
40	Chinese Trades	1904	£5.00	£200.00
50	Danish Athletes	1906	£8.00	—
28	Dominoes	1908	£4.25	—
48	Fairy Tales	1928	£2.50	—
25	New York Views	1908	£7.50	—
53	Playing Cards	1908	£8.00	—
M50	Wild Animals	1930	£1.00	—

(2) SERIES WITH BRAND NAMES

(A) Albert Cigarettes (Belgium Etc.)

Qty		Date	Odds	Sets
L50	Aeroplanes (Civils)	1935	£3.75	—
50	Artistes De Cinema (1-50)	1932	£1.50	—
50	Artistes De Cinema (51-100)	1933	£1.50	—
50	Artistes De Cinema (101-150)	1934	£1.50	—
M48	Beauties	1928	£1.50	—
M75	Belles Vues De Belgique	1926	£1.60	£120.00
M50	Birds, Beasts & Fishes	1934	£2.50	—
M50	Butterflies (Girls)	1926	£2.50	—
M50	Cinema Stars, Set 1 (Brown)	1927	£1.50	—
M100	Cinema Stars, Set 2	1928	£1.50	—
M208	Cinema Stars, Set 3 (Unnumbered)	1928	£1.50	—
M100	Circus Scenes	1930	£1.75	—
M100	Famous Beauties	1916	£3.00	—
M100	La Faune Congolaise	1934	£1.00	—
M50	L'Afrique Equatoriale De L'Est A L'Ouest	1932	£1.75	—
M50	Les Grands Paquebots Du Monde	1924	£3.00	—
M50	Merveilles Du Monde	1927	£3.00	—
M50	Women of Nations	1922	£3.00	—

(B) Atlas Cigarettes (China)

Qty		Date	Odds	Sets
50	Buildings	1907	£3.00	—
25	Chinese Beauties	1912	£1.75	—
50	Chinese Trades, Set 4	1908	£1.75	—
85	Chinese Trades, Set 6	1912	£1.75	—

(C) Battle Ax Cigarettes

Qty		Date	Odds	Sets
M100	Famous Beauties	1916	£3.00	—
M50	Women of Nations	1922	£3.75	—

Cameo Cigarettes (Australia)

Qty		Date	Odds	Sets
50	Horses of To-Day	1906	£7.50	

(D) Copain Cigarettes (Belgium)

Qty		Date	Odds	Sets
52	Birds of Brilliant Plumage (P/C Inset)	1927	£4.25	—

(E) Domino Cigarettes (Mauritius)

Qty		Date	Odds	Sets
25	Animaux et Reptiles	1961	—	£2.00
25	Coursaires et Boucaniers	1961	—	£2.00
25	Figures Historiques, Une Serie	1961	—	£2.00
25	Figures Historiques, Seconde Serie	1961	—	£7.50
25	Fleurs De Culture	1961	—	£2.00
25	Les Oiseaux et L'Art Japonais	1961	—	£12.50
25	Les Produits Du Monde	1961	—	£2.00
50	Voitures Antiques	1961	—	£46.00

(F) Eagle Bird Cigarettes (China & Siam)

Qty		Date	Odds	Sets
50	Animals & Birds	1909	£1.50	£75.00
50	Aviation Series	1912	£1.75	—

Qty		Date	Odds	Sets
25	Birds of the East	1912	£1.50	—
25	China's Famous Warriors	1911	£1.50	—
25	Chinese Beauties, 1st Series (2 Types)	1908	£2.50	—
25	Chinese Beauties, 2nd Series (2 Types)	1909	£1.50	—
50	Chinese Trades	1908	£1.50	—
25	Cock Fighting	1911	£2.50	£62.50
60	Flags & Pennons	1926	£1.00	£60.00
50	Romance of the Heavens	1929	£1.50	£75.00
50	Siamese Alphabet	1922	£1.00	£50.00
50	Siamese Dreams & Their Meaning (2 Types)	1923	80p	£40.00
50	Siamese Horoscopes	1916	80p	£40.00
50	Siamese Play—Inao	1916	£1.00	—
50	Siamese Play—Khun Chang Khun Phaen 1	1917	80p	£40.00
50	Siamese Play—Khun Chang Khun Phaen 2	1917	80p	£40.00
36	Siamese Play—Phra Aphai, 1st	1918	80p	£28.00
36	Siamese Play—Phra Aphai, 2nd	1919	80p	£28.00
150	Siamese Play—Ramakien I	1913	70p	£105.00
50	Siamese Play—Ramakien II	1914	80p	£40.00
50	Siamese Uniforms	1915	£1.25	£62.50
50	Views of Bangkok	1928	£1.00	£50.00
50	Views of Siam (2 Types)	1928	75p	£37.50
30	War Weapons	1914	£1.50	£45.00
(G)	**Gold Dollar Cigarettes (Germany)**			
M270	Auf Deutscher Scholle	1934	£1.00	—
M270	Der Weltkrieg (1914)	1933	£1.00	—
M270	Deutsche Kolonien	1931	£1.00	—
M270	Die Deutsche Wehrmacht	1935	£1.00	—
?50	Do You Know?	1928	£3.75	—
B100	Filmbilder	1935	75p	£75.00
B100	In Prarie Und Urwald	1930	75p	£75.00
100	Wild-West	1932	75p	£75.00
(H)	**Kong Beng Cigarettes (China)**			
50	Animals	1912	£4.00	—
(I)	**Mascot Cigarettes (Germany)**			
100	Cinema Stars	1931	£1.75	—
M208	Cinema Stars	1924	£1.75	—
(J)	**Motor Cigarettes (Denmark)**			
50	Aviation Series	1911	£6.25	—
50	Butterflies & Moths	1911	£3.75	—
50	Flag Girls of All Nations	1908	£6.25	—
50	Girls of All Nations	1908	£6.25	—
	Old Judge Cigarettes (Australia)			
50	Horses of To-Day	1906	£7.50	—
FS50	Views of the World	1908	£6.25	—
(K)	**Pedro Cigarettes (India)**			
50	Actors & Actresses	1906	£2.50	—
37	Nautch Girls (Red Border, 3 Types)	1907	£1.50	—
40	Nautch Girls (Coloured)	1907	£1.50	—
52	Nautch Girls (P/C Inset)	1907	£1.75	—
(L)	**Pinhead Cigarettes (China)**			
50	Chinese Modern Beauties	1912	£1.00	£50.00
33	Chinese Heroes, Set 1	1912	£1.00	—
50	Chinese Heroes, Set 2	1913	£1.00	—
50	Chinese Trades, Set III (2 Types)	1908	£1.00	£50.00

BRITISH AMERICAN TOBACCO CO. LTD. (B.A.T.)—cont.

Qty		Date	Odds	Sets
50	Chinese Trades, Set IV	1909	£1.00	£50.00
50	Chinese Trades, Set V	1910	£1.00	£50.00
50	Types of the British Army	1909	£1.75	—
(M)	**Railway Cigarettes (India)**			
37	Nautch Girl Series (2 Types)	1907	£1.25	£45.00
(N)	**Shantung Cigarettes (China)**			
50	Chinese Curios	1928	£4.00	—
(O)	**Sunflower Cigarettes (China)**			
50	Chinese Trades	1906	£4.00	
(P)	**Teal Cigarettes (Siam)**			
30	Chinese Beauties	1917	£2.50	—
50	Cinema Stars (Blue Back)	1930	£1.00	£50.00
50	Cinema Stars (Red Back)	1930	£1.00	£50.00
30	Fish Series	1916	£1.50	£45.00
L15	Fish Series (Double Cards)	1916	£3.75	—
50	War Incidents	1916	£1.50	£75.00
(Q)	**Tiger Cigarettes (India)**			
52	Nautch Girl Series (P/C Inset, 4 Types)	1911	£1.25	—
	Vanity Fair Cigarettes (Australia)			
50	Horses of To-Day	1906	£7.50	—

(3) SERIES WITH PRINTED BACK NO MAKER'S NAME OR BRAND
(See also Imperial Tobacco Co. (Canada & India), United Tobacco Co.)

Qty		Date	Odds	Sets
250	Actresses "ALWICS" (Design Back)	1906	£1.75	—
50	Aeroplanes (Gilt Border)	1926	£1.25	£62.50
50	Aeroplanes of Today	1936	50p	£25.00
25	Angling	1930	£2.00	£50.00
25	Animaux Prehistoriques	1925	£3.00	—
L25	Arabic Proverbs (Silk)	1913	£10.00	—
50	Arms & Armour	1910	£3.00	—
L50	Arms of the British Empire (Silk, Blue Back)	1911	£2.50	£125.00
L50	Arms of the British Empire (Brown Back)	1911	£3.75	—
25	Army Life	1908	£4.00	—
50	Art Photogravures	1912	80p	—
1	Australia Day	1915	—	£7.50
L50	Australian Wild Flowers (Silk)	1913	£3.00	£150.00
22	Automobilien	1923	£5.00	—
75	Aviation	1910	£2.00	—
50	Aviation Series	1911	£1.60	£80.00
50	Beauties, Red Tinted (Design Back)	1906	£1.60	—
52	Beauties, Tobacco Leaf Back (P/C Inset)	1908	£1.75	£93.75
52	Beauties, Tobacco Leaf Back (No Inset)	1908	£3.00	—
F50	Beauties	1925	80p	—
BF50	Beauties (Hand Coloured)	1925	80p	—
F50	Beauties, 2nd Series	1926	60p	£30.00
F50	Beauties, 3rd Series	1926	60p	£30.00
F50	Beauties of Great Britain	1930	40p	£20.00
F50	Beautiful England	1928	30p	£15.00
50	Best Dogs of their Breed	1916	£2.00	£100.00
L50	Best Dogs of their Breed (Silk)	1913	£4.00	£200.00
50	Billiards	1929	£1.00	£50.00
50	Birds Beasts & Fishes	1937	30p	£15.00
M50	Birds Beasts & Fishes	1937	£1.00	£50.00
24	Birds of England	1924	£2.00	£50.00
50	Boy Scouts	1930	£1.25	£62.50

Qty		Date	Odds	Sets
50	Britain's Defenders (Blue Front)	1914	£1.00	—
50	Britain's Defenders (Mauve Front)	1914	80p	£40.00
50	British Butterflies	1930	60p	£30.00
50	British Empire Series	1913	£1.75	—
25	British Trees & Their Uses	1930	£1.50	£37.50
50	British Warships and Admirals	1915	£2.00	£100.00
50	Butterflies & Moths	1911	£1.00	—
50	Butterflies (Girls)	1928	£3.00	£150.00
M50	Butterflies (Girls)	1928	£3.00	£150.00
M50	Celebrities of Film and Stage (2 Types)	1930	£1.00	—
LF48	Channel Islands, Past & Present (2 Types)	1939	20p	£9.50
40	Characters from the Works of Dickens	1919	—	£39.00
38/40	Characters from the Works of Dickens	1919	50p	£19.00
50	Cinema Artistes (Black & White 1-50)	1928	75p	—
50	Cinema Artistes (Black & White 101-150)	1930	75p	—
60	Cinema Artistes, Set 1 (Brown, 2 Types)	1929	75p	—
50	Cinema Artistes, Set 2 (Brown, 2 Types)	1931	75p	—
M48	Cinema Artistes, Set 3	1932	£1.00	—
48	Cinema Celebrities (C)	1935	50p	£25.00
L48	Cinema Celebrities (C)	1935	75p	£37.50
L56	Cinema Celebrities (D)	1937	£1.75	—
50	Cinema Favourites	1929	£1.75	—
50	Cinema Stars, Set 2 (1-50)	1928	60p	—
50	Cinema Stars, Set 3 (51-100)	1930	60p	—
50	Cinema Stars, Set 4 (101-150)	1932	60p	—
100	Cinema Stars (Coloured)	1931	£1.25	—
F50	Cinema Stars, Set 1	1924	75p	—
F50	Cinema Stars, Set 2	1924	60p	£30.00
F50	Cinema Stars, Set 3	1925	80p	—
MF52	Cinema Stars, Set 4	1925	£1.00	—
MF52	Cinema Stars, Set 5	1926	£1.00	—
MF52	Cinema Stars, Set 6	1927	£1.25	—
LF48	Cinema Stars, Set 7	1927	£1.50	—
F50	Cinema Stars, Set 8	1928	80p	—
F50	Cinema Stars, Set 9 (51-100)	1929	80p	—
F50	Cinema Stars, Set 10 (101-150)	1930	80p	—
F50	Cinema Stars, Set 11 (151-200)	1931	80p	—
110	Crests & Badges of the British Army (Silk)	1915	£2.00	—
M108	Crests & Badges of the British Army (Silk)	1915	£1.50	—
M50	Crests & Colours of Australian Universities, Colleges & Schools (Silk)	1916	£2.00	—
25	Derby Day, Series A	1914	£6.25	—
50	Do You Know?	1923	30p	£15.00
50	Do You Know? 2nd Series	1931	30p	£15.00
25	Dracones Posthistorici	1938	£5.00	—
25	Dutch Footballers	1913	£5.00	—
25	Dutch Scenes	1928	£1.75	£43.75
50	Engineering Wonders (2 Types)	1930	40p	£20.00
40	English Costumes of Ten Centuries	1919	£1.00	£40.00
F25	English Cricketers	1926	£1.75	£43.75
26	Etchings (of Dogs)	1926	80p	£20.00
F50	Famous Bridges	1935	50p	£25.00
50	Famous Footballers, Set 1	1923	£1.50	£75.00
50	Famous Footballers, Set 2	1924	£1.50	£75.00

BRITISH AMERICAN TOBACCO CO. LTD. (B.A.T.)—cont.

Qty		Date	Odds	Sets
50	Famous Footballers, Set 3	1925	£1.50	£75.00
25	Famous Racehorses	1926	£1.80	£45.00
25	Famous Railway Trains	1929	£1.50	£37.50
50	Favourite Flowers	1923	50p	£25.00
50	Film and Stage Favourites	1926	80p	£40.00
75	Film Favourites	1928	80p	£60.00
50	Flags of the Empire	1928	60p	£30.00
50	Foreign Birds	1930	50p	£25.00
50	Game Birds and Wild Fowl	1929	80p	£40.00
LF45	Grace and Beauty (1-45)	1938	25p	£11.25
LF45	Grace and Beauty (46-90)	1939	20p	£9.00
LF48	Guernsey, Alderney & Sark	1937	20p	£10.00
LF48	Guernsey, Alderney & Sark, Second Series	1938	20p	£10.00
L80	Guernsey Footballers, Priaulx League	1938	25p	£20.00
F52	Here There & Everywhere	1929	25p	£12.50
25	Hints & Tips for Motorists	1929	£1.75	—
48	Hints on Association Football (Chinese)	1934	20p	£7.00
F50	Homeland Events	1928	50p	£25.00
50	Horses of Today	1906	£3.75	—
32	Houses of Parliament (Red Back)	1912	£1.50	£48.00
32	Houses of Parliament (Brown Back with Verse)	1912	*£6.25*	—
50	Indian Chiefs	1930	£4.60	£230.00
50	Indian Regiments Series	1912	£6.25	—
50	International Air Liners	1937	50p	£25.00
25	Java Scenes	1929	*£6.25*	—
LF48	Jersey Then & Now	1935	40p	£20.00
LF48	Jersey Then & Now, Second Series	1937	20p	£10.00
50	Jiu-Jitsu Series	1911	£2.00	—
?82	Joueurs de Football Belges	1923	*£4.25*	—
50	Keep Fit	1939	50p	£25.00
M60	La Belgique Monumentale & Pittoresque	1926	£2.50	—
50	Leaders of Men	1929	£1.75	—
50	Life in the Treetops	1931	40p	£20.00
50	Lighthouses	1926	75p	£37.50
40	London Ceremonials	1929	£1.00	£40.00
F50	London Zoo	1927	60p	£25.00
50	Lucky Charms	1930	£1.25	£62.50
25	Marvels of the Universe Series	1925	£2.00	£50.00
45	Melbourne Cup Winners	1906	£3.75	£168.75
50	Merchant Ships of the World	1925	£2.50	—
25	Merchant Ships of the World	1925	£2.50	—
25	Military Portraits	1917	£1.75	£43.75
LF36	Modern Beauties	1939	35p	£12.50
XF36	Modern Beauties	1936	75p	£27.00
36	Modern Beauties, First Series	1938	30p	£11.00
MF54	Modern Beauties	1937	60p	£33.00
36	Modern Beauties, Second Series	1938	20p	£7.50
MF54	Modern Beauties, Second Series	1938	60p	£33.00
XF36	Modern Beauties, Second Series	1936	45p	£16.00
MF36	Modern Beauties, Third Series	1938	60p	£22.00
XF36	Modern Beauties, Third Series	1936	25p	£9.00
MF36	Modern Beauties, Fourth Series	1939	60p	£22.00
XF36	Modern Beauties, Fourth Series	1937	20p	£7.50

Qty		Date	Odds	Sets
XF36	Modern Beauties, Fifth Series	1938	20p	£7.50
XF36	Modern Beauties, Sixth Series	1938	20p	£7.50
XF36	Modern Beauties, Seventh Series	1938	20p	£7.50
LF36	Modern Beauties, Eighth Series	1939	30p	£11.00
LF36	Modern Beauties, Ninth Series	1939	30p	£11.00
50	Modern Warfare	1936	50p	£25.00
M48	Modern Wonders	1938	£1.50	—
25	Modes of Conveyance	1928	£1.25	£31.25
48	Motor Cars (Coloured)	1926	£2.00	—
36	Motor Cars (Brown)	1929	£2.25	—
50	Motor Cycles	1927	£2.25	£112.50
F50	Native Life in Many Lands	1932	40p	£20.00
F50	Natural & Man Made Wonders of the World	1937	40p	£20.00
FS50	Nature Studies	1928	40p	£20.00
50	Naval Portraits	1917	£1.75	£87.50
32	Nederlandische Leger (Dutch Army)	1923	£3.75	£120.00
25	Notabilities	1917	£1.75	£43.75
25	Past & Present	1929	£1.50	£37.50
FS48	Pictures of the East	1930	40p	£20.00
M48	Picturesque China	1925	£1.00	£50.00
B53	Playing Cards	1940	20p	£5.00
36	Popular Stage, Cinema & Society Celebrities	1928	£2.00	—
25	Prehistoric Animals	1931	£1.50	£37.50
50	Prominent Australian & English Cricketers	1911	£25.00	—
25	Puzzle Series	1916	£3.00	—
50	Railway Working	1927	£1.00	£50.00
33	Regimental Pets	1911	£3.75	£125.00
50	Regimental Uniforms	1936	£1.00	£50.00
50	Romance of the Heavens (2 Types)	1929	50p	£25.00
FS50	Round the World in Pictures	1931	50p	—
50	Royal Mail	1912	£2.50	—
27	Rulers of the World	1911	£4.25	—
40	Safety First	1931	50p	£20.00
25	Ships Flags & Cap Badges, A Series	1930	£1.00	£25.00
25	Ships Flags & Cap Badges, 2nd Series	1930	£1.00	£25.00
F50	Ships and Shipping	1928	50p	£25.00
50	Signalling Series	1913	£1.75	—
100	Soldiers of World (Tobacco Leaf back)	1902	£8.00	—
50	Speed	1938	50p	£25.00
25	Sports & Games in Many Lands	1930	£1.50	£37.50
50	Stage & Film Stars	1926	£1.00	—
M50	Stars of Filmland	1927	£1.25	—
F50	The Royal Navy	1930	£1.50	—
F50	The World of Sport	1928	75p	£37.50
100	Transfers, Set 1	1930	£1.75	—
100	Transfers, Set 2	1930	£1.75	—
32	Transport of the World	1911	*£6.25*	—
20	Types of North American Indians	1931	£5.00	£100.00
F50	Types of the World	1936	50p	£25.00
F52	Ur Ollum Attum	1930	£2.50	—
FS270	Views of the World	1908	*£2.50*	—
48	Volaille, Pigeons & Chiens	1915	*£5.00*	—
25	Warriors of All Nations (Gold Panel)	1937	£1.00	£25.00
50	War Incidents (Blue Black)	1915	80p	£40.00

Qty		Date	Odds	Sets
50	War Incidents (Brown Back, Different)	1916	80p	£40.00
50	Warships	1926	£1.25	—
25	Whaling	1930	£1.50	£37.50
F50	Who's Who in Sport	1927	75p	£37.50
50	Wild Animals of the World (Tobacco Leaf Back)	1903	£5.00	—
25	Wireless	1923	£2.00	£50.00
50	Wonders of the Past	1930	60p	£30.00
50	Wonders of the Sea	1929	60p	£30.00
25	Wonders of the World	1928	60p	£15.00
40	World Famous Cinema Artistes	1933	75p	£30.00
L40	World Famous Cinema Artistes	1933	75p	£30.00
50	World's Products	1929	40p	£20.00
F50	Zoo	1935	50p	—
50	Zoological Studies	1928	40p	£20.00
B50	Zulu Chiefs	1932	£7.50	—

(4) SERIES WITH PLAIN BACKS

Qty		Date	Odds	Sets
50	Actors & Actresses "WALP"	1906	£1.50	£75.00
50	Actresses "ALWICS"	1907	£1.50	—
50	Actresses, Four Colours Surround	1905	£1.50	£75.00
30	Actresses, Unicoloured (Light Brown)	1910	60p	£18.00
30	Actresses, Unicoloured (Purple Brown)	1910	75p	£22.50
50	Animals & Birds	1912	£1.50	£75.00
60	Animals (Cut-Outs)	1912	£1.00	
50	Art Photogravures	1912	£1.25	—
50	Aviation Series	1911	£2.00	—
40	Beauties (Brown Tinted)	1913	£1.75	—
50	Beauties, Coloured Backgrounds	1911	£2.00	£100.00
50	Beauties, "LAWHA"	1906	£2.00	—
32	Beauties, Picture Hats I	1914	£1.50	£50.00
45	Beauties, Picture Hats II	1914	£1.50	£67.50
30	Beauties & Children	1912	*£3.00*	—
52	Birds of Brilliant Plumage (P/C Inset)	1914	£2.00	£100.00
30	Boy Scouts Signalling	1922	£2.00	£60.00
50	Butterflies & Moths	1910	£1.25	—
50	Cinema Artistes	1930	60p	—
50	Cinema Stars (1-50)	1927	60p	—
50	Cinema Stars (51-100)	1928	60p	—
50	Cinema Stars (101-150)	1930	60p	—
100	Cinema Stars (201-300)	1932	60p	—
50	Cinema Stars "BAMT"	1928	75p	£37.50
50	Cinema Stars "FLAG"	1929	60p	—
27	Dancing Girls	1913	£1.00	£27.00
32	Drum Horses	1910	£3.75	£120.00
50	English Period Costumes	1929	60p	£30.00
50	Flag Girls of All Nations	1911	£1.25	£62.50
165	Flags, Pennons & Signals	1907	50p	—
20	Flowers	1915	60p	£12.00
50	Girls of All Nations	1908	£1.50	£75.00
30	Heroic Deeds	1913	£1.25	—
25	Hindoo Gods	1909	£5.00	—
32	Houses of Parliament	1914	£2.50	—
25	Indian Mogul Paintings	1909	*£6.25*	—
53	Jockeys & Owners Colours (P/C Inset)	1914	£2.00	£106.00

BRITISH AMERICAN TOBACCO CO. LTD. (B.A.T)—cont.

Qty		Date	Odds	Sets
K36	Modern Beauties, 1st Series	1938	£1.50	—
36	Modern Beauties, 2nd Series	1939	£1.25	—
F48	Movie Stars	1928	£1.00	—
F50	New Zealand, Early Scenes & Maori Life	1929	£1.00	—
50	Poultry & Pigeons	1926	£2.00	—
25	Products of the World	1914	80p	—
50	Royal Mail	1912	£3.75	—
36	Ships & Their Pennants	1913	£1.50	£54.00
75	Soldiers of the World	1904	£6.25	—
30	Sporting Girls	1913	£2.00	—
50	Sports of the World (Brown)	1917	£2.00	—
50	Sports of the World (Coloured)	1917	£1.50	£75.00
M50	Stars of Filmland	1927	£1.25	—
25	The Bonzo Series	1923	£2.25	£56.25
32	Transport of the World	1917	75p	£24.00
50	Types of the British Army (Numbered)	1908	£1.25	£62.50
50	Types of the British Army (Unnumbered)	1908	£1.50	—
F50	Types of the World	1936	£1.50	—
F50	Units of the British Army & R.A.F.	1930	£1.25	—
FS50	Views of the World	1908	£1.00	—
50	War Leaders and Scenes	1916	£4.25	—
M50	Women of Nations (Flag Girls)	1922	£2.00	—

BRITISH-AUSTRALASIAN TOBACCO CO. (Australia)

?252	Flags of all Nations (2 Types)	1910	£5.00	—

BRITISH CIGARETTE CO. (China)

25	Actresses and Beauties (FECKSA)	1900	£50.00	—
25	South African War Scenes	1900	£17.50	£437.50

BRITISH LEAF TOBACCO CO. (India)

?20	Cinema Stars	1930	£6.25	—

BRITISH NEW GUINEA DEVELOPMENT CO.

50	Papuan Series 1	1910	£31.25	—

BROWN & WILLIAMSON TOBACCO CORPORATION (U.S.A.)

B50	Modern American Warplanes, Series A	1940	80p	£40.00
B50	Modern Warplanes, Series B	1941	£1.00	£50.00
B50	Modern Warplanes, Series C	1942	£1.00	£50.00
50	Movie Stars	1940	£3.00	—

D. BUCHNER & CO. (U.S.A.)

B45	Actors	1888	£17.50	—
X?100	Actresses	1888	£20.00	—
X?60	American Scenes with a Policeman	1888	£35.00	—
B120	Baseball Players	1888	£50.00	—
X?10	Butterflies & Bugs	1888	£42.50	—
P200	Defenders & Offenders	1888	£30.00	—
B31	Jockeys	1888	£25.00	—

D. BUCHNER & CO. (U.S.A.) —cont.

Qty		Date	Odds	Sets
X52	Morning Glory Maidens	1888	£31.25	—
X31	Morning Glory Maidens & American Flowers	1888	*£50.00*	—
X25	Musical Instruments	1888	£37.50	—
X25	New York City Scenes	1888	£37.50	—
B101	Police Inspectors	1888	£17.50	—
X100	Police Inspectors & Captains	1888	£17.50	—
X12	Presidential Puzzle Cards	1888	£50.00	—
X25	Yacht Club Colors	1888	£37.50	—

CALCUTTA CIGARETTE CO. (India)

25	Actresses (Blue Front)	1906	£17.50	—
25	Actresses (Brown Front)	1906	£22.50	—

A. G. CAMERON & CAMERON (U.S.A.)

?35	Actresses (Burdick 488)	1887	£45.00	—
24	Occupations for Women	1893	£37.50	—
F?	Photographic Cards	1893	£3.00	—
25	The New Discovery	1829	£21.50	—

V. CAMILLERI (Malta)

BF104	Popes of Rome	1922	£1.25	£130.00

CAMLER TOBACCO COY. (Malta)

F250	Footballers	1926	£2.50	—
B96	Maltese Families' Coats of Arms	1925	75p	£72.00

CASTELANO BROS. (India)

52	Beauties, Playing Card Inset	1899	£20.00	—

C. COLOMBOS (Malta)

F?200	Actresses	1902	£2.50	—
MF?53	Actresses	1902	£10.00	—
50	Actresses (Coloured)	1900	£7.50	—
BF?57	Celebrities	1900	£12.50	—
F136	Dante's Divine Comedy	1914	£1.50	£200.00
MF72	Famous Oil Paintings, Serie A	1910	60p	£42.50
MF108	Famous Oil Paintings, Serie B	1911	60p	£65.00
MF240	Famous Oil Paintings, Serie C	1912	60p	£145.00
MF100	Famous Oil Paintings, Serie D	1913	60p	£60.00
XF?91	Famous Oil Paintings	1911	£4.25	—
BF100	Life of Napoleon Bonaparte	1914	£1.50	£150.00
BF70	Life of Nelson	1914	£1.50	£105.00
BF70	Life of Wellington	1914	£1.50	£105.00
MF100	National Types and Costumes	1908	£1.75	£175.00
F?25	Opera Singers	1899	£21.50	—
120	Paintings and Statues	1913	50p	£60.00
B112	Royalty and Celebrities	1908	£2.00	£225.00

COLONIAL TOBACCOS (PTY.) LTD. (South Africa)

X150	World's Fairy Tales	1930	£3.00	—

CONDACHI BROS (Malta)

Qty		Date	Odds	Sets
25	The Bride Retires	1905	£17.50	—

D. CONDACHI & SON (Malta)

?10	Beauties	1910	£15.00	—

CONGRESS CUT PLUG (U.S.A.)

X?	Actresses	1890	£35.00	—

CONSOLIDATED CIGARETTE CO. (U.S.A.)

25	Ladies of the White House	1893	£21.50	—
B14	Ladies of the White House	1898	£27.50	£385.00
B25	Turn Cards	1894	£37.50	—
M25	Turn Cards	1894	£42.50	—

A. G. COUSIS & CO. (Malta)

254	Actors & Actresses	1924	50p	—
KF100	Actors & Actresses (Hand Coloured)	1906	£1.25	—
F100	Actors & Actresses (Hand Coloured)	1906	£1.25	—
F?	Actresses (Cairo Address)	1907	*£25.00*	—
KF100	Actresses, Serie I	1907	£1.00	—
KF80	Actresses, Serie II	1907	£1.00	—
F1900	Actresses, Serie I to Serie XIX	1907	£1.25	—
KF?2000	Actresses (Unnumbered)	1905	50p	—
F?1300	Actresses (Unnumbered)	1905	60p	—
MF?150	Actresses (White Border)	1902	£6.25	—
KF100	Actresses, Partners & National Costumes (Cousis')	1906	£1.25	—
KF200	Actresses, Partners & National Costumes (Cousis's)	1906	£1.25	—
F100	Actresses, Partners & National Costumes	1906	£1.50	—
50	Beauties, Couples & Children (Red Back)	1923	£1.50	—
MF50	Beauties, Couples & Children, Collection No. 1	1908	£1.75	—
MF50	Beauties, Couples & Children, Collection No. 2	1908	£1.75	—
MF50	Beauties, Couples & Children, Collection No. 3	1908	£1.75	—
F100	Bullfighters	1901	£4.25	—
F402	Celebrities (Numbered)	1906	60p	—
KF?2161	Celebrities (Unnumbered)	1905	60p	—
F?2161	Celebrities (Unnumbered)	1905	60p	—
XF?30	Celebrities & Warships (White Border)	1902	£7.50	—
MF72	Grand Masters of the Order of St. John	1909	£1.75	—
F100	National Costumes	1908	£1.50	—
MF100	Paris Exhibition, 1900	1900	*£18.75*	—
MF102	Paris Series	1902	*£18.75*	—
MF182	Popes of Rome (To A.D. 1241)	1904	£1.00	£180.00
MF81	Popes of Rome (Dubec, After A.D. 1241)	1904	£1.75	—
F100	Statues & Monuments (Numbered)	1905	£1.25	—
F100	Statues & Monuments (Unnumbered)	1905	£1.25	—
KF127	Views of Malta	1903	£1.00	—
F?100	Views of Malta (Numbered)	1903	75p	—
BF?127	Views of Malta (Numbered)	1903	75p	—

A. G. COUSIS & Co. (Malta) — cont.

Qty		Date	Odds	Sets
BF?65	Views of Malta (Unnumbered)	1903	75p	—
F?30	Views of the Mediterranean	1903	*£3.75*	—
BF?100	Views of the Mediterranean	1903	*£3.75*	—
F?557	Views of the World	1903	75p	—
BF?557	Views of the World	1903	75p	—
F99	Warships (White Border)	1910	£1.75	£175.00
KF850	Warships	1904	60p	—
BF850	Warships	1904	80p	—
BF?75	Warships & Liners (Dubec)	1904	£3.00	—
BF?25	Warships & Liners (Excelsior)	1904	£3.00	—
MF?50	Warships & Liners (Superior)	1904	*£3.75*	—

CRESCENT CIGAR FACTORY (U.S.A.)

T?12	Actresses	1886	£45.00	—

CROWN TOBACCO CO. (India)

X24	Actresses	1900	£37.50	—
96	National Types, Costumes & Flags	1900	£25.00	—
T96	National Types, Costumes & Flags	1900	*£37.50*	—
MF?	Photo Series	1900	*£37.50*	—

CHARLES C. DAVIS & CO. (U.S.A.)

?15	Actresses	1890	£42.50	—

DIAMOND INDIAN CIGARETTES

?25	Beauties	1924	£10.00	—

DIXSON (Australia)

50	Australian M.P.s & Celebrities	1900	£10.00	—

DOMINION TOBACCO CO. (Canada)

100	Photos (Actresses, Plum Background)	1905	£18.75	—
50	Photos (Actresses ALWICS)	1905	£18.75	—
50	The Smokers of the World	1904	£30.00	—

DOMINION TOBACCO CO. LTD (New Zealand)

50	Coaches and Coaching Days	1927	£1.00	£50.00
50	People and Places Famous in New Zealand History	1933	£1.50	£75.00
50	Products of the World	1929	80p	£40.00
50	U.S.S. Co's Steamers	1928	£1.75	—

DRUMMOND TOBACCO CO. (U.S.A.)

?20	Actresses	1895	*£50.00*	—
?50	Bathing Girls	1895	£50.00	—
25	Beauties "CHOAB"	1897	*£75.00*	—
X?25	Girls	1896	£45.00	—

DUDGEON & ARNELL (Australia)

Qty		Date	Odds	Sets
B16	1934 Australian Test Team	1934	£3.75	£60.00
B55	Famous Ships	1933	£2.00	£110.00

W. DUKE & SONS LTD. (U.S.A.)

Qty		Date	Odds	Sets
50	Actors and Actresses, Series 1	1889	£10.00	£500.00
B50	Actors and Actresses, Series 1	1889	£31.25	—
50	Actors and Actresses, Series 2	1889	£10.00	£500.00
B50	Actors and Actresses, Series 2	1889	£31.25	—
X30	Actors and Actresses (As Above)	1889	£20.00	—
X25	Albums of American Stars	1886	£35.00	—
X25	Battle Scenes	1887	£20.00	—
X25	Beauties, Black Border	1886	£17.50	£437.50
X25	Beauties, Folders	1886	£37.50	—
X25	Bicycle and Trick Riders	1891	£22.00	—
X25	Breeds of Horses	1892	£20.00	£500.00
X25	Bridges	1888	£18.75	£468.75
X25	Burlesque Scenes	1889	£20.00	—
50	Coins of all Nations	1889	£10.00	£500.00
X25	Comic Characters	1887	£18.75	£468.75
X25	Cowboy Scenes	1888	£22.50	—
X50	Fairest Flowers in the World	1887	£20.00	—
F45	Famous Ships	1884	£6.25	—
50	Fancy Dress Ball Costumes	1887	£10.00	£500.00
B50	Fancy Dress Ball Costumes	1887	£31.25	—
X50	Fancy Dress Ball Costumes	1887	£20.00	—
50	Fishers and Fish	1888	£10.00	£500.00
X25	Fishers and Fishing	1888	£20.00	—
X25	Flags & Costumes	1892	£22.00	£550.00
50	Floral Beauties & Language of Flowers	1893	£10.00	£500.00
X25	French Novelties	1891	£20.00	—
X25	Gems of Beauty (2 Types)	1884	£20.00	—
50	Great Americans	1888	£10.50	£525.00
X16	Great Americans	1888	£20.00	—
25	Gymnastic Exercises (Duke in Blue)	1887	£18.75	£468.75
25	Gymnastic Exercises (Duke in Brown)	1887	£18.75	£468.75
X25	Habitations of Man	1890	£18.75	£468.75
50	Histories of Generals (Booklets)	1889	£15.00	£750.00
X50	Histories of Generals	1889	£20.00	—
50	Histories of Poor Boys & Other Famous People (Booklets)	1889	£16.00	£800.00
50	Holidays	1890	£10.00	£500.00
X25	Illustrated Songs	1893	£20.00	—
X25	Industries of the States	1889	£22.00	—
50	Jokes (2 Types)	1890	£11.25	£562.50
X25	Jokes	1890	£18.75	—
X25	Lighthouses (Die Cut)	1890	£20.00	£500.00
X25	Miniature Novelties	1891	£17.50	£437.50
50	Musical Instruments	1888	£15.00	£750.00
X25	Musical Instruments of the World	1888	£20.00	—
36	Ocean & River Steamers	1887	£18.75	£675.00
F?	Photographic Cards	1885	60p	—
MF?	Photographic Cards	1885	£1.50	—
XF?	Photographic Cards	1885	£1.50	—

W. DUKE & SONS LTD. (U.S.A.)—cont.

Qty		Date	Odds	Sets
53	Playing Cards (2 Types)	1888	£8.75	£462.50
50	Popular Songs and Dancers	1894	£15.00	—
50	Postage Stamp (3 Types)	1889	£11.25	£562.50
X25	Presidential Possibilities	1888	£18.75	£468.75
X15	Puzzles	1887	£25.00	—
50	Rulers, Flags & Arms (Folders)	1888	£11.25	£562.50
X50	Rulers, Flags and Coats of Arms	1889	£17.50	—
50	Scenes of Perilous Occupations	1888	£15.50	£775.00
X25	Sea Captains	1887	£25.00	—
50	Shadows	1889	£10.00	£500.00
X25	Snapshots from "Puck"	1889	£18.75	£468.75
X25	Stars of the Stage, (White Border)	1891	£18.75	£468.75
X25	Stars of the Stage, 2nd Series	1891	£20.00	£500.00
X25	Stars of the Stage, 3rd Series	1892	£18.75	£468.75
X25	Stars of the Stage, 4th Series (Die Cut)	1893	£20.00	£500.00
48	State Governors, Arms & Maps (Folders)	1888	£11.25	£540.00
X48	State Governors, Arms & Maps	1888	£17.50	—
X25	Talk of the Diamond	1893	£28.00	—
50	The Terrors of America & Their Doings	1889	£11.25	£562.50
M50	The Terrors of America & Their Doings	1889	£31.25	—
X50	The Terrors of America & Their Doings	1889	£18.75	—
50	Tinted Photos	1887	£15.00	—
50	Tinted Photos (Die Cut)	1887	£10.00	—
X25	Transparencies	1888	£45.00	—
X24	Tricks with Cards	1887	£25.00	—
X25	Types of Vessels (Die Cut)	1889	£20.00	£500.00
50	Vehicles of the World	1888	£15.00	—
X50	Yacht Club Colors of the World	1890	£20.00	—
50	Yacht Colors of the World	1890	£10.00	£500.00
B50	Yacht Colors of the World	1890	£31.25	

PRINTED ALBUMS (EXCHANGED FOR COUPONS)

		Date	Odds	Sets
	Costumes of All Nations (3 Series)	1890	—	£75.00
	Governors, Coats of Arms & Maps	1889	—	£55.00
	Postage Stamp Album	1889	—	£70.00
	Shadows	1889	—	£65.00
	Sporting Girls	1888	—	£165.00
	The Heroes of the Civil War	1889	—	£130.00
	The Rulers, Flags, Coats of Arms	1889	—	£65.00
	The Terrors of America	1889	—	£65.00
	Yacht Colors of the World (3 Series)	1890	—	£80.00

DUNGEY, RALPH & CO (Australia)

50	Australian Footballers	1906	£20.00	—
?55	Australian Racehorses	1906	£20.00	—

EAGLE CIGARETTES (Australia)

F50	Actresses (Photographic)	1890	£62.50	—

EGYPTIAN CIGARETTE COY. (Malta)

F120	Actresses	1906	£4.25	—
XF30	Actresses	1906	£18.75	—
264	Decorations & Medals	1908	£6.25	—
F100	Maltese Band Players	1910	£10.00	—

EGYPTIAN CIGARETTES MFG. CO. (China)

Qty		Date	Odds	Sets
?50	Actresses	1900	£37.50	—
25	Armies of the World	1900	£40.00	—
?	Beauties	1900	*£50.00*	—
30	Beauties "Nymphs"	1900	£40.00	—
?30	Chinese & South African Series	1900	*£50.00*	—
25	National Flags & Flowers—Girls	1900	£45.00	—
30	Old Masters	1900	£37.50	—
?55	Russo-Japanese War Series	1903	*£42.50*	—
25	Types of British & Colonial Troops	1900	£37.50	—
25	Warships	1900	£30.00	—

H. ELLIS & CO. (U.S.A.)

25	Breeds of Dogs (6 Types)	1890	£35.00	£875.00
25	Costumes of Women	1890	£50.00	—
25	Generals of the Late Civil War	1890	£60.00	—
F?	Photographic Cards	1887	£4.00	—

D. FANCIULLI & CO. (Malta)

50	Il Paradiso Perduto	1906	£5.00	—

LA FAVORITA (Canary Islands)

M30/58	Flags & Soldiers (Silk)	1915	60p	£18.00

JOHN FINZER & BROS. (U.S.A.)

X10	Inventors & Inventions	1891	£25.00	£250.00

G. W. GAIL & AX (U.S.A.)

X25	Battle Scenes	1891	£22.00	—
X25	Bicycle and Trick Riders	1891	£28.00	—
X25	French Novelties	1891	£20.00	—
X25	Industries of the States	1891	£22.00	—
X25	Lighthouses (Die Cut)	1891	£20.00	—
X25	Navy Library	1890	*£31.25*	—
X25	Novelties (Die Cut)	1890	£25.00	—
XF?	Photographic Cards	1885	£1.75	—
X25	Stars of the Stage	1891	£20.00	—

GENERAL CIGAR CO. LTD. (Canada)

X36	Northern Birds	1977	80p	£30.00

GENESEE TOBACCO WORKS (U.S.A.)

?50	Actresses	1888	£37.50	—

G. G. GOODE LTD. (Australia)

17	Prominent Cricketer Series	1924	£45.00	—

GOODWIN & CO. (U.S.A.)

50	Champions (2 Types)	1888	£20.00	—
50	Dogs of the World (3 Types)	1890	£15.00	£750.00
50	Flowers	1890	£15.00	£750.00

GOODWIN & CO. (U.S.A.)—cont.

Qty		Date	Odds	Sets
50	Games and Sports Series	1889	£17.50	£875.00
50	Holidays	1889	*£18.75*	—
50	Occupations for Women	1887	£50.00	—
?25	Old Judge Cards	1886	£50.00	—
F?	Photographic Cards	1886	£1.50	—
50	Vehicles of the World	1888	*£18.75*	—

PRINTED ALBUMS (EXCHANGED FOR COUPONS)

	Champions	1888	—	*£312.50*
	Floral Album	1890	—	*£100.00*
	Games & Sports	1889	—	*£175.00*

L. O. GROTHE LTD. (Canada)

52	Bridge Hands (3 Types)	1927	£4.00	—

THOS. W. HALL (U.S.A.)

B153	Actors & Actresses (Dull Background)	1881	£5.00	—
B112	Actors & Actresses (Black Background)	1882	£6.25	—
B?297	Actors & Actresses (Fancy Corners)	1884	£15.00	—
B?154	Actors & Actresses (Sun's Rays)	1890	£10.00	—
B?52	Actresses (Tiled Wall)	1888	£15.00	—
B?11	Actresses (No Borders, Hall on Front)	1892	£25.00	—
B25	Actresses (No Borders, No Hall on Front)	1892	£20.00	£500.00
T20	Actresses ("Ours")	1885	£50.00	—
B12	Athletes	1881	£42.50	—
B8	Presidential Candidates & Actresses	1880	£50.00	—
B22	Presidents of the United States	1888	£21.50	—
25	Theatrical Types	1890	£25.00	£625.00

HARTLEY'S TOBACCO CO. (S. Africa)

L19	S. African English Cricket Tour 1929	1929	£45.00	—

S. F. HESS & CO. (U.S.A.)

F?	Photographic Cards	1885	£5.00	—
55	Poker Puzzle Cards (2 Types)	1890	£37.50	—
25	Terms of Poker Illustrated	1890	£37.50	—

WM. G. HILLS (U.S.A.)

X25	Actresses	1888	£45.00	—

HILSON CO. (U.S.A.)

T25	Battleships & Signal Flags	1901	£17.50	£437.50
T25	National Types	1901	£17.50	£437.50

IMPERIAL CIGARETTE & TOBACCO, CO. (Canada)

?24	Actresses	1900	£40.00	—

IMPERIAL TOBACCO CO. OF CANADA LTD (Canada)

50	Actresses, Framed Border (Plain Back)	1910	£2.00	£100.00
L55/66	Aircraft Spotter Series (Packets)	1941	50p	£27.50

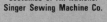

GEPPETTO & PINOCCHIO

Pinocchio.
Anon. U.S. Trade

Costumes of All Nations.
Singer Sewing Machine Co.

Useful Birds of America.
Church & Dwight

Horse Pictures.
Cowans

MARCOS 3 LITRE

Super Cars.
Sanitarium

CHURCHMAN'S CIGARETTES

THE PENANG-SINGAPORE EXPRESS, F.M.S. RAILWAYS

Empire Railways.
Churchman

Golden Age of Sail.
Player (Doncella)

CROSSLEY

Motor Cars.
U.T.C. (S.Africa)

LAMBERT & BUTLER'S CIGARETTES.

SCOTT SQUIRREL.

Motor Cycles.
Lambert & Butler

LAMBERT & BUTLER'S CIGARETTES.

VICKERS MONOPLANE.

Aviation.
Lambert & Butler

Transport Through the Ages.
Brooke Bond

IMPERIAL TOBACCO CO. OF CANADA LTD. (Canada)—cont.

Qty		Date	Odds	Sets
60	Animals (Millbank, 4 Types)	1916	60p	£36.00
L55	Animal With Flag (Silk)	1915	£2.25	£125.00
50	Arms of the British Empire	1911	£1.75	—
50	Around the World Series (Numbered)	1912	£3.00	—
50	Around the World Series (Unnumbered)	1912	£3.75	—
50	Aviation Series	1910	£1.75	—
90	Baseball Series	1912	*£15.00*	—
30	Beauties—Art Series (Plain Back)	1911	£8.75	—
30	Beauties—Art Series (Bouquet Cigarettes)	1902	£37.50	—
50	Beauties (Coloured, Black Border)	1912	£2.00	£100.00
25	Beauties—Girls in Costume	1904	£35.00	—
24	Beauties—Smoke Girls	1904	£37.50	—
M50	Birds, Beasts & Fishes (2 Types)	1924	£1.25	£62.50
30	Bird Series	1910	£1.25	£37.50
X100	Birds of Canada	1924	£2.00	—
X100	Birds of Canada (Western Canada)	1925	£4.00	—
50	Boy Scouts	1911	£3.50	£175.00
50	British Birds	1923	50p	£25.00
50	British Man of War Series (Plain Back)	1910	£7.50	£375.00
50	Buildings (Plain Back)	1902	£7.50	—
50	Butterflies & Moths	1911	£1.50	—
L24	Canada's Corvettes, 1st Series	1943	£6.25	—
L24	Canada's Corvettes, 2nd Series	1944	£6.25	—
50	Canadian Historical Portraits	1913	£2.50	—
48	Canadian History Series	1926	80p	£40.00
50	Canadian History Series (Anon)	1926	£1.00	—
P50	Canadian History Series (Silk)	1914	£9.00	—
T118	Canadian Miscellany (Silk)	1912	£3.00	—
50	Children of All Nations	1924	60p	£30.00
23	Dogs Series	1924	80p	£18.00
50	Dogs, 2nd Series	1925	75p	£37.50
50	Famous English Actresses	1924	80p	£40.00
50	Film Favourites (4 Types)	1926	£2.50	—
50	Fish & Bait	1924	90p	£45.00
50	Fishes of the World	1924	75p	£37.50
50	Fish Series	1912	£1.50	—
50	Flower Culture in Pots	1925	50p	£25.00
50	Fowls, Pigeons & Dogs	1911	£2.00	—
30	Game Bird Series	1925	60p	£18.00
L55	Garden Flowers (Silk)	1913	£2.00	£110.00
G5	Garden Flowers (Silk)	1913	£15.00	—
50	Gardening Hints	1923	40p	£20.00
L25	Heraldic Signs & Their Origin	1925	£1.00	£25.00
45	Hockey Players	1912	*£6.25*	—
36	Hockey Series (Coloured)	1911	*£6.25*	—
50	Hockey Series (Blue)	1910	*£6.25*	—
50	"How to do It" Series	1911	£2.00	£100.00
50	How To Play Golf	1925	£3.75	£187.50
50	Infantry Training (4 Types)	1915	£1.80	£90.00
100	Lacrosse Series, Set 1	1910	£3.00	£300.00
100	Lacrosse Series, Set 2	1911	£3.00	—
50	Lacrosse Series, Set 3	1912	£3.00	—
50	L'Histoire Du Canada	1914	£1.00	—
M48	Mail Carriers and Stamps	1903	£17.50	—

IMPERIAL TOBACCO CO. OF CANADA LTD. (Canada)—cont.

Qty		Date	Odds	Sets
50	Merchant Ships of the World	1924	75p	£37.50
25	Military Portraits (2 Types)	1914	£1.75	£43.75
50	Modern War Weapons	1915	£3.00	£150.00
56	Motor Cars	1921	£1.00	£56.00
50	Movie Stars	1925	75p	
50	Music Hall Artistes (Plain Back)	1911	£1.75	£87.50
50	Naval Portraits (2 Types)	1915	£2.00	£100.00
25	Notabilities (2 Types)	1915	£1.75	£43.75
L55	Orders & Military Medals (Silk)	1915	£2.00	£110.00
L50	Pictures of Canadian Life (2 Types)	1912	£5.00	—
52	Poker Hands (Many Types)	1924	75p	£39.00
25	Poultry Alphabet	1924	£1.00	£25.00
50	Prominent Men of Canada	1912	£2.50	
50	Railway Engines (3 Types)	1924	75p	£37.50
L55	Regimental Uniforms of Canada (Silk)	1914	£2.50	£137.50
P25	Rulers with Flags (Silk)	1910	£8.75	—
127	Smokers Golf Cards (2 Types)	1926	£2.50	£315.00
50	The Reason Why	1924	80p	£40.00
25	The World's Dreadnoughts	1910	£2.00	—
50	Tricks & Puzzles Series	1911	£3.00	£150.00
50	Types of Nations	1910	£1.75	—
25	Victoria Cross Heroes (Blue Back)	1915	£1.50	£37.50
L45	Views of the World	1912	£4.25	—
L25	Wild Animals of Canada	1912	£7.50	—
B144	World War I Scenes & Portraits	1916	£1.50	£215.00
X49	Yacht Pennants & Views (Silk)	1915	£4.25	£200.00

IMPERIAL TOBACCO CO. OF INDIA LTD. (India)

25	Indian Historical Views	1910	£1.25	£31.25
40	Nautch Girl Series (Pedro Cigarettes)	1908	£1.50	£60.00
40	Nautch Girl Series (Railway Cigarettes)	1908	£1.50	£60.00
52	Nautch Girl Series (P/C Inset, Pedro)	1908	£1.50	£78.00
52	Nautch Girl Series (P/C Inset, Railway)	1908	£1.50	£78.00
K52	Miniature Playing Cards	1933	75p	—
52	Playing Cards (3 Types)	1919	£1.50	—
1	Present Ticket	1917	—	£2.50

IMPERIAL TOBACCO CO. (NFLD) LTD (Canada)

B52	Playing Cards	1930	£5.00	—

JACK & JILL CIGARS (U.S.A.)

T25	Actresses "JAKE"	1890	£44.00	—

JAMAICA TOBACCO CO.

F?104	Miniature Post Card Series	1915	£5.00	—

KENTUCKY TOBACCOS (PTY) LTD. (S. Africa)

L120	The March of Mankind	1940	£1.00	£120.00

KEY WEST FAVORS (U.S.A.)

T25	Actresses "JAKE"	1890	£44.00	—

KHEDIVIAL COMPANY (U.S.A.)

Qty		Date	Odds	Sets
B10	Aeroplane Series No. 103 (2 Types)	1912	£10.00	£100.00
B10	Prize Dog Series No. 102 (2 Types)	1911	£12.50	—
M25	Prize Fight Series No. 101 (2 Types)	1910	£12.50	£125.00
M25	Prize Fight Series No. 102	1911	£15.00	—

WM. S. KIMBALL & CO. (U.S.A.)

Qty		Date	Odds	Sets
?25	Actresses, Collotype	1887	£50.00	—
72	Ancient Coins (2 Types)	1888	£21.00	—
48	Arms of Dominions	1888	£15.00	—
50	Ballet Queens	1889	£15.00	£750.00
X20	Beautiful Bathers (2 Types)	1889	£21.50	—
52	Beauties, Playing Card Insets	1895	£15.00	£780.00
50	Butterflies	1888	£16.00	—
50	Champions of Games and Sports (2 Types)	1888	£20.00	—
50	Dancing Girls of the World	1889	£15.00	£750.00
50	Dancing Women	1889	£15.00	£750.00
50	Fancy Bathers	1889	£15.00	£750.00
X25	French Novelties	1891	£27.50	—
X25	Gems of Beauty	1891	£30.00	—
50	Goddesses of the Greeks & Romans	1889	£16.00	—
X25	Household Pets	1891	£21.50	—
X15	National Flags	1887	£21.50	—
F?	Photographic Cards	1886	£2.50	—
XF?	Photographic Cards	1886	£3.75	—
X20	Pretty Athletes	1890	£21.50	—
50	Savage & Semi Barbarous Chiefs & Rulers	1890	£17.50	£875.00
L?25	Wellstood Etchings	1887	*£62.50*	—

PRINTED ALBUMS (EXCHANGED FOR COUPONS)

		Date	Odds	Sets
	Ancient Coins	1888	—	*£85.00*
	Ballet Queens	1889	—	*£80.00*
	Champions of Games & Sports	1888	—	*£85.00*
	Dancing Girls of the World	1889	—	*£80.00*
	Dancing Women	1889	—	*£80.00*
	Fancy Bathers	1889	—	*£80.00*
	Goddesses of the Greeks & Romans	1889	—	*£80.00*
	Savage & Semi Barbarous Chiefs & Rulers	1890	—	*£90.00*

KINNEY BROS. (U.S.A.)

Qty		Date	Odds	Sets
25	Actresses "Set 1"	1893	£6.25	£150.00
25	Actresses "Set 2"	1895	£10.00	—
50	Actresses (Group 2)	1891	£4.25	—
50	Actresses (Group 3)	1892	£4.25	—
50	Actresses (Group 4, Coloured)	1893	£4.25	—
150	Actresses (Group 4, Sepia, Plain Back)	1893	£1.75	—
25	Animals	1890	£12.50	£312.50
10	Butterflies of the World (White)	1888	£12.50	£125.00
50	Butterflies of the World (Gold)	1888	£10.00	£500.00
25	Famous Gems of the World	1889	£12.50	£312.50
25	Famous Running Horses (American)	1890	£14.00	£350.00
25	Famous Running Horses (English)	1889	£12.00	£300.00
F45	Famous Ships	1887	£7.50	—
25	Great American Trotters	1890	£16.00	—

KINNEY BROS. (U.S.A.)—cont.

Qty		Date	Odds	Sets
52	Harlequin Cards	1888	£12.50	£650.00
53	Harlequin Cards, Series 2	1889	£12.50	£662.50
L?4	Inaugural Types	1888	£75.00	—
X50	International Cards	1888	£27.50	—
K25	Jocular Oculars (2 Types)	1887	£35.00	—
25	Leaders	1889	£15.00	£375.00
50	Magic Changing Cards	1889	£15.50	—
50	Military Series A (Series 7)	1887	£3.75	£187.50
50	Military Series B (Series 8)	1887	£3.75	£187.50
30	Military Series C (Series 9)	1887	£4.25	£127.50
50	Military Series D (Coloured Background)	1887	£3.75	£187.50
50	Military Series E (1886)	1887	£3.75	£187.50
18	Military Series F (U.S. Continental)	1887	£3.75	£67.50
3	Military Series F (Vatican)	1887	£31.25	—
5	Military Series F (Decorations)	1887	£31.25	—
51	Military Series G (U.S. Army & Navy)	1887	£3.00	£150.00
85	Military Series H (U.S. State Types)	1887	£3.00	£255.00
60	Military Series I ("I.S.C" in 3 Lines)	1887	£6.25	—
50	Military Series J (English/Ngsny)	1887	£12.50	—
49/50	Military Series K (1853)	1887	£8.00	—
50	Military Series L (Foreign Types)	1887	£4.25	£212.50
15	Military Series M (French Army/Navy)	1887	£3.00	£45.00
5	Military Series M (State Seals)	1887	£25.00	—
50	National Dances (White Border)	1889	£10.00	£500.00
25	National Dances (No Border)	1889	£12.50	£312.50
25	Naval Vessels of the World	1889	£16.00	£400.00
50	New Year 1890 Cards	1889	£16.00	—
K25	Novelties (Circular, Thick Cards)	1888	£17.50	—
K50	Novelties (Circular, Thin Cards)	1888	£7.50	£375.00
75	Novelties (Die Cut)	1888	£6.00	£450.00
14	Novelties (Oval)	1888	£25.00	—
44	Novelties (Rectangular)	1888	£8.00	£350.00
F?	Photographic Cards	1886	75p	—
LF?	Photographic Cards	1886	£1.75	—
50	Surf Beauties	1889	£15.50	£775.00
1	Sweet Caporal Calendar	1890	—	£50.00
52	Transparent Playing Cards (3 Types)	1890	£12.50	£650.00
25	Types of Nationalities (Folders, 4 Types)	1890	£18.75	—

PRINTED ALBUMS (EXCHANGED FOR COUPONS)

		Date	Odds	Sets
	Butterflies	1889	—	£85.00
	Celebrated American & English Running Horses	1890	—	£95.00
	Leaders	1889	—	£65.00
	Liberty Album	1889	—	£65.00
	National Dances	1889	—	£95.00
	Natural History	1890	—	£65.00
	Reigning Beaties	1889	—	£90.00
	Singers & Opera Houses	1889	—	£95.00
	Surf Beauties	1889	—	£90.00

KRAMERS TOB. CO (PTY) LTD. (S. Africa)

50	Badges of South African Rugby Football Clubs (Multi-Backed)	1933	£4.25	—

LEWIS & ALLEN CO. (U.S.A.)

Qty		Date	Odds	Sets
X120	Views & Art Studies	1912	£4.25	—

LIGGETT & MYERS TOBACCO CO. (U.S.A.)

?30	Actresses	1890	£37.50	—

LONE JACK CIGARETTE CO. (U.S.A.)

25	Inventors and Inventions	1887	£42.50	—
50	Language of Flowers (3 Types)	1888	£20.00	—
F?	Photographic Cards	1886	£4.25	—

P. LORILLARD CO. (U.S.A.)

25	Actresses (Coloured)	1888	£18.75	£468.75
B20	Actresses (Irregular Gold Frame)	1889	£18.75	—
B?150	Actresses (Fancy Surrounds)	1889	£18.75	—
B75	Actresses (Plain Surround)	1890	£15.00	—
X25	Actresses (Burdick 263)	1889	£17.50	£406.25
X25	Actresses (Burdick 264-1)	1890	£17.50	£406.25
X25	Actresses (Burdick 264-2)	1890	£18.75	—
X25	Actresses (Burdick 264-3, Grey Border)	1890	£18.75	—
X25	Actresses in Opera Roles	1892	£31.25	—
T25	Ancient Mythology Burlesqued	1893	£17.50	£437.50
T50	Beautiful Women	1893	£17.50	£875.00
X25	Boxing Positions & Boxers	1887	£43.75	—
M?10	Busts of Girls (Die Cut)	1886	£75.00	—
X25	Circus Scenes	1888	£50.00	—
X?10	Everyday Annoyances	1886	£75.00	—
25	National Flags	1888	£20.00	—
T52	Playing Card Inset Girls	1885	£21.50	—
X50	Prizefighters	1887	£45.00	—
X?15	Song Album	1887	£50.00	—
T25	Types of Flirtation	1892	£43.75	—
T25	Types of the Stage	1893	£17.50	£437.50

W. C. MACDONALD INC. (Canada)

?350	Aeroplanes & Warships	1940	60p	—
53	Playing Cards (Many Printings)	1927	40p	—

B. & J. B. MACHADO (Jamaica)

25	British Naval Series	1916	£12.50	—
F50	Popular Film Stars	1926	£3.25	—
F52	Stars of the Cinema	1926	£3.25	—
50	The Great War—Victoria Cross Heroes	1916	£12.50	—
F50	The Royal Family at Home and Abroad	1927	£3.00	—
F50	The World of Sport	1928	£3.00	—

MACLIN-ZIMMER (U.S.A.)

X53	Playing Cards (Actresses)	1890	£18.75	£1000.00

MALTA CIGARETTE CO.

Qty		Date	Odds	Sets
135	Dante's Divine Comedy	1905	£9.00	—
M36	Maltese Families Arms & Letters	1905	£5.00	—
?41	Prominent People	1905	£9.00	—

H. MANDELBAUM (U.S.A.)

20	Comic Types of People	1890	£43.50	—
36	Flags of Nations	1890	£31.25	—

MARBURG BROS (U.S.A.)

50	"National Costume" Cards (2 Types)	1887	£42.50	—
50	Typical Ships	1887	£50.00	—

MASPERO FRERES LTD. (Palestine)

50	Birds, Beasts & Fishes	1925	£3.00	—

S. MATTINNO & SONS (Malta)

X36	Britain Prepared Series	1940	£2.50	—

P. H. MAYO & BROTHER (U.S.A.)

B25	Actresses (Fancy Frame)	1890	£17.50	£437.50
?25	Actresses (Sepia)	1886	£50.00	—
M25	Actresses (Black Border)	1890	£20.00	—
L12	Actresses (Diagonal)	1888	£43.75	—
?50	Actresses (Burdick 488, 2 Types)	1888	£20.00	—
X25	Actresses	1887	£37.50	—
28	Baseball Game (Die Cut)	1890	£37.50	—
40	Baseball Players	1892	£50.00	—
35	College Football Stars	1892	£37.50	—
20	Costumes & Flowers	1892	£22.00	—
19	Costumes of Warriors & Soldiers	1892	£22.00	—
25	Headdresses of Various Nations	1890	£25.00	—
?100	National Dances (Die Cut)	1890	£37.50	—
M25	National Flowers (Girl & Scene)	1891	£22.00	£550.00
20	Naval Uniforms	1892	£22.00	—
F?	Photographic Cards	1887	£4.25	—
24	Presidents of U.S.	1888	£31.25	—
35	Prizefighters (2 Types)	1890	£20.00	—
20	Shakespeare Characters	1891	£22.00	£550.00
X12	The Seasons	1888	£45.00	—
X15	Wings of Birds of Plumage	1888	£45.00	—

M. MELACHRINO & CO. (Malta)

52	Peuples Exotiques "1 Serie"	1925	60p	£30.00
52	Peuples Exotiques "2 Serie"	1925	60p	£30.00
52	Peuples Exotiques "3 Serie"	1925	60p	£30.00

MEXICAN PUFFS (U.S.A.)

20	Actresses, Blue Border	1890	£50.00	—

MIFSUD & AZZOPARDI (Malta)

KF59	First Maltese Parliament	1922	£3.75	—

MRS. G. B. MILLER & CO. (U.S.A.)

Qty		Date	Odds	Sets
X?	Actresses & Celebrities	1885	£45.00	—
X?	Alphabet Cards	1887	£42.50	—
22	Photographs of all the Presidents	1888	£50.00	—

L. MILLER & SONS (U.S.A.)

49	Animals & Birds	1900	£43.75	—
X25	Battleships	1900	£20.00	£500.00
X100	Beauties "THIBS" (2 Types)	1900	£50.00	—
X25	Generals & Admirals (Spanish War)	1900	£21.00	—
X24	Presidents of U.S.	1900	£16.25	£390.00
X50	Rulers of the World	1900	£16.00	£800.00

CHAS. J. MITCHELL (Canada)

26	Actresses "FROGA" (Brown Back)	1900	£20.00	—
26	Actresses "FROGA" (Green Back)	1900	£20.00	—
26	Actresses "FROGA" (Playing Card Back)	1900	£31.25	—

MONARCH TOBACCO WORKS (U.S.A.)

X?4	American Indian Chiefs	1890	£50.00	—

MOORE & CALVI (U.S.A.)

X53	Beauties, Playing Card Inset, Set 1	1886	£20.00	£1050.00
X53	Beauties, Playing Card Inset, Set 2	1890	£17.50	£925.00
X53	Beauties, Playing Card Inset, Set 3	1890	£17.50	£925.00
X10	Rope Knots	1888	£45.00	—

MURAI BROS. (Japan)

50	Actresses "ALWICS"	1910	£7.50	£375.00
50	Beauties	1902	£9.00	£450.00
24	Beauties "HUMPS"	1900	£18.75	—
50	Chinese Trades	1905	£18.75	—
50	Dancing Girls of the World	1900	£20.00	—
32	Flowers	1900	£18.75	—
25	Japanese Personalities	1900	£31.25	—
?50	Japanese Subjects — Symbol Inset	1900	£31.25	—
26	Phrases and Advertisements	1900	£17.50	£450.00
50	World's Distinguished Personages	1900	£20.00	—
50	World's Smokers	1900	£18.75	—

NATIONAL CIGARETTE & TOBACCO CO. (U.S.A.)

?12	Actresses	1886	£50.00	—
25	National Types (Sailor Girls)	1890	£17.50	£437.50
F?	Photographic Cards	1888	£3.00	—

NATIONAL CIGARETTE CO. (Australia)

13	English Cricket Team, 1897-8	1897	£187.50	—

NATIONAL TOBACCO WORKS (U.S.A.)

Qty		Date	Odds	Sets
GF?	Actresses, Etc, (Newsboy)	1900	£10.00	—
G100	Actresses (Coloured)	1900	£20.00	—

OLD FASHION FINE CUT (U.S.A.)

TF?	Photographic Cards	1890	£5.00	—

OMEGA CIGARETTE FACTORY (Malta)

KF96	Cinema Stars	1936	£1.25	—
F?	Maltese Footballers	1928	£8.50	—

OXFORD CIGARETTE CO. (Malta)

MF24	Egyptian Scenes (Anonymous)	1926	£7.50	—

PENINSULAR TOBACCO CO. LTD. (India)

50	Animals and Birds	1910	£1.50	—
52	Birds of Brilliant Plumage (P/C Inset)	1916	£2.50	—
25	Birds of the East, 1st Series	1912	£1.25	£31.25
25	Birds of the East, 2nd Series	1912	£1.25	£31.25
25	China's Famous Warriors (2 Types)	1912	£1.50	£37.50
25	Chinese Heroes	1913	£1.50	—
50	Chinese Modern Beauties	1912	£3.00	—
50	Chinese Trades, Set 3	1912	£2.00	—
50	Chinese Trades, Set 5	1913	£2.00	—
30	Fish Series	1916	£1.50	£45.00
25	Hindoo Gods	1909	£1.60	£40.00
37	Nautch Girl Series (3 Types)	1910	£4.00	—
25	Products of the World	1915	£1.25	£31.25

PIZZUTO (Malta)

50	Milton's "Paradise Lost"	1910	£4.25	—

THE PLANTERS STORES (India)

50	Actresses "FROGA"	1900	£20.00	—
25	Beauties "FECKSA"	1900	£25.00	—

POLICANSKY BROS. (South Africa)

M50	Birds, Beasts & Fishes (Nassa Cigarettes)	1924	£4.25	—
50	South African Fauna (2 Types)	1925	£6.25	—

RED MAN CHEWING TOBACCO (U.S.A.)

X40	American Indian Chiefs	1952	£4.50	£180.00

D. RITCHIE & CO. (Canada)

30	Actresses "RITAN"	1887	£25.00	£750.00
?33	Actresses ("Our Production" Back)	1889	£37.50	—
?29	Actresses ("Derby" Front)	1889	£37.50	—
52	Beauties P/C Inset (Several Types)	1888	£20.00	—
36	Flags of All Nations	1888	£50.00	—
52	Playing Cards	1888	£21.50	—

RITMEESTER CIGARS

Qty		Date	Odds	Sets
X28	Austrian Cavalry (Cigar Bands)	1976	60p	£18.00
X28	French Cavalry (Cigar Bands)	1976	75p	£21.25
X28	German Cavalry (Cigar Bands)	1976	50p	£14.00

D. E. ROSE & CO. (U.S.A.)

G28	Imperial Cards	1890	£28.50	—

RUGGIER BROS. (Malta)

M50	Story of the Knights of Malta	1924	£3.00	£150.00

RUMI CIGARETTES (Germany)

B56	Beauties (Franks)	1901	£30.00	—

JOHN SCERRI (Malta)

147	Beauties & Children (Black & White)	1930	60p	£90.00
180	Beauties & Children (Unicoloured)	1930	£12.50	—
?100	Beauties & Children (Large Numerals)	1930	£9.25	—
45	Beauties & Children (Coloured)	1930	80p	—
BF50	Beautiful Women	1931	£1.25	—
BF480	Cinema Artists	1931	£1.25	—
BF180	Cinema Stars	1931	£1.25	—
BF50	Famous London Buildings	1934	£2.50	—
F60	Film Stars (First Serie)	1931	£1.25	—
F60	Film Stars (Second Serie)	1931	£1.25	—
52	Interesting Places of the World	1934	40p	£20.00
F25	International Footballers	1933	£3.75	—
401	Malta Views	1928	50p	—
BF51	Members of Parliament — Malta	1928	40p	£20.00
146	Prominent People	1930	75p	—
BF100	Scenes from Films	1932	£1.00	—
LF100	Talkie Stars	1932	£1.25	—
B100	World's Famous Buildings	1931	50p	£50.00

J. J. SCHUH TOBACCO CO. (Australia)

60	Australian Footballers A (½ Length)	1920	£3.00	£180.00
40	Australian Footballers B (Rays)	1921	£3.25	£130.00
60	Australian Footballers C (Oval Frame)	1922	£6.25	—
60	Australian Jockeys	1921	£3.00	£180.00
F72	Cinema Stars (Black & White)	1924	£1.00	£72.00
60	Cinema Stars (Coloured)	1924	£1.00	£60.00
L12	Maxims of Success	1917	£37.50	—
F72	Official War Photographs (2 Types)	1918	£2.00	£144.00
F104	Portraits of our Leading Footballers	1920	£2.00	£210.00

G. SCLIVAGNOTI (Malta)

50	Actresses & Cinema Stars	1923	£1.50	£75.00
MF71	Grand Masters of the Order of Jerusalem	1898	£6.25	—
F102	Opera Singers	1898	£6.25	—
M100	Opera Singers	1898	£6.25	—
B?47	Scenes with Girls	1905	£25.00	—

SINSOCK & CO. (China)

Qty		Date	Odds	Sets
?50	Chinese Beauties	1905	£10.00	—

SNIDERS & ABRAHAMS PTY LTD (Australia)

Qty		Date	Odds	Sets
30	Actresses (Gold Background)	1905	£4.25	£127.50
14	Actresses (White Borders)	1905	£4.25	£67.50
20	Admirals & Warships of the USA (2 Types)	1908	£5.00	—
2	Advertisement Cards	1905	£18.75	—
60	Animals (Green, Descriptive Back)	1912	£2.50	—
60	Animals & Birds (2 Types)	1912	£2.00	—
15	Australian Cricket Team	1905	£18.75	—
16	Australian Football—Incidents in Play	1906	£5.00	£80.00
72	Australian Footballers—Series A (Full Length)	1904	£6.25	—
76	Australian Footballers—Series B (½ Length)	1906	£5.00	—
76	Australian Footballers—Series C (½ Length)	1907	£5.00	—
56	Australian Footballers—Series D (Head/Shoulders)	1908	£3.75	£200.00
140	Australian Footballers-Series D (Head/Shoulders)	1909	£3.75	—
60	Australian Footballers-Series E (Head in Oval)	1910	£3.75	£225.00
60	Australian Footballers-Series F (Head in Rays)	1911	£3.75	—
60	Australian Footballers-Series G (With Pennant)	1912	£3.00	—
60	Australian Footballers-Series H (Head in Star) 2 Types	1913	£2.50	—
60	Australian Footballers-Series I (Head in Shield) 2 Types	1914	£2.50	—
56	Australian Footballers-Series J (½-¾ Length)	1910	£5.00	—
48	Australian Jockeys (Blue Back)	1907	£2.00	£96.00
60	Australian Jockeys (Brown Back)	1908	£2.50	£150.00
56	Australian Racehorses (Horizontal Back)	1906	£2.50	£140.00
56	Australian Racehorses (Vertical Back)	1907	£2.50	—
40	Australian Racing Scenes	1911	£2.50	£100.00
?133	Australian V.C.'s and Officers	1917	£3.75	—
?63	Belgian Views	1916	£2.50	—
12	Billiard Tricks	1908	£6.25	—
60	Butterflies & Moths (Captions in Capitals)	1914	£1.25	£75.00
60	Butterflies & Moths (Captions in Small Letters)	1914	£1.25	£75.00
60	Cartoons & Caricatures (2 Types)	1907	£4.25	—
12	Coin Tricks	1908	£5.00	£60.00
64	Crests of British Warships (2 Types)	1915	£3.75	—
40	Cricketers in Action	1906	£25.00	—
12	Cricket Terms	1905	£16.00	£192.00
32	Dickens Series	1909	£3.00	£196.00
16	Dogs (4 Types)	1910	£5.00	£80.00
90	European War Series	1916	£3.00	—
6	Flags (Shaped Metal)	1915	£2.00	—
6	Flags (Shaped Card)	1915	£2.00	—
60	Great War Leaders & Warships (3 Types)	1915	£2.00	£120.00
30	How to Keep Fit	1907	£4.00	£120.00

SNIDERS & ABRAHAMS PTY LTD. (Australia)—cont.

Qty		Date	Odds	Sets
60	Jokes (3 Types)	1906	£2.00	£120.00
12	Match Puzzles	1908	£5.00	£60.00
48	Medals & Decorations	1915	£4.00	—
M48	Melbourne Buildings	1914	£5.00	—
25	Natives of the World	1904	£8.75	£218.75
12	Naval Terms	1905	£5.00	£60.00
29	Oscar Asche, Lily Brayton & Lady Smokers	1911	£3.75	£112.50
40	Shakespeare Characters	1909	£3.75	£150.00
30	Signalling Series	1916	£4.25	—
?14	Statuary	1905	£6.25	—
60	Street Criers in London, 1707	1914	£5.00	—
32	Views of Victoria in 1857 (2 Types)	1906	£6.25	—
FS?250	Views of the World	1908	£2.00	—

SOUTH INDIAN TOBACCO MFG CO.

25	Actresses "ALWICS"	1905	£7.50	—
?25	Moslem Personalities	1905	£7.50	—

SPANISH FOUR (U.S.A.)

X25	Actresses (Coloured)	1890	£40.00	—
X?	Actresses (Sepia)	1890	£30.00	—

SPAULDING & MERRICK (U.S.A.)

M25	Actresses	1888	£50.00	—
B24/25	Animals	1890	£20.00	£480.00

STAR TOBACCO CO. (India)

?25	Beauties STARA (2 Types)	1898	£37.50	—
52	Beauties (P/C Inset) (3 Types)	1898	£18.75	—
52	Heroes of the Transvaal War (P/C Inset)	1901	£42.50	—
52	Indian Native Types (P/C Inset)	1898	£20.00	£1000.00

J. W. L. STUBBS (New Zealand)

M?44	Barques and Sailing Boats	1926	£15.00	—
F?150	Photographic Cards	1926	£9.00	—

SUB ROSA CIGARETTES (U.S.A.)

?10	Actresses	1885	£45.00	—

SURBRUG CO. (U.S.A.)

B10	Aeroplane Series No. 103	1912	£10.00	—
B10	Prize Dog Series No. 102	1911	£12.50	—
M25	Prize Fight Series No. 101 (2 Types)	1910	£12.50	—

CIE. DE TABAC TERREBONNE (Canada)

30	Bingo-Puzzle	1924	£3.75	—
30	Bingo-Puzzle, 2nd Serie	1925	£3.75	—
30	Bingo-Puzzle, 3rd Series	1926	£3.75	—
30	Bingo-Puzzle, 4th Series	1927	£3.75	—
30	Bingo-Puzzle, 5th Series	1928	£3.75	—

TOBACCO PRODUCTS CORPORATION (Canada & U.S.A.)

Qty		Date	Odds	Sets
?45	Canadian Sports Champions	1917	£7.50	—
60	Do You Know?	1918	£4.25	—
60	Hockey Players	1918	£7.50	—
220	Movie Stars	1915	£1.50	—
120	Movie Stars (Portrait in Oval)	1915	£1.50	—
L?50	Movie Stars	1915	£2.50	—
L?100	Movie Stars, Series No. 3	1916	£2.20	—
?180	Movie Stars, Series No. 4	1916	£1.80	—
L100	Movie Stars, Series No. 5	1916	£2.20	—
18	Ship Picture Letters	1915	£6.25	—

TUCKETT LTD. (Canada)

B52	Aeroplane Series	1930	£3.00	£156.00
B52	Aviation Series (2 Types)	1930	£3.00	£156.00
25	Autograph Series (2 Types)	1913	£25.00	—
?50	Beauties & Scenes (2 Types)	1910	£4.25	—
25	Boy Scout Series	1914	£12.50	—
M8	British Gravures	1923	£7.50	—
L8	British Gravures	1923	£7.50	—
F100	British Views Plain Backs	1912	£1.50	£75.00
F?250	British Views (3 Types)	1912	£1.25	—
F80	British Warships (2 Types)	1914	£6.25	—
F50	Canadian Scenes	1912	£1.25	—
?50	Card Trick Series	1928	£4.25	—
M48	Delivering Mail (Stamps)	1910	£12.50	—
?110	Girls and Warships	1924	£9.25	—
52	Playing Card Premium Certificates	1930	£6.25	—
60	Regimental Badges	1924	£9.25	—
B52	Tucketts Auction Bridge Series	1930	£4.25	—

TURKISH-MACEDONIAN TOBACCO CO. (Holland)

ANONYMOUS SILKS

M21	Arms of Holland & European Towns	1926	£3.00	—
19	Celebrities (White)	1926	£4.25	—
M30	Celebrities (Coloured)	1926	£3.75	—
M19	Decorations and Medals	1926	£4.25	—
101	Dutch Celebrities	1926	£3.00	—
M12	Film Stars	1926	£6.25	—
M249	Flags, Arms and Standards	1926	£1.50	—
D166	Flags and Arms, Series 2	1926	£1.75	—
M20	Flowers	1926	£3.75	—
?4	Girls from Dutch Provinces	1926	£7.50	—
M50	Girls of Many Lands (Black Silk)	1926	£3.00	—
B50	Girls of Many Lands (White Silk)	1926	£3.00	—
M54	Illustrated Initials	1926	£2.50	—
M20	Javanese Figures	1926	£3.00	—
M36	National Costumes	1926	£3.00	—
D62	National Flags	1926	£2.50	—
M141	National Flags (Paper Backs)	1926	£2.50	—
M16	Nature Calendar	1926	£3.00	—
M6	Ships of All Ages	1926	£6.25	—
?85	Sporting Figures (Series A-E)	1926	£3.75	—
25	Sporting Figures (CA1-25)	1926	£3.75	—

TURKISH-MACEDONIAN TOBACCO CO. (Holland) — cont.

Qty		Date	Odds	Sets
M77	Town & Other Arms of Holland & Colonies	1926	£2.50	—
X18	Town Arms of Holland	1926	£3.75	—
M26	World Celebrities	1926	£5.00	—
M?120	Youth Series and Miscellaneous	1926	£2.50	—

U. S. TOBACCO CO. (U.S.A.)

X25	Actresses	1890	£37.50	—

UNITED CIGAR STORES (U.S.A.)

L25	The Aviators (2 Types)	1911	£12.50	£312.50

UNITED TOBACCO COMPANIES (SOUTH) LTD (S. Africa)

Qty		Date	Odds	Sets
50	Aeroplanes of Today (2 Types)	1936	80p	£40.00
50	African Fish	1937	£1.00	£50.00
?6	All Sports Series	1926	£18.75	—
L?6	All Sports Series	1926	£18.75	—
50	Animals & Birds (2 Types)	1923	£5.00	—
L24	Arms & Crests of South African Universities & Schools	1930	75p	£18.75
FS50	Beauties of Great Britain	1930	75p	—
L52	Boy Scout, Girl Guide & Voortrekker Badges ...	1932	£1.00	£52.00
B50	British Aeroplanes	1933	£1.00	£50.00
L20	British Butterflies (Silk)	1924	£8.00	—
L30	British Roses (Silk)	1924	£8.00	—
L62	British Rugby Tour of South Africa	1938	80p	£50.00
50	Children of All Nations	1928	75p	£37.50
50	Cinema Stars (Flag Cigarettes)	1922	£1.25	—
X?12	Conundrums	1910	£40.00	—
40	Cricketers & Their Autographs (Plain Back)	1922	£18.75	—
60	Do You Know?	1930	50p	£30.00
50	Do You Know? 2nd Series	1930	50p	£25.00
50	Do You Know? 3rd Series	1931	50p	£25.00
30	Do You Know? (Different)	1933	60p	£18.00
50	Eminent Film Personalities	1930	£1.25	—
50	English Period Costumes	1932	80p	£40.00
L50	Exercises for Men and Women	1932	75p	£37.50
96	Fairy Tales	1926	80p	—
24	Fairy Tales (Folders)	1926	£7.50	—
25	Famous Figures from South African History	1932	£1.50	£37.50
L100	Famous Works of Art	1939	20p	£15.00
L120	Farmyards of South Africa	1934	30p	£36.00
L65	Flags of All Nations (Silk)	1910	£2.50	—
25	Flowers of South Africa	1932	£1.25	£31.25
FS52	Here There and Everywhere	1930	60p	£30.00
L50	Household Hints	1926	£1.00	—
B50	Humour in Sport	1929	£1.50	£75.00
25	Interesting Experiments	1930	£1.00	£25.00
L100	Medals & Decorations of the British Commonwealth of Nations	1941	60p	£60.00
50	Merchant Ships of the World	1925	80p	£40.00
30	Merrie England Studies — Female	1914	£6.50	—
B52	Miniature Playing Cards (Flag)	1938	75p	—

Qty		Date	Odds	Sets
53	Miniature Playing Cards (Lifeboat)	1938	£1.25	—
53	Miniature Playing Cards (Lotus)	1938	£1.25	—
53	Miniature Playing Cards (Rugger)	1938	£1.50	—
50	Motor Cars	1928	£2.50	£125.00
FS50	Nature Studies	1930	60p	—
X28	1912-13 Springboks	1912	£30.00	—
X?12	Nursery Rhymes	1910	£40.00	—
M25	Old Masters (Silk)	1926	£7.50	—
L100	Our Land	1938	20p	£15.00
B150	Our South African Birds	1942	25p	£37.50
L150	Our South African Birds	1942	20p	£25.00
B100	Our South African Flora	1940	20p	£12.50
L100	Our South African Flora	1940	20p	£10.00
B100	Our South African National Parks	1941	20p	£12.50
L100	Our South African National Parks	1941	20p	£10.00
L200	Our South Africa—Past & Present	1938	20p	£25.00
X60	Ozaka's System of Self Defence	1911	£37.50	—
L24	Pastel Plates	1930	75p	£18.00
L88	Philosophical Sayings	1938	80p	—
L50	Pictures of South Africa's War Effort	1940	20p	£10.00
FS48	Pictures of the East	1930	50p	£25.00
25	Picturesque People of the Empire	1929	£1.00	£25.00
L50	Pottery Types (Silk)	1926	£5.00	—
M50	Pottery Types (Silk)	1926	£6.25	—
L50	Racehorses—South Africa (Set 1)	1929	£1.00	£50.00
L52	Racehorses—South Africa (Set 2) (2 Types)	1930	£1.00	£52.00
50	Regimental Uniforms (2 Types)	1937	£1.00	£50.00
50	Riders of the World (Firms Name)	1931	80p	£40.00
50	Riders of the World (C.T. Ltd)	1931	80p	£40.00
50	Safety First	1936	60p	£30.00
L52	S. A. Flora (2 Types)	1935	30p	£16.00
B40	Ships of All Times	1931	£1.25	£50.00
10	Silhouettes of M.L.A.'s	1914	£20.00	—
25	South African Birds, 1st Series	1927	£1.00	£25.00
25	South African Birds, 2nd Series	1927	£1.00	£25.00
L52	South African Butterflies	1937	60p	£30.00
L52	South African Coats of Arms	1931	40p	£20.00
L17	South African Cricket Touring Team	1929	£10.50	£175.00
L17	S.A. Cricket Touring Team (Autographed)	1929	£10.50	£175.00
B100	South African Defence	1941	20p	£20.00
L50	South African Flowers (Silk)	1913	£3.00	—
L50	South African Flowers (Second Series)	1913	£3.00	—
L50	South African Places of Interest	1934	20p	£10.00
L65	South African Rugby Football Clubs	1933	75p	£50.00
L52	Sports & Pastimes in South Africa	1936	90p	£47.00
L47	Springbok Rugby & Cricket Teams	1931	£1.75	£82.25
FS50	Stereoscopic Photographs, Assorted Subjects	1928	60p	—
FS50	Stereoscopic Photographs of South Africa	1929	75p	—
25	"Studdy Dogs" (Bonzo)	1925	£2.50	—
B50	Tavern of the Seas	1939	40p	£20.00
50	The Story of Sand	1934	75p	—
50	The World of Tomorrow	1938	60p	£30.00
?84	Transfers	1925	£4.25	—
L40	Views of South African Scenery	1918	£3.75	£150.00

UNITED TOBACCO COMPANIES (SOUTH) LTD (S. Africa) — cont.

Qty		Date	Odds	Sets
L36	Views of South African Scenery, 2nd Series	1920	£3.75	£137.50
25	Warriors of All Nations (Swords at Base)	1937	£1.00	£25.00
25	What's This—Troublesome Things & Their Remedy	1929	£1.25	£31.25
50	Wild Animals of the World	1932	£1.00	£50.00
25	Wild Flowers of South Africa, A Series	1925	80p	£20.00
25	Wild Flowers of South Africa, 2nd Series.........	1926	80p	£20.00
B40	Wonders of the World	1931	80p	£32.00
B100	World-Famous Boxers	1939	£1.50	—

UNIVERSAL TOBACCO CO. (India)

Qty		Date	Odds	Sets
F50	Actresses (Plain Back)	1900	£16.00	—
F50	Actresses (Printed Back)	1900	£17.50	—

UNIVERSAL TOBACCO CO. (PTY) LTD. (S. Africa)

Qty		Date	Odds	Sets
835	Flags of All Nations	1935	60p	—
B?368	Park Lane Fashions	1934	£5.00	—

S. W. VENABLE TOBACCO CO. (U.S.A.)

Qty		Date	Odds	Sets
X?56	Actresses	1888	£25.00	—
X8	Baseball Scenes	1888	£55.00	—
X?2	Sea Shore Scenes	1888	£55.00	—

R. WHALEN & CO. (U.S.A.)

Qty		Date	Odds	Sets
L25	Actresses	1890	£44.00	—

WYNEN ZIGARETTEN (Germany)

Qty		Date	Odds	Sets
50	Tanzerinnen Aller Welt	1900	£30.00	—

GEO. F. YOUNG (U.S.A.)

Qty		Date	Odds	Sets
X?76	Actresses	1889	£21.50	—
X8	Baseball Scenes	1888	£55.00	—
X10	National Sports—Girls	1887	£55.00	—
X?	Photographic Cards	1886	£3.00	—
X2	Seashore Scenes	1888	£55.00	—

SILKS

In the world of cigarette card collecting silks is the name given to all items woven in, or printed on, fabrics of all sorts, including satin, canvas, blanket and leather.

Many tobacco and a few other trade firms issued silks in the early part of this century. The best known of these are Godfrey Phillips in Britain, mainly with their B.D.V. brand, the American Tobacco Co. in the U.S.A. and the British American Tobacco Co. in the Commonwealth, usually under the names of their subsidiaries such as the I.T.C. (Canada) or United Tobacco Co. (South Africa). Among trade issues the majority were given away with magazines such as Happy Home and My Weekly. Noteworthy however are the series of cabinet size silks given with each Christmas number of 'The Gentlewoman' between 1890 and 1915.

In some cases the subjects on silks are repeats of card issues, such as 'Best Dogs of their Breed', but the majority are new subjects, and cover a very wide range of interests. These include Flags, Regimental Badges and Colours, County Cricket Badges, Famous Queens, Paintings, Red Indians, Great War Leaders, Dogs, Flowers and even Automobile Pennants. Manufacturers encouraged the smokers to use the satin issues to make cushion covers and the like—I.T.C. of Canada issued large centrepieces for this purpose, and Godfrey Phillips even issued a set of CARDS entitled 'Prizes for Needlework'.

Silks are often thought of as a specialised subject, but the general collector should consider some of these as an attractive addition to his album. We can supply an illustrated book listing all known British silks for £4.50 (post paid).

OKAPI - CONGO

37

ROSE COLOURED STARLING   B.D.V. CIGARETTES

The Leicestershire Regiment.
17th Foot.

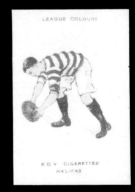

LEAGUE COLOURS

B.D.V. CIGARETTES
HALIFAX

BENEVOLENT PROTECTIVE
ORDER OF ELKS

OLD MILL CIGARETTES

JAPAN

MARGUERITE

ERRORS & VARIETIES

In view of the enormous number of cards that has been produced, most of which have detailed descriptions, it is hardly surprising that mistakes occur occasionally. In some cases these were brought to light at an early stage, and a corrected card was also issued, but sometimes the error remained undetected until many years after the set appeared.

Some of the mistakes can best be described as 'Howlers', and among the best known are Carreras Figures of Fiction showing Uncle Tom with white feet, Pattreiouex Coastwise giving the date of the Battle of Trafalgar as 1812 and Player Sea Fishes with three versions of the Monk (or Angel) Fish, one of which states that it is inedible, while another describes its flesh as 'quite wholesome'. Gallaher, in its Great War Series, showed a Tommy with his rifle sloped on the wrong shoulder, and Carreras Britains Defence No.47 can be found with the picture upside down. Most of these have been illustrated elsewhere, so we have shown here a different selection, with no comments other than—find the mistake for yourself.

Varieties occur as the result of deliberate changes by the issuer. Common examples of this are the updating of army ranks and decorations, new sports statistics, and changes of rank or title caused by a death. The most fruitful series for a study of varieties are probably in the series of Guinea Gold cards and also Wills Transvaal series, where over 250 different cards can be collected within the 66 numbers of the series.

Three books including all known British varieties are listed on page 12.

Part 3

NON-TOBACCO ISSUES

INDEX OF BRANDS (Non-Tobacco)

A-1 DAIRIES LTD. (Tea)

Qty		Date	Odds	Sets
25	Birds and their Eggs	1965	—	£7.50
25	Butterflies & Moths	1964	—	£1.50
25	The Story of Milk	1967	—	£2.50

A-1 DOLLISDALE TEA

25	Do you know about Shipping & Trees?	1963	—	£1.50

A.B.C. (Cinemas)

10	Animals	1952	£1.50	£15.00
10	An Adventure in Space	1950	£2.05	£20.50
10	Birds	1958	—	£5.00
10	Birds & Birdwatching	1953	£2.20	—
10	British Athletes	1955	—	£4.40
20	British Soldiers (Black Back)	1949	30p	£6.00
20	British Soldiers (Brown Back)	1949	20p	£4.00
10	Colorstars, 1st	1962	—	£3.00
10	Colorstars, 2nd	1962	£1.55	—
10	Colorstars, 3rd	1962	95p	—
10	Dogs	1957	—	£9.50
L16	Film Stars	1935	£3.75	—
10	Film Stars	1948	75p	£7.50
10	Horses	1958	—	£5.00
10	Interesting Buildings	1956	—	£4.40
10	Journey by Land	1954	£1.75	—
10	Journey by Water	1954	£1.75	—
10	Journey to the Moon	1955	—	£6.25
10	Parliament Buildings	1957	—	£5.00
10	Railway Engines	1951	£2.50	£25.00
10	Scenes from Films	1953	£1.50	—
10	Sea Exploration	1957	—	£4.40
10	Sea Scenes	1958	—	£4.40
10	Sports on Land	1956	—	£5.00
12	Star Series	1936	£3.15	—
10	Travel of the Future	1956	—	£5.00
10	Water Sports	1956	—	£4.40

A. & B. C. GUM
40 Page Illustrated Reference Book — £2.75

M120	All Sports Series	1954	£1.75	—
P17	Banknotes	1971	£2.50	—
X55	Batman (Pink Back, Fan Club Panel)	1966	£1.50	£82.50
X55	Batman (Numbered Pink Back, No Panel)	1966	95p	£52.25
X55	Batman (Numbered on Front)	1966	£1.55	£85.25
X44	Batman (1A-44A)	1966	£1.00	£44.00
X44	Batman (1B-44B)	1966	£2.50	—
X38	Batman (Black Back)	1966	£1.25	£47.50
B1	Batman Secret Decoder	1966	—	£12.50
X38	Batman (Black Back, Dutch)	1966	£2.50	£95.00
X73	Battle Cards	1966	75p	£57.50
X66	Battle of Britain	1970	65p	£43.00
X60	Bazooka Joe and his Gang	1968	£2.80	—
X60	Beatles (Black & White)	1964	£2.20	£132.00
X45	Beatles, 2nd Series	1965	£3.75	—
X40	Beatles (Coloured)	1965	£3.75	£150.00

A. & B. C. GUM—cont.

Qty		Date	Odds	Sets
K120	Car Stamps	1971	£2.50	—
X21	Car Stamps Albums	1971	£5.00	—
X45	Champions	1969	£1.25	£56.25
L?56	Christian Name Stickers	1967	£1.90	—
X15	Civil War Banknotes	1965	£2.20	£33.00
X88	Civil War News	1965	£1.00	£100.00
X43	Comic Book Foldees	1968	£1.00	£43.00
P24	Crazy Disguises	1970	£6.25	—
X48	Cricketers	1959	£1.25	£60.00
X48	Cricketers 1961 Test Series 94 x 68mm	1961	£1.55	£75.00
X48	Cricketers 1961 Test Series 90 x 64mm	1961	£1.75	£84.00
X66	Elvis Presley Series	1956	£5.00	—
X36	Exploits of William Tell	1960	50p	£18.00
22	Famous Indian Chiefs	1968	£1.75	—
X54	Fantastic Twisters	1972	£3.75	—
M48	Film & TV Stars	1953	£1.75	£87.50
M48	Film & TV Stars No. 2 Series (49-96)	1953	£1.75	£87.50
M48	Film & TV Stars No. 3 Series (97-144)	1953	£1.75	£87.50
X48	Film Stars (Plain Back)	1954	£1.25	£62.50
X73	Flags (Cut-Outs)	1971	50p	£36.50
L80	Flags of the World	1960	50p	£40.00
X80	Flags of the World	1959	50p	£40.00
40	Flag Stickers	1966	£3.15	—
X46	Footballers (Planet, 1-46)	1958	15p	£7.00
X46	Footballers (Without "Planet" 1-46)	1958	95p	—
X46	Footballers (Planet, 47-92)	1958	£1.90	—
X46	Footballers (Without "Planet" 47-92)	1958	£1.90	—
X49	Footballers (Football Quiz, 1-49)	1959	£1.25	£61.25
X49	Footballers (Football Quiz, 50-98)	1959	£1.75	—
X42	Footballers (Black Back, 1-42)	1960	90p	£38.00
X42	Footballers (Black Back, 43-84)	1960	£1.00	£42.00
XF64	Footballers (Plain Back)	1961	95p	£61.00
XF44	Footballers (Plain Back, Scottish)	1961	£3.75	—
X82	Footballers (Bazooka)	1962	£2.20	—
X55	Footballers (Make-a-Photo, 1-55)	1963	£1.55	—
X55	Footballers (Make-a-Photo, 56-110)	1963	£1.55	—
X81	Footballers (Make-a-Photo, Scottish)	1963	£3.75	—
X58	Footballers (Quiz, 1-58)	1964	£1.05	£61.00
X45	Footballers (Quiz, 59-103)	1964	£2.00	—
X46	Footballers (Quiz, 104-149)	1964	£3.15	—
X81	Footballers (Quiz, Scottish)	1964	£3.75	—
X55	Footballers (In Pairs, 1-110)	1966	£1.25	—
X55	Footballers (In Pairs, 111-220)	1966	£1.50	—
X55	Footballers (In Pairs, Scottish)	1966	£1.90	—
X55	Footballers (Star Players)	1967	30p	£16.50
P12	Footballers	1967	£2.50	£30.00
X54	Footballers (Yellow, 1-54)	1968	90p	£49.00
X47	Footballers (Yellow, 55-101)	1968	75p	£35.25
M20	Football Emblems	1968	£2.50	—
E26	Football Team Pennants	1968	£3.15	—
X65	Footballers (Football Facts, 1-64)	1969	65p	£42.25
X54	Footballers (Football Facts, 65-117)	1969	45p	£24.25
X55	Footballers (Football Facts, 117-170)	1969	45p	£24.75
MF36	Footballers	1969	95p	—

A. & B. C. GUM—cont.

Qty		Date	Odds	Sets
X42	Footballers (Football Facts, Scottish, 1-41)	1969	£2.50	—
X35	Footballers (Football Facts, Scottish, 42-75)	1969	£3.15	—
MF15	Footballers (Scottish)	1969	£2.50	—
X85	Footballers (Orange Back, 1-85)	1970	15p	£10.00
X85	Footballers (Orange Back, 86-170)	1970	15p	£8.00
X85	Footballers (Orange Back, 171-255)	1970	40p	£34.00
72	Football Colour Transparencies	1970	£1.50	—
P14	Footballers, Pin-Ups	1970	£1.90	£26.50
X85	Footballers (Green Back, Scottish, 1-85)	1970	65p	—
X86	Footballers (Green Back, Scottish, 86-171)	1970	75p	—
P28	Footballers, Pin-Ups (Scottish)	1970	£2.80	—
X109	Footballers (Did You Know, 1-109)	1971	20p	£22.00
X110	Footballers (Did You Know, 110-219)	1971	20p	£22.00
X71	Footballers (Did You Know, 220-290)	1971	30p	£21.00
X73	Footballers (Did You Know, Scottish, 1-73)	1971	15p	£6.50
X71	Footballers (Did You Know, Scottish, 74-144)	1971	£1.00	—
16/23	Football Club Crests	1971	30p	£5.00
16	Football Club Crests (Scottish)	1971	95p	£15.00
X109	Footballers (Orange/Red, 1-109)	1972	15p	£10.50
X110	Footballers (Orange/Red, 110-219)	1972	15p	£12.50
B22	Football Card Game	1972	40p	£8.75
M23	Footballers, Superstars	1972	£1.75	—
X89	Footballers (Rub Coin, Scottish, 1-89)	1972	80p	—
X89	Footballers (Orange/Red, Scottish, 90-179)	1972	£1.00	—
M32	Footballers (Autographed Photos)	1973	80p	£25.00
X131	Footballers (Blue Back, 1-131)	1973	15p	£19.75
X130	Footballers (Blue Back, 132-263)	1973	30p	—
X90	Footballers (Red Back, Scottish, 1-90)	1973	95p	—
X88	Footballers (Red Back, Scottish, 91-178)	1973	95p	—
E16	Football Giant Team Posters	1973	£2.50	—
X132	Footballers (Red Back, Rub Coin)	1974	15p	£20.00
X132	Footballers (Green Back, Scottish, Rub Coin)	1974	40p	£53.00
X40	Fotostars	1961	65p	£26.00
X66	Funny Greetings	1961	75p	£50.00
X66	Funny Valentines	1961	75p	£50.00
X36	Golden Boys (Matt)	1958	95p	£34.00
XF40	Golden Boys (Glossy)	1958	£1.75	£70.00
L27	Grand Prix	1970	20p	£5.50
D200	Hip Patches	1968	£1.25	—
X55	Huck Finn	1968	30p	£16.50
X60	Kung Fu	1974	40p	£24.00
X55	Land of the Giants	1969	£1.40	£77.00
X55	Lotsa Laffs	1970	40p	£22.00
X84	Love Initials	1970	30p	—
X36	Magic	1967	40p	£14.50
L1	Magic Circle Club Application	1969	—	£6.25
X74	Man on the Moon	1969	50p	£37.00
X55	Mars Attacks	1965	£8.15	£450.00
X52	Mickey Takers	1970	£1.90	—
B24	Military Emblem Stickers	1966	£2.50	—
X55	Monkees (Black & White)	1967	65p	£35.75
X55	Monkees (Coloured)	1967	65p	£35.75
X30	Monkees Hit Songs	1967	80p	£24.00
X49	Nutty Initial Stickers	1968	£1.90	—
E16	Olympic Posters	1972	£2.50	—
X36	Olympics	1972	£1.55	£56.00
X50	Outer Limits	1966	£1.90	£95.00
X55	Partridge Family	1972	30p	£16.50
X120	Planes	1960	50p	£60.00
X44	Planet of the Apes	1968	65p	£28.50
X33	Put-on Stickers	1969	£1.90	—

A. & B. C. GUM —cont.

Qty		Date	Odds	Sets
X48	Railway Quiz	1958	65p	£31.25
X72	Railway Quiz	1959	95p	£69.00
M24	Royal Portraits	1953	£2.00	£48.00
M34	Silly Stickers	1966	*£1.90*	—
X25	Sir Francis Drake	1961	£1.00	£25.00
X88	Space Cards	1958	90p	£79.00
X44	Stacks of Stickers	1971	£1.55	£68.25
X55	Star Trek	1969	£2.80	£154.00
X66	Superman in the Jungle	1968	95p	£62.75
X16	Superman in the Jungle (Jig-Saw)	1968	£1.90	£30.50
X25	The Girl from U.N.C.L.E.	1965	£1.25	—
X36	The High Chaparral	1969	50p	£18.00
X54	The Legend of Custer	1968	75p	£40.50
L55	The Man from U.N.C.L.E.	1965	65p	£35.75
X40	The Rolling Stones	1965	£4.40	—
X50	Top Stars	1964	£1.75	£87.50
X40	Top Stars (Different)	1964	£1.75	£70.00
X56	TV Westerns	1959	75p	£42.00
X44	Ugly Stickers	1967	£1.25	£55.00
P88	Wacky Plaks	1962	£1.25	£110.00
E16	Wanted Posters	1968	£3.75	—
X70	Who-Z-At Star?	1958	80p	£56.00
X55	Winston Churchill Cards	1965	20p	£11.00
X37	World Cup Footballers	1970	£1.00	£37.00
30	World Cup Football Stickers	1966	£3.75	—
E16	World Cup Posters	1966	£2.50	—
X66	You'll Die Laughing (Creature Feature)	1974	25p	£16.50
X48	You'll Die Laughing (Purple Back)	1967	40p	£19.00

A.H.C. (Confectionery)

25	Tropical Birds (Anon.)	1955	—	£1.55
25	Wonders of the Universe	1955	—	£1.55

ABBEY GRANGE HOTEL

15	Fighting Vessels	1986	—	£2.50

P. A. ADOLPH ("Subbuteo")

24	Famous Footballers 1st	1954	—	£5.00
24	Famous Footballers 2nd	1954	—	£5.00

A. W. ALLEN (Confectionery, Australia)

32	Bradman's Records	1931	£15.00	—
72	Butterflies & Moths	1920	£1.25	—
36	Cricketers (Brown Front)	1932	£8.15	£295.00
36	Cricketers (Brown Front, Different)	1933	£8.15	—
36	Cricketers (Flesh Tinted, Frame Back)	1934	£5.00	£180.00
36	Cricketers (Flesh Tinted, No Frame)	1936	£5.00	£180.00
36	Cricketers (Coloured)	1938	£5.00	£180.00
M24	Fliers	1926	£3.75	—
144	Footballers (Striped Colours)	1933	£1.05	—
72	Footballers (Pennants)	1934	£1.05	—
49	Kings & Queens of England	1937	95p	£46.50
36	Medals	1938	£1.00	—
36	Soldiers of the Empire	1938	£1.25	—
36	Sports & Flags of Nations	1936	£1.55	£56.00
M24	Wrestlers	1926	£3.15	£75.50

ALMA CONFECTIONERY

Qty		Date	Odds	Sets
48	James Bond 007 Moonraker	1980	£1.25	—

JAMES ALMOND (Confectionery)

25	Sports and Pastimes	1925	£6.25	—

AMABALINO PHOTOGRAPHIC (Commercial)

L30	Display Fireworks	1988	—	£6.25

AMALGAMATED PRESS LTD.

24	Aeroplanes (Plain Back)	1933	£1.90	—
32	Aeroplanes & Carriers	1932	£1.90	—
M32	Australian & English Cricket Stars	1932	£6.25	£200.00
M12	Catchy Tricks & Teasers	1933	£1.55	£18.75
M16	England's Test Match Cricketers	1928	£6.25	£100.00
M22	English League (Div. 1) Footer Captains	1926	£1.75	£38.50
M16	Exploits of the Great War	1929	£1.00	£16.00
16	Famous Aircraft	1927	£2.20	£35.00
M16	Famous Australian Cricketers	1929	£6.25	£100.00
16	Famous Film Stars	1927	£3.75	£60.00
M24	Famous Footer Internationals	1926	£1.75	£42.00
M22	Famous Shipping Lines	1926	£3.75	£82.50
M32	Famous Test Match Cricketers	1926	£3.75	£120.00
24	Famous Trains & Engines	1932	£1.55	£37.25
16	Fighting Planes of the World	1934	£1.90	—
32	Football Fame Series	1936	£1.75	£56.00
M16	Great War Deeds	1927	£1.00	£16.00
M32	Great War Deeds (Different)	1928	£1.00	£32.00
M16	Heroic Deeds of the Great War	1927	£1.00	£16.00
32	Makes of Motor Cars & Index Marks	1923	£1.75	£56.00
32	Mechanical Wonders of 1935	1935	£1.90	—
32	Modern Motor Cars	1926	£3.75	—
24	Motors (Plain Back)	1933	£1.90	—
24	Ships of the World (Champion)	1924	£1.75	£42.00
33	Ships of the World (Different, Anon.)	1935	£2.00	—
BF66	Sportsmen	1922	40p	£26.50
32	Sportsmen of the World	1934	95p	£30.50
M12	Sports Queeriosities	1933	£2.00	£24.00
M24	The Great War 1914-1918	1928	£1.00	£24.00
M16	The Great War 1914-1918 New Series	1929	£1.00	£16.00
M16	The R.A.F. at War (Plain Back)	1940	£2.50	—
M32	Thrilling Scenes from the Great War	1927	£1.00	£32.00
M16	Thrills of the Dirt Track	1929	£3.75	£60.00
M16	Tip Top Tricks and Teasers	1927	£1.90	£30.50
M14	V.C.'s & Their Deeds of Valour (Plain Back)	1928	£2.50	—
M24	Wonderful London	1926	£3.15	£75.00

AMANDA'S FLOWERS

L12	Flower Children	1990	—	£3.75

AMARAN TEA

Qty		Date	Odds	Sets
25	Coins of the World	1964	—	£3.00
25	Dogs' Heads	1965	—	£2.20
25	Do you Know?	1969	—	£2.00
25	Flags & Emblems	1964	—	£2.50
25	Naval Battles	1971	—	£4.40
25	Old England	1969	—	£1.50
25	Science in the 20th Century	1966	—	£1.50
25	The Circus	1966	—	£1.90
25	Veteran Racing Cars	1965	—	*£9.50*

AMPOL (Oil, Australia)

M32	Cars of To-day	1958	—	£10.75

THE ANGLERS MAIL (Periodical)

E3	Terminal Tackle Tips	1976	—	£1.50

ANGLING TIMES (Magazine)

M24	Collect-Cards (Fish)	1988	—	£3.00

ANGLO-AMERICAN CHEWING GUM LTD.

L36	Kidnapped (Thriller Chewing Gum)	1935	£2.20	—
X66	The Horse	1966	15p	£10.00
40	Underwater Adventure	1966	—	£3.00
50	Zoo Stamps of the World	1966	45p	£22.50

ANGLO CONFECTIONERY LTD.

X66	Captain Scarlet & The Mysterons	1968	£1.55	£102.25
L12	Football Hints (Folders)	1970	65p	£7.75
L84	Football Quiz	1969	45p	£37.75
X66	Joe 90	1968	£1.25	£82.50
L66	National Team Colours	1970	£2.00	£132.00
X84	Railway Trains & Crests	1974	50p	£42.00
X66	Space	1967	40p	£26.50
X66	Tarzan	1967	25p	£16.50
X66	The Beatles—Yellow Submarine	1968	£4.00	—
X66	The Horse	1966	80p	—
L56	The New James Bond	1970	£2.50	—
L64	U.F.O.	1971	40p	£25.50
M24	Vintage Cars Series	1970	£2.50	£60.00
L78	Walt Disney Characters	1971	£1.90	£150.00
L66	Wild West	1970	40p	£26.50
L48	World Cup 1970	1970	80p	£38.50

ANONYMOUS—TRADE ISSUES

K24	Animal Jungle Game	1965	—	£3.00
50	Animals of the World	1954	—	£3.00
25	Aquarium Fish (Plain Backs)	1961	—	£1.50
25	Bridges of the World	1958	—	£1.50
25	British Uniforms of the 19th Century	1957	—	£1.50
26	Boy Scouts Signalling	1910	£4.40	—
20	Budgerigars	1960	25p	£5.00

ANONYMOUS — TRADE ISSUES — cont.

Qty		Date	Odds	Sets
25	Cacti	1961	—	£1.50
25	Careless Moments	1922	—	£8.75
25	Castles of Britain	1962	—	£1.90
25	Children of All Nations	1958	—	£1.50
25	Dogs	1958	—	£2.50
25	Do you Know	1963	—	£1.50
25	Evolution of the Royal Navy	1957	—	£1.50
25	Family Pets	1964	—	£2.50
25	Flags & Emblems	1961	—	£1.50
25	Flowers	1971	—	£2.20
25	Football Clubs & Badges	1962	—	£1.90
25	Jockeys and Owners Colours	1963	—	£3.75
50	Mars Adventure	1958	—	£31.25
100	Miscellaneous Subjects (Gum)	1965	—	£8.15
25	Modern Aircraft	1958	—	£1.50
X12	Motor Cycles (Collectors Series)	1987	—	£2.50
25	Musical Instruments	1971	—	£2.20
25	Pigeons	1971	—	£3.75
25	Pond Life	1963	—	£1.50
M24	R.A.F. Badges	1985	—	£3.75
1	Soldier — Bugler	1965	—	£1.25
25	Sports of the Countries	1967	—	£3.00
25	The Circus	1966	—	£3.00
25	The Wild West	1960	—	£1.50
1	Venice in London	1965	—	75p

SILK ISSUES

M4	Great War Incidents	1916	£9.40	—
M10	Review Titles Travestied	1915	£12.50	—
M4	Warships	1915	£9.40	—

BELGIAN ISSUES

X100	Famous Men	1938	—	£9.40

U.S. ISSUES

X30	Aeroplanes & Insignia	1945	—	£25.00
M48	America at War (101-148)	1942	—	£62.50
M48	America at War (501-548)	1943	—	£75.00
M48	America at War (601-648)	1943	—	£75.00
10	Boy Scouts	1926	—	£10.00
M48	Disney Characters	1942	£2.00	£10.00
10	Film Stars "A"	1926	—	£7.50
10	Film Stars "B"	1926	—	£7.50
10	Film Stars "C"	1926	—	£7.50
M60	Pinocchio (Bread Issue)	1950	—	£25.00
10	Presidents "A"	1926	—	£7.50
10	Presidents "B"	1926	—	£7.50
10	Western Pioneers	1926	—	£9.40

SPANISH ISSUES

X32	Footballers (P/C Backs)	1930	75p	£24.00

APLIN & BARRETT (Cheese)

X25	Whipsnade	1937	90p	£22.50

ARBUCKLE COFFEE CO. (U.S.A.)

Qty		Date	Odds	Sets
P50	Animals	1890	£3.75	£187.50
P50	Cooking Subjects	1890	£3.75	—
P100	General Subjects (Unnumbered)	1890	£5.00	—
P50	General Subjects (51-100)	1890	£4.40	—
P50	History of Sports & Pastimes of the World	1893	£4.40	£220.00
P50	History of United States & Territories	1890	£3.15	£157.50
P50	Illustrated Atlas of U.S.	1890	£4.00	£200.00
P50	Illustrated Jokes	1890	£4.40	—
P50	Principal Nations of the World	1890	£3.15	£157.50
P50	Views from a Trip Around the World	1890	£3.15	£157.50

ARDMONA (Tinned Fruit, Australia)

X50	International Cricket Series III	1980	—	£8.15

ARMITAGE BROS. LTD. (Pet Foods)

25	Animals of the Countryside	1964	—	£1.50
25	Country Life	1968	—	£1.50

ARROW CONFECTIONERY CO.

12	Conundrums	1904	£25.00	—
12	Shadowgraphs	1904	£25.00	—

ASKEY'S (Biscuits)

25	People & Places	1971	—	£2.50
25	Then & Now	1971	—	£2.50

AUSTRALIAN DAIRY CORPORATION

X63	Kanga Cards (Cricket)	1985	—	£7.50
X50	Super Cricket Card Series, 1982-3	1983	—	£7.50
X50	Super Cricket Card Series, 1983-4	1984	—	£7.50

AUSTRALIAN LICORICE PTY. LTD.

?27	Australian Cricketers	1930	£7.50	—
24	Australian Cricketers	1931	£7.50	£180.00
24	English Cricketers (Blue Back)	1928	£7.50	£180.00
24	English Cricketers (Brown Back)	1930	£7.50	—
18	English Cricketers ("18 in Set")	1932	£7.50	£135.00
12	South African Cricketers	1931	£7.50	£90.00

AUTOBRITE (Car Polish)

25	Vintage Cars	1965	—	£5.00

AUTOMATIC MACHINE CO.

25	Modern Aircraft	1958	—	£3.00

AUTOMATIC MERCHANDISING CO.

X25	Adventure Twins & The Treasure Ship	1958	—	£15.00

AVON RUBBER CO. LTD.

Qty		Date	Odds	Sets
30	Leading Riders of 1963	1963	—	£25.00

B.B.B. PIPES

25	Pipe History	1926	£6.25	—

B.T. LTD. (Tea)

25	Aircraft	1961	—	£5.00
25	British Locomotives	1961	—	£5.00
25	Do you Know	1967	—	£4.40
25	Holiday Resorts	1963	—	£1.90
25	Modern Motor Cars	1962	—	£9.40
25	Occupations	1962	—	£5.00
25	Pirates & Buccaneers	1961	—	£5.00
25	The West	1964	—	£3.00

BADSHAH TEA CO.

25	British Cavalry Uniforms of the 19th Century	1963	—	£7.50
25	Butterflies & Moths	1971	—	£1.50
25	Fish & Bait	1971	—	£1.50
25	Fruits of Trees & Shrubs	1965	—	*£3.00*
25	Garden Flowers	1963	—	£4.40
25	Naval Battles	1971	—	£5.00
25	People & Places	1970	—	£1.50
25	Regimental Uniforms of the Past	1971	—	£2.20
25	Romance of the Heavens	1968	—	£18.75
25	Wonders of the World ("Series of 50")	1970	—	£1.50

BAILEY'S (Toffee)

25	War Series (Ships)	1916	£10.50	—

J. BAINES (Commercial)

L?200	Football Cards (Shaped)	1897	£4.40	—

BAKE-A-CAKE LTD.

56	Motor Cars	1952	£2.20	£123.50

BARBERS TEA LTD.

1	Advertising Card—Cinema & T.V. Stars	1955	—	£1.00
1	Advertising Card—Dogs	1956	—	50p
1	Advertising Card—Railway Equipment	1958	—	£1.25
25	Aeroplanes	1956	—	£5.00
24	Cinema & Television Stars	1955	—	£20.00
24	Dogs	1961	—	£1.90
5	Ferry to Hong Kong	1957	£5.00	—
25	Locomotives	1956	—	£10.00
24	Railway Equipment	1958	—	£7.50

JOHN O. BARKER (IRELAND) LTD. (Gum)

Qty		Date	Odds	Sets
X24	Circus Scenes	1970	—	£12.50
X24	Famous People	1970	—	£12.50
25	The Wild West	1970	*£1.90*	—

BARRATT & CO. LTD. (Confectionery)

Qty		Date	Odds	Sets
M30	Aircraft (Varnished)	1941	£2.50	—
M30	Aircraft (Unvarnished)	1943	£2.80	—
25	Animals in the Service of Man ,,,,,,,,,,,,,,,,,,,,,,	1964	—	£1.90
16	Australian Cricketers, Action Series	1926	£8.75	—
15	Australian Test Players	1930	£15.00	—
25	Birds	1960	—	£4.40
50	Botany Quest	1966	£1.25	£62.50
25	British Butterflies	1965	£1.90	£47.50
25	Butterflies & Moths	1969	—	£1.50
25	Cage & Aviary Birds	1960	—	£4.40
50	Captain Scarlet & The Mysterons	1967	75p	£37.50
50	Cars of the World	1965	£1.00	£50.00
B122	Characters from Film Cartoons	1940	£4.40	—
K4	Coronation & Jubilee Medallions	1902	£18.75	—
25	Coronation, 1911	1911	£12.50	—
20	Cricket Team Folders	1933	£10.00	—
?260	Cricketers, Footballers & Football Teams	1925	£6.25	—
L60	Disneyland "True Life"	1956	75p	£45.00
L50	F.A. Cup Winners	1935	£6.25	—
25	Fairy Stories	1926	£2.00	£50.00
12	Famous British Constructions, Aircraft	1925	£15.50	—
B?240	Famous Cricketers (Various Series)	1936	£6.25	—
35	Famous Film Stars	1961	£1.00	£35.00
B248	Famous Footballers (Various Series)	1936	£2.50	—
B79	Famous Footballers (Non-Descriptive)	1947	£2.50	—
B50	Famous Footballers, New Series	1950	£2.00	—
B50	Famous Footballers, New Series (Different)	1952	£2.00	—.
B50	Famous Footballers, Series A1	1953	£1.55	£77.50
B50	Famous Footballers, Series A2	1954	£1.55	£77.50
B50	Famous Footballers, Series A3	1955	£1.55	—
60	Famous Footballers, Series A4	1956	£1.50	—
60	Famous Footballers, Series A5	1957	£1.25	£75.00
60	Famous Footballers, Series A6	1958	£1.25	£75.00
60	Famous Footballers, Series A7	1959	£1.25	£75.00
50	Famous Footballers, Series A8	1960	£1.25	£62.50
50	Famous Footballers, Series A9	1961	£1.25	£62.50
50	Famous Footballers, Series A10	1962	75p	£37.50
50	Famous Footballers, Series A11	1963	£1.25	£62.50
50	Famous Footballers, Series A12	1964	£1.25	£62.50
50	Famous Footballers, Series A13	1965	£1.25	£62.50
50	Famous Footballers, Series A14	1966	£1.00	£50.00
50	Famous Footballers, Series A15	1967	—	£5.00
32/50	Famous Sportsmen	1971	—	£3.75
B45	Fastest on Earth	1953	95p	£42.75
32	Felix Pictures	1930	£15.50	—
25	Fish & Bait	1962	—	£4.40
12	Football Action Caricatures	1928	£9.40	—
100	Football Stars	1930	*£9.40*	—
50	Football Stars	1974	£1.25	—

BARRATT & CO. LTD. (Confectionery) — cont.

Qty		Date	Odds	Sets
?69	Football Team Folders	1933	£5.00	—
B66	Football Teams — 1st Division	1930	£5.00	—
48	Giants in Sport	1959	£2.00	—
C12	Gold Rush (Packets)	1960	£4.40	—
25	Headdresses of the World	1962	—	£5.00
25	Historical Buildings	1960	—	£2.50
48	History of the Air	1959	90p	£43.25
32	History of the Air	1959	£2.50	—
25	History of the Air	1960	—	£5.00
25	Interpol	1964	£2.00	£50.00
50	Leaders of Sport	1927	£6.25	—
35	Magic Roundabout	1968	—	£4.40
25	Merchant Ships of World (Black Back)	1962	—	£6.25
25	Merchant Ships of World (Blue Back)	1962	—	£2.50
L40	Modern Aircraft	1957	£1.00	£40.00
B45	Modern British Aircraft	1959	£1.90	—
13	National Flags	1914	£15.50	—
64	Natural History (Plain Back)	1940	£3.75	—
B24	Naval Ships (Plain Back)	1939	£5.00	—
B6	Our King & Queen (Plain Back)	1940	£6.25	—
25	People & Places	1965	—	£1.50
25	Pirates & Buccaneers	1960	—	£3.00
P25	Pop Stars	1980	—	£7.50
12	Prominent London Buildings	1912	£12.50	—
30	Robin Hood	1961	£1.25	£37.50
36	Sailing into Space	1959	£1.90	—
50	Soccer Stars	1973	75p	£37.50
50	Soldiers of the World	1966	—	£7.50
16	South African Cricketers	1929	£11.00	—
25	Space Mysteries	1965	—	£3.00
L20	Speed Series	1930	£5.00	—
50	Tarzan	1967	—	£12.50
35	Test Cricketers, Series A	1956	£3.15	£110.25
48	Test Cricketers, Series B	1957	£5.00	—
50	The Secret Service	1970	—	£18.75
24	The Wild West	1961	—	£2.50
25	The Wild West (Different)	1963	—	£2.50
50	The Wild Wild West	1969	—	£37.50
25	The Young Adventurer	1965	£1.90	£47.50
50	Thunderbirds	1967	£2.50	£125.00
50	Thunderbirds, 2nd Series	1968	80p	£40.00
50	Tom & Jerry	1970	—	£7.50
50	Trains	1970	—	£7.50
50	Trains of the World	1964	—	£10.00
35	TV's Huckleberry Hound & Friends	1961	£1.25	£43.75
35	TV's Sea Hunt	1961	£1.55	£54.25
35	TV's Yogi Bear	1969	£1.50	£52.50
35	TV's Yogi Bear & Friends	1971	—	£2.00
70	U.F.O.	1971	—	£22.00
1	Victory V Sign	1940	—	£7.50
B35	Walt Disney Characters	1956	£1.75	£61.25
50	Walt Disney Characters, 2nd Series	1957	£1.65	£82.50
36	Walt Disney's Robin Hood	1957	£1.00	£36.00
35	Walt Disney's True Life	1962	£1.00	£35.00

BARRATT & CO. LTD. (Confectionery)—cont.

Qty		Date	Odds	Sets
25	Warriors Through the Ages	1962	—	£3.00
25	What do you Know?	1964	—	£1.55
X72	Wild Life	1972	40p	£29.00
M50	Wild Animals by George Cansdale	1954	£1.25	£62.50
36	Wild West Series No.1	1959	£1.25	£45.00
25	Willum	1961	£1.90	£47.50
50	Wisecracks	1970	—	£3.00
50	Wisecracks, 2nd Series	1970	—	£6.25
50	Wisecracks, 3rd Series	1971	—	£7.50
50	Wonders of the World	1962	—	£3.00
25	World Locomotives	1961	—	£6.25
50	Wunders Der Welt	1968	—	£4.40
50	Zoo Pets	1964	£1.00	£50.00

GEO. BASSETT & CO. LTD. (Confectionery)

Qty		Date	Odds	Sets
25	Motor Cars—Vintage & Modern	1968	—	£6.25
25	Nursery Rhymes	1966	—	£1.90
25	Popular Dogs	1967	—	£3.00
70	U.F.O.	1974	—	£7.50
25	Victoria Cross Heroes in Action	1970	—	£2.50

BARRATT DIVISION

Qty		Date	Odds	Sets
50	Age of the Dinosaurs	1979	30p	—
40	Ali-Cat Magicards	1978	40p	£16.00
50	Asterix in Europe	1977	15p	£3.75
50	Athletes of the World	1980	15p	£6.25
48	Bananaman	1986	—	£3.00
M20	Battle (Packets)	1985	95p	£19.00
50	Cricket	1978	£2.50	—
50	Cricket, 2nd Series	1979	£1.55	£77.50
48	Dandy-Beano Collection	1989	—	£5.00
50	Disney—Health & Safety	1977	—	£3.75
50	Football Action	1977	65p	£32.50
50	Football Action	1978	75p	—
50	Football 1978-79	1979	50p	£25.00
50	Football 1979-80	1980	25p	£12.00
50	Football 1980-81	1981	20p	£10.00
50	Football 1981-82	1982	30p	£15.00
50	Football 1982-83	1983	40p	£20.00
50	Football 1983-84	1984	15p	£4.50
50	Football 1984-85	1985	15p	£4.50
48	Football 1985-86	1986	15p	£6.25
48	Football 1986-87	1987	15p	£5.00
48	Football 1987-88	1988	—	£5.00
48	Football 1988-89	1989	—	£5.00
48	Football 1989-90	1990	—	£5.00
50	Football Stars	1974	—	£6.25
50	Football Stars 1975-6	1975	65p	—
48	Hanna Barbera's Cartoon Capers	1984	25p	£12.00
24	Holograms (Plain Backs)	1986	30p	£7.50
24	Holograms (Red Backs)	1986	—	£5.00
50	House of Horror	1982	40p	£20.00
40	Knight Rider	1987	15p	£6.00
50	Living Creatures of our World	1979	15p	£7.50

GEO. BASSETT & CO. LTD. (Confectionery)—cont.

Qty		Date	Odds	Sets
50	Play Cricket	1980	20p	£10.00
25	Pop Stars	1974	—	£1.90
L5	Scratch and Match	1990	—	£3.75
35	Secret Island, 1st Series	1976	40p	£14.00
40	Secret Island, 2nd Series	1976	—	£3.00
M20	Sky Fighters (Packets)	1986	65p	£13.00
50	Space 1999	1976	20p	£10.00
50	Super Heroes	1984	50p	—
50	Survival on Star Colony 9	1979	20p	£10.00
40	Swim and Survive	1983	15p	£5.00
B20	The A Team	1986	—	£9.50
50	The Conquest of Space	1980	25p	£12.50
50	Tom & Jerry	1974	65p	—
50	World Cup Stars	1974	—	£3.75
50	World of the Vorgans	1978	30p	£15.00
50	World Record Breakers	1983	50p	£25.00
49/50	Yogi's Gang	1976	—	£6.25

BATTLE PICTURE WEEKLY

80	Weapons of World War II	1975	—	£20.00

BATTLEAXE TOFFEE

24	British and Empire Uniforms	1915	£20.00	—

BAYTCH BROS. (Commercial)

64	Fighting Favourites	1951	£3.75	—

BEANO LTD. (Gum)

1	Bang-o-Spacesuit Coupon	1950	—	45p
25	Fascinating Hobbies	1950	£1.25	—
50	Modern Aircraft (Beano)	1951	—	£25.00
50	Modern Aircraft (British Educational)	1951	—	£4.40
50	Ships of the Royal Navy	1955	—	£3.75
50	The Conquest of Space	1956	—	£3.75
50	This Age of Speed No.1 (Aeroplanes)	1954	—	£9.50
50	This Age of Speed No.2 (Buses & Trams)	1954	—	£18.75
50	Wonders of Modern Transport (Aircraft)	1955	—	£22.00
25	Wonders of the Universe (Foto Gum)	1960	—	£1.50

S. N. BEATTIE & CO. (Commercial)

24	Safety Signs	1955	£1.90	£45.50

J. J. BEAULAH (Canned Goods)

1	Boston Stump	1953	—	45p
25	Coronation Series	1953	—	£31.25
24	Marvels of the World	1954	—	£1.50
24	Modern British Aircraft	1953	—	£2.50

THE BEEHIVE STORES

25	British Uniforms of the 19th Century	1959	—	£10.00

BELLS SCOTCH WHISKY

Qty		Date	Odds	Sets
40/42	Other Famous Bells (Shaped)	1975	30p	£12.00

J. BELLAMY & SONS LTD. (Confectionery)

25	Vintage & Modern Trains of the World	1975	—	£4.40

VAN DEN BERGHS LTD. (Margarine Etc.)

60	Countryside Cards	1975	50p	—
L24	Pirates	1965	£1.55	£37.25
M12	Recipes from Round the World	1958	£1.55	£18.75
M12	Regional Recipes	1958	£1.55	£18.75
L24	This Modern World	1965	£1.25	£30.00

DE BEUKELAER (Biscuits)

KF100	All Sports	1932	30p	£30.00
KF900	Film Stars (101-1000)	1932	65p	—
KF100	Film Stars (1001-1100)	1937	65p	£65.00
KF100	Film Stars (B1-100)	1935	75p	—
132	Film Stars (Gold Background)	1939	40p	£53.00
K160	Film Stars (Gold Background)	1936	80p	—
M125	Pinocchio Series	1940	80p	—
M60	Sixty Glorious Years	1940	95p	—
M100	Snow White Series	1940	65p	—

J. BIBBY & SONS LTD. (Cooking Fat)

L25	Don't You Believe It	1955	75p	£18.75
L25	Good Dogs	1955	£2.00	£50.00
L25	How What and Why	1955	75p	£18.75
L25	Isn't it Strange	1955	75p	£18.75
L25	They Gave it a Name	1955	£2.00	£50.00
L25	This Wonderful World	1955	£1.00	£25.00

BIRCHGREY LTD. (Sporting Promotions)

L20	American Golfers	1990	—	£8.50
L25	Panasonic European Open	1989	—	£15.00
L15	The Ryder Cup	1988	—	£15.00

ALFRED BIRD & SONS (Custard)

K48	Happy Families	1938	80p	£38.50

BIRDSEYE FROZEN FOODS

T12	England's Football Team	1980	—	£18.75

BIRKUM (Cheese, Denmark)

25	Motor Cars	1956	—	£9.40

Nowadays one is accustomed to reading of multi-national corporations. Surprisingly many of the larger cigarette card issuers were such almost a century ago. Duke issued cards in South Africa, Goodwin in Australia, Allen & Ginter in Britain and the Canadian firm Ritchie in Germany, Australia, India and England. The American Tobacco Co. issued many cards in Britain with its Old Gold brand, and eventually through its purchase of Ogden, which precipitated the Tobacco War. British firms flourished in their expected spheres of influence, the British Empire, with many issues in Malta, India and Australia. In some cases a series was prepared specifically for one country, but often a set would be issued in several areas.

Sometimes the series had to be adapted to suit the requirements of the country in which it was to be issued. The text of the New Zealand version of Godfrey Phillips Annuals was amended to show different dates for "planting out", while Ardath changed just one card of the Mitchell Our Empire set to include the current New Zealand Prime Minister. In the case of the Player Hints on Association Football the fronts were re-drawn to show Oriental features for the B.A.T. Chinese set.

The criterion in this catalogue for determining whether series should be shown in Part 1 or Part 2 is generally based on the main location of the issuer rather than the area of issue. So all American based Companies will be found in Part 2. Ritchie, which issued cards in Britain, is essentially a Canadian firm, so is also in Part 2. Firms such as International Tobacco Co. and A. & M. Wix, which were based in England, but most of whose issues were abroad, are nevertheless shown in Part 1. One major exception is British American Tobacco Co., which was incorporated in Britain, but all of whose cigarettes were sold abroad, and is therefore shown in Part 2. The decision has in several cases been marginal, and entirely subjective, so when in doubt consult BOTH sections!

B.A.T. ISSUES

In 1902 at the conclusion of the "Tobacco War", the British American Tobacco Co. was incorporated in Britain for the purpose of marketing all I.T.C. and A.T.C. tobacco products in countries other than the U.S.A., Cuba, Great Britain and Ireland.

In many British Empire countries B.A.T. began to market under the name of a subsidiary Company. In Canada it was the Imperial Tobacco Co. of Canada, while in India the Imperial Tobacco Co. of India shared the stage with the Peninsular Tobacco Co. In South Africa the dominant name was United Tobacco Co. and in South America Cia Chilena and Cia Nobleza. In Australia the majority of issues bore the Wills name, either with Capstan or Vice-Regal, except that some also appeared as Havelock Cigarettes, with no issuer's name. Brands in New Zealand appeared under the names of Lambert & Butler, Player and Wills, as well as the local Dominion Tobacco Co; local arrangements were made with companies such as Ardath, as may be deduced from their issue in New Zealand of their versions of sets such as Churchman Eastern Proverbs, Player Tennis and Ogden Swimming Diving & Life Saving.

Card issues appeared with all the above firms' names, as well as some, particularly earlier issues such as the tobacco war Beauties, which have the B.A.T. name. There were also many in foreign languages such as Motor Cigarettes (Portugal), Albert (Belgium) and Gold Dollar (Germany), as well as a number in Chinese and Siamese characters. A large section of B.A.T.'s card output however appears with no clues as to the issuer, both with printed backs (often mentioning cigarettes) and with plain backs.

When the B.A.T. issue utilises the name of a British firm, such as Ogden or Wills, then in the Catalogue the cards will be found listed under that firm, often in a separate group. Anonymous series that were issued exclusively in Canada or South Africa are included in Part 2 under Imperial Tobacco Co. of Canada or United Tobacco Co. respectively. All other Anonymous sets known to have been produced by B.A.T. are listed under that firm in Part 2.

A more detailed explanation of the foundation and ramifications of B.A.T. may be found in the B.A.T. Reference Book, price £12.50.

BISHOPS STORTFORD DAIRY FARMERS (Tea)

Qty		Date	Odds	Sets
25	Dogs' Heads	1967	—	£5.75
25	Freshwater Fish	1964	—	£8.15
25	Historical Buildings	1964	—	£5.00
25	History of Aviation	1964	—	£6.25
25	Passenger Liners	1965	—	£2.50
25	Pond Life	1966	—	£1.50
25	Science in the 20th Century	1966	—	£1.50
25	The Story of Milk	1966	—	£2.50

BLAKEY BOOT PROTECTORS

72	War Series	1916	£4.40	—

BLUE BAND SERIES (Stamps)

24	History of London's Transport	1954	—	£7.50
24	History of London's Transport, 2nd Series	1955	1.90	£45.50
16	See Britain by Coach	1954	—	£1.50

BLUE BIRD STOCKINGS

P12	Exciting Film Stars	1963	—	£7.50
24	Star Cards	1963	£3.15	—

BLUE CAP LTD. (Cheese)

K144	Flixies	1952	50p	£72.00

PACKAGE SERIES

12	Animal Series D	1953	95p	—
8	Animal Series E	1953	£1.25	—
12	Farm Series A	1953	65p	£7.75
12	Farm Series B	1953	65p	£7.75
12	Farm Series C	1953	65p	£7.75
12	Sports Series D	1953	£1.25	—
8	Sports Series E	1953	£1.90	—

E. H. BOOTH & CO. LTD. (Tea)

25	Badges & Uniforms of Famous British Regiments & Corps	1967	—	£1.90
25	Ships & Their Workings	1971	—	£3.75

BOUCHERE'S FIRM

50	War Portraits	1916	£31.25	—

BOW BELLS (Periodical)

BF6	Handsome Men on the British Screen	1922	£2.50	£15.00

BOYS CINEMA (Periodical)

BF6	Famous Film Heroes	1922	£2.20	£13.00
M24	Famous Heroes	1922	£1.55	£37.50
F7	Film Stars (Anon)	1930	£2.20	—
MF8	Film Stars (Brown Front)	1930	£2.50	£20.00
MF8	Film Stars (Black Front)	1931	£2.50	£20.00

BOYS COMIC LIBRARY

Qty		Date	Odds	Sets
4	Heroes of the Wild West	1910	£10.50	—

BOYS FRIEND (Periodical)

3	Famous Boxers Series	1911	£6.25	£18.75
3	Famous Flags Series	1911	£5.00	£15.00
3	Famous Footballers Series	1911	£6.25	£18.75
3	Famous Regiments Series	1911	£5.00	£15.00
BF4	Footballers (½ Length)	1923	£2.00	£8.00
BF5	Footballers (2 per Card)	1922	£2.00	£10.00
BF15	Rising Boxing Stars	1922	£1.25	£18.75

BOYS MAGAZINE (Periodical)

M8	Boxers	1922	£3.75	£30.00
B8	Coloured Studies—Famous Internationals	1922	£3.15	£25.00
M10	Cricketers	1922	£6.25	£62.50
F10	Famous Cricketers Series	1929	£5.00	£50.00
F12	Famous Footballers Series	1929	£2.50	£30.00
BF10	Football Series	1922	£1.55	£15.50
M30	Footballers (Picture 49 x 39mm)	1922	£2.00	—
B64	Footballers & Sportsmen (Picture 56 x 35mm) .	1922	£2.80	—
12	Zat Cards (Cricketers)	1930	£6.25	£75.00
M11	Zat Cards (Cricketers)	1930	£7.50	£82.50

BOYS REALM (Periodical)

BF15	Famous Cricketers	1922	£2.20	£33.00
BF9	Famous Footballers	1922	£1.90	£17.00

C. & T. BRIDGEWATER LTD. (Biscuits)

KF48	Coronation Series	1937	20p	£6.25
KF96	Film Stars, 1st (CE Over No.)	1932	20p	£19.00
KF96	Film Stars, 2nd (E Below No.)	1933	20p	£19.00
KF96	Film Stars, 3rd (Black & White)	1934	30p	£29.00
KF48	Film Stars, 4th	1935	20p	£8.50
KF48	Film Stars, 5th	1937	65p	—
KF48	Film Stars, 6th (F Before No.)	1938	65p	—
F48	Film Stars, 7th	1939	50p	£24.00
KF48	Film Stars, 8th	1940	20p	£6.50
KF48	Radio Stars, 1st (Black & White)	1935	45p	£21.75
KF48	Radio Stars, 2nd (Coloured)	1936	20p	£7.50

JOHN M. BRINDLEY (Printers)

30	Australian Cricketers	1986	—	£10.65
20	Car Badges & Emblems	1987	—	£5.00
30	Cricketers, A Series	1985	—	£12.50
30	Cricketers, 2nd Series	1985	—	£12.50
X16	Cricketers, Howzat, 3rd Series	1985	—	£10.00
30	Cricketers, 4th Series	1986	—	£10.00
X20	Cricketers, 5th Series (Sketches)	1986	—	£10.00
25	Cricketing Greats	1987	—	£3.75
30	Cricket, The Old School	1987	—	£9.40
20	Golfers	1987	—	£7.50

JOHN M. BRINDLEY (Printers)—cont.

Qty		Date	Odds	Sets
20	Locos	1987	—	£3.00
30	London, Brighton & South Coast Railway	1986	—	£6.25
20	Military	1987	—	£3.00
25	Old Golfing Greats	1987	—	£3.75
20	Racing Series	1987	—	£4.40

BRITISH AUTOMATIC CO. (Weight)

Qty		Date	Odds	Sets
24	British Aircraft	1950	65p	£15.50
24	British Birds	1950	75p	£18.00
24	British Locomotives	1948	30p	£7.25
36	British Motor Cars	1954	£1.90	—
44	Coronation Information	1953	£1.00	—
32	Dogs, A Series	1953	20p	£6.50
32	Dogs (A Series, No "Weigh Daily", as 2nd)	1953	65p	£21.00
32	Dogs, 2nd Series	1953	50p	£16.00
24	Famous Trains of the World, 1st Series	1952	50p	£12.00
24	Famous Trains of the World, 2nd Series	1952	50p	£12.00
30	Fortunes, 1st Series	1950	65p	—
32	Fortunes, 2nd Series	1953	50p	£16.00
32	Fortunes, 3rd Series	1954	65p	—
24	Freshwater Fish	1950	75p	£18.00
24	History of Transport	1948	15p	£2.50
44	Jokes	1951	30p	£13.25
24	Olympic Games	1952	£1.75	—
37	Quotations	1951	65p	—
24	Racing & Sports Cars	1957	£1.25	£30.00
24	Space Travel	1955	£1.00	£24.00
24	Speed	1949	20p	£4.75
24	Sportsmen	1955	£1.55	£37.25
20	Twenty Questions	1952	95p	£19.00
24	Warships of the World	1954	15p	£3.75
1	Watch your Weight	1950	—	65p

BRITISH TELECOM

Qty		Date	Odds	Sets
T11	Football Clubs	1987	—	£2.50

BROOKE BOND & CO. LTD. (Tea)
(Special albums available for most series—ask for quote)

Qty		Date	Odds	Sets
50	Adventurers & Explorers	1973	15p	£3.50
50	African Wild Life	1962	15p	£5.00
25	A Journey Downstream	1990	20p	£4.00
L25	A Journey Downstream (Double Cards)...........	1990	50p	£12.50
50	Asian Wild Life	1962	15p	£5.00
50	Bird Portraits (no address)	1957	£1.00	—
50	Bird Portraits (with address)	1957	30p	£15.00
20	British Birds	1954	75p	£15.00
50	British Butterflies	1963	15p	£5.00
50	British Costume	1967	15p	£4.00
50	British Wild Life (Brooke Bond Great			
	Britain Ltd.)	1958	60p	£30.00
50	British Wild Life (Brooke Bond Tea Ltd.)	1958	40p	£20.00
50	British Wild Life (Brooke Bond & Co. Ltd.)	1958	60p	£30.00

BROOKE BOND & CO. LTD. (Tea)—cont.

Qty		Date	Odds	Sets
50	Butterflies of the World	1964	15p	£4.00
12	Chimp Stickers	1986	25p	£3.00
50	Discovering our Coast	1989	15p	£3.50
L25	Discovering our Coast (Double Cards)	1989	40p	£10.00
50	Famous People	1969	15p	£3.50
50	Features of the World	1984	15p	£4.00
L25	Features of the World (Double Cards)	1984	40p	£10.00
50	Flags & Emblems of the World	1967	15p	£5.00
50	Freshwater Fish	1960	15p	£5.00
50	History of Aviation	1972	15p	£3.50
50	History of the Motor Car	1968	15p	£4.00
40	Incredible Creatures (Last Line Sheen Lane)	1985	15p	£6.00
40	Incredible Creatures (Last Line Walton...)	1986	15p	£6.00
40	Incredible Creatures (Last Line P.O. Box ..)	1986	15p	£3.50
40	Incredible Creatures (Thick Cards, Stickers)	1987	£1.75	—
40	Incredible Creatures (Green Back, Irish)	1986	20p	£8.00
L20	Incredible Creatures (Double, Sheen)	1986	60p	—
L20	Incredible Creatures (Double, Walton)	1986	80p	—
L20	Incredible Creatures (Double, PO Box)	1986	75p	—
50	Inventors and Inventions	1975	15p	£3.50
40	Olympic Greats	1979	15p	£4.00
50	Out into Space (Issued with...)	1956	£2.50	—
50	Out into Space (Issued in...)	1958	50p	£25.00
40	Play Better Soccer	1976	15p	£2.50
40	Police File	1977	15p	£2.50
P10	Poly Filla Modelling Cards	1974	25p	£2.50
50	Prehistoric Animals	1972	15p	£3.50
50	Queen Elizabeth I—Queen Elizabeth II	1982	15p	£3.50
L25	Queen Elizabeth I—II (Double Cards)	1982	50p	—
40	Small Wonders	1981	15p	£3.00
12	The Language of Tea	1988	20p	£2.50
25	The Magical World of Disney	1989	20p	£4.00
L25	The Magical World of Disney (Double Cards)	1989	60p	£15.00
50	The Race into Space	1971	15p	£3.50
50	The Saga of Ships	1970	15p	£3.50
50	The Sea—Our Other World	1974	15p	£3.50
50	Transport through the Ages	1966	15p	£3.50
50	Trees in Britain	1966	15p	£3.50
50	Tropical Birds	1961	15p	£4.50
40	Unexplained Mysteries of the World	1987	15p	£3.50
L20	Unexplained Mysteries (Double Cards)	1988	40p	£8.00
40	Vanishing Wildlife	1978	15p	£3.00
50	Wild Birds in Britain	1965	15p	£3.50
50	Wild Flowers, 1st Series	1955	£1.00	£50.00
50	Wild Flowers, 2nd Series (with Issued by)	1959	20p	£10.00
50	Wild Flowers, 2nd Series (no Issued by)	1959	£1.00	£50.00
50	Wild Flowers, 3rd Series	1964	15p	£5.00
50	Wild Life in Danger	1963	15p	£3.50
50	Wonders of Wildlife	1976	15p	£3.50
40	Woodland Wildlife	1980	15p	£2.50

BLACK BACK REPRINTS

Qty		Date	Odds	Sets
50	African Wild Life	1973	—	£3.00
50	British Butterflies	1973	—	£3.00
50	British Costume	1973	—	£3.00

BROOKE BOND & CO. LTD. (Tea)—cont.

Qty		Date	Odds	Sets
50	Famous People	1973	—	£3.00
50	Flags & Emblems of the World	1973	—	£6.25
50	Freshwater Fish	1973	—	£3.00
50	History of the Motor Car	1974	—	£3.00
50	Queen Elizabeth I—Queen Elizabeth II	1987	—	£3.00
40	Small Wonders	1988	—	£2.50
50	The Race into Space	1974	—	£3.00
50	The Saga of Ships	1973	—	£3.00
50	Transport through the Ages	1973	—	£6.25
50	Trees in Britain	1973	—	£3.00
50	Tropical Birds	1974	—	£3.00
40	Vanishing Wildlife	1988	—	£2.50
50	Wild Birds in Britain	1973	—	£3.00
50	Wild Flowers, Series 2	1973	—	£3.00
50	Wild Life in Danger	1973	—	£3.00

CARD GAMES BASED ON REGULAR SERIES

Qty		Date	Odds	Sets
L36	British Costume Snap Game	1974	—	£4.00
L36	Flags & Emblems Snap Game	1974	—	£4.00
L36	Motor History Snap Game	1974	—	£4.00

CANADIAN ISSUES

Qty		Date	Odds	Sets
48	African Animals	1964	—	£3.75
48	Animals & Their Young ("Products")	1972	—	£3.75
48	Animals & Their Young (Tea/Coffee)	1972	£3.75	—
48	Animals of North America	1960	—	£25.00
48	Birds of North America	1962	—	£18.75
48	Butterflies of North America	1965	—	£37.50
48	Canadian/American Songbirds	1966	—	£22.00
48	Dinosaurs	1963	—	£62.50
48	Exploring the Oceans	1971	—	£3.75
48	Indians of Canada	1974	—	£5.00
48	North American Wildlife in Danger	1970	—	£3.75
48	Songbirds of North America (Red Rose/Blue Ribbon)	1959	—	£50.00
48	Songbirds of North America (Red Rose Only, "Album available")	1959	£1.90	—
48	Songbirds of North America (Red Rose Only, "Mount Your Collection")	1959	£1.90	—
48	The Arctic	1973	—	£3.75
48	The Space Age	1969	—	£3.75
48	Transportation through the Ages (Top Line Black)	1967	—	£9.50
48	Transportation through the Ages (Top Line Red)	1967	£1.90	—
48	Trees of North America	1968	—	£9.50
48	Tropical Birds (Top Line Black)	1964	—	£12.50
48	Tropical Birds (Top Line Red)	1964	£1.90	—
48	Wild Flowers of North America	1961	—	£25.00

RHODESIAN ISSUES

Qty		Date	Odds	Sets
50	African Birds	1965	95p	—
50	African Wild Life	1963	£1.50	£75.00
50	Asian Wild Life	1963	£1.25	£62.50
50	Butterflies of the World	1966	£1.25	£62.50
50	Tropical Birds	1962	£1.25	£62.50
50	Wildlife in Danger	1964	£1.55	—

BROOKE BOND & CO. LTD. (Tea)—cont.

	Qty		Date	Odds	Sets
SOUTH AFRICAN ISSUES					
	50	Our Pets	1967	£1.25	£62.50
	50	Out into Space	1966	£1.15	£57.50
	50	Wild Van Afrika (Bilingual)	1965	£1.25	£62.50
	50	Wild Van Afrika (One Language)	1965	£2.00	—
U.S.A. ISSUES					
	48	Animals of North America (Black Back)	1960	£5.00	—
	48	Animals of North America (Blue Back)	1960	£4.40	—
	48	Birds of North America	1962	£3.15	—
	48	Butterflies of North America	1964	£2.20	—
	48	Canadian/American Song Birds	1966	£1.15	£57.50
	48	Dinosaurs	1963	£3.15	—
	48	Tropical Birds	1964	£2.20	—
	48	Wild Flowers of North America	1961	£2.20	—

BROOK MOTORS

G12	Motor Cycles (Cut from Calendars)	1975	—	£5.00
P12	Steam Engines	1973	—	£9.40
P12	Steam Engines (Different)	1970	—	£25.00
P12	The Traction Engine	1967	—	£18.75
P12	Veteran Cars	1961	—	£15.00

DAVID BROWN (Tractors)

XF3	Is Your Slip Showing?	1954	—	£3.75

BROWN & POLSON (Custard)

X25	Recipe Cards	1925	£3.15	—

BROWNE BROS. LTD. (Tea)

25	Birds	1964	—	£7.50
25	British Cavalry Uniforms of the 19th Century	1964	—	£8.15
25	Garden Flowers	1965	—	*£12.50*
25	History of the Railways, 1st	1964	—	£7.50
25	History of the Railways, 2nd	1964	—	£7.50
25	Passenger Liners	1966	—	*£12.50*
25	People & Places	1965	—	£1.50
25	Tropical Birds	1966	—	£1.50
25	Wonders of the Deep	1965	—	£1.90
25	Wonders of the World	1970	—	£5.00

BUCHANAN'S (Jam)

24	Birds and their Eggs	1924	£6.25	—

JOHNNY BUNNY (Medicines)

25	Football Clubs and Badges	1958	—	£18.75

BUNSEN CONFECTIONERY CO.

?100	Famous Figures Series	1925	£7.50	—

BURDALL & BURDALL (Gravy Salt)

Qty		Date	Odds	Sets
30	Wild Animals	1924	£4.40	—

BURGER KING (Restaurants, U.S.A.)

X36	The Empire Strikes Back	1981	—	£8.75

BURTONS WAGON WHEELS (Biscuits)

25	Indian Chiefs	1972	—	£5.00
L7	Pictures of the Wild West	1983	£1.25	£8.75
25	The West	1972	—	£1.90
25	Wild West Action	1972	—	£1.90

BUTTAPAT DAIRIES

?24	People of the World	1915	£12.50	—

C. & G. CONFECTIONERY LTD.

25	Box of Tricks, 1st Series	1965	£1.00	—
25	Box of Tricks, 2nd Series	1965	£1.00	—

CBS IRONMONGERY LTD.

30	Glamorgan Cricketers	1984	—	£12.50

CADBURY BROS. LTD. (Chocolate)

T12	Antartic Series	1913	£18.75	—
X6	Bay City Rollers	1975	—	£1.50
L12	Birds in Springtime	1983	—	£3.00
6	Bournville Series B	1906	£15.00	£90.00
P3	Bournville Views (Script at Side)	1906	£1.90	£5.70
P6	Bournville Views (Block at Side)	1906	£2.50	£15.00
P6	Bournville Views (White Borders)	1906	£2.50	£15.00
P8	Bournville Views (Gravure)	1906	£2.50	—
6	Bournville Village Series	1906	£15.00	—
P25	British Birds (Reward Cards)	1910	£6.25	—
12	British Birds & Eggs	1910	£7.50	—
P12	British Birds & Their Eggs (Reward Cards)	1910	£6.25	—
P32	British Butterflies & Moths (Reward Cards)	1910	£3.75	£120.00
6	British Colonies, Maps & Industries	1908	£12.50	£75.00
120	British Marvels	1936	65p	—
120	British Marvels, Series 2	1936	65p	—
12	British Trees Series	1911	£4.40	£53.00
80	Cadbury's Picture Making	1936	£1.00	—
12	Cathedral Series	1913	£4.40	£53.00
6	Colonial Premiers Series	1908	£12.50	£75.00
12	Constellations Series	1912	£5.00	£60.00
24	Copyright (Inventors) Series	1914	£9.40	—
1	Coronation	1911	—	£17.50
48	Dangerous Animals	1970	—	£6.25
6	Dog Series	1908	£22.50	—
C12	English Industries	1908	£21.50	—
25	Fairy Tales	1924	£1.50	£37.50
27	Famous Steamships	1923	£1.50	£40.50

CADBURY BROS. LTD. (Chocolate)—cont.

Qty		Date	Odds	Sets
12	Fish	1910	£9.40	—
P6	Fish & Bait Series	1909	£22.00	
12	Flag Series	1912	£1.55	£18.50
C6	Flag Series (Joined Pairs)	1912	£3.15	£19.00
C12	Flag Series (Different)	1910	£15.00	—
X12	Flight (Birds)	1982	50p	£6.00
32	Happy Families	1950	£1.25	—
1	Largest Steamers in the World	1907		£18.75
6	Locomotive Series	1906	£18.75	—
12	Match Puzzles	1906	£20.00	—
6	Old Ballad Series	1906	£15.50	—
X6	Panama Series	1910	£18.75	—
X5	Pop Stars	1975	40p	£2.00
1	Poster Series	1910	—	£22.50
X8	Prehistoric Monsters	1975		£1.90
P6	Rivers of the British Isles (Reward Cards)	1910	£10.50	£63.00
24	Shadow Series	1914	£8.15	—
6	Shipping Series (4 sizes)	1910	£7.50	—
T6	Sports Series	1906	*£22.50*	—
24	Strange But True	1970	—	£1.50
12	The Age of the Dinosaur	1971	—	£1.50
25	Transport	1925	20p	£5.00
L6	Wildlife Stickers	1986	—	£1.90

CADET SWEETS ("C.S.")

Qty		Date	Odds	Sets
25	Arms & Armour	1961	—	£1.50
50	Buccaneers	1957	—	£6.25
50	Buccaneers (Different)	1959	—	£12.50
25	Daktari	1969	—	£3.00
50	Doctor Who and The Daleks	1965	£2.00	£100.00
25	Dogs, 1st Series	1958	—	£4.50
25	Dogs, 2nd Series	1958	—	£4.50
25	Evolution of the Royal Navy	1959	—	£1.90
B22	Famous Explorers (Packets)	1960	£4.40	—
50	Fifty Years of Flying	1953	—	£25.00
50	Footballers	1956	—	£5.00
50	Footballers (Different) Large Wording	1959	—	£4.50
50	Footballers (Different) Small Wording	1959	—	£4.50
50	Footballers & Club Colours	1963	—	£3.75
25	How?	1969	—	£2.20
50	Motor Cars	1954	—	£10.00
25	Prehistoric Animals	1961	—	£7.50
50	Railways of the World (Cadet)	1956	—	£4.50
50	Railways of the World (Paramount Laboratories)	1956	—	£8.15
50	Railways of the World (Paramount Sweets)	1956	—	£7.50
50	Record Holders of the World	1956	—	£3.75
25	Record Holders of the World (Different)	1962	—	£1.90
25	Ships through the Ages, 1st Series	1963	—	£1.90
25	Ships through the Ages, 2nd Series	1963	—	£1.90
50	Stingray	1965	—	£25.00
48	The Adventures of Rin Tin Tin	1960	—	£6.25
50	The Conquest of Space	1957	—	£4.40
25	Treasure Hunt	1964	—	£1.90

CADET SWEETS ("C.S.")—cont.

Qty		Date	Odds	Sets
50	U.N.C.L.E.	1966	—	£31.25
25	What Do You Know?	1965	—	£10.00

A. J. CALEY & SON (Confectionery)

K24	Film Stars	1930	£5.00	—
10	Passenger Liners	1939	£6.25	—
48	Wisequacks (Mickey Mouse Weekly)	1932	£2.50	—

CALTEX OIL (Australia)

P6	Stargazer (Haley's Comet)	1986	—	£1.25

F. C. CALVERT & CO. LTD. (Toothpaste)

25	Dan Dare Series	1954	£1.40	£35.00

CANDY GUM

50	Autosprint	1975	—	£3.75
50	Autosprint (Plain Back)	1975	—	£5.00
30	Autosprint, 2nd Series	1975	—	£3.00
30	Autosprint, 2nd Series (Plain Back)	1975	—	£3.75

CANDY NOVELTY CO.

B25/50	Dog Series—A1 Set	1953	—	£1.50

CANNINGS (Jam)

25	Types of British Soldiers	1914	£10.00	—

F. CAPERN (Bird Seed)

?10	British Birds	1925	£9.40	—
P54	Cage Birds	1926	£1.55	—
24	Picture Aviary	1964	—	£10.00
1	Picture Aviary Introductory Card	1964	—	20p

CAPEZIO (Ballet Shoes, U.S.A.)

XF12	Famous Dancers Gallery	1950	—	£18.75

CARD INSERT LTD.

1	Famous Footballers	1953	—	£1.90

CARR'S BISCUITS

M30	Animals of the World	1930	£6.25	—
E20	Cricketers	1967	£1.75	£35.00

CARSON'S CHOCOLATE

72	Celebrities	1902	£10.00	—

CARTER'S LITTLE LIVER PILLS

Qty		Date	Odds	Sets
28	Dominoes	1911	80p	£22.50

F. C. CARTLEDGE (Razor Blades)

X48	Epigrams "A"	1939	20p	£7.50
X64	Epigrams "B"	1939	20p	£9.50
X96	Epigrams "C"	1941	20p	£19.00
50	Famous Prize Fighters	1938	£1.25	£57.50

CASH & CO. (Shoes)

20	War Series	1916	£7.50	—

CASSELLS (Periodical)

M6	British Engines	1923	£7.50	£45.00
B12	Butterflies & Moths Series	1923	£5.00	£60.00

CASTROL OIL

X18	Famous Riders	1958	£1.55	£28.00
X24	Racing Cars	1958	£1.00	£24.00

CAVE AUSTIN & CO. LTD. (Tea)

20	Inventors Series	1923	£8.15	—

CEDE LTD.

25	Coins of the World	1956	—	£3.00

CENTRAL ELECTRICITY AUTHORITY

B10	Interesting Careers	1961	—	£1.25

CEREBOS (Salt)

100	Sea Shells	1925	£1.00	£100.00

CEYLON TEA CENTRE

24	The Island of Ceylon	1955	—	£1.50

CHANNEL 4/CHEERLEADER PRODUCTIONS (TV)

L20	All Time Great Quarterbacks	1989	—	£7.50

H. CHAPPEL & CO. (Confectionery)

10	British Celebrities	1905	£25.00	—

CHARTER TEA & COFFEE CO. LTD.

25	Prehistoric Animals, 1st Series	1962	—	*£12.50*
25	Prehistoric Animals, 2nd Series	1962	—	*£12.50*
25	Strange But True, 1st Series	1961	—	£4.40
25	Strange But True, 2nd Series	1961	—	£4.40
25	Transport through the Ages, 1st Series	1961	—	£5.00
25	Transport through the Ages, 2nd Series	1961	—	£5.00

CHEF & BREWER

Qty		Date	Odds	Sets
L20	Historic Pub Signs	1984	—	£6.25

CHIVERS & SONS LTD. (Preserves)

Qty		Date	Odds	Sets
L125	Firm Favourites	1932	£1.55	—
P6	Studies of English Fruits, Series 1	1924	£3.75	£22.50
P6	Studies of English Fruits, Series 2	1924	£3.75	£22.50
24	Wild Wisdom	1964	£1.55	—
48	Wild Wisdom in Africa	1964	£1.55	—
48	Wild Wisdom, River and Marsh	1964	£1.55	—

PACKAGE ISSUES

Qty		Date	Odds	Sets
L15	Children of other Lands	1952	65p	£9.75
L15	Chivers British Birds	1951	65p	£9.75
L20	On Chivers Farms	1951	65p	£13.00

CHIX CONFECTIONERY CO. LTD.

Qty		Date	Odds	Sets
M12	Batman (Packets)	1990	—	£4.50
X50	Famous Footballers	1960	£1.25	—
X48	Famous Footballers No.1 Series	1953	£1.00	£48.00
X48	Famous Footballers No.2 Series	1956	£1.00	£48.00
X48	Famous Footballers No.3 Series	1958	£1.00	£48.00
X50	Famous Last Words	1970	65p	—
X24	Footballers (Portrait & Action) 1-24	1956	—	£2.50
X24	Footballers (Portrait & Action) 25-48	1956	—	£2.50
L50	Funny Old Folk	1970	—	£10.75
L50	Happy Howlers	1970	65p	£32.50
L50	Krazy Kreatures from Outer Space	1970	*65p*	*£31.25*
L50	Military Uniforms	1970	—	£15.75
L50	Moon Shot	1966	£1.00	—
X50	Popeye	1960	£2.00	—
X24	Scottish Footballers	1960	£3.15	£75.00
L50	Ships of the Seven Seas	1968	£1.50	—
X50	Soldiers of the World	1962	65p	£32.50
X50	Sports through the Ages	1968	£1.75	—
96	TV & Radio Stars	1954	£1.00	—
X50	Wild Animals	1960	£1.25	—

CHU-BOPS (U.S.A.)

Qty		Date	Odds	Sets
L8	Elvis Record Covers	1980	—	£12.50

CHUMS (Periodical)

Qty		Date	Odds	Sets
BF23	Cricketers	1923	£2.50	£57.50
BF20	Football Teams	1922	£1.55	£31.00
F8	Football Teams New Series	1923	£1.90	£15.00
X10	Real Colour Photos (Footballers)	1922	£3.75	—

CHURCH & DWIGHT (Baking Soda, U.S.A.)

Qty		Date	Odds	Sets
M60	Beautiful Birds, New Series	1899	£2.80	£168.00
M60	Beautiful Birds of America	1898	£3.75	£225.00
M60	Beautiful Flowers	1899	£2.50	£150.00
X10	Birds of Prey	1976	—	£4.00

CHURCH & DWIGHT (Baking Soda, U.S.A.)—cont.

Qty		Date	Odds	Sets
M30	Champion Dog Series	1902	£6.25	—
M30	Dairy Animals	1905	£4.40	—
M30	Fish Series	1900	£2.50	£75.00
M30	Game Bird Series	1904	£3.15	£94.50
M60	Interesting Animals	1903	£3.15	£189.00
M30	Mother Goose Series	1900	£4.40	—
M30	New Series of Birds	1908	£1.90	£57.00
M30	New Series of Dogs	1910	£6.25	—
M30	Useful Birds of America	1915	£1.90	£57.00
M30	Useful Birds of America, 2nd Series	1918	£1.90	£57.00
M30	Useful Birds of America, 3rd Series	1922	£1.90	£57.00
M30	Useful Birds of America, Series 4	1924	£1.90	£57.00
M15	Useful Birds of America, Series 5	1924	£1.50	£22.50
M15	Useful Birds of America, Series 6	1924	£1.50	£22.50
M15	Useful Birds of America, Series 7	1924	£1.50	£22.50
M15	Useful Birds of America, Series 8	1924	£1.50	£22.50
M15	Useful Birds of America, Series 9	1926	30p	£4.50
M15	Useful Birds of America, Series 10	1926	40p	£6.00

CLASSIC IMPORTS

25	Ladies of the White House (Consolidated Cigarette Co.)	1989	—	£7.50

THE CLASSIC MOTOR CYCLE

16	Motor Races 1931 (Ogden Reprints)	1989	—	£1.25

CLEVEDON CONFECTIONERY LTD.

50	British Aircraft	1958	£1.55	—
25	British Orders of Chivalry & Valour	1960	£1.90	—
50	British Ships	1959	£1.90	—
B50	British Trains & Engines	1958	£3.15	—
25	Dan Dare	1961	£2.50	—
40	Did You Know?	1963	£1.90	—
40	Famous Cricketers	1959	£6.25	—
25	Famous Cricketers	1962	£6.25	—
50	Famous Football Clubs	1964	£1.00	£50.00
50	Famous Footballers	1961	£2.00	—
50	Famous International Aircraft	1963	90p	£40.00
B50	Famous Screen Stars	1959	£1.75	—
40	Film Stars	1958	£1.75	—
50	Football Club Managers	1959	£3.75	—
50	Hints on Association Football	1961	£1.55	—
50	Hints on Road Safety	1962	£1.55	—
50	International Sporting Stars	1960	£1.00	£50.00
B50	Regimental Badges	1959	£2.20	—
X25	Sporting Memories	1962	£2.80	—
50	The Story of the Olympics	1961	£1.00	—
50	Trains of the World	1962	£1.25	£62.50
B60	Wagon Train	1963	£2.50	—

CLEVELAND (Petrol)

P20	Golden Goals	1970	—	£15.75

CLOVER DAIRIES LTD.

Qty		Date	Odds	Sets
25	Animals & Reptiles	1970	—	£1.50
25	British Rail	1973	—	£1.50
25	People & Places	1972	—	£1.50
25	Prehistoric Animals	1965	—	£1.50
25	Science in the 20th Century	1971	—	£1.50
25	Ships & Their Workings	1971	—	£1.50
25	The Story of Milk	1970	—	£2.50
25	Transport through the Ages	1971	—	£1.50

COCA COLA (Drinks)

M100	Our Flower Paradise (S. Africa)	1960	—	£18.75
X96	The World of Nature (U.S.A.)	1960	—	£15.00

COFTON COLLECTIONS (Shop)

25	Dogs, 1st Series	1988	—	£4.40
25	Dogs, 2nd Series	1988	—	£4.40
25	Dogs, 3rd Series	1988	—	£4.40
L20	Worcestershire County Cricketers	1989	—	£6.25

CECIL COLEMAN LTD. (Confectionery)

24	Film Stars	1935	£4.40	—

COLGATE-PALMOLIVE (Toiletries)

D24	Famous Sporting Trophies	1979	—	£4.40
P4	Royal Britain	1951	£1.55	£6.00

COLINVILLE LTD. (Gum)

M56	Look'n See	1958	£3.75	—
L25	Prairie Pioneers	1959	£2.00	£50.00
L28	Space Fantasy, 1st Series (1-28)	1959	£2.20	—
L28	Space Fantasy, 2nd Series (29-56)	1959	£2.20	—

COLLECTABLES OF SPALDING (Shops)

25	British Cavalry Uniforms	1987	—	£4.50
25	Military Maids	1987	—	£4.50
25	Warriors through the Ages	1987	—	£4.50

COLLECTOR & HOBBYIST (Periodical)

25	Fascinating Hobbies	1950	—	£1.50

COLLECTORS SHOP

25	Bandsmen of the British Army	1960	—	£9.40
3	Bonus Cards	1961	95p	—
2	Bonus Cards 1961-62	1961	—	£2.50
25	Butterflies & Moths	1961	—	£7.50

COLT 45 (Drink)

Qty		Date	Odds	Sets
X5/6	Advertising Slogans (Silk)	1976	£2.50	£12.50
X4	American Scenes (Beer Mats)	1975	—	£2.50

COMET SWEETS

25	A. & M. Denis on Safari, 1st Series	1961	—	£1.90
25	A. & M. Denis on Safari, 2nd Series	1961	—	£1.90
25	Modern Wonders (Black Back)	1961	—	£1.50
25	Modern Wonders (Blue Back)	1961	—	£10.00
25	Olympic Achievements, 1st Series	1960	—	£2.50
25	Olympic Achievements, 2nd Series	1960	—	£2.50
M22	Olympic Achievements (Package)	1960	£4.40	—

COMIC LIFE (Periodical)

BF4	Sports Champions	1922	£3.15	£12.50

COMMODEX (Gum)

L88	Operation Moon	1969	95p	£83.50
L120	Super Cars	1970	75p	—

COMMONWEALTH SHOE & LEATHER CO. (U.S.A.)

M12	Makes of Planes	1930	£1.90	£22.75

COMO CONFECTIONERY PRODUCTS LTD.

L25	History of the Wild West, 1st	1963	£1.55	—
L25	History of the Wild West, 2nd	1963	—	£6.25
50	Lenny's Adventures	1961	75p	£37.50
50	Noddy & His Playmates	1962	—	£8.25
L25	Noddy's Adventures, 1st Series	1958	75p	—
L25	Noddy's Adventures, 2nd Series	1958	90p	—
25	Noddy's Budgie & Feathered Friends, 1st	1964	90p	—
25	Noddy's Budgie & Feathered Friends, 2nd	1964	75p	—
L50	Noddy's Friends Abroad	1959	95p	—
L50	Noddy's Nursery Rhyme Friends	1959	90p	—
L50	Sooty's Adventures	1960	90p	—
L50	Sooty's New Adventures, 2nd	1961	—	£7.50
50	Sooty's Latest Adventures, 3rd	1963	80p	—
25	Speed, 1st Series	1962	£1.25	—
25	Speed, 2nd Series	1962	—	£3.75
25	Supercar, 1st Series	1962	£2.20	—
25	Supercar, 2nd Series	1962	£1.50	£37.50
25	Top Secret, 1st Series	1965	£1.05	—
25	Top Secret, 2nd Series	1965	£1.05	—
L26	XL5, 1st Series	1965	£7.50	—
L26	XL5, 2nd Series	1966	£7.50	—

COMPTON'S GRAVY SALT

22	Footballers, Serie A (Black)	1924	£5.00	—
22	Footballers, Serie A (Coloured)	1924	£5.65	—
22	Footballers, Serie B (Black)	1924	£5.00	—
22	Footballers, Serie B (Coloured)	1924	£6.25	—

COMPTON'S GRAVY SALT —cont.

Qty		Date	Odds	Sets
22	Footballers, Serie C	1924	£6.25	—
22	Footballers, Serie D	1924	£6.25	—

COOPER & CO. LTD. (Tea)

50	Do You Know?	1962	—	£3.75
25	Inventions & Discoveries, 1st Series	1962	—	£18.75
25	Inventions & Discoveries, 2nd Series	1962	—	£18.75
25	Mysteries & Wonders of the World, 1st	1961	—	£1.90
25	Mysteries & Wonders of the World, 2nd	1961	—	£1.50
25	Prehistoric Animals, 1st Series	1962	—	£18.75
25	Prehistoric Animals, 2nd Series	1962	—	£18.75
25	Strange But True, 1st Series	1961	—	£1.50
25	Strange But True, 2nd Series	1961	—	£1.50
24	The Island of Ceylon	1955	£1.90	—
25	Transport through the Ages, 1st Series	1961	—	£3.75
25	Transport through the Ages, 2nd Series	1961	—	£3.00

CO-OPERATIVE SOCIETIES (Shops)

D306	Espana '82. Complete with Album	1982	—	£9.50
	Special Poster for above (only if ordered at the same time)	1982	—	65p
B48	World Cup Teams & Players, Complete with Poster	1982	—	£3.75

COUNTY PRINT SERVICES (Commercial)

X24	Cricket Teams 1884-1900	1990	—	£6.25
50	Cricketers 1890	1989	—	£7.50
50	Cricketers 1896	1989	—	£7.50

COW & GATE (Baby Food)

X24	Advertisement Cards	1928	£1.25	£30.00
X48	Happy Families	1928	65p	£31.25

COWANS (Confectionery, Canada)

24	Dog Pictures	1930	£3.75	£90.00
24	Horse Pictures	1930	£3.75	—
24	Learn to Swim	1929	£3.75	—
24	Noted Cats	1930	£3.75	£90.00

CRESCENT CONFECTIONERY CO.

100	Sportsmen	1928	£10.50	—

CROMWELL STORES

25	Do You Know?	1963	—	£5.00
25	Racing Colours	1963	—	£5.00

CROSBIE (Preserves)

K54	Miniature Playing Cards	1938	65p	—

JOSEPH CROSFIELD & SONS LTD. (Soap)

Qty		Date	Odds	Sets
36	Film Stars	1924	£4.40	—

CRYSELCO ELECTRIC LAMPS

X25	Beautiful Waterways	1939	65p	£16.25
X25	Buildings of Beauty	1938	75p	£18.75
X12	Interesting Events of 60 Years Ago	1955	—	£18.75

D. CUMMINGS & SON (Commercial)

64	Famous Fighters	1947	£1.25	£80.00

DAILY EXPRESS (Newspaper)

X59	Car Cards	1971	—	£3.00

DAILY HERALD (Newspaper)

32	Cricketers	1954	£2.20	—
32	Footballers	1954	80p	—
32	Turf Personalities	1955	15p	£3.75

DAILY ICE CREAM CO.

24	Modern British Locomotives	1954	—	£9.50

DAILY MAIL (Newspaper)

P176	War Photographs	1916	95p	—

DAILY MIRROR (Newspaper)

B72	Chart Toppers	1989	—	£4.40
M100	Star Soccer Sides	1972	25p	£25.00

DAILY SKETCH (Newspaper)

40	World Cup Souvenir	1970	80p	£32.00

DAINTY NOVELS

10	World's Famous Liners	1912	£10.00	—

DANDY GUM

M200	Birds (F1-200)	1968	—	£50.00
K50	Bird Series (Transfers)	1950	£1.25	—
M160	Cars and Bikes	1977	50p	—
M97	Film & Entertainment Stars (Serie G)	1968	30p	£29.00
M116	Flag Parade	1965	—	£20.00
M160	Flag Parade	1978	—	£31.25
M55	Football World Cup (Playing Card Inset)	1986	—	£8.15
B72	Motor Cars	1966	50p	—
B53	Our Modern Army (Playing Card Inset)	1958	—	£35.00
B43/53	Our Modern Army (Playing Card Inset)	1958	15p	£6.25
B53	Pin Ups (Playing Card Inset)	1956	£1.25	£66.25
B53	Pin Ups (Playing Card Inset, Different)	1978	—	£6.25

THEMATIC COLLECTING

Many people come into the hobby not because of an interest in cards themselves, but as an extension of an already existing interest. For there cannot be one subject that is not covered by at least one set of cards, in every case with an illustration and often with informative text.

One of the most popular themes to be collected is sport, and particularly cricket, golf and soccer. The value to the enthusiast can be shown by series such as Taddy County Cricketers and Prominent Footballers which depicted almost every first class player of the time, and the series of 2,462 different Footballers issued in the 1920's by Godfrey Phillips with their Pinnace Cigarettes. In the U.S.A. Baseball is the main cartophilic interest, while in Canada it is hockey. Other games sought by collectors are tennis, billiards, chess and archery.

Militaria, shipping and cinema are other themes that were issued in large numbers and have many devotees. Subjects such as aviation, opera, motoring, music hall and railways are also extensively covered, as are modern subjects such as space exploration and television. The significance of most of these is that they are contemporary records, and one can trace the development of the subject through a period of nearly a century.

E. HENDREN.

ARCHERY

TURF CIGARETTES

DANNY KAYE

CHURCHMAN'S CIGARETTES

GENE TUNNEY

WAR SERIES

GENERAL JOFFRE.
Commander-in-Chief French Army.

PROMINENT FOOTBALLERS.

W. J. LYON.
PRESTON NORTH END.

STANLEY HOLLOWAY.

Tobacco Companies occasionally felt the need to reprint their own cards; the most notable example of this was Player after the Great War not having any new series prepared, and therefore re-issuing 'Cries of London 2nd Series, Miniatures, Players Past & Present and Characters from Dickens. However a new dimension was achieved by Brooke Bond, who have reprinted many of their earlier sets (with a different coloured back) SOLELY FOR SELLING TO COLLECTORS.

Several other commercial reprints appeared before Murray Cards (International) Ltd., began their "Nostalgia" reprints; these are carefully selected old series, which are very difficult to obtain in the original form, such as Wills 1896 Cricketers, Cope Golfers and Player Military Series. More recently Victoria Gallery have printed under license from Imperial Tobacco Co. a number of their series, including two that were never actually issued! There have also been a number of reprints in North America, mainly of Baseball and Hockey cards, but also of the modern set, Mars Attacks. All these cards are clearly marked to show that they are reprints.

Early fears about the proliferation of reprints have proved to be unfounded. Their advantages are that on the one hand they have made available to a large number of collectors, cards that they would otherwise be unable to obtain or afford. In the other case they have fulfilled a demand for cards to be sold commercially in frames, and thereby relieved some of the pressure on supply of the originals, to the benefit of general collectors. In no case has the presence of reprints adversely affected the value of the originals.

One problem that has arisen, is the attempt by some dishonest people to remove all mention of the reprint and attempt to pass the cards off as originals. This has also happened in the case of Taddy Clowns and Wills Advertisement Cards, which have been cut from book illustrations and doctored. It therefore behoves the collector to be extremely careful when offered such rarities, or better still only to buy from a reputable dealer.

DANDY GUM—cont.

Qty		Date	Odds	Sets
M70	Pop Stars (Serie P)	1977	25p	£17.50
M56	Rock Stars (Playing Card Inset)	1987	—	£7.50
M100	Soldier Parade	1970	—	£25.00
M72	Veteran & Vintage Cars (V1-72)	1966	65p	£46.75
M100	Wild Animals (H1-100)	1969	—	£18.75
M200	Wonderful World (Y1-200)	1978	—	£31.25

LIAM DEVLIN & SONS (Confectionery)

M36	Coaching Gaelic Football	1960	£3.75	—
48	Corgi Toys	1971	—	£31.25
50	Do You Know?	1964	—	£3.00
B50	Famous Footballers (New Series)	1952	£3.75	—
B50	Famous Footballers (A1)	1953	£3.00	—
B50	Famous Footballers (A2)	1954	£3.00	—
50	Famous Footballers (A3)	1955	£3.00	£150.00
B54	Famous Speedway Stars	1960	£6.25	—
B45	Fastest on Earth	1953	£2.20	—
36	Flags of the Nations	1960	£1.90	—
48	Gaelic Sportstars	1960	£3.15	—
48	Irish Fishing	1962	—	£8.75
50	Modern Transport	1966	—	£3.75
48	Our Dogs	1963	£3.00	—
48	Right or Wrong?	1963	£2.50	—
B35	Walt Disney Characters	1956	£2.50	—
B48	Wild Animals by George Cansdale	1954	£2.50	—
48	Wild Wisdom	1970	£1.55	—
50	Wonders of the World	1972	—	£3.00
100	World Flag Series	1970	£3.75	—

DICKSON ORDE & CO. (Confectionery)

50	Footballers	1960	—	£3.75
25	Ships through the Ages	1961	£1.00	—
25	Sports of the Countries	1962	—	£2.20

DINKIE PRODUCTS LTD. (Hair Grips)

L24	Films (Plain Backs)	1952	£1.90	—
L20	Gone with the Wind (Series 5)	1948	£2.50	—
X20	M.G.M. Films (Series 3)	1948	—	£20.00
L24	M.G.M. Films (Series 7)	1949	—	£20.00
L24	M.G.M. Films (Series 9)	1950	—	£20.00
L24	M.G.M. Films (Series 10)	1951	£2.50	—
L24	M.G.M. Films (Series 11)	1951	£2.50	—
L24	Paramount Pictures (Series 8)	1950	—	£20.00
X24	Stars & Starlets (Series 1)	1947	—	£20.00
X20	Stars & Starlets (Series 2)	1947	—	£20.00
L24	Warner Bros. Artistes (Series 4)	1948	—	£20.00
L24	Warner Bros. Films (Series 6)	1949	—	£20.00

DIRECT TEA SUPPLY CO.

25	British Uniforms of the 19th Century	1958	—	£15.75

DISNEY MAGAZINE

Qty		Date	Odds	Sets
P8	Disney Characters	1987	—	£6.25

F. M. DOBSON (Confectionery)

X144	Flags of the World	1980	—	£12.50
100	Newcastle & Sunderland's 100 Greatest Footballers	1982	—	£4.40
2	Error Cards	1982	—	75p

A. & J. DONALDSON (Commercial)

?500	Sports Favourites	1953	£4.00	—

DONRUSS (Gum, U.S.A.)

X59	B.M.X. Card Series	1984	—	£9.40
X56	Dallas	1981	—	£6.25
X66	Disneyland	1965	—	£37.50
X66	Elvis	1978	—	£12.50
X66	Freddie and the Dreamers	1965	—	£25.00
X66	Magnum P.I.	1983	—	£7.50
X66	M.A.S.H.	1982	—	£7.50
X99	Moonraker	1979	—	£10.75
X66	1980 P.G.A. Tour	1981	—	£50.00
X66	1981 P.G.A. Tour	1982	—	£50.00
X66	Rock Stars	1978	—	£9.40
X66	Sgt. Peppers Lonely Hearts Club Band	1978	—	£8.75
X78	The Dark Crystal	1982	—	£6.25
X74	Tron	1983	—	£5.00

DOUBLE DIAMOND (Beer)

P5	Puzzle Pictures (Beer Mats)	1976	—	£1.90

DRYFOOD LTD. (Confectionery)

50	Animals of the World	1956	—	£3.00
K50	Zoo Animals	1955	—	£3.00

DUCHESS OF DEVONSHIRE DAIRY CO. LTD.

L25	Devon Beauty Spots	1936	£3.75	£93.75

DUNHILLS (Confectionery)

25	Ships & Their Workings	1962	—	£5.00

DUNKIN (Confectionery, Spain)

X88	Martial Arts	1976	—	£31.25
M50	Motor Cycles of the World	1976	£1.00	£50.00

DUNNS (Chocolate)

60	Animals	1924	£3.75	—

DUTTON'S BEER

Qty		Date	Odds	Sets
12	Team of Sporting Heroes	1981	—	£1.25

THE EAGLE (Periodical)

M12	Marvels of this Modern Age (with Album)	1965	—	£3.75
16	Wallet of Soccer Stars	1965	—	£4.40

EAST KENT NATIONAL BUS CO.

L8	British Airways Holidays	1984	—	£1.25

J. EDMONDSON & CO. (Confectionery)

26	Actresses "FROGA"	1901	£42.50	—
4	Aeroplane Models	1939	£10.00	—
?40	Art Picture Series	1914	£10.00	—
15	Birds & Their Eggs	1924	£6.25	—
?20	Boy Scout Proficiency Badges	1924	£15.00	—
20	British Ships	1925	£1.55	£31.00
20	Dogs	1924	£5.00	—
20	Famous Castles	1925	£4.40	—
40	Flags of all Nations	1923	£4.40	—
24	Pictures from the Fairy Stories	1930	£3.75	—
24	Popular Sports	1930	£5.00	—
25	Sports & Pastimes Series	1916	£8.75	—
12	Throwing Shadows on the Wall	1937	£2.00	£25.00
25	War Series	1916	£10.00	—
12	Woodbine Village	1936	£2.00	£25.00
26	Zoo Alphabet	1935	£4.40	—

EDWARDS & SONS (Confectionery)

27	Popular Dogs	1954	£1.90	—
12	Products of the World	1957	—	£1.25
25	Transport Present & Future (Descriptive)	1956	—	£1.50
25	Transport Present & Future (Non-Descriptive)	1955	—	£1.90
25	Wonders of the Universe	1956	—	£1.50

ELECTROLUX (Leisure Appliances)

P16	Weekend Tours	1990	—	£5.75

ELKES BISCUITS LTD.

25	Do You Know?	1964	—	£1.90

ELY BREWERY CO. LTD.

B24	Royal Portraits	1953	£1.25	£30.00

EMPIRE MARKETING BOARD

12	Empire Shopping	1926	£2.00	£24.00

H. E. EMPSON & SONS LTD. (Tea)

Qty		Date	Odds	Sets
25	Birds	1962	—	£5.00
25	British Cavalry Uniforms of the 19th Century ...	1963	—	£9.40
25	Garden Flowers	1966	65p	£16.25
25	History of the Railways, 1st Series	1966	75p	£18.75
25	History of the Railways, 2nd Series	1966	75p	£18.75
25	Passenger Liners	1964	50p	£12.50
25	Tropical Birds	1966	50p	£12.50
25	Wonders of the Deep	1965	—	£1.90

ENGLISH & SCOTTISH C.W.S. (Shops)

50	British Sports Series	1904	£25.00	—
25	Humorous Peeps into History (1-25)	1927	£2.00	£50.00
25	Humorous Peeps into History (26-50)	1928	£3.75	—
25	In Victoria's Days	1930	£2.00	£50.00
X12	The Rose of the Orient Film Series	1925	30p	£3.50
X12	The Rose of the Orient 2nd Film Series	1925	40p	£4.75
X12	The Story of Tea (Blue Back)	1925	45p	£5.25
X12	The Story of Tea (Brown Back, Different)	1925	40p	£4.75

ESKIMO FOODS

P4	The Beatles	1965	—	£25.00

JOHN E. ESSLEMONT LTD. (Tea)

25	Before our Time	1966	—	£2.50
25	Into Space	1966	—	£2.50

ESSO PETROLEUM CO.

M16	Squelchers (Football)	1970	80p	£12.50

ESTA MEDICAL LABORATORIES INC. (U.S.A.)

E6	Curiosa of Conception	1960	—	£6.00

EVERSHED & SON LTD. (Soap)

25	Sports and Pastimes	1914	£10.00	—

EVERY GIRL'S PAPER

BF17	Film Stars	1924	£2.50	£42.50

EWBANKS LTD. (Confectionery)

25	Animals of the Farmyard	1960	—	£1.50
25	British Uniforms	1956	—	£1.90
25	Miniature Cars & Scooters	1960	—	£2.50
50	Ports & Resorts of the World	1960	—	£3.00
25	Ships Around Britain	1961	—	£1.50
25	Sports & Games	1958	—	£2.50
25	Transport through the Ages (Black Back)	1957	—	£1.50
25	Transport through the Ages (Blue Back)	1957	—	£9.50

EXPRESS WEEKLY (Periodical)

Qty		Date	Odds	Sets
25	The Wild West (No Overprint)	1958	—	£2.50
25	The Wild West (Red Overprint)	1958	—	£1.50

FACCHINO'S CHOCOLATE WAFERS

100	Cinema Stars	1936	35p	£35.00
50	How or Why!	1937	40p	£20.00
50	People of All Lands	1937	£1.25	—
50	Pioneers	1937	£1.00	£50.00

FAITH PRESS (Commercial)

10	Boy Scouts (LCC)	1928	£3.45	£34.50

FAMILY STAR (Periodical)

K52	Fortune Telling Cards	1952	—	£10.50

FARM TO DOOR SUPPLIES (LUTON) LTD.

25	Castles of Great Britain	1965	£2.50	—
25	Cathedrals of Great Britain	1964	£2.50	—

FARROWS (Sauces)

50	Animals in the Zoo	1925	£3.75	—

FAX-PAX (Commercial)

X36	ABC and Numbers	1987	—	£3.50
X36	Alphabet Spelling	1988	—	£3.50
X40	Castles	1990	—	£3.50
X40	Cathedrals & Minsters	1989	—	£3.50
X36	Equestrian	1987	—	£3.50
X36	Fables	1987	—	£3.50
X36	Football Greats	1989	—	£3.50
X36	Football Stars	1989	—	£3.50
X36	Golf	1987	—	£10.00
X40	Historic Houses	1990	—	£3.50
X36	Kings & Queens	1988	—	£3.50
X36	London	1987	—	£3.50
X36	Nursery Rhymes	1987	—	£3.50
X40	Scotland's Heritage	1990	—	£3.50
X38	Tennis	1987	—	£7.50

ALEX FERGUSON (Confectionery)

41	V.C. Heroes	1916	£15.00	—

FILM PICTORIAL (Periodical)

P2	Film Stars (Silk)	1923	£18.75	—

JOHN FILSHILL LTD. (Confectionery)

24	Birds & Their Eggs	1924	£3.75	—
25	Footballers	1924	£6.25	—

FINDUS (Frozen Foods)

Qty		Date	Odds	Sets
20	All About Pirates	1967	—	£3.75

FINE FARE TEA

25	Inventions & Discoveries, 1st Series	1965	—	£5.00
25	Inventions & Discoveries, 2nd Series	1965	—	£5.00
12	Your Fortune in a Tea-cup	1966	—	£2.50

FISH MARKETING BOARD

18	Eat More Fish	1930	£1.90	—

FIZZY FRUIT (Confectionery)

25	Buses and Trams	1959	—	£15.00

FLEER GUM INC. (U.S.A.)

X40	Crazy Magazine Covers, 3rd	1981	—	£6.25
X66	Gomer Pyle, U.S.M.C.	1965	—	£15.75
X72	Here's Bo!	1980	—	£4.50
E12	Here's Bo Posters	1980	—	£3.00
X66	McHale's Navy	1965	—	£15.75

FLEETWAY PUBLICATIONS LTD.

P28	Football Teams	1959	£1.00	£28.00
P2	Pop Stars (Roxy)	1961	—	£1.25
50	Star Footballers of 1963	1963	50p	£25.00

FLORENCE CARDS (Commercial)

24	Luton Corporation Tramways	1983	—	£1.50
T20	Tramway Scenes	1985	—	£1.50

FORD MOTOR CO. LTD.

M50	Major Farming	1955	£4.00	—

FOSTER CLARK PRODUCTS (Malta)

50	The Sea—Our Other World	1974	—	£9.00

FOSTER'S LAGER

P4	How to Order your Fosters (Beermats)	1988	—	£1.00

A. C. W. FRANCIS (Confectionery, Grenada)

25	Football Clubs & Badges	1967	—	£10.00
25	Pond Life	1967	—	£6.25
25	Sports of the Countries	1967	—	£7.50

LES FRERES (Shop)

25	Aircraft of World War II	1964	—	£5.00

J. S. FRY & SONS LTD. (Confectionery)

Qty		Date	Odds	Sets
3	Advertisement Cards	1910	£18.75	—
50	Ancient Sundials	1924	£2.00	£100.00
50	Birds & Poultry	1912	£1.55	£77.50
24	Birds & Their Eggs	1912	£2.00	£48.00
15	China & Porcelain	1907	£10.00	£150.00
P2	Coronation Postcards	1911	£7.50	—
25	Days of Nelson	1906	£6.00	£150.00
25	Days of Wellington	1906	£5.00	£125.00
25	Empire Industries	1924	£3.15	—
50	Exercises for Men & Women	1926	£3.15	—
48	Film Stars	1934	£1.50	—
50	Fowls, Pigeons & Dogs	1908	£2.20	£110.00
P12	Fun Cards	1972	—	£1.25
25	Match Tricks	1921	*£18.75*	—
15	National Flags	1908	£3.75	£56.25
50	Nursery Rhymes	1917	£1.90	£95.00
50	Phil May Sketches	1905	£2.20	£110.00
25	Red Indians	1927	£3.15	—
25	Rule Britannia	1915	£4.40	£110.00
50	Scout Series	1912	£3.75	£187.50
48	Screen Stars	1928	£1.90	—
120	This Wonderful World	1935	95p	—
50	Time & Money in Different Countries	1908	£2.00	£100.00
50	Tricks & Puzzles (Black Back)	1924	£1.75	£87.50
50	Tricks & Puzzles (Blue Back)	1918	£2.00	£100.00
6	War Leaders (Campaign Packets)	1915	£17.50	—
25	With Captain Scott at the South Pole	1913	£5.00	£125.00

CANADIAN ISSUES

Qty		Date	Odds	Sets
50	Children's Nursery Rhymes	1912	£7.50	—
25	Radio Series	1912	£5.00	—
50	Scout Series—Second Series	1913	£6.25	—
50	Treasure Island Map	1912	£4.40	—

G. B. & T. W. (Commercial)

L20	Golfing Greats	1989	—	£8.50

GARDEN NEWS

T6	Flowers	1988	—	£1.50
T6	Vegetables	1988	—	£1.50

GAUMONT CHOCOLATE BAR

F50	Film Stars	1936	£1.75	—

GAYCON PRODUCTS LTD. (Confectionery)

25	Adventures of Pinky & Perky, 1st Series	1961	£1.00	—
25	Adventures of Pinky & Perky, 2nd Series	1961	£1.00	—
50	British Birds & Their Eggs	1961	—	£3.75
25	British Butterflies	1962	—	£12.50
25	Do You Know?, 1st Series	1964	£1.00	—
25	Do You Know?, 2nd Series	1964	£1.00	—
50	Flags of All Nations	1963	80p	—

GAYCON PRODUCTS LTD. (Confectionery) — cont.

Qty		Date	Odds	Sets
25	History of the Blue Lamp, 1st Series	1962	—	£7.50
25	History of the Blue Lamp, 2nd Series	1962	—	£7.50
30	Kings & Queens	1961	—	£1.90
25	Modern Motor Cars	1959	£1.55	—
25	Modern Motor Cars of the World, 1st Series	1962	£1.90	—
25	Modern Motor Cars of the World, 2nd Series	1962	£1.90	—
25	Red Indians, 1st Series	1960	—	£4.50
25	Red Indians, 2nd Series	1960	—	£4.50
25	Top Secret, 1st Series	1963	£1.25	—
25	Top Secret, 2nd Series	1963	£1.25	—

GEES FOOD PRODUCTS

Qty		Date	Odds	Sets
30	Kings & Queens	1961	—	£7.50
16	See Britain by Coach	1959	—	£1.25

GEM LIBRARY (Periodical)

Qty		Date	Odds	Sets
BF4	Footballers—Autographed Action Series	1923	£2.20	£8.80
BF6	Footballers—Autographed Real Action Photo Series	1922	£1.90	£11.50
BF15	Footballers—Special Action Photo	1922	£1.75	£26.25
L16	Marvels of the Future	1929	£2.00	£32.00

ALFRED GERBER (Cheese)

Qty		Date	Odds	Sets
M143	Glorious Switzerland	1952	80p	—

GIRLS FRIEND (Periodical)

Qty		Date	Odds	Sets
B6	Actresses (Silk)	1913	£8.75	£52.50

GIRLS MIRROR (Periodical)

Qty		Date	Odds	Sets
BF10	Actors & Actresses	1922	£2.00	£20.00

GIRLS WEEKLY

Qty		Date	Odds	Sets
12	Flower Fortune Cards	1912	£10.00	—

GLAMOUR (Magazine)

Qty		Date	Odds	Sets
F52	Pop Singer Card Game	1957	50p	£26.00

GLENGETTIE TEA

Qty		Date	Odds	Sets
25	Animals of the World	1964	—	£1.50
25	Birds & Their Eggs	1970	—	£3.00
25	British Locomotives	1959	—	£2.20
25	Do You Know?	1970	—	£1.50
25	Historical Scenes	1968	—	£1.50
25	History of the Railways, 1st Series	1974	—	£1.50
25	History of the Railways, 2nd Series	1974	—	£1.50
25	International Air Liners	1963	—	£1.50
25	Medals of the World (Black Back)	1959	—	£1.50
25	Medals of the World (Blue Back)	1959	—	£9.40
25	Modern Transport (Black Back)	1963	—	£8.15

GLENGETTIE TEA — cont.

Qty		Date	Odds	Sets
25	Modern Transport (Blue Back)	1963	—	£9.40
25	Naval Battles	1971	—	£1.50
25	Rare British Birds	1967	—	£3.75
25	Sovereigns, Consorts & Rulers of G.B., 1st	1970	—	£9.40
25	Sovereigns, Consorts & Rulers of G.B., 2nd	1970	—	£9.40
25	The British Army (Black Back)	1976	—	£1.50
25	The British Army (Blue Back)	1976	—	£1.50
25	Trains of the World	1966	—	£1.50
25	Veteran & Vintage Cars	1966	—	£15.00
25	Wild Flowers	1961	—	£3.00

GLENTONS LTD. (Shop)

24	World's Most Beautiful Butterflies	1910	£4.40	—

J. GODDARD & SONS LTD. (Metal Polish)

L4	Cleaning a Silver Teapot	1928	£2.50	—
L3	Four Generations	1923	75p	£2.25
L12	London Views	1925	65p	£7.75
L12	Old Silver	1924	75p	£9.00
L9	Old Silver at the Victoria & Albert Museum	1933	£1.50	£13.50
L12	Ports of the World	1928	£1.55	£18.50
L12	Present Day Silverware	1937	£1.00	£12.00
L4	Silverware with Flowers I	1928	£1.55	£6.25
L8	Silverware with Flowers II	1933	£1.90	£15.00
L2	Use & Cleaning of Silverware I	1926	65p	£1.30
L6	Use & Cleaning of Silverware II	1937	£3.15	—
L8	Views of Leicester	1934	£2.75	£22.00
L12	Views of Old Leicester	1928	£2.75	£33.00

GOLDEN FLEECE (Australia)

X36	Pedigree Dogs	1972	—	£10.50

GOLDEN GRAIN TEA

25	Birds	1970	—	£8.15
25	British Cavalry Uniforms of the 19th Century	1964	—	£4.40
25	Garden Flowers	1971	—	£1.50
25	Passenger Liners	1970	—	£1.50

GOLDEN WONDER (Potato Crisps)

24	Soccer All Stars	1978	—	£1.50
14	Space Cards (Round Corners)	1979	—	£1.25
14	Space Cards (Square Corners)	1979	—	£1.25
24	Sporting All Stars	1979	—	£1.50
24	TV All Stars	1979	—	£1.50
36	World Cup Soccer All Stars	1978	—	£3.50

GOODIES LTD. (Confectionery)

25	Flags & Emblems	1961	—	£2.50
25	Indian Tribes	1975	£1.00	£25.00
25	Mini Monsters	1975	90p	£22.50

GOODIES LTD. (Confectionery) — cont.

Qty		Date	Odds	Sets
24	Olympics	1972	£1.00	£24.00
25	Pirates	1976	£1.00	£25.00
25	Prehistoric Animals	1969	£1.25	—
25	Robbers & Thieves	1976	£1.00	£25.00
25	The Monkees, 1st Series	1967	40p	£10.00
25	The Monkees, 2nd Series	1968	£1.90	—
25	Vanishing Animals	1977	£1.00	£25.00
25	Weapons through the Ages	1974	90p	£22.50
25	Wicked Monarchs	1973	90p	£22.50
25	Wide World/People of Other Lands	1968	90p	£22.50
25	Wild Life	1977	£1.00	£25.00
25	World Cup '74	1974	£1.00	£25.00

D. W. GOODWIN & CO. (Flour)

36	Careers for Boys & Girls	1930	£6.25	—
24	Extra Rhymes, 2nd Series	1930	£9.40	—
36	Flags of all Nations	1930	£5.00	—
36	Jokes Series	1930	£6.25	—
?30	Optical Illusions	1930	£6.25	—
36	Ships Series	1930	£7.50	—
36	World Interest Series	1930	£5.00	—

WILLIAM GOSSAGE & SONS LTD. (Soap)

48	British Birds & Their Eggs	1924	£1.50	£72.00
48	Butterflies & Moths	1924	£1.00	£48.00

GOWERS & BURGONS (Tea)

25	British Birds & Their Nests	1970	—	£5.00
25	Family Pets	1964	—	£1.50
25	People & Places	1970	—	£1.50
25	Prehistoric Animals	1969	—	£12.50
25	Sailing Ships Through the Ages	1971	—	£12.50
25	The Circus	1964	—	£15.00
25	Veteran & Vintage Cars	1965	—	£12.50
25	Veteran Racing Cars	1964	65p	—

GRAIN PRODUCTS (New Zealand)

L20	Fire Engines	1988	—	£6.00
P10	Vintage & Veteran Cars	1985	—	£4.40

GRANGERS NO. "1"

12	Dr. Mabuse Series	1926	£6.25	£75.00

GRANOSE FOODS LTD.

M48	Adventures of Billy the Buck	1956	—	£3.00
M16	Air Transport	1957	—	£1.50
M16	Animal Life	1957	—	£1.25
25	Animals in the Service of Man	1965	£1.90	—
M16	Aquatic & Reptile Life	1957	—	£1.50
M48	King of the Air	1956	30p	—

GRANOSE FOODS LTD. —cont.

Qty		Date	Odds	Sets
M48	Life Story of Blower the Whale	1956	40p	—
M48	Lone Leo the Cougar	1955	40p	—
L20	150 Years of British Locomotives	1981	65p	—
M16	Our Winged Friends	1957	30p	—
M16	Plant Life	1957	*65p*	—
M48	Silver Mane the Timber Wolf	1955	—	£3.75
M16	Space Travel	1957	—	£3.00
M48	Tippytail the Grizzly Bear	1956	—	£3.00
M16	Water Transport	1957	—	£1.25
M16	World Wide Visits	1957	—	£1.25

GREGG (Jelly, New Zealand)

B48	Aquatic Birds	1974	—	£8.75
B40	Land Birds of New Zealand	1974	—	£9.40
B35	Rare and Endangered Birds	1974	—	£9.40
B40	Remarkable Birds of the World	1974	—	£9.40
B35	Unusual Birds of the World	1974	—	£9.40

HALPINS (Tea)

25	Aircraft of the World	1958	—	£1.50
L20	Aircraft of the World (Double, as above)	1958	—	*£7.50*
25	Nature Studies	1958	—	£2.50

HAMPSHIRE CRICKET CLUB

24	Sunday League Era	1987	—	£5.75

HAPPY HOME (Periodical)

B32	Child Studies (Silk)	1912	£8.75	—
M9	Flags (Silk)	1914	£5.00	£45.00
B9	Our Lucky Flowers (Silk)	1912	£10.00	—
K14	The Happy Home Silk Button (Silk)	1914	£5.00	£70.00
M12	Women on War Work (Silk)	1915	£5.00	£60.00

HARBOUR REPROGRAPHICS

30	Cricket, Surrey v Yorkshire	1988	—	£6.25

HARDEN BROS. & LINDSAY LTD. (Tea)

50	Animals of the World	1960	—	£7.50
50	British Birds & Their Eggs	1960	—	£15.00
50	National Pets	1961	—	£3.00

HARRISON (Pomade)

25	Beauties	1902	£18.75	—

JOHN HAWKINS & SONS LTD. (Cotton)

LF30	The Story of Cotton	1925	£3.75	£112.50

HEINZ (Foods)

E1	Australian Cricket Team	1964	—	£1.90

HERALD ALARMS

Qty		Date	Odds	Sets
10	Feudal Lords	1986	—	£6.25
X10	Feudal Lords	1986	—	£6.25

HERON PETROL

K16	Holidays	1960	95p	—

HERTFORDSHIRE POLICE FORCE

X12	Postage Stamps	1985	—	£3.75

HIGSONS (Brewery)

X?26	Famous Old Higsonians	1987	45p	—

JOHN HINDHAUGH & CO. (Bread)

25	Railway Engines	1913	£25.00	—

HITCHMAN'S DAIRIES LTD.

25	Aircraft of World War II	1966	—	£6.25
25	Animals of the World	1964	—	£6.25
25	British Birds & Their Nests	1970	—	£18.75
25	British Railways	1971	—	£1.90
25	Buses & Trams	1966	—	£1.90
25	Merchant Ships of the World	1970	—	£6.25
25	Modern Wonders	1962	—	£6.25
25	Naval Battles	1971	—	£1.50
25	People & Places	1971	—	£1.90
25	Regimental Uniforms of the Past	1973	—	£1.50
25	Science in the 20th Century	1966	—	£1.50
25	The Story of Milk	1965	—	£10.00
25	Trains of the World	1970	—	£12.50

HOADLEY'S CHOCOLATES (Australia)

50	British Empire Kings & Queens	1940	90p	£45.00
?33	Cricketers (Black Front)	1928	£8.75	—
36	Cricketers (Brown Front)	1933	£6.25	£225.00
50	Early Australian Series	1938	£1.00	£50.00
50	Empire Games and Test Teams	1932	£5.00	—
40	Test Cricketers	1936	£7.50	—
B36	Test Cricketers (Different)	1938	£9.40	—
50	The Birth of a Nation	1938	£1.00	£50.00
50.	Victorian Footballers (Heads, 1-50)	1938	£1.25	£62.50
50	Victorian Footballers (51-100)	1938	£1.25	£62.50
50	Victoria Footballers (Action)	1938	£1.25	£62.50
50	Wild West Series	1938	90p	£45.00

HOBBYPRESS GUIDES (Books)

X6	Horse Racing Series	1984	—	£1.25
20	Preserved Railway Locomotives	1983	—	£1.50
20	Preserved Steam Railways, 1st	1983	—	£1.25
20	Preserved Steam Railways, 2nd	1984	—	£1.25

HOBBYPRESS GUIDES (Books) — cont.

Qty		Date	Odds	Sets
X12	Railway Engines	1984	—	£3.75
X6	Railway Engines. 2nd Series	1984	—	£2.50
20	The World's Great Cricketers	1984	—	£3.75

THOMAS HOLLOWAY LTD. (Pharmaceutics)

X39	Natural History Series (Animals Heads)	1900	£4.40	£172.00
X39	Natural History Series (Birds)	1900	£4.40	£172.00
X60	Natural History Series (Full Length)	1900	£3.75	£225.00
X50	Pictorial History of the Sports and Pastimes of all Nations	1900	£6.25	£312.50

HOME & COLONIAL STORES LTD.

26	Advertising Alphabet	1914	£5.00	—
M100	Flag Pictures	1916	£2.50	—
M40	War Heroes	1916	£3.15	£126.00
M40	War Pictures	1916	£3.15	£126.00
100	War Pictures (Different)	1916	£2.50	£250.00

HOME COUNTIES DAIRIES TEA

25	Country Life	1964	—	£2.20
25	International Air Liners	1965	—	£1.50
25	The Story of Milk	1965	—	£1.90

HOME MIRROR (Periodical)

M4	Cinema Star Pictures (Silk)	1919	£8.15	—

HOME WEEKLY (Periodical)

12	Little Charlie Cards	1920	£15.00	—

GEORGE W. HORNER & CO. (Confectionery)

P24	Wireless Cards	1926	£9.40	—

HORNIMAN (Tea)

P10	Boating Ways	1910	£12.50	—
P12	British Birds & Eggs	1910	£12.50	—
48	Dogs	1961	—	£3.00
P10	Naval Heroes	1910	£12.50	£125.00
48	Pets	1960	—	£3.00
48	Wild Animals	1958	—	£3.00

HORSLEY'S STORES

25	British Uniforms of the 19th Century	1968	—	£6.25
25	Castles of Britain	1968	—	£7.50
25	Family Pets	1968	—	£5.00

VAN HOUTEN (Chocolate)

P12	How Nature Protects the Weak	1908	£6.25	£75.00

HULL CITY FOOTBALL CLUB

Qty		Date	Odds	Sets
X20	Footballers	1950	£2.80	£56.00

HUNT CROP & SONS (Vedast)

Qty		Date	Odds	Sets
15	Characters from Dickens	1912	£6.25	£93.75

HUNTLEY & PALMER (Biscuits)

Qty		Date	Odds	Sets
P12	Animals	1900	£5.00	£60.00
P12	Aviation	1900	*£37.50*	—
P12	Biscuits in Various Countries	1900	£4.40	£52.50
P6	Biscuits with Travellers	1900	£5.00	£30.00
P12	Children of Nations I (Gold Border)	1900	£4.40	£52.50
P12	Children of Nations II (White Border)	1900	£4.40	£52.50
P12	Children at Leisure & Play	1900	£5.00	£60.00
P12	Harvests of the World	1900	£12.50	—
P12	Hunting	1900	£6.25	£75.00
P8	Inventors	1900	£12.50	—
X12	Rhondes Enfantines	1900	£15.00	—
P12	Scenes with Biscuits	1900	£4.40	£52.50
X8	Shakespearian Series	1900	£5.00	£40.00
P12	Soldiers of Various Countries	1900	£9.40	£112.50
P12	Sports (Semi-Circular Background)	1900	£6.25	£75.00
P12	Sports (Plain Background)	1900	£6.25	£75.00
P12	The Seasons	1900	£7.50	—
P12	Travelling During the 19th Century	1900	£10.00	—
P12	Views of Italy & The French Riviera	1900	£6.25	—
P12	Warships of Nations	1900	£9.40	£112.50
P8	Watteau	1900	£5.00	£40.00
P8	Wonders of the World	1900	£10.00	—

HUSTLER SOAP

Qty		Date	Odds	Sets
20	Animals, 1st Series	1925	65p	£13.00
20	Animals, 2nd Series	1925	75p	£15.00
20	Animals, 3rd Series	1925	65p	£13.00
30	Regimental Nicknames	1924	£1.50	£45.00

R. HYDE & CO. LTD. (Bird Seed)

Qty		Date	Odds	Sets
80	British Birds	1928	75p	£60.00
80	Cage Birds	1930	75p	£60.00
80	Canary Culture	1930	65p	£60.00
M10	Cartoons	1908	£10.00	—
M24	Modern Wonders	1924	£7.50	£180.00

I.P.C. MAGAZINES LTD.

Qty		Date	Odds	Sets
M25	Lindy's Cards of Fortune	1975	—	£2.50
P2	Oink! Prime Porky Cards	1987	—	£1.90

JOHN IRWIN SONS & CO. LTD. (Tea)

Qty		Date	Odds	Sets
6	Characters from Shakespeare	1912	£15.00	£90.00
8	European War Series	1916	£12.50	£100.00

JACOB & CO. (Biscuits)

Qty		Date	Odds	Sets
D24	Banknotes that made History (with Album)	1975	—	£1.50
D32	Famous Picture Cards from History (with Album)	1978	—	£1.50
25	Vehicles of All Ages	1924	£2.00	£50.00
25	Zoo Series (Brown Back)	1924	£1.00	£25.00
25	Zoo Series (Green Back)	1924	65p	£16.25

JESK (Confectionery)

25	Buses & Trams	1959	—	£8.75

JIBCO (Tea)

28	Dominoes	1956	£2.50	—
K53	Miniature Playing Cards	1956	£2.50	—
K50	Puzzle Cards	1955	£2.50	—
K25	Screen Stars	1955	£2.20	—
K25	Screen Stars, 2nd Series	1956	20p	£5.00

JIFFI (Condoms)

M64	Kama Sutra	1989	—	£37.50

R. L. JONES & CO. LTD. (Drink)

24	Jet Aircraft of the World	1956	—	£1.50

JUBBLY (Drink)

50	Adventurous Lives	1967	—	£3.00

JUNIOR PASTIMES (Commercial)

52	Popular English Players	1951	£1.25	—
52	Popular Players (Footballers)	1951	£1.25	—
52	Popular Railway Engines	1951	£1.25	—
L80	Star Pix	1951	80p	—

JUST SEVENTEEN (Magazine)

T17	Posters	1986	—	£1.25

K. P. NUTS & CRISPS

12	Sports Adventure Series	1978	—	£7.50
20	Wonderful World of Nature	1983	40p	£8.00

KANE PRODUCTS LTD. (Confectionery)

36	ATV Stars (Packets)	1957	£1.55	—
50	British Birds & Their Eggs	1960	—	£22.00
25	Cricket Clubs & Badges	1957	—	£1.90
L50	Disc Stars	1960	65p	£32.50
X50	Disc Stars	1960	75p	£37.50
50	Dogs	1955	£1.25	£62.50
X72	Film Stars (Plain Back)	1955	75p	£54.00
50	Flags of All Nations	1959	—	£7.50

KANE PRODUCTS LTD. (Confectionery) —cont.

Qty		Date	Odds	Sets
25	Football Clubs & Colours	1956	—	£1.50
50	Historical Characters	1957	—	£3.00
25	International Football Stars	1957	—	£5.00
30	Kings & Queens	1959	—	£4.40
X30	Kings & Queens	1959	—	£5.75
25	Modern Motor Cars	1959	—	£7.50
50	Modern Racing Cars	1954	—	£4.50
25	National Pets Club, 1st Series	1958	—	£3.75
25	National Pets Club, 2nd Series	1958	£1.75	£43.75
25	1956 Cricketers, 1st Series	1956	—	£4.00
25	1956 Cricketers, 2nd Series	1956	—	£6.50
25	Red Indians, 1st Series	1957	—	£3.25
25	Red Indians, 2nd Series	1957	—	£3.25
25	Roy Rogers Colour Series	1958	60p	£15.00
25	Roy Rogers Series	1957	£1.20	£30.00
50	Space Adventure	1955	—	£22.00
50	20th Century Events	1955	£1.00	£50.00
K50	Wild Animals	1954	—	£3.00

KARDOMAH (Tea)

K?500	General Interest (Various Series)	1900	£2.50	—

M. & S. KEECH

15	Australian Cricket Team 1905	1986	—	£3.00
15	English Cricketers of 1902	1987	—	£3.00

KEILLER (Confectionery)

LF18	Film Favourites	1926	£5.00	—
25	Scottish Heritage	1976	—	£6.25

KELLOGG LTD. (Cereals)

16	A History of British Military Aircraft	1963	15p	£2.00
16	Animals (3D)	1971	£1.55	£24.75
12	Famous Firsts	1963	15p	£1.25
L20	Gardens to Visit	1988	—	£3.00
12	International Soccer Stars	1963	—	£1.50
40	Motor Cars (Black and White)	1949	£1.60	£64.00
40	Motor Cars (Coloured, as above)	1949	£1.80	£72.00
X56	Playing Cards	1986	—	£3.75
8	Prehistoric Monsters and the Present	1985	—	£1.50
16	Ships of the British Navy	1962	40p	£6.25
M6	Space (Surprise Gifts)	1989	—	£1.50
L4	Space Transfers	1988	—	£1.90
P4	Sticky Pix	1988	—	£3.00
12	The Story of the Bicycle	1964	£2.20	£26.25
16	The Story of the Locomotive, 1st Series	1963	40p	£6.25
16	The Story of the Locomotive, 2nd Series	1963	40p	£6.25
K8	Tony Racing Stickers	1988	—	£1.25
16	Veteran Motor Cars	1962	25p	£4.00

LIEBIG

OXO RECIPE NO 16
BROWN VEGETABLE SOUP

The Liebig Extract of Meat Co. Ltd. was formed in 1856 and was acquired by Brooke Bond in 1971. In Britain their product was renamed Oxo, which it is known as today. In a period of 100 years from 1872 the Company issued a large number of sets of cards, including postcards, menus, calendars, place cards and other novelty issues. The first series were issued in France, but eventually cards could be obtained all over Europe, in languages such as Danish, Czech, Spanish, and even Russian. Many series were printed in English, including the Oxo insert series, and issued in Britain and the U.S.A.

In all the company issued 2,000 different sets of cards. There covered an enormous variety of subjects, including the Trans-Siberian Railway, Shadowgraphs, Gulliver, Fans, Education in Ancient Greece, and the Left Bank of the Po. There is even a set showing the life of Justus von Liebig, founder of the firm, and another showing how the cards themselves are prepared and printed.

Because of the size of the subject a separate catalogue is available (price £4.00) listing all the issues, and a small selection of series is listed on page 227.

© Quaker Oats Limited 1982

Flintlock Duelling Pistol

The last few years have been but a trickle of cigarette cards, albeit in cigar packets such as Doncella and Tom Thumb. For the most part however collectors have had to be satisfied with trade cards for their new acquisitions.

The most significant of these has been Brooke Bond, which has been issuing cards continuously since 1954 (British Birds) and has now issued over 40 different sets, usually with special albums, in Britain, North America, and Africa. One would like to think that the success of the Company, which incidentally also owns Liebig, owes as much to the quality and appeal of the cards as to the tea itself. Its rivals failed to sustain any competition in card issues, although many, such as Lyons, Horniman and Lipton, made some attempts.

Confectionery is another prolific area for card collectors, chiefly with sweet cigarettes (now discreetly called "Candy Sticks") and bubble gum. Barratt/Bassett is the premier issuer of the former, and A. & B. C./Topps of the latter, although the competition in these items is intense. Many other firms appear in these pages, such as Dandy, Monty, Primrose & Somportex, and often collectors try to obtain the box or wrapper in addition to the set of cards.

Cereal products are also a fruitful source for the cartophilist. Kellogg,

Nabisco and Welgar regularly include among their free incentive inserts collectable series of cards, often in novel form such as transfers or cut-outs.

The last rewarding area for cards is that of periodicals. A new feature of these has been the appearance of Panini, with free inserts in magazines and newspapers, followed by the opportunity to complete the very long sets by purchasing packets of cards. Often these sets are of footballers, and Panini invests some of its profits (with further advertising) in sponsoring family enclosures at soccer grounds.

I FREE POP TOKEN

KELLOGG LTD. (Cereals) — cont.

CANADIAN ISSUES

Qty		Date	Odds	Sets
M150	General Interest, 1st Set	1940	£1.00	—
M150	General Interest, 2nd Set	1940	£1.00	—
M150	General Interest, 3rd Set	1940	£1.00	—

KENT COUNTY CRICKET CLUB

50	Cricketers of Kent	1986	—	£7.50

KIDDYS FAVOURITES LTD. (Commercial)

52	New Popular Film Stars	1950	95p	—
52	Popular Boxers	1950	£1.00	—
52	Popular Cricketers	1950	£2.50	—
65	Popular Film Stars	1950	95p	—
52	Popular Footballers	1950	£1.25	—
52	Popular Olympics	1950	95p	—
75	Popular Players (Hearts on Front)	1950	95p	—
52	Popular Players (Shamrocks on Front)	1950	£1.25	—
52	Popular Speedway Riders	1950	£1.90	—

KINGS OF YORK (Laundry)

25	Flags of All Nations (Silk)	1954	£1.50	£37.50
30	Kings & Queens of England	1954	—	£1.50

KINGS LAUNDRIES LTD. (Walthamstow, E. London)

25	Famous Railway Engines	1953	£2.20	—
25	Modern British Warplanes	1953	£1.75	—
25	Modern Motor Cycles	1953	£2.00	—
25	Radio & Television Stars	1953	£1.75	—

KINGS SPECIALITIES (Food Products)

26	Alphabet Rhymes	1915	£8.15	—
25	"Don'ts" or Lessons in Etiquette	1915	£6.25	—
25	Great War Celebrities	1915	£6.25	—
25	Heroes of Famous Books	1915	£5.00	—
25	King's "Discoveries"	1915	£5.00	—
25	King's "Servants"	1915	£5.00	—
25	Proverbs	1915	£6.25	—
37	Unrecorded History	1915	£5.00	—
100	War Pictures	1915	£7.50	—
25	Where King's Supplies Grow	1915	£5.00	—

KNOCKOUT (Periodical)

20	Super Planes of Today	1956	—	£1.90

KNORR (Cheese)

T6	Great Trains of Europe	1983	£1.25	£7.50

KRAFT CHEESE

12	Historic Military Uniforms	1971	—	£1.25

LACEY'S CHEWING GUM

Qty		Date	Odds	Sets
50	Footballers	1923	£7.50	—
?24	Uniforms	1923	£12.50	—

F. LAMBERT & SONS LTD. (Tea)

25	Before our Time	1961	—	£1.50
25	Birds & Their Eggs	1962	—	*£4.40*
25	Butterflies & Moths	1960	—	£1.50
25	Cacti	1962	—	£1.50
25	Car Registration Numbers, 1st Series	1959	—	£3.45
25	Car Registration Numbers, 2nd Series	1960	—	£6.25
25	Football Clubs & Badges	1958	—	£1.50
25	Game Birds & Wild Fowl	1964	—	£5.00
25	Historic East Anglia	1961	—	£1.50
25	Interesting Hobbies	1965	—	£8.15
25	Passenger Liners	1965	—	£8.15
25	Past & Present	1964	—	£1.50
25	People & Places	1966	—	*£3.75*
25	Pond Life	1964	—	£6.25
25	Sports & Games	1964	—	£1.50

LANCASHIRE CONSTABULARY

24	Cop-a-Cards	1987	—	£6.25
D11	Cop-a-Cards, Series 3	1989	—	£1.90
X12	Motor Cars	1987	—	£4.40

LANCASTER REPRINTS (Canada)

45	Hockey Players (I.T.C. Canada)	1987	—	£8.75
36	Hockey Series (I.T.C. Canada)	1987	—	£8.75

HERBERT LAND (Cycles)

30	Army Pictures, Cartoons, etc.	1915	£25.00	—

LEAF BRANDS INC. (Confectionery)

X50	Cliff Richard	1960	90p	£45.00
X50	Do You Know?	1961	15p	£5.00
X90	Famous Artistes	1960	80p	—
X50	Famous Discoveries & Adventures	1962	£1.00	—
X50	Footballers	1961	25p	£12.50
X40	The Flag Game	1960	25p	£10.00
X50	Totem Pole Talking Signs	1962	45p	£22.50

LETRASET

12	Star Wars	1978	—	£6.00

LEVER BROS. (Soap)

20	British Birds & Their Nests	1961	—	£1.25
F150	Celebrities	1900	£2.80	—
L39	Celebrities	1901	£4.40	£170.00

LIEBIG EXTRACT OF MEAT CO. (see also Oxo)

This firm issued nearly 2,000 different sets throughout Europe between 1872 and 1974. Because inclusion of all these in this volume would be impracticable we have produced a separate catalogue of Liebig cards. See separate announcement for details. Some recent issues are included below as a sample of the scope of these series.

Qty			Date	Odds	Sets
X6	1559	Antelopes	1953	—	£2.50
X6	1542	Astronomic Observations	1952	—	£3.00
X6	1751	Bilharziosis (Parasitic Disease)	1961	—	£3.50
X6	1610	Birds of the Beaches and Dunes	1954	—	£3.00
X6	1582	Boats Through the Ages	1954	—	£3.50
X6	1684	Buccaneers	1958	—	£3.50
X6	1563	Charles-Joseph, Prince of Ligne	1953	—	£3.00
X6	1776	Children's Games of Yesteryear	1962	—	£3.50
X6	1818	Dante's Paradise	1966	—	£3.50
X6	1777	Exploits of the Belgian Air Force	1962	—	£3.50
X6	1602	Famous Belgian Inventors and Thinkers	1954	—	£3.00
X6	1568	Forest Flowers	1953	—	£3.00
X6	1599	Francois Rabelais	1954	—	£3.00
X6	1536	Giant Flowers	1952	—	£3.00
X6	1579	Herb Teas	1953	—	£3.00
X6	1546	History of the Belgian Congo II	1952	—	£3.00
X6	1787	History of Military Engineering	1962	—	£7.00
X6	1794	History of Stringed Instruments	1963	—	£3.50
X6	1708	How Children are Carried	1959	—	£3.50
X6	1808	Medieval Armour	1965	—	£3.50
X6	1796	Ocean Birds	1963	—	£7.00
X6	1761	Owls	1961	—	£3.50
X6	1782	Painters of the Rissorgimento	1962	—	£3.50
X6	1647	Places of Pilgrimage	1956	—	£3.00
X6	1673	Pond Life	1957	—	£3.00
X6	1693	Prehistoric Plants Still Surviving	1958	—	£3.00
X6	1755	Scottish Clans	1961	—	£3.50
X6	1695	Spiders	1958	—	£3.00
X6	1735	State Prisons & Their Famous "Guests"	1960	—	£3.00
X6	1819	Story of the Motor Car	1966	—	£5.75
X6	1789	Stringed Weapons	1963	—	£3.50
X6	1576	Suliman The Magnificent	1953	—	£3.00
X6	1663	The Bersaglieri	1957	—	£3.50
X6	1650	The Earth's Varied Features II	1956	—	£3.00
X6	1591	The Empire of the Incas	1954	—	£3.00
X6	1628	The Exploitation of Methane	1955	—	£3.00
X6	1589	The Fall of Constantinople	1954	—	£3.00
X6	1699	The History of Italy XIII	1958	—	£3.00
X6	1723	The History of Moscow	1959	—	£3.00
X6	1745	The History of Roumania	1960	—	£3.00
X6	1635	The Left Bank of the River Po	1956	—	£3.00
X6	1810	The Life of Dante	1965	—	£3.50
X6	1566	The Minoan Civilization	1953	—	£3.00
X6	1618	The Processing of Rice	1955	—	£3.00
X6	1592	The Sea Shore	1954	—	£3.00
X6	1561	The Suez Canal	1953	—	£3.00
X6	1797	Tropical Birds	1963	—	£4.50
X6	1581	Virgil, The Poet	1953	—	£3.00
X6	1788	Well Known Tunnels	1962	—	£3.50
X6	1569	William The Silent	1953	—	£3.00

LIFEGUARD PRODUCTS (Soap)

Qty		Date	Odds	Sets
25	British Butterflies	1955	—	£1.50

JOSEPH LINGFORD & SON (Baking Powder)

36	British War Leaders	1949	—	£31.25

LIPTON LTD. (Tea)

60	Flags of the World	1967	—	£7.50
50	The Conquest of Space	1962	—	£4.40

LITTLE CHEF (Restaurants)

M8	Disney Characters	1990	—	£2.50

LITTLE OWL MAGAZINES

6	Masters of the Universe	1987	—	£5.60

LODGE SPARK PLUGS

T24	Cars	1960	£6.25	—

LONDESBORO' THEATRE

50	War Portraits	1916	£25.00	—

LONGLEAT HOUSE

25	Longleat House	1967	—	£1.50

LOT-O-FUN (Periodical)

BF4	Champions	1922	£3.15	£12.50

G. F. LOVELL & CO. (Confectionery)

Qty		Date	Odds	Sets
36	British Royalty Series	1910	£20.00	—
36	Football Series	1910	£22.00	—
25	Photos of Football Stars	1926	£7.50	—

J. LYONS & CO. LTD. (Ice Cream & Tea)

Qty		Date	Odds	Sets
40	All Systems Go	1968	80p	£32.00
48	Australia	1959	15p	£3.00
M20	Banknotes	1974	—	£6.25
M12	Beautiful Butterflies	1974	—	£1.90
25	Birds & Their Eggs	1962	—	£1.90
40	British Wildlife	1970	65p	£26.00
L16	Catweazle Magic Cards	1971	—	£1.50
M20	County Badge Collection	1974	—	£1.90
X12	Did You Know?	1983	30p	£3.60
40	European Adventure	1969	95p	—
40	Famous Aircraft	1965	20p	£8.00
40	Famous Cars	1966	95p	£38.00
40	Famous Locomotives	1964	£1.25	£50.00
48	Famous People	1966	45p	£21.50
D12	Farmyard Stencils	1977	—	£6.25
M14	Flowers (Cut-out)	1976	—	£18.75
32	HMS 1902-1962 (Descriptive)	1962	15p	£1.90
32	HMS 1902-1962 (Non-Descriptive)	1962	—	£1.90
X12	Horses in the Service of Man	1984	—	£3.00
L35	Illustrated Map of the British Isles	1959	40p	£14.00
40	International Footballers	1972	£1.00	£40.00
40	Into the Unknown	1969	75p	£30.00
15	Jubilee	1977	75p	£11.25
X10	Junior Champs	1983	—	£1.90
50	100 Years of Motoring	1964	75p	£37.50
40	On Safari	1970	75p	£30.00
40	Pop Scene	1971	80p	—
40	Pop Stars	1970	80p	£32.00
L10	Pop Stars (Shaped)	1975	—	£3.00
K48	Puzzle Series	1955	25p	—
40	Soccer Stars	1971	£1.00	£40.00
40	Space Age Britain	1968	75p	£30.00
40	Space Exploration	1963	80p	£32.00
25	Space 1999	1976	£1.00	—
25	Star Trek	1979	£1.90	—
50	Train Spotters	1962	40p	£20.00
K100	Tricks & Puzzles	1926	£1.25	—
40	Views of London	1967	80p	£32.00
48	What do you Know?	1957	15p	£3.00
24	Wings Across the World (Descriptive)	1962	15p	£1.50
24	Wings Across the World (Non-Descriptive)	1961	—	£3.00
24	Wings of Speed (Descriptive Back)	1961	15p	£1.50
24	Wings of Speed (Non-Descriptive)	1961	15p	£3.00

M. P. L. LTD. (Records)

Qty		Date	Odds	Sets
M5	Wings—Back to the Egg	1981	—	£2.50

MACFISHERIES (Shops)

Qty		Date	Odds	Sets
L12	Gallery Pictures	1924	65p	£7.75
L14	Japanese Colour Prints	1924	80p	£11.25
L12	Poster Pointers	1925	65p	£7.75
L12	Sporting Prints	1923	£1.00	£12.00

MACGIRR & CO. (Tea)

24	Birds & Their Eggs	1912	£5.00	—

MACROBERTSON (Confectionery, Australia)

24	Flags of All Nations	1916	£3.75	—
24	Naval & Military Decorations	1916	£5.00	£120.00
24	Sons/Allies of the Empire	1916	£5.00	—
50	Sports of the World	1916	£1.75	£87.50

McVITIE & PRICE (Food)

8	The European War Series	1916	£12.50	£100.00

MADISON CONFECTIONERY PRODUCTIONS LTD.

X31	Christmas Greeting Cards	1957	£1.25	—
X48	Disc Jockey, 1st Series	1957	65p	£31.25
X48	Disc Jockey, 2nd Series	1958	75p	£36.00
X50	Recording Stars	1958	65p	£32.50

MAGNET LIBRARY (Periodical)

BF15	Footballers	1922	£1.50	£22.50
BF6	Football Teams	1922	£2.00	£12.00
BF4	Football Teams	1923	£2.00	£8.00

MANCHESTER EVENING NEWS (Newspaper)

L30	Footballers	1976	—	£7.50

MAPLE LEAF GUM

K90	Motor Car & Motor Cycle Badges (Metal)	1960	65p	—
K75	National Flags (Metal)	1960	50p	—

R. MARCANTONIO LTD. (Ice Lollies)

50	Interesting Animals	1953	—	£3.00

A. T. MARKS (Commercial)

11	1892 Gloucestershire (Cricket)	1990	—	£1.75
11	1892 Middlesex (Cricket)	1990	—	£1.75
12	1903 Middlesex (Cricket)	1990	—	£1.75
12	1903 Yorkshire (Cricket)	1990	—	£1.75

MARLOW CIVIL ENGINEERING LTD.

Qty		Date	Odds	Sets
25	Famous Clowns	1990	—	£7.50

MARS CONFECTIONS LTD.

25	Ceremonies of the Coronation (Brown Back)	1937	60p	£15.00
25	Ceremonies of the Coronation (Blue Back)	1937	£3.15	—
50	Famous Aeroplanes, Pilots & Airports	1938	65p	£32.50
50	Famous Escapes	1937	65p	£32.50
50	Famous Film Stars	1939	65p	£32.50
25	Wonders of the Queen Mary	1936	65p	£16.25

JAMES MARSHALL (GLASGOW) LTD. (Food)

30	Colonial Troops	1900	£21.50	—
1	Marshall's Products Illustrated	1926	—	£3.75
40	Recipes	1926	£3.75	—

MASTER VENDING CO. LTD. (Gum)

X25	A Bombshell for the Sheriff	1959	65p	£16.25
X50	Cardmaster Football Tips	1958	50p	£25.00
X16	Cricketer Series—New Zealand 1958	1958	65p	£10.50
X50	Did You Know? (Football)	1959	20p	£10.00
X100	Jet Aircraft of the World	1958	65p	—
X100	Jet Aircraft of the World (German Text)	1958	75p	—
X25	Taxing the Sheriff	1959	30p	£7.50
X36	Tommy Steele	1958	£1.05	£37.50

J. JOHN MASTERS & CO. (Matches)

X12	Food from Britain	1987	—	£1.25

MATCH (Periodical)

X31	F.A. Cup Fact File	1986	—	£2.50

MAXILIN MARKETING CO.

25	Motor Cars	1951	—	£2.00

MAYNARDS LTD. (Confectionery)

12	Billy Bunter Series	1926	£18.75	—
?20	Football Clubs	1926	£9.40	—
18	Girl Guide Series	1921	£12.50	—
50	Girls of All Nations	1921	£3.75	£187.50
12	Strange Insects	1935	£3.75	£45.00
8	The European War Series	1916	£15.00	£120.00
12	Wonders of the Deep	1935	£3.75	£45.00
12	World's Wonder Series (Numbered)	1930	£3.75	£45.00
10	World's Wonder Series (Unnumbered)	1930	£4.40	£44.00

MAYPOLE (Grocers)

25	War Series	1915	£4.40	£110.00

MAZAWATTEE (Tea)

Qty		Date	Odds	Sets
X39	Kings and Queens	1902	£3.15	£125.00

MEADOW DAIRY CO.

50	War Series	1915	£5.00	—

J. F. MEARBECK (Printer)

30	Army Pictures, Cartoons, etc.	1915	£25.00	—

MELLINS FOOD

K2	Diamond Jubilee Coins	1897	£7.50	£15.00

MELOX (Dog Food)

L50	Famous Breeds of Dogs	1937	£3.75	£187.50
M32	Happy Families (Dogs)	1935	£5.00	£160.00

MERRYSWEETS LTD.

X48	Telegum TV Stars	1958	25p	£12.00
X48	Tracepiks	1960	£5.00	—
X48	World Racing Cars	1959	80p	£40.00

GEOFFREY MICHAEL PUBLISHERS LTD.

40	Modern Motor Cars	1949	—	£9.50

MIDLAND COUNTIES (Ice Cream)

12	Action Soldiers	1976	—	£3.00
M20	Banknotes	1974	—	£12.50
D12	Farmyard Stencils	1977	—	£2.50
M24	Kings of the Road	1977	—	£6.25
X10	Steam Power	1978	—	£2.50

MILK MARKETING BOARD

P10	Milk Recipe Cards	1979	—	£2.50
25	Prehistoric Animals	1963	—	£2.20

MILLER

MF20	Film Stars	1958	—	£7.50

MILLERS (Tea)

25	Animals & Reptiles	1962	—	£1.50

ROBERT R. MIRANDA LTD.(Confectionery)

50	150 Years of Locomotives	1956	—	£3.00
50	100 Years of Motoring	1955	—	£3.00
25	Ships Through the Ages	1957	—	*£6.25*
50	Strange Creatures	1961	—	£3.75

MISTER SOFTEE LTD. (Ice Cream)

Qty		Date	Odds	Sets
M12	Beautiful Butterflies	1977	30p	£3.60
B20	County Badge Collection	1976	15p	£2.50
L12	Did You Know?	1976	30p	£3.60
D12	Farmyard Stencils	1977	—	£3.75
M24	1st Division Football League Badges	1972	—	£4.40
M24	Kings of the Road	1977	25p	£6.00
G1	Map of the British Isles	1976	—	£1.50
15	Moon Mission	1962	—	£6.25
M24	Pop Discs	1972	65p	—
M10	Pop Stars (Shaped)	1975	75p	£7.50
X1	Secret Code Computer	1977	—	50p
D20	Sports Cups (Shaped)	1975	—	£6.25
M20	Stamp in a Million	1976	40p	£8.00
L10	Steam Power	1978	—	£3.00
P12	Top Ten (Blue Back)	1964	—	£3.00
20	Top Twenty	1963	45p	—
25	TV Personalities	1962	95p	—
P12	Your World	1963	—	£1.90

MITCHAM FOODS LTD.

Qty		Date	Odds	Sets
25	Aircraft of Today	1955	—	£3.00
25	Aquarium Fish, 1st Series	1957	—	£15.65
25	Aquarium Fish, 2nd Series	1957	—	£1.50
50	Butterflies & Moths	1959	95p	£47.50
25	Footballers	1956	—	£2.00
50	Mars Adventure	1958	£1.75	—
25	Motor Racing	1960	—	£9.50

MIZZ MAGAZINE

Qty		Date	Odds	Sets
P4	The Seasons	1986	—	£1.00

MOBIL OIL CO. LTD.

Qty		Date	Odds	Sets
M30	Football Club Badges (Silk)	1983	95p	£28.50
P40	Footy Photos 1965 (Australia)	1965	—	£10.65
X36	The Story of Grand Prix Motor Racing	1971	—	£1.90
25	Veteran & Vintage Cars	1962	—	£12.50
24	Vintage Cars	1966	—	£1.90

MODERN WEEKLY (Periodical)

Qty		Date	Odds	Sets
P3	Film Couples (Silk)	1923	£18.75	—

MOFFAT B. & G. Ltd. (Confectionery)

Qty		Date	Odds	Sets
D102	Money That Made History	1981	—	£6.25

THE MOLASSINE CO. (Dog Food)

Qty		Date	Odds	Sets
50	Dogs (Full Length)	1963	50p	£25.00
50	Dogs (Heads)	1964	£1.25	£62.50
25	Dogs at Work	1970	—	£1.90
12	Dogs of All Countries	1925	£6.25	£75.00
50	Puppies	1967	£1.25	£62.50

MONTAGUE MOTOR MUSEUM

Qty		Date	Odds	Sets
M24	Veteran & Vintage Cars	1965	£2.00	£48.00

MONTY GUM

M98	Bruce Lee	1980	—	£4.40
L50	Elvis	1978	—	£18.75
L72	Flag Parade	1972	—	£8.15
M100	Flags of All Nations	1980	—	£4.00
L56	Footballers (P/C Inset)	1970	£1.00	£56.00
M54	Hitmakers (P/C Inset)	1978	—	£10.00
L72	International Football Teams	1970	—	£37.50
M72	Kojak	1975	20p	£14.00
M54	Kojak (P/C Inset)	1976	—	£10.00
L56	Motor Cars (P/C Inset)	1956	—	£50.00
M263	Olympics	1984	—	£12.00
M100	Return of the Jedi	1983	—	£6.25
M100	The Cops, 1st Series	1976	15p	£12.50
M124	The High Chaparral	1970	—	£15.00

MORNING FOODS LTD.

1	Advertisement Card	1953	—	75p
F25	British Planes (Numbered)	1978	£1.50	—
F25	British Planes (Unnumbered)	1953	—	£6.25
F50	British Trains	1952	£3.15	—
25	British Uniforms	1954	—	£1.50
50	Modern Cars	1954	—	£4.40
50	Our England	1955	—	£3.00
25	Test Cricketers	1953	—	£8.25
12	The Cunard Line (Black Back)	1957	—	£1.25
12	The Cunard Line (Blue Back)	1957	—	£3.00
25	World Locomotives (Black Back)	1954	—	£1.50
25	World Locomotives (Blue Back)	1954	—	£7.50

E. D. L. MOSELEY (Confectionery)

B25	Historical Buildings	1954	—	£1.90

MOTOR CYCLE NEWS

24	'Best of British' Collection (With Folder)	1988	—	£1.90

V. MUHLENEN & CO. (Cheese)

B6	Swiss Views, Series III	1955	—	£4.40
B6	Swiss Views, Series IV	1955	—	£5.00

MURCO PETROLEUM

P28	English Counties	1986	—	£3.00
B50	World's Airlines	1978	—	£3.00

MUSEUM OF BRITISH MILITARY UNIFORMS

25	British Cavalry Uniforms	1987	—	£4.50
25	Military Maids	1987	—	£4.50
25	Warriors through the Ages	1987	—	£4.50

MUSGRAVE BROS. LTD. (Tea)

Qty		Date	Odds	Sets
25	Birds	1961	—	£1.90
20	British Birds	1960	£3.15	—
50	British Wild Life	1962	£3.75	—
50	Butterflies of the World	1964	£2.50	—
25	Into Space	1961	—	£1.50
25	Modern Motor Cars	1962	—	£6.25
25	Pond Life	1963	—	£5.00
25	Products of the World	1961	—	£1.50
50	Transport through the Ages	1966	£1.75	£87.50
25	Tropical Birds	1964	—	£1.50
25	Wild Flowers	1961	—	£1.50

MYERS & METREVELI (Gum)

KF48	Film Stars	1953	£1.55	—
X48	Film Stars & Biographies	1953	£2.50	—
X60	Hollywood Peep Show	1953	£2.50	—
L50	Spot the Planes	1953	£2.50	—

MY WEEKLY (Periodical)

M9	Battle Series (Silk)	1916	£5.00	£45.00
M12	Floral Beauties (Silk)	1914	£4.40	£52.50
M15	Language of Flowers (Silk)	1914	£4.40	£66.00
M54	Lucky Emblems (Silk)	1912	£6.25	—
M6	Lucky Flowers (Silk)	1913	*£9.40*	—
M12	Our Soldier Boys (Silk)	1915	£5.00	£60.00
M14	Soldiers of the King (Silk)	1915	£5.00	£70.00
M6	Sweet Kiss Series (Silk)	1913	£5.00	£30.00
M6	War Heroes (Silk)	1916	£5.00	£30.00

NABISCO FOODS LTD.

B5	Aces in Action	1980	£2.20	£11.00
M24	Action Shots of Olympic Sports	1980	65p	£15.50
12	British Soldiers	1971	—	£1.25
P20	Champions of Sport	1961	£1.50	—
P8	England's Soccer Stars Tactic Cards	1980	£1.55	£12.50
12	E.T.	1983	—	£4.40
L24	Footballers	1970	65p	£15.50
L10	History of Aviation	1970	£1.50	£15.00
P10	Kevin Keegan's Keep Fit with the Stars	1978	—	£5.65
P10	Motor Show	1960	£1.90	—
P6	Play 'n Score	1989	—	£5.00
L6	World Superstars & Sporting Trophies	1980	£1.55	—

AUSTRALIAN ISSUES

32	Leading Cricketers (Crispies etc.)	1948	£2.20	£70.00
M66	Popular Pets	1962	—	£10.00
L24	United Nations in Action	1968	—	£8.15

EDWARD NASSAR & CO. LTD. (Coffee, Gold Coast)

25	Transport, Present & Future	1955	—	£2.20

NATIONAL SPASTICS SOCIETY

Qty		Date	Odds	Sets
24	Famous County Cricketers (Booklet)	1958	—	£22.00
24	Famous Footballers	1959	—	£3.00

NEEDLER'S (Confectionery)

12	Military Series	1916	£18.00	—

NEILSON'S (Confectionery)

50	Interesting Animals	1954	—	£3.00

NELSON LEE LIBRARY (Periodical)

BF15	Footballers	1922	£1.75	£26.25
BF6	Modern British Locomotives	1922	£5.00	£30.00

NESTLE LTD. (Chocolate)

L12	Animal Bars (Wrappers)	1970	—	£1.25
24	Animals of the World	1962	—	£9.40
P12	British Birds (Reward Cards)	1900	£8.75	—
49	Happy Families	1935	65p	£31.75
144	Pictorial World Atlas	1934	£1.25	—
100	Stars of the Silver Screen, Volume I	1936	80p	£80.00
50	Stars of the Silver Screen, Volume II	1937	£1.25	—
136	This England	1936	50p	£68.00
T24	Wild Animals Serie II	1910	£5.00	—
156	Wonders of the World, Volume I	1932	45p	—
144	Wonders of the World, Volume II	1933	45p	—

NEW ENGLAND CONFECTIONERY CO. (U.S.A.)

M12	Real Airplane Pictures	1929	£2.00	£24.00

NEW HOLLAND MACHINE CO.

P12	Traction Engines	1960	£3.15	£37.75

NEWS CHRONICLE (Newspaper)

L13	Barrow RFC	1955	—	£1.90
L12	Bradford City FC	1955	—	£3.15
L11	Chesterfield FC	1955	—	£2.50
L12	Everton FC	1955	—	£3.75
L10	Everton FC (Different Back)	1955	—	£3.75
L14	Rochdale Hornets RFC	1955	—	£1.90
L13	Salford RFC	1955	—	£1.90
L17	Stockport County	1955	—	£2.50
L13	Swinton RFC	1955	—	£1.90
L12	The Story of Stirling Moss	1955	£1.90	—
L11	Workington AFC	1955	—	£1.90

NEWTON, CHAMBERS & CO. (Toilet Rolls)

P18	More Rhyme Time (19-36)	1934	£2.20	£39.50
P18	Nursery Rhymes (1-18)	1934	£2.20	£39.50

NEW ZEALAND MEAT PRODUCERS BOARD

Qty		Date	Odds	Sets
X25	Scenes of New Zealand Lamb	1930	£2.00	£50.00

NORTHAMPTONSHIRE COUNTY CRICKET CLUB

30	Northamptonshire Cricketers	1985	—	£9.00

NORTHERN CO-OPERATIVE SOCIETY LTD. (Tea)

25	Birds	1963	75p	—
25	History of the Railways, 1st Series	1964	—	£4.40
25	History of the Railways, 2nd Series	1964	—	£8.15
25	Passenger Liners	1963	—	£1.50
25	Then & Now	1963	—	£3.75
25	Tropical Birds	1962	—	£3.75
25	Weapons of World War II	1962	—	£6.25
25	Wonders of the Deep	1965	—	£1.50

NORTON'S (Shop)

25	Evolution of the Royal Navy	1965	—	£18.75

NOSTALGIA REPRINTS

50	Celebrated American Indian Chiefs (Allen & Ginter)...	1989	—	£7.50
50	Cope's Golfers	1984	—	£7.50
238	County Cricketers (Taddy)	1987	—	£24.00
50	Cricketers 1896 (Wills)	1983	—	£7.50
50	Cricketers 1901 (Wills)	1984	—	£7.50
50	Dickens Gallery (Cope)	1989	—	£7.50
50	Fruits (Allen & Ginter)	1989	—	£7.50
25	Humorous Golfing Series (Berlyn)	1989	—	£6.00
25	Leaders (Kinney)	1990	—	£6.00
50	Military Series (Player)	1984	—	£7.50
50	Shakespeare Gallery (Cope)	1989	—	£7.50
18	Spurs Footballers (Jones)	1987	—	£1.75

NUGGET POLISH CO.

X30	Allied Series	1910	£10.00	—
50	Flags of All Nations	1925	£3.50	—
X40	Mail Carriers and Stamps	1910	£10.00	£400.00

NUNBETTA (Grocer)

25	Motor Cars	1955	£3.75	—

O.V.S. TEA

K25	Modern Engineering	1955	—	£3.75

TONY L. OLIVER (Commercial)

25	Aircraft of World War II	1964	—	£25.00
50	German Orders & Decorations	1963	—	£10.00
50	German Uniforms	1971	—	£6.25
M25	Vehicles of the German Wehrmacht	1965	—	£20.00

O-PEE-CHEE CO. LTD. (Gum, Canada)

Qty		Date	Odds	Sets
X75	Ringside Action, 1st Series (Wrestlers)	1987	—	£7.50
X75	Wrestlers, 2nd Series	1988	—	£7.50

ORBIT (Commercial)

15	Engines of the L.N.E.R.	1986	—	£2.50
20	Famous Douglas Aeroplanes	1986	—	£2.50
28	Great Rugby Sides (NZ Tourists 1905)	1987	—	£2.50
16	New Zealand Cricketers 1958	1988	—	£4.25

ORPHEUS RECORDS

30	Opera Stars	1988	—	£10.00

OVALTINE (Beverage)

25	Do You Know?	1965	—	£7.50

OXO LTD. (Meat Extract)

K47	Advertisement Series	1926	£3.75	—
K20	British Cattle	1934	£2.00	£40.00
15	Bull Series	1937	£1.80	£27.00
K24	Feats of Endurance	1934	£2.00	£48.00
K20	Furs & Their Story	1932	£2.00	£40.00
K36	Lifeboats & Their History	1935	£2.20	£80.00
K30	Mystery Painting Pictures	1928	£2.20	£66.00
P6	Oxo Cattle Studies	1930	£14.00	—
25	Oxo Recipes	1936	£1.60	£40.00

P.M.R. ASSOCIATES LTD. (Commercial)

25	England, The World Cup, Spain '82	1982	—	£1.50

H. J. PACKER LTD. (Confectionery)

K30	Footballers	1924	£12.50	—
50	Humorous Drawings	1936	£2.20	£110.00

PAGE WOODCOCK WIND PILLS

20	Humorous Sketches by Tom Browne	1902	£17.50	—

PALMER MANN & CO. LTD. (Salt)

24	Famous Cricketers	1950	£9.40	—
24	Famous Footballers	1950	£5.00	—
12	Famous Jets	1950	£4.40	—
12	Famous Lighthouses	1950	£3.75	—

PALS (Periodical)

BF27	Australian Sportsmen	1923	£4.40	£118.00
B8	Famous Footballers	1922	£2.50	£20.00
BF12	Football Series	1922	£1.55	£18.50

PANINI (Commercial, with Albums)

Qty		Date	Odds	Sets
M220	A Team	1986	—	£15.00
M240	Auto 2000	1988	—	£15.00
M360	Disney Show (French)	1984	—	£15.00
M558	Football 81	1981	—	£15.00
M516	Football 82	1982	—	£15.00
M527	Football 83	1983	—	£15.00
M526	Football 84	1984	—	£15.00
M526	Football 85	1985	—	£15.00
M574	Football 86	1986	—	£15.00
M576	Football 87	1987	—	£15.00
M574	Football 88	1988	—	£15.00
M480	Football 89	1989	—	£15.00
M216	Masters of the Universe	1986	—	£15.00
M150	100 Years of Coca Cola Advertising	1986	—	£17.50
M360	Pinocchio (Italian)	1985	—	£15.00
M180	Return of the Jedi	1980	—	£15.00
M210	Rugby 83 (French)	1983	—	£15.75
M400	Space 1999, 1st Series	1976	—	£15.00
M400	Space 1999, 2nd Series	1978	—	£15.00
M256	Star Wars (Italian)	1978	—	£15.00
M204	Superman (Italian)	1979	—	£15.00
M400	Tarzan	1985	—	£15.00
X190	The Royal Family	1988	—	£15.00
M400	U.F.O.	1973	—	£15.00
M268	World of Cricket 83	1983	—	£17.50

JAMES PASCALL LTD. (Confectionery)

48	Boy Scout Series	1912	£6.25	—
24	British Birds	1925	£1.55	£37.25
30	Devon Ferns	1927	£1.50	£45.00
30	Devon Flowers	1927	£1.50	£45.00
24	Devon Worthies	1927	£1.55	£37.25
18	Dogs	1924	£2.50	£45.00
10	Felix the Film Cat	1928	£16.00	—
30	Flags & Flags with Soldiers	1905	£8.75	—
30	Glorious Devon	1929	£1.50	£45.00
36	Glorious Devon, 2nd Series (Black Back)	1929	£1.50	£54.00
36	Glorious Devon, 2nd Series (Green Back)	1929	£1.50	£54.00
36	Glorious Devon, 2nd Series (Non-Descriptive)	1929	£3.75	—
2	King George V & Queen Mary	1910	£20.00	—
44	Military Series	1912	£10.50	—
20	Pascall's Specialities	1926	£10.50	—
12	Royal Naval Cadet Series	1912	£10.50	—
?	Rulers of the World	1916	*£25.00*	—
65	Town and Other Arms	1914	£10.00	—
50	Tricks & Puzzles	1926	£2.50	£125.00
?13	War Portraits	1915	*£12.50*	—

J. PATERSON & SON LTD. (Biscuits)

M48	Balloons	1960	—	£15.00

PATRICK (Garages)

Qty		Date	Odds	Sets
T24	The Patrick Collection (Cars)	1986	—	£5.65
C24	The Patrick Collection (With Coupons)	1986	—	£10.00

GEORGE PAYNE (Tea)

25	American Indian Tribes	1962	—	£5.00
25	British Railways	1962	—	£1.90
12	Characters from Dickens Works (Numbered)	1912	£10.50	—
6	Characters from Dickens Works (Unnumbered)	1912	£12.50	—
25	Dogs' Heads	1963	—	£3.75
25	Science in the 20th Century	1963	—	£1.50

PEEK FREAN & CO. (Biscuits)

X12	English Scenes	1884	£6.25	£75.00
X4	Shakespeare Scenes	1884	£8.15	£32.50
X4	Views Abroad	1883	£10.50	£42.00

PENNY MAGAZINE

BF12	Film Stars	1931	£2.00	£24.00

PERFETTI (Gum)

40	Famous Trains	1983	£1.50	£60.00

PETERKIN (Foods)

B8	English Sporting Dogs	1930	£10.00	—

PETPRO LTD.

35	Grand Prix Racing Cars	1966	—	£2.00

PHILADELPHIA CHEWING GUM CORP.

X88	War Bulletin	1965	75p	£66.00

PHILATELIC POSTCARD PUBLISHING CO.

P10	Philatelic Anniversary Postcards Set 1	1983	—	£1.50

PHILLIPS (Tea)

25	Army Badges Past & Present	1964	—	£1.50
25	British Birds & Their Nests	1966	—	£25.00
25	British Rail	1965	—	£4.40

PLANET LTD. (Gum)

X50	Racing Cars of the World	1965	£1.25	£62.50

PLANTERS NUT & CHOCOLATE CO. (U.S.A.)

M25	Hunted Animals	1933	£2.00	£50.00

Celebrities of British History.
Carreras

Joachim Rossini

COLOMBOS CIGARETTES
Royalty and Celebrities. Colombos

MITCHELL'S CIGARETTES

H.R.H. PRINCESS ELIZABETH

A Gallery of 1934.
Mitchell

MARGOT FONTEYN

Famous People
John O. Barker. Also Lyons

Historical Characters. Kane

SIR HARRY LAUDER

Famous Scots. Ardath

Jackie Coogan

Famous Boys. Godfrey Phillips

BUTTERFLY
CIGARETTES.

SOUTHERN LYNX

Hignett Bros & Co Ltd
LIVERPOOL.

MANDRILL

Nº 18. MAGPIES.
COPE'S CIGARETTES

Animal Pictures. Hignett.
Also Church & Dwight

Animals at the Zoo.
Morris, Ardath

Pigeons.
Cope

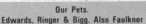

POMERANIAN

RINGER'S
CIGARETTES.

RABBITS.

Dogs and Their Treatment.
Drapkin

Our Pets.
Edwards, Ringer & Bigg. Also Faulkner

ANEMONES

Flowers.
Carreras

British Birds.
Carreras (Black Cat)

WILLS'S CIGARETTES.

WAYFARING TREE.

Flowering Trees & Shrubs.
Wills

PLUCK (Periodical)

Qty		Date	Odds	Sets
BF27	Famous Football Teams	1922	£1.50	£40.50

POLAR PRODUCTS LTD. (Ice Cream, Barbados)

25	International Air Liners	1970	—	£8.15
25	Modern Motor Cars	1970	—	£8.15
25	Tropical Birds	1970	—	£7.50
25	Wonders of the Deep	1970	—	£7.50

POLYDOR LTD. (Records)

16	The Polydor Guitar Album	1975	—	£3.50

H. POPPLETON & SONS (Confectionery)

50	Cricketers Series	1926	£18.75	—
16	Film Stars Series	1928	£4.40	—

POPULAR MOTORING (Periodical)

L4	P.M. Car Starter	1972	—	£1.25

POSTER STAMP ASSOCIATION

25	Modern Transport	1957	—	£1.90

PRESCOTT (Confectionery)

L36	Speed Kings	1966	—	£5.00

PRESCOTT-PICKUP & CO. (Commercial)

P60	Papal Visit	1982	—	£7.50
P70	Royal Family—Birth of a Prince	1982	—	£10.00

PRESTON DAIRIES (Tea)

25	Country Life	1966	—	£1.50

PRICES PATENT CANDLE CO. LTD.

P12	Famous Battles	1910	£8.15	£97.50

PRIMROSE CONFECTIONERY CO. LTD.

24	Action Man	1976	£1.00	—
50	Amos Burke—Secret Agent	1970	—	£32.50
50	Andy Pandy	1960	—	£7.50
50	Bugs Bunny	1964	—	£7.50
50	Burke's Law	1967	£1.55	—
25	Captain Kid	1975	—	£81.25
50	Chitty Chitty Bang Bang	1971	—	£4.00
50	Cowboy	1960	—	£5.00
25	Cup Tie Quiz	1973	—	£1.50
25	Dad's Army	1973	—	£1.50
50	Famous Footballers F.B.S.I.	1961	—	£6.00

PRIMROSE CONFECTIONERY CO. LTD.—cont.

Qty		Date	Odds	Sets
25	Football Funnies	1974	—	£1.50
25	Happy Howlers	1975	—	£1.50
50	Joe 90	1969	—	£35.00
50	Krazy Kreatures from Outer Space	1970	—	£4.60
50	Laramie	1964	—	£11.50
50	Laurel & Hardy	1968	—	£17.50
M22	Mounties (Package Issue)	1960	£5.00	—
50	Popeye	1960	£2.50	—
50	Popeye, 2nd Series	1961	—	£20.00
50	Popeye, 3rd Series	1962	—	£10.00
50	Popeye, 4th Series	1963	—	£10.00
50	Queen Elizabeth II	1969	—	£6.25
50	Quick Draw McGraw	1964	—	£9.00
50	Space Patrol	1970	—	£4.00
50	Space Race	1969	—	£3.00
12	Star Trek	1971	—	£2.00
50	Superman	1968	—	£8.00
50	The Flintstones	1963	—	£5.00
50	Yellow Submarine	1968	—	£62.50
50	Z Cars	1968	—	£4.60

PRINCE EDWARD THEATRE

XF?4	Josephine Baker Cards	1930	£8.15	—

S. PRIOR (Bookshop)

25	Do You Know?	1964	—	£12.50

PRIORY TEA CO. LTD.

50	Aircraft	1961	—	£7.50
50	Birds	1962	—	£9.40
24	Bridges	1960	—	£1.90
24	Cars	1958	£2.00	£50.00
50	Cars (Different)	1964	—	£8.75
50	Cycles & Motorcycles	1963	£1.00	£50.00
24	Dogs	1957	—	£1.50
24	Flowering Trees	1959	—	£1.50
24	Men at Work	1959	—	£1.90
24	Out & About	1957	—	£2.50
24	People in Uniform	1956	£1.00	£24.00
24	Pets	1957	—	£2.50
50	Wild Flowers	1963	50p	£25.00

PROPERT SHOE POLISH

25	British Uniforms	1955	—	£1.90

PUKKA TEA CO. LTD.

50	Aquarium Fish	1961	—	£31.25

PYREX LTD. (Glassware)

P16	Guide to Simple Cooking	1976	—	£1.90

QUADRIGA (Commercial)

Qty		Date	Odds	Sets
M126	Snooker Kings	1986	—	£7.00

QUAKER OATS

Qty		Date	Odds	Sets
X12	Armour through the Ages	1968	60p	£7.25
M4	Famous Puffers	1983	£3.75	£15.00
M54	Historic Arms of Merrie England	1938	65p	—
X8	Historic Ships	1967	£3.15	£25.00
M6	Honey Monster's Circus Friends	1985	75p	—
15	Honey Monster's Crazy Games Cards	1985	75p	—
M16	Jeremy's Animal Kingdom	1980	75p	£12.00
X4	Minibooks	1969	£1.90	£7.50
12	Monsters of the Deep	1984	75p	—
M6	Nature Trek	1976	25p	£1.50
X12	Prehistoric Animals	1967	£3.15	—
L8	Return to Oz	1985	95p	£7.50
X12	Space Cards	1968	£3.15	—
X12	Vintage Engines	1967	£3.15	—

PACKAGE ISSUES

Qty		Date	Odds	Sets
12	British Customs	1961	45p	£5.25
L36	British Landmarks	1961	50p	—
12	Characters in Literature	1961	75p	—
12	Exploration & Adventure	1974	75p	—
12	Famous Explorers	1961	45p	£5.25
12	Famous Inventors	1961	45p	£5.25
12	Famous Ships	1961	65p	—
12	Famous Women	1961	45p	£5.25
12	Fascinating Costumes	1961	45p	£5.25
12	Great Feats of Building	1961	40p	£4.75
L36	Great Moments of Sport	1961	£1.00	—
12	History of Flight	1961	50p	£6.00
12	Homes & Houses	1961	45p	£5.25
L36	Household Hints	1961	50p	—
12	National Maritime Museum	1974	95p	—
12	National Motor Museum	1974	£1.00	£12.00
12	On the Seashore	1961	45p	£5.25
L36	Phiz Quiz	1961	65p	—
L36	Railways of the World	1961	£1.50	—
12	Royal Air Force Museum	1974	£1.00	—
12	Science & Invention	1974	75p	£9.00
L36	The Story of Fashion	1961	45p	—
12	The Wild West	1961	50p	£6.00
12	Weapons & Armour	1961	50p	£6.00

QUEEN ELIZABETH LAUNDRY

Qty		Date	Odds	Sets
45	Beauties	1912	£12.50	—

QUEENS OF YORK (Laundry)

Qty		Date	Odds	Sets
30	Kings & Queens of England	1955	—	£22.00

QUORN SPECIALITIES LTD. (Foods)

Qty		Date	Odds	Sets
25	Fish and Game	1963	£2.00	—

RADIO FUN (Periodical)

Qty		Date	Odds	Sets
20	British Sports Stars	1956	—	£1.50

RADIO LANCASHIRE

P16	Personalities	1989	—	£1.50

RADIO REVIEW (Periodical)

L36	Broadcasting Stars	1936	£1.55	£55.75
E20	Broadcasting Stars	1936	£2.50	£50.00

RALEIGH BICYCLES

L48	Raleigh the All Steel Bicycle	1957	—	£48.00

REDDINGS TEA CO.

25	Castles of Great Britain	1965	90p	£22.50
25	Cathedrals of Great Britain	1964	90p	£22.50
25	Heraldry of Famous Places	1966	90p	£22.50
48	Ships of the World	1964	—	£3.75
25	Strange Customs of the World	1970	—	£1.50
48	Warriors of the World	1962	95p	£45.50

REDDISH MAID CONFECTIONERY

50	Famous International Aircraft	1963	£1.55	£77.50
25	Famous International Athletes	1964	£2.20	—
25	International Footballers of Today	1965	£2.50	—

RED HEART (Pet Food)

P6	Cats	1954	—	£18.00
P6	Dogs	1953	—	£15.00
P6	Dogs, 2nd Series	1953	—	£18.00
P6	Dogs, 3rd Series	1954	—	£18.00

RED LETTER (PERIODICAL)

P29	Charlie Chaplin Cards	1920	£8.15	—
M4	Luck Bringers (Silk)	1924	£18.75	£75.00
X98	Midget Message Cards	1920	£1.90	—

REEVES LTD. (Confectionery)

25	Cricketers	1912	£20.00	£500.00

REGENT OIL

X25	Do You Know?	1965	—	£1.50

RIDGWAY'S TEA

X20	Journey to the Moon (Package Issue)	1958	£3.75	—

RINGTONS LTD. (Tea)

Qty		Date	Odds	Sets
25	Aircraft of World War II	1962	—	£10.60
25	British Cavalry Uniforms of the 19th Century ...	1971	—	£4.40
25	Do You Know?	1964	—	£1.50
25	Fruits of Trees & Shrubs	1964	—	£1.50
25	Headdresses of the World	1973	—	£1.50
25	Historical Scenes	1964	—	£1.50
25	Old England	1964	—	£1.50
25	People & Places	1964	—	£1.90
25	Regimental Uniforms of the Past	1966	—	£3.75
25	Sailing Ships through the Ages	1967	—	£2.50
25	Ships of the Royal Navy	1961	—	£1.90
25	Sovereigns Consorts & Rulers, 1st Series	1961	—	£5.00
25	Sovereigns Consorts & Rulers, 2nd Series	1961	—	£5.00
25	The West	1968	—	£2.50
25	Then & Now	1970	—	£15.75
25	Trains of the World	1970	—	£1.50

RISCA TRAVEL AGENCY

25	Holiday Resorts	1957	—	£15.75

D. ROBBINS & CO. (Bread, U.S.A.)

P24	Frontiers of Freedom	1942	—	£31.25
P24	Good Neighbors of the Americas	1942	—	£31.25
P24	Modern Wonders of the World	1942	—	£31.25
P24	Our Friend — The Dog	1942	—	£60.00
P23/24	Story of Transportation	1942	—	£25.00

ROBERTSON LTD. (Preserves)

6	British Medals	1914	£12.50	—
10	Musical Gollywogs (Shaped)	1962	£1.50	—
10	Sporting Gollywogs (Shaped)	1962	£1.75	—

ROBERTSON & WOODCOCK LTD. (Confectionery)

50	British Aircraft Series	1930	£1.55	£77.50

C. ROBINSON ARTWORKSHOP (Commercial)

X16	The Pilgrims F.A. Cup Squad 1983-4	1984	—	£3.75

ROBINSON'S BARLEY WATER

X30	Sporting Records (with Folder)	1983	—	£1.90

ROBINSON BROS. & MASTERS (Tea)

25	Tea from the Garden to the Home	1930	£4.40	£110.00

ROCHE & CO. LTD. (Matches)

K49/50	Famous Footballers	1927	£3.00	—

THE ROCKET (Periodical)

Qty		Date	Odds	Sets
BF11	Famous Knockouts	1923	£5.00	£55.00

ROLLS ROYCE (Cars)

X25	Bentley Cars	1986	—	£10.75
X25	Bentley Cars, Second Edition	1987	—	£10.75
X25	Rolls Royce Cars	1986	—	£10.75
X25	Rolls Royce Cars, Second Edition	1987	—	£10.75

ROSSI'S (Ice Cream)

M48	Flags of the Nations	1975	15p	£5.00
25	The History of Flight, 1st Series	1963	—	£6.25
25	The History of Flight, 2nd Series	1963	—	£6.25
25	World's Fastest Aircraft	1964	—	£4.40

ROWNTREE & CO. (Confectionery)

K12	British Birds (Packet Issue)	1955	—	£4.40
25	Celebrities	1905	£17.50	—
X8	Circus Cut-Outs	1960	£2.50	—
M20	Merrie Monarchs	1978	—	£2.50
M18	Prehistoric Animals	1978	—	£3.00
L6	Punch & Judy Show	1976	75p	—
X42	Railway Engines (Caramac)	1976	—	£8.15
L2	Smartie Models	1976	—	£3.00
M10	Texan Tall Tales of the West	1977	75p	£7.50
48	The Old & The New	1934	£2.80	—
120	Treasure Trove Pictures	1932	75p	—
24	York Views	1924	£7.50	—

ROYAL LEAMINGTON SPA

25	Royal Leamington Spa	1975	—	£1.50

ROYAL NATIONAL LIFEBOAT INSTITUTION

M16	Lifeboats	1979	—	£1.25

ROYAL SOCIETY FOR THE PREVENTION OF ACCIDENTS

24	Modern British Cars	1954	65p	£15.50
22	Modern British Motor Cycles	1953	£1.75	£38.50
25	New Traffic Signs	1958	—	£3.75
24	Veteran Cars, 1st Series	1955	65p	£15.50
24	Veteran Cars, 2nd Series	1957	65p	£15.50

RUBY (Periodical)

T10	Famous Beauties of the Day	1923	£3.15	£31.50
T6	Famous Film Stars	1923	£3.75	£22.50

S & B PRODUCTS (Commercial)

?69	Torry Gillick's Internationals	1951	£3.75	—

SAGION STUFFING

Qty		Date	Odds	Sets
28	Dominoes Without the Dot	1939	20p	£5.00

J. SAINSBURY LTD. (Groceries)

M12	British Birds	1924	£4.40	£52.50
M12	Foreign Birds	1924	£4.40	£52.50

ST. GEORGE'S HALL

50	War Portraits	1916	£25.00	—

SANDERS BROS. (Custard)

25	Birds, Fowls, Pigeons & Rabbits	1925	£2.50	£62.50
20	Dogs	1926	£2.50	£50.00
25	Recipes	1924	£2.50	£62.50

SANITARIUM HEALTH FOOD CO. (Oceania)

X12	Animals of New Zealand	1974	—	£4.40
L30	Another Look at New Zealand	1971	—	£3.00
L30	Antarctic Adventure	1972	—	£4.40
X12	Bush Birds of New Zealand	1981	—	£3.00
L20	Cars of the Seventies	1976	—	£3.75
L20	Conservation—Caring for Our Land	1974	—	£2.50
L20	Discover Indonesia	1977	—	£2.50
L20	Exotic Cars	1987	—	£4.40
L24	Famous New Zealanders	1971	—	£3.75
L20	Farewell to Steam	1981	—	£4.40
M30	Fascinating Orient	1974	—	£2.50
M20	History of Road Transport—New Zealand	1979	—	£5.00
X12	Jet Aircraft	1974	—	£4.40
L20	Looking at Canada	1978	—	£2.50
L25	National Costumes of the Old World	1968	—	£4.40
X12	New Zealand Lakes, Series 2	1978	—	£3.00
L30	New Zealand National Parks	1973	—	£5.00
L20	New Zealand's Booming Industries	1975	—	£1.90
M30	New Zealand To-Day	1974	—	£3.75
L20	N.Z. Energy Resources	1976	—	£3.00
M20	N.Z. Rod and Custom Cars	1979	—	£5.00
X12	N.Z. Waterfalls	1981	—	£3.00
X12	N.Z.R. Steam Engines	1976	—	£6.25
X12	Our Fascinating Fungi	1980	—	£3.00
M20	Our South Pacific Island Neighbours	1974	—	£3.75
L20	Spectacular Sports	1974	—	£3.75
L20	Super Cars	1972	—	£5.00
L20	The Story of New Zealand Aviation	1977	—	£3.75
L20	The Story of New Zealand in Stamps	1977	—	£5.00
L20	Timeless Japan	1975	—	£3.00
L20	Vintage Cars	1973	—	£6.25
X12	Wild Flowers of N.Z.	1979	—	£3.00
L20	Your Journey Through Disneyland	1988	—	£4.40

SAVOY PRODUCTS LTD. (Foods)

Qty		Date	Odds	Sets
M56	Aerial Navigation	1926	90p	£50.00
M56	Aerial Navigation, Series B	1927	90p	£50.00
M56	Aerial Navigation, Series C	1928	90p	£50.00
M56	Famous British Boats	1928	90p	£50.00

SCANLEN'S (Gum, Australia)

M172	Cricket Series (Including Album)	1982	—	£17.50
M172	Cricket Series No.2 (Including Album)	1983	—	£17.50
X90	World Series Cricket	1982	—	£12.50

SCHELE (Commercial)

X48	Espana '82 (World Cup)	1982	—	£3.00

THE SCHOOL FRIEND (Periodical)

L6	Famous Film Stars	1927	£2.80	—
X10	Popular Girls of Cliff House School	1922	£8.15	—
XF6	Popular Pictures	1923	£2.50	—

THE SCHOOLGIRL (Periodical)

BF12	Zoological Studies	1923	£2.00	£24.00

THE SCHOOLGIRLS' WEEKLY (Periodical)

XF1	HRH The Duke of York	1922	—	£4.40
XF4	Popular Pictures	1922	£3.15	£12.50

SCOTTISH DAILY EXPRESS

X24	Scotcards (Soccer)	1972	£1.25	£30.00

THE SCOUT (Periodical)

L9	Birds' Eggs	1925	£3.50	£31.50
M12	Railway Engines	1924	£4.00	£48.00

SCRAPBOOK MINICARDS

27	Pendon Museum (Model Railway Etc.)	1978	—	£1.50

SECRETS (Periodical)

K52	Film Stars (Miniature Playing Cards)	1935	75p	—

SELLOTAPE PRODUCTS LTD. (Adhesive Tape)

35	Great Homes & Castles	1974	—	£8.15

SEYMOUR MEAD & CO. LTD. (Tea)

24	The Island of Ceylon	1964	—	£1.50

SHARMAN (Newspapers)

Qty		Date	Odds	Sets
T24	Golden Age of Flying	1979	—	£5.00
T24	Golden Age of Motoring	1979	—	£5.00
T24	Golden Age of Steam	1979	—	£5.00

EDWARD SHARP & SONS (Confectionery)

20	Captain Scarlet	1970	£2.50	£50.00
25	Hey Presto!	1970	—	£2.00
K53	Miniature Playing Cards	1924	£1.90	—
100	Prize Dogs	1924	£2.80	—

SHELL (Oil)

M16	Animals (3-D)	1975	65p	£10.25
14	Bateman Series	1930	£5.00	£70.00
P20	Great Britons	1972	50p	—
K16	Man in Flight (Medals) Including Mount	1970	65p	£10.25
M16	Wonders of the World (3-D)	1976	—	£6.25

AUSTRALIAN ISSUES

M60	Beetle Series (301-360)	1962	—	£10.00
M60	Birds (121-180)	1960	—	£17.50
M60	Butterflies and Moths (181-240)	1960	—	£10.00
M60	Citizenship Series	1965	—	£10.00
M60	Discover Australia with Shell	1959	—	£25.00
M60	Meteorology Series (361-420)	1963	—	£10.00
M60	Pets (481-540)	1964	—	£15.00
M60	Shells, Fish and Coral (61-120)	1959	—	£17.50
M60	Transportation Series (241-300)	1961	—	£17.50

NEW ZEALAND ISSUES

B48	Aircraft of the World	1970	—	£3.75
B60	Cars of the World	1970	—	£7.50
B48	Racing Cars of the World	1970	—	£9.50
40	Vintage Cars (Transfers)	1970	—	£5.00

SHELLEY'S ICE CREAM

25	Essex—County Champions	1984	20p	£5.00

SHEPHERD'S DAIRIES

100	War Series	1915	£5.00	—

SHERMAN'S POOLS LTD.

P8	Famous Film Stars	1940	25p	£2.00
P37	Famous Teams	1938	£1.55	£57.50
P2/37	Famous Teams (Aston Villa/Blackpool)	1938	—	65p
P38	Searchlight on Famous Players	1937	£1.90	—

SHIPTON

75	Trojan Gen Cards	1959	65p	£48.75

SHUREY'S PUBLICATIONS LTD.

P?750	Views (Various Printings)	1906	75p	—

SIDELINES (Commercial)

Qty		Date	Odds	Sets
L23	19th Century Cricket Teams	1988	—	£3.00

SILVER KING & CO. (Theatrical)

1	Advertisement Card	1905	—	£8.15

SINGER SEWING MACHINE CO.

53	Beauties (Playing Card Inset)	1898	£10.00	£530.00
P36	Costumes of All Nations	1892	£4.40	£158.00
P18	Costumes of All Nations (Different)	1894	£7.50	£135.00

SKETCHLEY CLEANERS

25	A Nature Series	1960	—	£4.40
25	Communications	1960	—	£6.25
25	Tropical Birds	1960	—	£7.50

SLADE & BULLOCK LTD. (Confectionery)

25	Cricket Series	1924	£42.50	—
25	Football Terms	1924	£10.00	—
25	Modern Inventions	1925	£6.25	£156.25
20	Now & Then Series	1925	£8.15	—
25	Nursery Rhymes	1925	£12.50	—
25	Science & Skill Series	1925	£8.15	—
25	Simple Toys & How to Make Them	1925	£9.40	—

P. SLUIS (Bird Food)

X30	Tropical Birds	1962	—	£6.25

SMART NOVELS (Periodical)

BF12	Stage Artistes & Entertainers	1924	£2.50	—

JOHN SMITH (Brewers)

P5	Limericks (Beer Mats)	1976	—	£1.90

SNAP CARDS (Gum)

L50	ATV Stars, 1st Series	1959	75p	£37.50
L48	ATV Stars, 2nd Series	1960	50p	£24.00
L50	Associated Rediffusion Stars	1960	75p	£37.50
L50	Dotto	1959	65p	£32.50

H. A. SNOW (Films)

12	Hunting Big Game in Africa	1923	£4.40	£52.50

SOCCER BUBBLE GUM

M48	Soccer Teams No. 1 Series	1956	—	£15.00
M48	Soccer Teams No. 2 Series	1958	£1.25	—

SODASTREAM (Confectionery)

Qty		Date	Odds	Sets
25	Historical Buildings	1957	—	£1.50

SOMPORTEX Ltd. (Gum Vending)

X72	Adventures of Sexton Blake	1968	50p	£36.00
L60	Famous TV Wrestlers	1966	£1.50	£90.00
X60	Film Scene Series James Bond 007	1966	£1.90	—
L72	John Drake Danger Man	1966	£1.90	—
L50	The Exciting World of James Bond 007	1965	£1.90	—
L72	The Saint	1967	£2.20	—
L71/72	Thunderball	1967	65p	£46.00
X73	Thunderbirds (Coloured)	1967	£1.90	£137.00
L72	Thunderbirds (Black/White)	1967	£1.90	£135.00
X72	Thunderbirds (Black/White)	1967	£1.55	£110.00
X36	Weirdies	1968	75p	£27.00
26	You Only Live Twice (Film Strips)	1969	£3.75	—

SONNY BOY

50	Railway Engines	1960	—	£4.00

SOUTH AFRICAN EGGS

L6	Oeufs Travel Collection	1988	—	75p

SOUTHSEA MODELS

30	Victorian & Edwardian Soldiers in Full Dress	1988	—	£6.25

SOUTH WALES CONSTABULARY

X36	British Stamps	1983	—	£7.50
X36	Castles & Historic Places of Wales	1988	—	£9.40
X36	Merthyr Tydfil Borough Council	1987	—	£9.40
X37	Payphones Past and Present	1987	—	£17.25
X36	Rhymney Valley	1986	—	£7.50
X35	The '82 Squad (Rugby)	1982	65p	£31.25

SPAR GROCERS

30	Disney Characters	1974	—	£32.50
X30	Disney on Parade	1972	—	£17.50

SPILLERS NEPHEWS (Biscuits)

25	Conundrum Series	1910	£15.00	—
40	Views of South Wales & District	1910	£15.00	—

SPORT AND ADVENTURE (Periodical)

M46	Famous Footballers	1922	£1.50	£69.00

SPORT IN PRINT (Commercial)

M64	Nottinghamshire Cricketers	1989	—	£10.00

SPRATTS PATENT LTD. (Pet Food)

Qty		Date	Odds	Sets
K100	British Bird Series (Numbered)	1935	£1.90	—
K50	British Bird Series (Unnumbered)	1935	£1.55	—
42	British Birds	1926	£2.50	£105.00
36	Champion Dogs	1926	£6.25	—
K20	Fish	1935	£7.50	—
K100	Poultry Series	1935	£3.15	—
25	The Bonzo Series	1924	£3.75	£93.75

STAMP CORNER

25	American Indian Tribes	1963	—	£20.00

STAR JUNIOR CLUB

10	Animals	1960	£1.00	£10.00
10	Sports & Games (Numbered)	1960	£1.25	£12.50
5	Sports & Games (Unnumbered)	1960	£1.50	£7.50

STAVELEY'S (Shop)

24	World's Most Beautiful Birds	1924	£3.75	—

STEAM RAILWAY (Magazine)

16	Railway Cigarette Cards	1988	—	75p

STOKES & DALTON (Cereals)

M20	The Crimson Cobra	1950	£1.50	£30.00

STOLL (Films)

25	Stars of To-Day	1930	£5.00	—
25	The Mystery of Dr. Fu-Manchu	1930	£7.50	—

STOLLWERCK (Chocolate)

T144	Animal World	1902	90p	£130.00
F?100	Views of the World	1915	£3.75	—

THE SUN (Newspaper)

M134	Football Swap Cards	1970	25p	£33.50
M52	Gallery of Football Action	1975	95p	£50.00
M6	How to Play Football	1975	£1.25	£7.50
M54	Page 3 Playing Cards	1979	—	£5.00
40	Pocket Book of Soccer Stickers (With Folders)	1989	—	£3.00
150	Royal Album Stickers (& Album)	1989	—	£5.00
1000	Soccercards	1980	—	*£50.00*
P50	3D Gallery of Football Stars	1975	90p	—

SUNBLEST (Bread, Australia)

M24	Sports Action Series	1975	—	£5.00
M25	Sunblest Explorer Cards	1975	—	£3.75

Hunted Animals.
Planters

Comics.
Welch

Illustrated Jokes.
Arbuckle

Butterflies of North America.
Brooke Bond

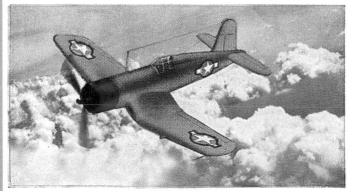

CORSAIR F4U

Aeroplanes & Insignia.
Anon. U.S. Trade

2. OWZATICUS

Prehistorigum.
Unusually Funny Factory

Fascinating Facts.
Woolworth

A Journey Downstream.
Brooke Bond

GEORGE WASHINGTON.

Leaders.
Kinney (Nostalgia Reprints)

Famous Clowns.
Marlow Civil Engineering

Disney Home Video.
Trio Bars